The Bible, the Supernatural, and the Jews

McCandlish Phillips

16750

The Bible,
the Supernatural,
and the Jews

BETHANY FELLOWSHIP, INC.
Minneapolis, Minnesota

ISBN 0-87123-036-4

Revised 1973
Published by Bethany Fellowship, Inc.
6820 Auto Club Road, Minneapolis, MN 55438

The author and publisher gratefully acknowledge permission to reprint the following:

Excerpts from the article "Pay Now, Kill Later," *Newsweek*, October 18, 1965. © Newsweek, Inc., 1965.

Excerpts from the article "Sirhan Through the Looking Glass," reprinted by permission from *Time*, The Weekly Newsmagazine; © Time, Inc., 1969.

Excerpts from *Mademoiselle*, "Special Magical Mystery Issue." © 1968 by The Conde Nast Publications, Inc.

Excerpts from the article "Release from Depression," by Derek Prince. © 1968 by Christian Life Publications, Inc., Wheaton, Illinois.

Excerpts from Martin Ebon, *Test Your ESP.* © 1969 by The New American Library and World Publishing Company.

Excerpts from Mary Barnard, *The Mythmakers.* © 1966 by Ohio University Press.

Excerpts from R. Gordon Wasson, "The Hallucinogenic Fungi of Mexico." Courtesy of the author.

Excerpts from Dudley Young, "The Magic of Peyote," *The New York Times Book Review*, September 29, 1968. © 1968 by The New York Times Company. Reprinted by permission.

Excerpts from Frederick Swain, "The Mystical Mushroom," reprinted from *Tomorrow*, Autumn, 1962, now *Studies in Comparative Religion*, Pates Manor, Bedfont, Middlesex, England.

For

Hannah Lowe

To whom I am indebted

beyond my knowledge

By Way of Preface
and Acknowledgment

The writer was seated at his typewriter, diligently writing *another* book when, suddenly and with no prior announcement, a theme was struck and words began to flow with such rapidity that, in three and a half days' time, 167 pages piled up beside his table. They were all of a piece, unchaptered. He read them and discovered that they had little to do with the book that he was writing. In his perplexity, he carried them to Robert Gutwillig, the editor who had contracted with him for the *other* book, and laid them on his desk. "This is an entirely different book," the editor said after scanning them.

I am reminded of the Biblical account of the birth of Perez and Zerah to Tamar: "When the time of her delivery came, there were twins in her womb. And when she was in labor, one put out a hand; and the midwife took and bound on his hand a scarlet thread, saying, 'This came out first.' But as he drew back his hand, behold, his brother came out; and she said, 'What a breach you have made for yourself!' Therefore his name was called Perez." Genesis 38:27–29.

This manuscript, then, is Perez. When I look on it, I say with mild astonishment at least, "What a breach you have made for yourself!" The other is Zerah. It appeared first, but it will be second.

Like any child, Perez had to be nourished and fattened, so the 167 pages became 519 pages of manuscript, of which Mary Yastishak typed more than 400 pages, a service for which I am deeply grateful. Her sister, Julie Yastishak, extended her vocation as a researcher into evening and weekend hours and found records and checked facts necessary to the accuracy of the manuscript.

The broad outline of a book concerning the future role of the Jews in world history came during a series of Bible studies in the Book of Daniel, held in a living room overlooking Broadway in Morningside Heights, Manhattan, where the church of the New Testament Missionary Fellowship meets. Two years later the first words were written. I remember distinctly what impelled that start. In one of the early morning prayer meetings of the church, Ruth Johnson, now a nurse at Cali, Colombia, South America, prayed so urgently for the welfare of the Jews that her words fused two years of intention into immediate action. That morning I wrote a letter outlining the book; later in the week I sent it, with a sample chapter, to Robert Gutwillig. His generosity and strong encouragement in regard to both books were indispensable, for which I want to thank him here.

I have as deep a debt to Frank S. Boshold, a minister of my church, who, when certain towering doubts about continuing to write arose, spoke the unequivocal words of counsel without which this book would not have been published. He also read every line of the manuscript, suggesting additions and deletions and rephrasings with a swift intelligence. He graciously gave me permission to condense his translation of *Blumhardt's Battle: A Conflict With Satan,* a landmark document in German Protestant literature, and to use it as the basis of the chapter titled "A Victim of Magic."

Thanks are due also to Mrs. Jeanette Green for assistance in typing and manuscript proofreading. Her instant availability was a great help at times when deadlines could not otherwise have been met. My thanks also to Calvin B. Burrows and Benjamin Gravely; and to Philip K. Chamberlain and Mark Lindberg, Yale undergraduates, each of whom spent hours reading the original manuscript aloud while I checked it against the final typed version.

To James O. Wade, who succeeded Robert Gutwillig as editor in the last days of the preparation of the manuscript, go my thanks for possessing that deliberate restraint writers most admire, but do not unfailingly find, in editors—a restraint that gives a writer latitude to say what he wants to say, in the way he chooses to say it. Coming to it, as he did, near the end, his work has speeded the manuscript to completion.

The members of the church prayed almost daily during the many months that this book was in preparation. I am grateful to them all. Among them was Mrs. Charlotte Sheinkin, whose unflagging interest in the work was expressed in repeated requests for that enablement to be given to the writer which can come only from the One Who Is the "Alpha and Omega, the first and the last" and Who says, "What you see, write in a book." Revelation 1:17,19.

There is not the slightest possibility that this book would have been written apart from the unforgettable encounter of a wonderful morning in September 1950, when a man named Charles W. Campbell and his wife, Evelyn, took me to hear a minister who spoke the words by which faith arose in me and the irrevocable persuasion of the prophet Isaiah that "the grass withers, the flower fades; but the Word of our God shall stand forever."

McCandlish Phillips

Note on Scriptural Texts

The Scripture texts quoted in this book are taken chiefly from the King James version, and also from the Revised Standard Version. There are several citations from the "Living Bible" series by Kenneth N. Taylor, published by Tyndale House, Wheaton, Illinois.

There are some cases where the Scripture texts quoted are a blend of two versions. Where it makes the meaning more plain, the author has taken a phrase from one version and inserted it in the text of the other. His aim throughout has been to convey the words of Scripture with beauty and always with the greatest possible clarity.

Contents

Part I

Journey Into
the Supernatural

The Chariots of Israel:
More Than Meets the Eye

Once, when the king of Syria was at war against Israel, his secretly devised plans were repeatedly frustrated because the king of Israel always seemed to know exactly what they were. The king suspected a spy in his own camp, but one of his servants said, "Elisha, the prophet who is in Israel, tells the king of Israel the words that you speak in your bedchamber."

Elisha was in a city called Dothan, the servant said.

So the king sent "horses and chariots and a great army, and they came by night and surrounded the city." An army was sent to seize one man.

"When the servant of the man of God rose early in the morning and went out, behold, an army with horses and chariots was round about the city." Elisha was encircled and trapped.

"And the servant said, 'Alas, my master! What shall we do?' And Elisha answered, 'Fear not, for they that are with us are more than they that are with them.' "

That seemed an odd declaration, because *no* soldiers were with Elisha.

"And Elisha prayed and said, 'Lord, I pray thee, *open his eyes that he may see.'* And the Lord opened the eyes of the young man; and he saw, and behold, the mountain was full of horses and chariots of fire round about Elisha." II Kings 6:8–17.

In this account—and at many other points in the Bible—the Scriptures tell of forces and events in the physical and natural realm and of forces and concurrent events in the spiritual and supernatural realm. There was something visible going on and something invisible going on in the same place at the same time, and both had a bearing on the event. Here, for a brief moment, the unseen veil that separates the two was drawn back, so the young man who at first had seen only the army of Syria saw another army camped in that place, the army of the Lord.

What he saw was not a vision but reality. He saw real horses and real chariots on that mountain, but they existed on a different plane of reality than the one on which man dwells. They could come into the natural order and affect it, but they were not a part of the natural order. They exist in an order beyond or above that of the natural, called the supernatural. They are not less real because of their invisibility to man.

For the outcome of this confrontation between natural and supernatural forces see the chapter of the Bible listed above. It is sufficient here to say that Elisha was not seized or harmed, nor were any of the Syrian troops killed, and the last word on it is that "the Syrians came no more on raids into the land of Israel."

There had been one previous occasion on which Elisha had seen a sight like the one he saw that morning. It was while he was serving as a young man under the prophet Elijah.

Elijah was one of the holiest and mightiest prophets in the history of Israel. He is one of two men of whom it is told in the Old Testament that they were taken into heaven without suffering physical death. The other is Enoch.

Elisha had been servant to Elijah and when the day came for Elijah to be taken from the earth, Elisha knew what was going to happen. He followed the older man closely that day, refusing suggestions that he stay behind.

At the end, the old prophet turned to the young man and said, "Ask what I shall do for you before I am taken from you." Elisha said, "I pray you, let a double portion of your spirit be upon me." He was asking that the power of God that had made Elijah a prophet and a worker of miracles rest upon him, but in double measure.

Elijah said, "You have asked a hard thing. Nevertheless, *if you see me* when I am taken from you, it will be done for you; but if not, it shall not be so."

"It came to pass, as they still went on, and talked, that, behold, there appeared a chariot of fire, and horses of fire, and separated the two of them. And Elijah went up by a whirlwind into heaven.

"And Elisha saw it and he cried, 'My father, my father! The *chariots of Israel and the horsemen thereof!*' And he saw him no more."

The condition had been fulfilled. For a moment Elisha had seen things invisible to the human eye, and that made him call out in astonishment and awe. He saw forces assigned as protectors of Israel—real, powerful, efficient forces that the human eye cannot see, because they are not physical but spiritual, not natural but supernatural.

Because they are on a different plane than that of the natural and the physical, in their comings and goings they are, with very rare exceptions, unseen and unheard by man.

That is true of the supernatural forces of God. But it is equally true of the supernatural forces of evil. Both are invisible and both affect events on earth to a degree unsuspected by most men.

Once, when King David had obeyed the will of Satan in a certain matter and disobeyed the will of God, the Bible says that "God sent the angel to Jerusalem to destroy it, but when he was about to destroy it, the Lord saw, and he repented of the evil, and he said to the destroying angel, 'It is enough; now stay your hand.'

"And the angel of the Lord was standing by the threshing floor of Ornan the Jebusite"—notice that it was a very specific angel standing at a very specific place—"and David lifted his eyes and *saw the angel of the Lord* standing between earth and heaven, and in his hand a drawn sword stretched out over Jerusalem. . . .

"Now Ornan was threshing wheat; he turned and *saw the angel*, and his four sons who were with him hid themselves." I Chronicles 21:15,16,20.

It was given to David and to Ornan to see beyond the natural into the supernatural and to see, taking place in the supernatural, an event that had the most immediate and momentous bearing on the safety of the city of Jerusalem.

There are events occurring on the earth in our generation that are affected not only by what men do and say in the natural realm but by invisible forces that are operating in the supernatural realm. The Bible reveals that the primary initiative in certain events of history does not proceed from the will of man but from the will of powers beyond man in the supernatural. These powers seek to make human beings the instruments of their policy. Since some of the powers are evil, and since their desire is to increase the sum of strife and suffering and death among mankind, it is urgent to know something about them.

The Door That Can Never Be Opened Again

Supernaturalism in many forms has been flooding in upon the American culture in recent months, creating a sudden and widespread interest in clairvoyance, psychicism, necromancy, occultism, witchcraft, out-of-body travel, transcendental meditation, extrasensory perception, precognition, and various forms of mysticism, fetishism, spiritism. New as they may seem to the American consciousness, they are ancient supernatural practices that have found expressions in many cultures at various times in history. For many people they have, it must be acknowledged, the magnetism of fascination, but these things should not be entered into out of uninformed curiosity, without some knowledge of the possible consequences of even a limited amount of experimentation with them or exposure to them.

If you would not thrust your hand into a snake pit, you should not permit yourself to be drawn into an involvement with one or another form of occultism, even in a tentative and purely experimental way, without knowing that it is possible for you to step over a threshold and past a door that will slam shut behind you as soon as you stand on the far side of it—slam shut so tight that nothing you can do can ever get that door open again so that you can get back out.

That does happen. I have seen it happen. I have been told by others that something like this was happening to them but that somehow, somehow they got out of it in time. I have heard from the lips of still others that they wish that they had never become involved in what they are in, but they say that they are helpless to do anything about it now. For them there is no exit.

There is no knowing how quickly this irrevocable entrapment in the supernatural may occur. For some the process is a slow one. They can go for months, perhaps for years, without feeling or observing effects which they regard as damaging. For others a single experiment, entered into in a casual or ignorant way, is enough to carry them past the point of no return.

The supernatural is a tremendously potent realm. A person may pull what looks to be a small trigger and find that he has set off what for him proves to be a kind of nuclear fission of the human psyche. The powers are far, far beyond the capacity of man to handle.

If you are a Jew, there is a risk for you in involvement or experimentation with certain areas of the supernatural beyond the degree of risk run by a Gentile, as great as that is. A Jew who steps into these areas for whatever reason is more likely to experience destructive effects in his person immediately, or very soon, than a Gentile is. The door that can never be opened again slams shut faster on a Jew than on a non-Jew. This is not an impenetrable mystery. There are definite reasons for it, and I will go into them later.

Two months ago I watched in closeup the disintegration of a young Jew who went out of his mind as the direct and traceable result of having watched an Indian yogi on television. That gave him a mild taste of the occult. He took a deep dive into it, read widely in some of its literature, and began doing and saying strangely irrational things. He took some marijuana. He lost his hold on reality, and the unreality that seized his mind was of an especially preposterous kind. Six months ago he was a rational, effective human being of more than ordinary capacity and initiative. Now he is a futile and oddly warped individual. When he talks, half the time he sounds about eighty percent rational, the rest of the time he sounds a hundred percent out of his mind. He is one victim of new currents that are moving in our society. He was taken unawares. I know another young Jew, twenty-four years old, who believes that a certain notorious, self-proclaimed Christ-figure in India is the Messiah, and who has become absorbed in that conviction to the exclusion of almost everything else. He is in it to the point of mental aberration. He says frankly that when the idea concerning the Indian came over him, he knew it was wrong and he tried to resist, but he could not. In both of these cases, drugs taken in small amounts served as avenues into the supernatural for these young Jews and helped to undermine their self-control and loose them from their senses.

I know another Jew, now forty-five years old, who has spent the last four years in a mental institution, away from his family and away from the good job he had held for twenty years, because he dipped into supernaturalism, out of fascination, and got in over his head. Most of his trouble came because he met an elderly "prophetess" whose words and visions got hold of him. He went to her for advice on several occasions and submitted to her magic religious formulas for sickness. Some of it came through reading about the supernatural exploits of medieval so-called saints and some of it came through the use of religious medals. I warned him repeatedly and strongly against these things, until the time when his wife had him committed to a mental hospital and he was put through a series of electroshock treatments, which do not appear to have helped him. The last time I saw him he appeared to me to be hopelessly insane.

These things do not happen merely by chance. There are active, intelligent, invisible spiritual forces at work today who select particular individuals—especially young Jews—and seek to get them interested in, and then into, the supernatural. These forces have an entire program or path of spiritual ruination laid out for an individual, including events that seem to be "providential," and if the individual goes along with it and steps along that path, step by step, he cooperates in a program for his own destruction. If he knew what those forces are, and what they design to do, he would not allow them to make him their victim.

These powers of evil are skilled at planting events, coincidences, and signs in the lives of those they are after. They present themselves as good and they offer what they do as the acts of a benign providence. The Bible exposes them for what they are.

These spiritual forces are now massively at work in North America, multiplying and spreading the means that are useful to them in hooking individuals on supernaturalism. In doing that, they are also working to subvert parts of the American culture by thoroughly infiltrating it with a broad variety of corrupt and dangerous supernatural practices.

It is no accident—it is a program—that suddenly the motion

pictures, the national magazines, the bookstores and book stands are heavily freighted with graphic accounts of various adventures in supernaturalism. These accounts succeed in introducing super-naturalism into the consciousness of millions of people. For some it is only a brush, a matter of passing curiosity. Upon others it exerts the almost irresistible magnetism of a deep fascination. They feel themselves being drawn into new levels of experience. They are aware that a force is being exerted upon their souls to draw them on into places where they have not been before, into explorations of the supernatural, into the discovery of strange new powers. The line of least resistance is to go right along as you feel yourself being drawn or "led"—and that is exactly what is happen-ing—without stopping to be sure what the outcome of it will be. By such acquiescent, sometimes eager submissiveness some are led into things that they don't know how to handle.

A few months ago I met a young Jew, a college sophomore, who almost immediately impressed me as having a beautifully balanced combination of good attributes. He was bright, alert, quick of mind and quick of step, naturally and easily personable, just a bit dapper, genuinely willing to be helpful, and he had plenty of well-directed initiative. There was nothing sour or sluggish about him.

One afternoon it seemed to me important that I take a few minutes to talk with him about what he believed. I did, and I am glad that I did. He was interested in talking on the subject and, in the course of a ten-minute conversation, he told me that his col-lege-age brother had died in an automobile accident recently. The conversation, brief as it was, opened up an area of discussion that I believe proved critically important to him a short time later. I should add that, in a day when some teen-agers and college stu-dents seem in so many ways to be driven and bedeviled, he seemed to be entirely clear of hangups. I found myself wondering how and why he had escaped and seemed to enjoy an exemption from the contaminations of today.

He switched from a midwest college to one in New York City and found lodgings on Manhattan's upper West Side. About three weeks later he came to me and said, with a kind of taut urgency, "I've got to talk to you." He said that he had "just happened" to see a copy of a magazine lying on the desk near him, that he picked it up and read through Bishop Pike's account of his conver-sational exchanges with what the Bishop took to be his late son. That night, he said, he took a walk around his new neighborhood "to see where the good pizza is, the good hamburgers," and he "just happened" to look up and spot the upstairs shop of a reader and adviser.

"I just felt drawn," he said, "strongly drawn to go up there" to ask her if she could put him into contact with his dead brother. "Yes," she told him, "but not now. You'll have to come back."

There it was—two coincidences and a strangely compelling urge, and this young Jew was on the verge of getting involved in things against which the Bible gives the most clear-cut warnings to the Jews.

I believe that, without knowing it in any way, this young man was beginning to fall into a carefully arranged trap, designed to give evil supernatural powers an access to his soul, his inner being, that they had not previously had.

The next day I opened up the Bible and showed him several passages directly bearing on the thing he was dipping into. After he had seen them he said, "I won't go near that place again." If he sticks to that decision, made in the light of what the Bible says about the matter, he will keep out of a danger zone in the supernatural.

For this young man, a magazine article that he chanced to read triggered a desire to probe into the supernatural. For another, mentioned earlier, a television broadcast sent him on a quest through the pages of books on psychicism. For another, trouble in the supernatural began when he heard a talk by a Harvard student who had spent a few months in India and who came back to herald the news of an Indian Christ. For another, a chance meeting at work with a woman who claimed certain prophetic powers set him on the course that led to his confinement to a mental institution.

This book is not a condemnation of the supernatural. There is a hunger and a longing in man for contact with something above and beyond him, something that is eternal and sure. There is a human need for supernatural experience, a deep and legitimate need. Others, out of ignorance or prejudice, may deny the supernatural and scoff at it. I do not. I know that it is real. I have had experience with the supernatural.

Everyone knows that there are fakers and gyp artists and charlatans among those who deal in the supernatural realm, but there are also individuals who do in fact possess certain powers and who are able to exercise them and to produce results by them, if not always, sometimes. The fakers can do you no good; the others may do you great harm.

For those who do exercise supernatural powers, the right question is not whether their powers are real. The right question is: Where, exactly where, do they obtain those powers?

Most American synagogues and churches are stone dead to the supernatural or even stoutly and rigidly antagonistic to it. The Bible, however, is not an anti-supernatural book. It is just the opposite. It is a book filled from beginning to end with accounts of that which is supernatural. The Bible is not only a book *about* the supernatural. The Bible is a supernatural book.

Most synagogues and churches, by denying and cutting out or shutting out genuine supernatural experiences that the Bible says human beings ought to have, have created a tremendous void that is now being filled in the most destructive way by books that anyone can pick from a drugstore rack.

Since the churches won't give them what God wants the people to have, traffickers in the supernatural are giving them substitutes, in what is becoming a wide-open market in black magic.

The Bible recognizes this human desire to know more than may be known by natural means of cognition. It would be correct to say that the Bible is an anti-materialistic (though not an ascetic) book with a very strong emphasis on, and an invitation to, the supernatural. It promises that "your young men shall see visions, and your old men shall dream dreams."

Some people have a kind of thirst for the supernatural. It makes a difference whether they seek to quench that thirst at a well whose waters are poisoned, or at a well whose waters run pure.

Not all that is supernatural is good. There is plenty that is supernatural—genuinely supernatural—that is evil. It would be far better for a man to have no experience of the supernatural whatever than for him to have experience with supernatural powers of evil.

Supernaturalism has come into this country in a rush and it is here to stay, whether we like it or not. Wearing blinders will not help. Americans need desperately to know what the Bible says about it, before tragedy strikes homes and families who don't know what is happening to their young members, or why.

It is important for everyone to know of this, but it is particularly important for Jews to know. If Jewish parents and Jewish students knew what the Bible laid down concerning the supernatural, and why, it would help them to be on guard against that which is deadly in it.

Occultism and supernaturalism are growing rapidly in America. Since we are going to have it, we better be sure we know what we are getting. If you are a Jew, of whatever age, you better be doubly sure you don't get the wrong kind.

The Bible is a safe, sure guide to the supernatural. It distinguishes sharply and adamantly between two enormously potent supernatural realms, as between two irreconcilable forces. These two are in conflict, in the earth and in the heavens. As to their effect upon the earth, which of them shall prevail in human affairs in this generation, man must choose between them.

To make that choice, he needs information. The following chapters will lay down the Biblical guidelines on the supernatural, exposing that which is harmful or destructive and illuminating, on the basis of the Biblical accounts, that which is full of power and blessing for man.

Looking into the supernatural with the Bible as our guide, we can learn how to distinguish that which will do us evil from that which will do us good.

The Impenetrable Order

In the creation there is a physical order and a spiritual order, both of which are real. The physical universe is natural. The spiritual order is supernatural. There are facts that may be known about both, but not by the same means.

Man's body, and the five senses that go with it, is a part of the physical creation. Those senses are able to observe and to take in information, facts, about the natural universe—and that is all. They cannot observe the supernatural order. Your senses give you your relationship to the whole physical universe. They are the mediators and sentinels between you and all the rest of the physical creation. You know of it and learn of it by exercising them.

There it ends. They provide you with no information about the supernatural order. They afford you no relationship to it. Your ears are deaf to it, your eyes are blind to it.

The Bible says:

> The things which are seen are temporal, but the things which are unseen are eternal. II Corinthians 4:18a.

We know the first part of that statement to be true. The earth, the sun, the moon, the stars, the whole physical creation will wear out.

Psalm 102 says: "Of old hast thou laid the foundation of the earth, and the heavens are the work of thy hands. They shall perish but thou shalt endure. Yea, all of them shall wax old like a garment; as a vesture thou shalt change them, and they shall be changed. But thou art the same, and thy years shall have no end."

The earth and everything that is in the physical realm will "wax old like a garment" and "they shall perish."

We give ready assent to the statement that "the things which are seen are temporal." We know that to be the fact. We are much less sure that "the things which are unseen are eternal."

Notice that the verse does not refer to ideas, to values and concepts; it refers to *things*. It speaks of temporal things and it speaks of eternal *things*. The contrast is not between natural stuff and spiritual values, as though a man could read the verse and say, "Sure, money and clothes wear out, but love goes on forever." To say that is to spiritualize the verse falsely.

In order for something which is unseen to our eyes to be eternal, it has to be a real thing. It has to exist. A figment of the imagination may be unseen, but it does not exist, so it cannot be eternal.

The unseen things the Scripture says are eternal are things that have objective existence. They have that existence not on the natural and physical plane but on the spiritual and supernatural plane.

The natural man, in full possession of his physical faculties and senses, is constitutionally incapable of discovering anything on the spiritual plane. That is as true as that a standard band radio does not receive short-wave signals. The atmosphere may be charged with such signals but the standard band radio is as dead to them as the leg of a table is.

The Bible declares that the natural man does not receive spiritual truths. "They are folly to him, and he is *not able* to understand them because they are spiritually discerned." I Corinthians 2:14.

Since he cannot, it is an easy thing for him to assert that if something can't be seen it is not real, does not exist. Yet visibility is not the test of existence.

Science, the investigative exercise of the natural senses, is defined as "systematic knowledge of the physical and material world" gained by skilled observation, by measurement. The human baby is an infant scientist as he discovers the uses and proportions of things and his own proportions in respect to them. He does this by watching them, handling and feeling them, by tugging at them. On a far more sophisticated level the scientist learns the size and shape and the weight and motion of things by careful observation with his senses. Man has devised numberless tools and instruments that help him to observe things more exactly. These tools are really extensions of his senses. They enable man to use his senses to search out finer data and to make far more precise measurements than could be made by the unaided senses.

Science is able also to use methods of observation to determine certain laws that apply in the natural realm, including the laws of mathematics.

There are limits upon what man can discover by the scientific method. The whole physical universe is unlimitedly open to man to explore by the exercise of his senses, directed by his intelligence, as far as his ingenuity will allow him. Matter and energy, substance and structure, in all of their manifold forms may be explored endlessly by the intelligent use of the physical senses—for that is the realm of which they are a part and in which they freely and effectively operate.

Man may unlock secret after secret in chemistry, in biology, in nuclear physics, in geology, in astronomy by the rigorous application of the scientific method. The natural realm is vast and man is free to search it to the utmost. But beyond it he cannot go by any scientific method. Man's senses reach an end of what they can discover when they reach the end of the physical creation.

There are some who assert that God does not exist because He cannot be observed by man. Some scientists and some university professors are especially prone to this point of view. Their eminence in one realm tends to blind men to their incompetence in another.

When a scientist, however brilliant and accomplished in his field, steps out of it and seeks to use the authority obtained in his discipline as a warrant to make pronouncements in an entirely unrelated area, it is an act of sheer arrogance. He leaves the bank in which he has huge deposits and walks into another, in which he has none, and swaggers as importantly there as in the place where his capital actually is. He is entitled to be hustled out as a pauper.

This is particularly so with regard to any attempt to apply credentials earned in the natural realm to the spiritual and supernatural realm. We know it is possible for a man to be an intellectual genius and a moral idiot; it is equally possible for a man of the highest attainment in the arts, letters, or science to be entirely ignorant regarding the spiritual and supernatural.

Speculation, of course, and intuition may range beyond the physical universe, and they can construct any system men may fancy, but nothing of what they suppose is subject to any verification. All of it may be the sheerest fiction.

The natural man, whatever his gifts, remains fixedly inexpert in comprehending that which is beyond the physical creation. He may posit anything he wishes, but he cannot prove any of it.

My concern is not with what may be thought to be or with what may be imagined to be, but only with what may be *known* to be.

The senses of man, expert as they are in the physical realm, are deaf and dumb and blind in the realm of the spiritual and supernatural. Beyond that, speculation adduces exactly nothing. Yet man is entitled to know of those unseen things which are supernatural and eternal.

He Comes As Wind

Since nothing beyond the vast physical creation, consisting of matter and energy and all their interactions and relations, can be scientifically shown to be the case, we must seek another method.

The natural man is limited to the natural realm, where he has his existence. But that which has its existence in the spiritual realm is not limited to the spiritual realm. It may enter into the natural realm and do so with very pronounced effects upon it.

The chariots and the horsemen of Israel that Elisha's servant was permitted to see were supernatural and normally unseen, but they had taken their stations in the natural order and they were there to take effective action to protect the prophet Elisha and the nation Israel.

There are spiritual forces at work today causing changes of astonishing magnitude in human affairs. If we fail to recognize them we shall continue to be utterly helpless in dealing with their effects.

That there is a God is entirely outside of the capacity of science and the physical senses to discover by any method whatever. God is not found in the realm of the natural but in the realm of the spiritual.

If that were the last word on the matter, we would be blind and unknowing forever. But it is not the last word. The Bible says:

> *Eye* has not seen, *ear* has not heard, neither have entered into the heart of man, the things which God has prepared for them that love him. But *God has revealed them to us by his Spirit,* for the Spirit searches all things, even the deep things of God.... The things of God *no man knows,* but the Spirit of God" knows them and reveals them to man. I Corinthians 2:9–11.

There it is. If man is to know anything at all about the realm of the spiritual and the supernatural, it must be given to him by revelation. Revelation is a one-way avenue. It comes from the spiritual plane to the natural plane. It never runs the other way.

Until the young man's eyes were opened by God, in response to the prayer of Elisha, he saw nothing, knew nothing, suspected nothing of the chariots and the horsemen of Israel that were camped in that place.

The initiative in scientific discovery lies wholly with man. The initiative in spiritual revelation lies wholly with God. Men can know only what God elects to reveal to them about the spiritual and the supernatural.

If we are truthful, we are obliged to admit that we can know nothing whatever of life after death apart from revelation. We can know nothing whatever about heaven or hell apart from revelation. We can know nothing about angels or demons apart from revelation.

God has chosen to make an extensive revelation to man regarding these things. He has chosen to do so in a way that makes them readily intelligible to human beings.

There is a line of communication from the supernatural into the natural order. The personal agent of this communication is the Spirit of God, the Holy Spirit.

The Holy Spirit—He is a living Person—dwells in the spiritual order and He enters the natural order unseen. There are absolutely no limits on where He may go. In the Bible He is likened, in His comings and goings, to the wind: "The wind blows where it wills, and you hear the sound of it, but you do not know whence it comes or whither it goes. . . ." (John 3:8.) Unseen the Holy Spirit comes, unseen He goes, yet there are the effects of His wonderful presence among men.

There are no limits whatever on what the Holy Spirit may know, "for the Spirit searches all things, even the deep things of God." This passage also declares that "*no one* comprehends the thoughts of God except the Spirit of God." I Corinthians 2:11.

The Holy Spirit takes of the truths of God, and of the spiritual realm, and conveys them according to the will of God, to men. In this He uses words primarily but occasionally also visions (pictures) and dreams as means of communication, so that what is revealed is made plainly intelligible to man.

Prophecy is an aspect of this revelation. True prophecy comes from God. Prophecy comes initially in the form of the spoken word through the lips of a prophet. It is imparted to a man or a woman by the Holy Spirit, and then, as the prophet speaks it out, men hear it and receive the prophecy.

Prophecy does not come because man wills it, but because God gives it.

Speaking of the Hebrew prophets, the New Testament says (here I am going to quote both the King James and the Revised Standard Version translations), in II Peter 1:20,21:

> First of all you must understand this, that no prophecy of scripture is a matter of one's own interpretation, because no prophecy ever came by the impulse of man, but *men moved by the Holy Spirit spoke from God. RSV*

> Knowing this first, that no prophecy of the scripture is of any private interpretation. For the prophecy came not in old time by the will of man, but holy men of God spake as they were moved by the Holy Spirit. *KJV*

A true prophecy originates with God. It is given to a selected individual by the inspiration of the Holy Spirit. As that individual speaks it out spontaneously, without premeditation, men hear a message borne from heaven to earth by the Spirit of God. The words of a prophecy spoken in this way are pure. They cannot fail because they express the intention of God in regard to the matter of which they speak.

With few exceptions, a prophecy exists first in the form of the spoken word. It is often also transcribed in some way and so exists in the permanent form of the written word. That is why we have today many of the words spoken by the ancient prophets of Israel recorded in the pages of the Bible.

God channels His revelations to the human race through men who are holy and chosen by Him to declare that which He gives to them—such men as Moses, David, Joshua, Isaiah, Daniel, Joel, Micah, and scores of other inspired prophets of Israel.

The prophets of Israel did not speak their own minds. Each of them spoke publicly that which the Holy Spirit imparted to him from God. You can get some idea of the mode of prophecy and of what is accurately claimed for it from the following declarations:

"The Lord called Moses and spoke to him . . . saying, 'Speak to the people of Israel and say to them. . . .' " Leviticus 1:1,2.

"And the Lord said to Moses, 'Speak. . . .' " Leviticus 21:1.

"And the Lord said to Moses, 'Tell. . . .' " Leviticus 22:1.

"The Lord said to Moses, 'Say to the people of Israel. . . .' " Leviticus 23:1.

"The Lord said to Moses, 'Command. . . .' " Leviticus 24:1,2. All of these are instances of revelation to Moses by God.

"And *the Spirit of God came upon Azariah* the son of Oded, and he went out to meet King Asa, and said to him, 'Hear me, Asa, and all Judah and Benjamin, the Lord is with you, while you are with him. If you seek him, he will be found by you, but if you forsake him, he will forsake you . . . be strong therefore, and let not your hands be weak, for your work shall be rewarded.' " II Chronicles 15:1,2,7.

Ezekiel says: "In the eleventh year, in the third month, on the first day of the month, the word of the Lord came to me, 'Son of man, say. . . .' " Ezekiel 31:1,2.

Jeremiah says: "Now the word of the Lord came to me saying, 'Before I formed you in the womb I knew you, and before you were born I consecrated you; I appointed you a prophet to the nations.' " Jeremiah 1:4,5.

"The word that came to Jeremiah from the Lord, 'Thus says the Lord, the God of Israel: Write in a book all the words that I have spoken to you.' " Jeremiah 30:1,2.

Isaiah prophesied to the *nation:* "Therefore thus says the Lord, the Lord of hosts, 'O my people, who dwell in Zion, be not afraid of the Assyrians when they smite . . . For in a very little while my indignation will come to an end, and my anger will be directed to their destruction. And the Lord of hosts will wield against them a scourge. . . .' " Isaiah 10:24-26.

Isaiah prophesied to an *individual:* "Then the word of the Lord came to Isaiah, 'Go and say to Hezekiah, Thus says the Lord, the God of David your father: I have heard your prayer, I have seen your tears. Behold, I will add fifteen years to your life. I will deliver you and this city out of the hand of the king of Assyria, and defend this city.' " Isaiah 38:4-6.

"And the word of the Lord came to Zechariah, saying, 'Thus says the Lord of hosts: Render true judgments, show kindness and mercy. . . .' But they refused to hearken. . . They made their hearts like adamant lest they should hear the law and the *words which the Lord of hosts had sent by his Spirit through the prophets.*

"Therefore great wrath came from the Lord of hosts. 'As I called, and they would not hear, so they called, and I would not hear,' says the Lord of hosts, 'and I scattered them with a whirlwind among all the nations which they had not known.' " Zechariah 7:8-14.

These examples could be multiplied more than a hundredfold from the Old Testament. The prophets received the Word of God directly from God by the activity of the Holy Spirit, and they spoke it and wrote it.

Some of them also received revelation by visions, and they spoke and wrote what they saw. Genesis 15:1 says, "After these things the *word* of the Lord came to Abram in a vision. . . ."

Dreams are another means by which God sometimes conveys His truth to men. Jacob's son Joseph received revelation from God by dreams. The prophet Daniel interpreted prophetic dreams. The prophet Joel, speaking the word of the Lord, declared:

"I will pour out *my Spirit* on all flesh; your sons and your daughters shall *prophesy,* your old men shall dream *dreams,* and your young men shall see *visions."* Joel 2:28.

The active personal agent in communicating God's truth to man is the Spirit of the Lord. The direct result of the coming of the Holy Spirit upon men and women is sometimes seen in inspired prophecies . . . dreams . . . visions.

Testing Prophets and
Dreamers of Dreams

Though they are the means God uses to convey His revelations to men, prophecy, dreams, or visions do not in themselves have any claim whatever to expressing truth. More false prophecy is uttered in the world than true prophecy, and by no close margin. Dreams flicker through our sleep like surrealist films in montage. Visions may, and often do, come from mental derangement or from evil spirits. It is only when the Holy Spirit uses these means that the content of the prophecy, the dream, or the vision is truth.

It is important to understand that factual accuracy does not constitute evidence that a prophecy or a dream or a vision is from God. Factual accuracy is not an adequate test of the divine inspiration of any prophecy.

The law of Moses speaks this word regarding prophecy: "If a prophet arises among you, or a dreamer of dreams, and gives you a sign or a wonder, and the sign or the wonder which he tells you *comes to pass,* and if he says, 'Let us go after other gods,' which you have not known . . . *you shall not listen to the words of that prophet* or that dreamer of dreams; for the Lord your God is testing you to know whether you love the Lord your God with all your heart and with all your soul [and] that prophet or that dreamer of dreams shall be put to death." Deuteronomy 13:1–5.

True prophecy is, of course, always factually accurate, but that is not the acid test of it. The acid test of all prophecy is whether it is in or out of accord with the Scriptures. A prophecy may be factually accurate and spiritually wrong. In that case it is a counterfeit of divinely inspired prophecy designed to impress men intellectually but deceive them spiritually.

Such prophecy can be supremely deceiving precisely because it is factually accurate. In the Mosaic warning just above, a prophet gives out a distinct sign or portent. That sign comes to pass exactly as he said it would. The human instinct is to proclaim the man a true prophet, to listen to him with close attention and respect, and to give roughly equal weight to the rest of what he says. Having accredited himself in the popular imagination as a true prophet, he then gives a piece of spiritual counsel. That counsel is false and stands in direct contradiction to the First Commandment. The prophet is therefore a false prophet. In the law of Moses, he was put to death so as to cleanse the land of an individual of evil religious bent. It was a better thing for such a man to die than for the land to become populated with false prophets speaking words contrary to the word of God and leading many people astray.

Israel was a nation placed under the law of God, not under a human law, and that law required the penalty of death in this and certain other cases, just as our law does in certain instances. It would not do in our diverse and pluralistic society for there to be any supreme religious authority empowered to declare what is and what is not spiritually genuine and to enforce that judgment. But we do not have on that score to be made into the victims of false prophecy.

A prophecy can be supernatural, factually accurate and false! It is very likely that such a prophecy is factually accurate *because* it is supernatural. But it does not proceed from God, and the man or woman who speaks it is not a man or woman of God.

There are many false prophets and there is much false prophecy circulating in the United States today. False prophets have been coming very prominently to the fore in recent years. We can accurately define a false prophet as an individual who is spiritually connected to the supernatural, who speaks at times under the influence of supernatural powers, but whose authority as a prophet does not proceed from God and whose words and counsel are not in accord with the Word of God. In God's eyes, such a person is a great offender, because he deals in the supernatural —but not by God's commission!—and he dispenses spiritual counsel—in contradiction to God's Word!

Among the leading false prophets, by the terms of this Biblical definition, whose statements are widely known in the United States today are:

The late Bishop James A. Pike. His experiments with the supernatural were in the most direct and explicit contradiction to the Word of God.

Jeane Dixon. She has supernatural powers that do not proceed from God. Some of her prophecies may be factually accurate—

some clearly are, most are dead wrong—but she uses means that take a person into the supernatural by agents other than the Spirit of God.

Timothy Leary. He is under the strong influence of supernatural powers. He has become the single individual most responsible for the introduction into America of spiritual practices contrary to the Holy Scriptures.

There are many others. Some of them meet and pass the test of factual accuracy at times. That does not make them less false, it only makes them more dangerous and more deceptive to the uninformed.

A false prophet must be distinguished from a phony prophet. A false prophet has certain supernatural powers and uses them. A phony prophet is an outright fake. A false prophet may be utterly sincere and unaware of his falsity. A phony prophet knows he is a fake. A false prophet may practice gross spiritual deception without knowing it, because he himself is thoroughly deceived. A phony prophet knows exactly the deceptions he practices and how he practices them. He does not believe in what he is doing. A phony can be discovered in his *methods,* if they are inspected closely enough. A false prophet can be clearly identified by his or her disagreement with the Word of the God of Israel as recorded in the Bible.

The late Harry Houdini, the extraordinary escape artist and magician, made himself the chief scourge of phony trance mediums because he knew and could expose the contrived means by which they produced their purportedly supernatural effects. Such people preyed upon the naive and gullible and took their money by fakery, and Houdini showed it for what it was.

Such people are still around and they still deceive the ignorant, but we are mainly troubled now by quite a different breed. Bishop Pike was assuredly not a fake. He surely believed in what he was doing and in what he was saying. He cannot be faulted on the grounds of objective sincerity. He was deceived. His deception, joined to his very great abilities as a writer and a popularizer, was much more likely to deceive intelligent people than the duplicities of a fake.

It is a singularly interesting and significant fact that, almost 12 years ago, when supernatural gifts of the Holy Spirit that are specifically described and approved in the Bible began occurring in churches in his Episcopal diocese in California, Bishop Pike argued against them and sought to impede their exercise. Then he became engaged in promulgating in our culture by the considerable means at his disposal supernatural practices that the Bible specifically identifies as contrary to the will of God because they are harmful to man.

The term medium is a very apt one. One definition is: *"A person serving . . . as an instrument through which another personality or a supernatural agency is alleged to manifest itself: a spiritualistic medium."*

A medium stands between the natural realm and the supernatural realm and permits himself to become the channel through which supernatural powers manifest themselves to man. The Bible clearly and repeatedly warns worshipers of God to have nothing to do with mediums at any time.

The late Rev. Arthur Ford, a prominent medium, reportedly held the séance in which Bishop Pike received messages from what he took to be his dead son. Many mediums who conduct séances are outright fakes, but it would seem unlikely that Mr. Ford was a fake. It is probable that he was, in fact, a medium.

At this point we must ask a medium *from* what *to* what? Mr. Ford claimed to be a medium between dead human beings and living human beings. When he conducted the séance for Bishop Pike he apparently succeeded in speaking certain facts about the dead son to Bishop Pike. It is easy to conclude that he brought forth statements of factual accuracy by using supernatural powers. It is yet more precise to say that Mr. Ford brought forth certain words by *being used* by certain supernatural powers. His spiritual accessibility to these powers made him a medium.

I do not dispute that a spirit took hold of Mr. Ford during this séance. I do not dispute in any way the likelihood that what Mr. Ford said was spoken under the immediate influence of supernatural powers. But the terrible fact is that the spirit that takes hold of a medium is not the spirit of a deceased human being but an evil spirit. The voice that speaks through the vocal organs of a medium in a séance is not the voice of a dead human being. It is the voice of an evil spirit impersonating the dead human being.

A medium who is not a fake, who is sincere in his practice and in his adventures in the supernatural, brings men and women into direct contact with evil spirits. These evil spirits are engaged in active opposition to the will of God because they are the enemies of God. Their purpose is to draw human beings away from the truths of God, which set men free, and get them involved in practices against their well-being.

Evil spirits are not mortal. They are at least as old as human history, possibly a great deal older. Their knowledge of events and personalities of the past can be impressive.

It is because evil spirits are skillful and potent enemies of the human mind and soul that God warns us in His word to have nothing to do with mediums. A man is not wise to venture into and become spiritually involved in supernatural areas that are dangerous to him—as dangerous in their way as high-voltage wires.

Evil spirits will ultimately destroy the man who yields to their deceptive fascinations.

God wants man to know of, and to experience, that which is supernatural. But He speaks in the Scriptures to keep man away from that which is bad for him and to lead him to that which will do him good.

It is as though a table were spread with mushrooms, half of them tender, succulent, and fully edible, half of them deadly, all looking pretty much alike. Your friend will tell you which are which. He will say, "Eat all you can of that, and keep away from all of that." He will identify them with precision for your benefit.

Then along comes your enemy, who wants you to be destroyed, and he says, "Look, dig in! Eat anything that looks good and tastes good! If you listen to that narrow-minded, illiberal maker of distinctions you'll starve. Your friend doesn't want you to have any mushrooms." But the truth is he does. Your friend just doesn't want you to get any that will kill you.

Because there is a supernatural realm and because that realm impinges on human affairs, God has deliberately chosen to make a revelation to man regarding the supernatural that is fully adequate to keep any man who will pay it heed out of trouble. That revelation is found in the Bible. The Scriptures of the Old and New Testaments are the written Word of God, committed by the Holy Spirit to certain chosen Jewish men. They constitute a full and reliable declaration of what is true on the spiritual plane.

Whether by word or by vision, any revelation of which the Holy Spirit is the communicator from God to man is the truth about the facts of which it speaks.

The passage, quoted partially earlier, on the role of the Holy Spirit in revealing truths of the spiritual realm to man reads in major part:

"As it is written, 'Eye has not seen, nor ear heard, neither have entered into the heart of man the things which God has prepared for them that love him,' but God has revealed them to us by his Spirit. For the Spirit searches all things, even the deep things of God. For what man knows the thoughts of a man except by the spirit of man which is in him? So also no one comprehends the thoughts of God except the Spirit of God.

"Now we [who are believers] have received not the spirit of the world, but the Spirit which is of God, that we might understand the gifts bestowed on us by God. And we impart this in words not taught by human wisdom but taught by the Spirit, interpreting spiritual truths to those who possess the Spirit." I Corinthians 2:9–13.

The passage declares that the Word of God is given to man by the Holy Spirit so "that we might understand" what is true and know what spiritual and supernatural gifts belong to men and women who truly believe in the God of Israel.

When I speak of the spiritual and the supernatural realm I speak of that which lies beyond the physical and natural realm, beyond the reach of man's mind and senses, where God reigns, undiscoverable by man except by revelation.

A Lady Named Lowe

A wonderful instance of God's effective communication to man by the Holy Spirit occurred in a church at Birmingham, England, several years ago. A friend and associate of mine, Mrs. Hannah Lowe, a missionary of more than thirty years standing to Bogota, Colombia, had spent some months working with orphans at Bethlehem, Jordan. On her way back to South America she stopped in England. She wanted to visit Coventry, where her late husband's father and grandfather were born.

In London she met some Pentecostal people and it was suggested that she speak in several churches while in England, spending two nights in each church. Pentecostal churches frequently meet two or more nights in the week.

On a very cold night in late autumn Mrs. Lowe arrived to speak in the Birmingham church. The people were scattered about the church auditorium and she asked if they would move in closer to the pulpit. They would be more comfortable that way and she would not have to raise her voice to reach the last row of the pews. Nearly everyone moved, but one woman sat in an end seat in the last row, next to a radiator, and did not budge. Mrs. Lowe surmised that she felt extra cold and did not want to give up her place by the radiator. Mrs. Lowe told of her missionary work in Colombia.

As she finished, a vision flashed onto her consciousness. It was a picture—as vivid as a color slide—of an elephant with a bell standing in the thick green growth of a jungle.

She was standing on the platform with the minister seated nearby. She did not know what the vision signified. While she pondered, a man in the congregation gave out a message in tongues. She wondered if the vision might be related to the content of his message.

The picture of the elephant was gone, but a second picture took its place. Mrs. Lowe saw milestones set at the side of a woodland road.

In a moment a third picture succeeded it. The experience was very much like a succession of photographic slides in brilliant focus. They came rapidly. The message in tongues was still going on.

This third picture was of an hourglass. The yellow sand had almost all sifted through to the bottom half.

By now someone was speaking out an interpretation in English of the message in tongues, but it had nothing to do with the visions Mrs. Lowe saw.

A fourth picture flashed on. It was a beautiful picture of a lonely beach in wintertime, a frosty scene at the edge of the sea. The sun shone overhead, but it looked small and feeble to impart much warmth. The waves were crashing in and as tongues of the sea licked the rocks, they almost caught and froze there. A thin film of ice clung to the rocks, but the sun was just strong enough to keep the water from forming solid ice.

As Mrs. Lowe wondered what to make of the visions, the four pictures were presented again, very rapidly, one by one in the same order, and they were as exact in their detail and as vivid as at the first: The elephant in the jungle with the bell. The milestones strung along the roadside. The hourglass with the sand almost run out. The beach, and the waves that were not quite freezing as they washed over the rocks.

"I realized that I had something, but I did not know what I had," Mrs. Lowe says. There were only two alternatives. To declare the visions to the church or to remain silent and ponder them, hoping later to understand their meaning. The second course is easier and safer. The first involves the risk of sounding foolish. The visions bore no relation whatever to anything that had been spoken during the evening.

"I put out what I can only call a platform of faith and then I stepped on it," Mrs. Lowe said. "I said aloud, 'I don't want to fail the Lord tonight.'"

Mrs. Lowe did not know in her mind what to say next, but she opened her mouth and heard herself say these words:

"There is someone here tonight who has a call to India."

It was clear now that the elephant in the jungle signified India.

There was a momentary pause and Mrs. Lowe spoke again. *"You're not young anymore,"* she said. The words interpreted the vision of the milestones along the road, the passing of years. ("It was as if the Lord pieced it all together for me," Mrs. Lowe explained. "I would not have known how to bring it out, but the words came and I just stood there and listened to them myself.")

She spoke a few short sentences that conveyed the sense of the four-part vision in simple words.

"Time is running out for you," she said. *"You do not have much longer to decide."* These words matched the picture of the sand running out in the hourglass.

"Already your heart is becoming icy. A little longer and it will freeze entirely, but there is still a little warmth and it has not frozen yet. The sun of righteousness, God's Son, has warmed your heart even though that has seemed weak to you and He has kept your heart up until this time. Much time has passed. Now there is only a little time left, and He calls you to India."

A deep hush had fallen over the whole church, all eyes were fixed on her, and Mrs. Lowe felt very lonely. But she went on.

"Is there anyone here who answers to this description?" she asked. "Will you come to the altar?"

("The thought that came to me was, 'There is no one here who will answer to that call. At the end you will just say there *is* someone who didn't want to answer and try to excuse yourself by that.' I was in a 'Lord, I believe; help my unbelief' situation. The enemy, Satan, was there with suggestions to try to defeat the purpose of God.")

At this invitation, the woman seated at the rear of the hall, apart from the rest of the congregation, got up, came quickly down the side aisle and dropped to her knees at the altar railing, praying and weeping.

As she did that, other members of the congregation moved forward in a state of high interest, and some of them were crying, too. And the minister seemed to be profoundly affected.

The minister stepped to the lectern and said, "We know that our guest here has just come from Bethlehem and has no way of knowing what we have suffered for eight years, and in less than eight minutes she has told the history of what has been going on here. I perceive that this is the gift of the word of wisdom and the gift of the word of knowledge." (He named two specific gifts of the Holy Spirit of which the Scriptures speak.)

The minister then said to Mrs. Lowe, "Will you please step down and pray for our sister as we all gather around her?" Several of the members of the congregation were weeping quietly as Mrs. Lowe prayed for the woman.

"What has happened?" Mrs. Lowe thought. She had never been in the church, had never heard of it, had never met any of its people. The wisdom of God saw to that. The content of her message was such that it could not have been received if there had been premeditation to it.

After the service, the minister and his wife told Mrs. Lowe the woman's story. She was in her thirties. She had been born in India, and her parents had brought her home to England and to Birmingham when she was a child.

Eight years prior to that memorable evening, the woman had received what she believed to be the call of God to go to India as a missionary.

A missionary to India had passed through the church, had spoken eloquently, and the young woman had gone forward to the altar railing as a way of declaring that she desired to go as a missionary to India. The church stood behind her in the decision and money was supplied for her passage and for clothing and equipment.

She packed her belongings, bade her farewells, and traveled into Europe with the lady missionary to India. But something went wrong, there was some misunderstanding, and the missionary left her in Europe and went on alone. The young woman, uncertain about what to do next, got in touch with the church and was told to come back.

Almost immediately members of the church were torn between two opinions. Some said the woman's call to India was genuine but that an unfortunate circumstance had barred her way. Others said no. The call was not genuine. It had been a false emotional surge and the proof of that was that it had come to nothing. She should never have gone. These opinions solidified into factions that deeply split the church.

The young woman did not know the answer herself. The outcome of her uncompleted journey had dealt a blow to the faith in which she thought she had gone out. Yet she could not shake off the conviction that God had called her to India. Caught between two strong and contrary opinions, she did not know how to act.

There the matter stood for eight long years. The church remained divided on the question, and the woman remained rather remote from the other members in her bewilderment.

Exactly two days before the meeting at which Mrs. Lowe spoke, as the woman later related, she had remarked that her heart was growing cold. She did not feel she was getting anywhere or that she could just keep on with things the way they were.

As she heard the background to the events of the evening, Mrs. Lowe began to understand why the few words she had spoken had been so swift and deep in their effect—upon the woman, upon the minister, upon the congregation.

The woman knew that her own spiritual state had been portrayed with great precision in the sentences Mrs. Lowe spoke, each of which cut straight to the core of her great perplexity, even down to the fact that her heart was growing cold, upon which she herself had remarked two days before. Those sentences were a marvelously supernatural confirmation of her original call to India. The manner in which they came carried the assurance, as the Bible puts it, "that your faith might not rest in the wisdom of men but in the power of God."

The church members who had judged the case wrongly—regarding the circumstance of an impediment to the woman's journey to India as plausible evidence of a divine veto—now saw their error, and the division in the church over the matter was thoroughly healed. So it was that a few words spoken, not by human knowledge or insight but in a wisdom imparted by the Holy Spirit, resolved a severe perplexity that had vexed the church for eight years. The pictures and the words cut like a sharp sword through a knot that could not be untied. The more church members had pulled on that knot the tighter it had become.

The next night a radiant woman, who looked to be in her twenties, rushed up to Mrs. Lowe, who did not immediately recognize her. "I'm Dorothy, I'm the one you prayed for last night," the woman said. "I live in a rooming house and when I got to the door the lady there said, 'What has happened, what has happened to you?' But I said, 'Don't speak to me now,' and I ran up to my room and got down by my bed and cried out in thankfulness to God."

Mrs. Lowe returned to Colombia. One morning a long letter came from India, signed by Dorothy. "Here I am," she wrote. "I know I'm in the will of the Lord. After you left, the people in the church sacrificed and did everything they could to get me the passage on the boat. The church members went to the wharf with me and, as I left, they sang a verse from 'Onward Christian Soldiers'—the one about 'We are not divided, all one body we. . . .' "

It is a wonderfully refreshing thing to attend church services where something real happens—where there is spiritual reality, not just ritual.

Rote and ritual are substitutes for reality. They preempt the time, filling it with prescribed and preset forms, so that an individual knows what will be going on every minute during the period of worship. It can make worship the dullest of experiences, apart from and irrelevant to life. Men won't swallow that sort of thing in any line but religion. If they went into a cafeteria and ordered a meal and were served food substitutes they would complain: "These aren't carrots."

"You're right, sir," says the server. "They're not real carrots. They're our ritual carrots. They look like carrots, have the same color, but we make them out of sawdust. Real carrots vary so much in quality. Sometimes they're tender, sometimes they're tough. You can't count on them. The quality of these ritual carrots never varies. They always taste like sawdust."

People would not stick with that cafeteria for another meal. They'd get right out and find a place that served fresh carrots. Yet some people will drag on year after year after year in synagogue and church services that are ritualized, repetitive, predictable, and full of a kind of mortuary solemnity that makes you want to get back out into the real world.

Ritual crowds God out and stuffs a service up with filler. God has promised to dwell in the midst of His people and to speak to them directly, according to their present needs, through His prophets. When a prophet, or a prophetess, speaks by the momentary inspiration of the Holy Spirit the words may come like lightning or like dew but they are always fresh and arresting and right to the point of immediate need.

In their profound distrust of the supernatural, in their militant avoidance of it, and in their insistence on stale rote, houses of worship have won a reputation among the young as the dullest places in town. Instead of obtaining their knowledge of the supernatural from church and synagogue and Scripture, young people are obtaining it where they can get it, and most of what they are getting now are the deadly counterfeits of Satan.

God, Who does not want young feet to be taken in snares, has given an accurate chart to the channels of the supernatural in the Bible, with areas of danger clearly marked. God is a good Father, and He wants us to have what is good and to avoid what is evil in the supernatural.

"What father among you, if his son asks for a fish, will instead of a fish give him a serpent? Or if he asks for an egg, will give him a scorpion?" the Bible asks. "If you then, who are evil, know how to give good gifts to your children, how much more will the heavenly Father give the Holy Spirit to those who ask him!"

Unpremeditated prophecy comes forth frequently in worship services I attend. Sometimes it is addressed to particular individuals, sometimes to the congregation, sometimes it speaks more broadly to national and world affairs.

On July 4, 1964, I heard a prophecy warning of grave disruptions to the nation. I was not able to record it word by word, but the bulk and gist of it follows. The tone in which it was spoken, which added much to its impact on those who heard it, was filled with urgency and grief, as though a father were telling his son of an unseen mortal danger. The prophecy:

"O my people. Do you see that I have given America a broad land, flowing with good things? Do you see her harvest fields rippling with wheat, fields that roll like oceans? Do you see her streets lined with comfortable, protected homes, spacious homes —lined with homes for ten thousands of miles? Yet now I tell you that all this—all this that America enjoys—her fields, her homes— stands in danger of destruction. All this is in danger of destruction because of race hatred and race injustice in your land. O my people, pray!"

It was a few days later that the summer riots that were to tear like claws at parts of many cities began breaking out. That would seem to be the beginning of the prophesied destruction the nation must suffer if it fails swiftly to repair this grievous injury and sin.

Hatred and injustice bring judgment. Usually God warns once, twice, perhaps three times of the gathering storm of wrath. Then, if the warning is not effectively heeded, the storm breaks in great fury.

The warnings of God come in prophecy and in events, events that clearly delineate the nature of the sin that must be put out of a nation's life if it is to avoid wrath. The sin of slavery brought upon this nation the terrible judgment of the Civil War. Before it came, there were rumblings and prophetic warnings and clear depictions of the nature of the sin that offended God—especially in a nation so thoroughly aware of the declarations of the Hebrew prophets regarding injustice and God's hatred of it.

On various occasions I have heard Mrs. Lowe speak un-premeditated prophecy. The words have been recorded. On June 1, 1964, Mrs. Lowe spoke the following prophecy:

"Pray much for My people Israel, for Israel shall come into her own. The time is nearly here. My sovereign hour has nearly struck and you should pray more into the light and ask for the light that you may know how to come in and go out, that you may know more of my plan for My people and My call to them. 'Jerusalem, Jerusalem.' And though the call for them in that day was almost in vain, because their house was left unto them desolate; behold, have I forsaken them, that I should not take them again unto Myself? I shall hold them and I shall feed them, and some of them shall come into My body, My perfect plan for them. And Israel shall yet come into My perfect plan for her.

"I would ask you to hold steady at this time and to believe for them and to call for them. And as you call to Me, I will call to them; and as you intercede, it will be My intercession through you, for you cannot intercede, only as I give you the power and strength to intercede. And this intercession and travail is sure, for when Zion travails she brings forth.

"I would have you call upon Me at this time that My plan might be accomplished. You see this plan. It has seemed at times to become bright and then becomes dull and then bright again. It is only because there has to be a readiness, there has to be an hour. As you have seen the plan seemingly grow dim for them, it was only to do other things until the time would come when this would be brought forth, so the time is now almost upon them and upon you, My children."

The prophecy speaks of the full restoration of the people of Israel to the center of God's will for them, a position they have not occupied in the world since Old Testament days. That is what is meant by the phrase "Israel shall come into her own"—into that unclouded relationship to God that He has always intended for the Jews, though it shall come only after a time of national tribulation.

On July 7, 1968, Mrs. Lowe spoke a prophecy that came with such astonishing speed that tongue could hardly keep its pace. The words poured out at a rate much quicker than that of rapid speech; yet they came with what I can only call the anointing of God, by the Holy Spirit. Fortunately, the entire prophecy was tape-recorded:

"Yea, didn't I form man? Did I not form one man in the beginning and then the woman? Were they not perfect before Me? And was not even Satan, Lucifer himself, when I created him, was he not perfect until pride was found in his heart? And did he not become the king of pride, and did he not rebel? And was he not cast down? Yea, I kept Adam and Eve. Was not the garden perfect that I put them in? Was this not a possession of Mine, a place of a treasure that I had in them and in My garden? And yet they rebelled and yet they turned away. And did I not call Israel? And have you not known and have you not read how I washed her and I dressed her and did everything for her? Was she not to be a jewel? Was she not to be a treasure to the nations round about? Did I not ask her to keep herself pure? Did I not ask her to keep her skirts and her body all pure for me, that I would be her only lover and she would be My own choice elect, My wife, My Ishshah?

"And yet did they not all turn? Did not the enemy turn himself against Me and say, 'I will'? And did not the woman and the man turn to their own ways? And did not Israel turn to her own ways?

"And have I not kept My purpose and My plan, not allowing it to be contaminated or mixed with any other plan? Yea, I say to you that I have not allowed My plan ever to be dragged down, and though the enemy has sought to drag My plan down and though man has gone in with the enemy and with flesh to drag down My plan, My plan cannot be contaminated.

"There is a highway, a highway of holiness and no unclean thing shall walk therein. And so, as you see, there are few in the way. There are so few because of the cleanness of the way. There can be nothing of the enemy upon it.

"And did I not call your own nation that your own feet stand upon this day? Did I not call your Puritan fathers? Are they not called Puritans? Were some not Pilgrims over the face of the earth, as they wandered from the places where they were held in bondage, to seek My will, and did I not make a country? Did I not have a country formed and planned after My own will, to become a treasure in the earth, to be a nation which would call out to men and women because of the brightness and the clearness and the purity of the treasure and because of the light that would shine forth through My treasure? And have they not failed Me?

"Yea, they have failed Me until you see that the enemy would take vengeance against Me and against My plan to drag this country even to the dregs of misery and even to the bottom of hell. The enemy shakes his fist and says, 'Who can do this?' But yea, I will have My people.

"Is it not a temptation to be like other people? Is it not a temptation—as Israel once said, 'Nay, but we have no king. We must have a king before us, because we have no king to go out ahead of us physically. We want to see a king. We want to see a king with armor. We want to see a king who rides forth in great pomp in front of us.' And yea, did I not give them a king? Was there not a temptation to be as the other nations? Was it not Israel that called out, 'We will have no king but Caesar. We don't want the king who says he is the king. We will not accept him.' And is there not a temptation many times to be as other people, to be as other nations, to get in with those round about?

"But I would have you take hold this day with those who are holding on steadily for the clarity and the pureness of the vision that I have given. You cannot afford to be as others, you cannot afford to look around and see if you could only be as that one, if you could only have this or the other. But I say to you, keep your garments pure. Keep yourself spotless from the world. Keep yourself. Yea, they who live in Me shall walk in a godly way and without the spots and stains of sin—not like other nations, not like other peoples round about. For I do not do with the multitude. Yea, I need not arms. Yea, I need not the arms of men and the clamor and the clang of the armaments of men because hell is underneath of it. And cursed is the one who leans upon the flesh and makes flesh his arm.

"I will show you absolutely what you shall do that you may ride forth in absolute victory, for My plan will burst forth. I have a plan for you and you are in My plan, as long as your eyes are single to My glory and purity prevails among you. Yea, I will keep you as Mine own. Keep your eyes upon Me and be not cast down. Be not cast down but look unto Me and I will bring you through speedily, saith the Lord to you. For I the Lord have said this, and will I not perform it? For I am not a man that I should lie or the son of man that I should repent. I have spoken and who can disannul it, saith the Lord. Hallelujah."

On May 2, 1965, I heard Mrs. Lowe speak a prophecy concerning destruction. It had two parts, indicating two phases of God's dealing with the nations: The first phase is that of warning. The second is that of judgment. The prophecy spoke of "rumblings and shakings" in the earth, disturbances that would be pronounced in their force, yet take only a small toll:

"Thus says the Lord, I am going to shake the nations with earthquakes that they might know that I am God and turn to Me. You will see that the shakings will cause much damage, but few lives will be taken by them, for I would bring forth salvation and not destruction. I am starting with the shakings, that they might turn to Me. You will see, you will notice, how few lives are taken as I shake the earth."

That was the first part of the prophecy. The second part follows:

"I have said that I would shake the earth. I am about again to thunder throughout this earth and I will move upon this United States in such a way as you cannot imagine. This shall be shaken, this United States, from center to circumference, and buildings, yea, buildings shall topple and fall to the ground. There shall be ashes, there shall be rubble. All of this that is big with men, which they have built up, up, will be down before them as so much rubble, and the stench of the corpses of men shall smell in the streets. The noise of tumult and the noise of battle would not be any greater than that which I will do with My own hands, for I will send out lightnings and I will send forth thunders and I will discomfit them, saith the Lord.

"So I ask you, My children, to be faithful to Me, faithful unto death. I will give you the crown of life. You can never put a crown upon yourself. No man can crown himself. All these things that are of men are in vain, crying themselves and putting crowns upon their heads, but they shall topple and fall to the ground. They are not My crowns. My crowns are given by Me. I give My crowns to those I want to have them. No man can crown himself. Neither can any man crown another man. This cannot be. I give crowns. Be faithful unto death, and I will give you the crown of life, for it is the crown of life that you will receive; yea, eternal life. I will give you eternal life, and I will give a crown of joy to those who follow Me all the way through, saith the Lord.

"Yea, once more will I speak; yea, once more will I speak, and you shall see, and what you shall see—you shall see crumbling, you shall see ashes, you shall see debris, and men shall not know how to get away; for this shall come, yea, even shortly. And yea, as you have prayed of the Bridegroom calling to the bride: He is winning her and wooing her—'Come out of her, My people, and be a separate people and I shall be your Lord, and you shall be My sons and daughters, saith the Lord.' "

Journey Into the Supernatural: Knowing What Is

There are in the creation orders of beings who are intelligently active but unseen by man. They are capable of thought, of speech, of volition, of worship, of love, or of hate. One of these invisible orders of beings is that known as angels. They are servants of God, active on behalf of His will in the universe.

To reject this thought too quickly, to insist that all intelligent beings or that all beings whatever must be corporeal, and therefore visible to human sight when in range of it, is to be materialistic to the point of obtuseness. Science has lately discovered, for instance, that there is matter and also anti-matter. "Research in physics has revealed the existence of mirror-image counterparts to all the particles composing matter on this planet," a news report said.

Physicists say there may be worlds, there may be galaxies made up of anti-matter. Some go farther. Isaac Asimov suggested that "somewhere, entirely beyond our reach or observation, there may be an anti-universe made up almost entirely of anti-matter." The universe that we know may be a kind of obverse of another universe, coexistent and concurrent, that we do not know.

The structure of reality as it is revealed in the Bible is not the same as that commonly conceived by man. God has not limited Himself to flesh and blood in creating orders of intelligent beings.

Most Americans would say that they inhabit a universe in which men are intelligent beings, a universe in which there probably are but possibly are not other highly intelligent beings dwelling elsewhere in space, and in which there is, somewhere, a supreme being, God.

Some men inhabit a universe, as they suppose, in which there is no God. The Bible says of them, "The fool has said in his heart, 'There is no God.'" Psalm 53:1.

The Bible presents a distinctly different picture of reality.

It declares that the God Who revealed Himself to Israel is the creator and ruler of the universe.

It reveals that there is an order of intelligent created beings who are the servants of God, called angels.

It reveals man as a created order of intelligent beings made in the likeness of God. Man stands a little lower on the scale of creation than the angels.

The Bible reveals an order of intelligent beings, who are in active rebellion against God, called evil spirits or demons.

The Bible declares that they are led by an intelligent personality called Satan.

What is set forth here is what the Bible affirms to be the case, from the Book of Genesis to the Book of Revelation, the first and last books of the Bible. If a man fails to grasp this, he cannot understand much of the Bible, because that is the structure of reality in which all the earthly events of the Bible—past and future —are set.

They are set in that structure because *that is what is.*

This can be ignored, but it cannot be escaped. Saying that demons do not exist in no way prevents them from intruding into the lives and the affairs of your family. The tragic fact today is that families whose members ignore large segments of this reality are becoming the victims of intelligent forces of evil whose activity they do not even vaguely suspect. This is especially true among the young people, and parents are wholly unprepared to cope with that which has come to destroy their young.

Never in American history has there been a time when people more need to know what is behind the eruptions and disruptions that are beginning to rend society and disfigure history. Ignorance of these things is not God's program for man; it is the program of evil forces whose interest it is to conceal their activities from their intended victims. The Bible focuses the floodlight of revelation upon these forces, so that men may know of them and how to deal effectively with them.

What we need to know about is reality, spiritual reality as well as physical reality. What is important is reality, not fantasy.

I make this point because the assertion that there are invisible orders of beings is no license for creative acts of the mind. If we say that there are such orders of beings, the next question is: Well, where do we go from here? If we go out on a tangent of our imagination, or of someone else's possibly more fruitful imagination, we can people a universe full of non-corporeal, invisible, but *wholly imaginary* beings: hobgoblins and elves and ghosts and anything else that may strike your fancy or haunt your superstition. We know that superstition and old wives' tales and false religions have sometimes made men's lives grim with their unwarranted imaginings.

I do not want any part of any system of thought that populates men's minds with phantoms that do not, in fact, exist. On the other hand I want to know, exactly, the orders of beings that do, in fact, exist and that operate intelligently and purposefully in the creation. I want to know the whole extent of reality, as far as it may be known, visible and invisible, but I do not want to go one step beyond reality into fantasy and superstition. And, since neither the investigations of science or the speculations of my mind can tell me anything about this that is in any degree reliable, I am dependent on revelation.

The Biblical revelation—properly understood and not distorted or extended in any way by unwarranted exercises of the imagination—offers us a reliable, and in some respects a distinctly verifiable, guide to reality. It tells us of the existence and the activities of one order of invisible beings, having two categories: angels and demons. That is not revealed as a matter of curiosity, but because we need to know it.

The rational man ought to agree that if God declares by revelation that there is a being called Satan who actively and radically opposes all the purposes of God among men and who works with skill and inexhaustible energy against the best interests of men, it is a good thing for man to know it. In the Biblical revelation, Satan is fully exposed as the enemy of God and man.

By the same token, Satan seeks desperately to conceal the fact of his existence. His methods depend for their effectiveness on the concealment both of their source and their purpose. Satan does not want you to believe that he exists. He wants you to believe positively that he does *not* exist. Then he may go about his business against you and against your family unsuspected and undetected.

Rational men, accustomed as they are to equating the name of Satan with a variety of purely fantastic caricatures, are a little too quick to smile knowingly when his name is mentioned. One of Satan's devices has been to promote ridiculous caricatures of himself that are so evidently not of reality that rational men associate his name with that which is mythical. Because of this, intelligent people have too readily come to equate the name and person of Satan with a scheme of thought that is fanciful, at best, or grotesque and absurd, and therefore intellectually contemptible.

The Bible is not talking about that kind of figure at all. Satan bears about as much resemblance to the figures in these myths as the God of the Hebrews does to Santa Claus.

Dismiss your familiar sharp-eared Mephistopheles entirely when considering Satan as revealed in the Bible. Your association of the two confounds reality with mythic unreality.

That will make you do one of two things, neither of which is right. If you are superstitious, or irrational, you may adopt myths or fables for reality.

But if you are intelligent and rational, you are more likely to dismiss spiritual reality solely on the ground of the evident untenability of the mythic unreality with which you are already so familiar.

Either way, you get a badly distorted picture of reality. The Bible will give you a balanced, factual, and demonstrably useful picture of reality regarding the things which are supernatural.

I say "useful" and "verifiable" because what the Bible says can be checked against human experience. If you match actual human experience with the revelation, you find that the experience confirms the revelation, and the revelation explains the experience —and tells you what to do about it. There are events and experiences occurring today that are not intelligible in any terms but those of the Biblical revelation.

Without the Bible's light upon them, we are helpless and bewildered by them. With that light, we not only can understand them, but we can take effective action concerning them.

The chapters that follow set forth what the Bible teaches to be the case about the unseen activity of spiritual beings and spiritual forces that affect men, nations, and history.

Part II

The Biblical
Structure of Reality

The Invisible God:
"I AM"

The central declaration of the Scriptures is that God *is*.
The constant affirmation of the Scriptures is that God *acts*.

It has always been a wonder to me that some men can read the
Bible right through and leave God out of it. That is a tremendous
feat of intellectual excision. Everything is attributed to nature and
man, nothing is attributed to God. The presupposition behind it
is that there is no God. It requires a deliberate and selective blindness that screens out much of what the Bible is about.

If a man reads the Bible that way, he fails completely to understand it. As a record of events, the Bible goes beyond the telling
of the event to reveal what lies behind the event. More precisely,
it goes beyond the event to tell who—whose intelligence and will
—lies unseen behind the event.

The Bible is a book that pierces beyond the natural into the
supernatural. A man who reduces it, by mental fiat, to the dead
level of the natural, censors out of the Bible exactly what the book

was given to make clear to man. He lays an edict upon his understanding not to grasp what the Bible is about.

The Bible asserts, uniformly and from the beginning to end, that there are different levels of intelligent and active life: beasts, man, angels, demons, Satan, God. More are unseen than are seen. All but the beasts are intelligent agents whose actions profoundly affect human history. To smash them all down to a single level of existence is to read the Bible with resolute unintelligence.

The intelligent way to read the Bible is not to lump everything together without discrimination, assigning to man or to nature the acts of God. The intelligent and discriminate way to read the Bible is to assign the acts of man to man, the acts of Satan to Satan, the acts of God to God, the acts of angels to angels, and the acts of demons to demons. To do that illuminates events. Not to do so obscures their causes. There are events today that are not intelligible apart from the Biblical structure of reality.

The central declaration of the Scriptures is that God is. When God commissioned Moses to lead the people of Israel, Moses wondered if the people would accept his commission as genuinely divine. God said to Moses, "Say this to the people of Israel: 'I AM has sent me to you.' "

Through Isaiah God said, "For I am God, and there is no other; I am God, and there is none like me, declaring the end from the beginning, and from ancient times things not yet done." Isaiah 46:9-10.

"In the beginning God . . ." are the first words of the Bible. Look at the first chapter of Genesis: "And God said. . . ." "And God saw. . . ." "And God made. . . ." "And God called. . . ." "And God set. . . ." "So God created. . . ." "And God blessed them. . . ." "So God created man. . . ." "And God saw everything that he had made, and behold, it was very good." The Bible is in large part an account of God in action.

The God of the Scriptures is a God of intelligent and purposeful and efficient activity. He is a God Who acts—Who acts in human history. He is a God Who speaks, and the signature of His divinity is that what He speaks far in advance is fully acted out in history.

In Genesis, and throughout the Bible, we see God exercising attributes of volition and intelligence and personality and speech of which man is capable on a diminished scale, because man is made in the image of God.

There are scholars who scoff at this as "an anthropomorphic God." They fail to grasp that God deliberately speaks to man about Himself in terms understandable to man. When the infinite God speaks to finite man, He speaks in terms measured to the mind and experience of man, just as a parent in speaking to a child brings his words and illustrations within the range of a child's comprehension. If God is like man it is because the faculties with which man is endowed are in major respects God-like.

Genesis declares that "God said, 'Let us make man in our image, after our likeness, and let them have dominion. . . . So God created man in his own image, in the image of God created he him; male and female created he them. And God blessed them. . . ." (Genesis 1:26–28.) God endowed the first man Adam with attributes of will and intelligence and speech, so that man was like his creator.

Man was made in the image of God, but sin entered the human race and man is now a badly marred image of God. Psalm 82:6 says, *"You are gods,* and all of you are children of the most high, but you shall die like men . . ."

The Invisible God

The Bible says that "God is a spirit." (John 4:24.) He is invisible and He is immortal.

The invisible God has expressed Himself in the physical creation. His creative hand is seen in the natural order, but He does not dwell on that plane. Romans 1:20 says, "Ever since the creation of the world his invisible nature, namely, his eternal power and deity, have been clearly seen in the things that have been made."

God is a spirit, invisible to the eye of man, and He dwells on the spiritual plane. He is supernatural—that is, above nature. All that we see in the natural realm, from the intricate design of the atom to the great balanced wheels of the stars and galaxies, is the product of God's creative genius and His infinite power. Nature is His handiwork. The Milky Way alone is a system of over a hundred billion stars.

"No one has ever seen God," the Bible says in John 1:18. He cannot be discovered in any way other than by His own self-revelation made to man at times and by the means of His own choosing. The Scriptures—the sum of revelation after revelation given to Hebrew men over many centuries—are the appointed means that God uses to convey to mankind the truth about Who He is, what

His purposes are, and about the intelligent forces that operate in the supernatural realm.

God chose the Hebrew people to be the recipients and heralds of His revelation of Himself to mankind, and it is with the patriarchs that this unfolding revelation of God began.

God commenced His public revelation of Himself with Abraham and continued and expanded it through Isaac, Jacob, Joseph, Moses, David, and the Hebrew prophets.

A man may learn something *about* God through teaching, but he only comes to *know* God by a direct, personal revelation to himself.

Jacob had learned about God and about the acts of God from his fathers, but he did not know God until God revealed Himself to Jacob. That is the difference between head knowledge and heart knowledge. A man may be told all about a certain young woman —her birthplace, her background, her schooling, her character, her activities—and he may have a very complete and accurate *concept* of what she is like, but it is not until he meets her that he begins to know her as she really is.

Jacob made a journey from his father's house to his uncle's house. Chapter 28 of Genesis says, "Jacob left Beersheba and went toward Haran. And he came to a certain place, and stayed there that night, because the sun had set. Taking one of the stones of the place, he put it under his head and lay down in that place to sleep. And he dreamed that there was a ladder set up on the earth, and the top of it reached to heaven; and behold, the angels of God were ascending and descending upon it! And behold, the Lord stood above it and said, 'I am the Lord, the God of Abraham your father, and the God of Isaac; the land on which you lie I will give to you and to your descendants. . . . Behold, I am with you and will keep you wherever you go and will bring you back to this land . . . .'

"Then Jacob awoke from his sleep and said, 'Surely the Lord is in this place, and *I did not know it.*' And he was afraid and said, 'How awesome is this place! This is none other than the house of God and this is the gate of heaven.' " Jacob named that place Bethel, "the house of God."

It was, by all appearances, an entirely ordinary place when Jacob stopped there to rest on his journey. The sun had set, darkness had settled over the land, and Jacob could find no shelter or comfort except a stone for his pillow. God was invisible to Jacob's eye there. The place did not impress him. He took a stone, lay down, and went to sleep. Bethel was different only because God chose at that place, on that night, to reveal Himself to Jacob.

Jacob knew nothing of God, sensed nothing of the presence of God by his own faculties at that place—"the Lord is in this place, and *I did not know it*"—until God deliberately broke through the unseen veil that divides the natural from the supernatural and revealed Himself to Jacob there. Then that ordinary place seemed "awesome . . . the house of God . . . the gate of heaven."

Jacob could have strained his natural faculties to their utmost and not have discerned anything more about that place than its physical attributes. The natural senses cannot penetrate into the supernatural at any time. They are stone dumb to the presence of God, or angels, or evil spirits, in any place. They can know nothing about it at all.

God used three means of communication in revealing Himself to Jacob. Jacob received the revelation of God by a dream, by a vision, and by words—the words that God spoke to him that night.

God had spoken previously to Abraham: "To your descendants I give this land, from the river of Egypt to the great river, the river Euphrates . . . ." (Genesis 15:18.) The subsequent revelation spoken to Jacob was in strict accord with the revelation previously received by Abraham. That was an evidence of its validity. Supernatural revelations that contradict the Word of God—they regularly occur—are not of God. They are borne in upon men by evil spirits, and they are meant to deceive. The Scriptures warn against them. One such revelation occurred in the Middle East in 1968, when a virgin figure appeared as by a vision in a church and promised the enemies of Israel success in eradicating her.

There at Bethel, God spoke to Jacob: "I am the Lord, the God of Abraham your father and the God of Isaac; the land on which you lie I will give to you and to your descendants; and your descendants shall be like the dust of the earth, and you shall spread abroad to the east and to the north and to the south; and by you and your descendants shall all the families of the earth bless themselves. Behold, I am with you and will keep you wherever you go, and will bring you back to this land; for I will not leave you until I have done that of which I have spoken to you." Genesis 28:13–15.

Bethel was the beginning of Jacob's personal knowledge of God. No longer was it by family tradition and teaching alone that he knew of God. Now he knew God for himself. Later, at Peniel, Jacob was to experience a greater and more thoroughly transforming revelation of God that would alter his character permanently and cause his name to be changed, from Jacob (which means a supplanter) to Israel (which means prince with God).

This God Who revealed Himself to Jacob at Bethel is the God Who Is. He identified Himself to Jacob as the God of Abraham, because that is exactly Who He Is. This was not because Abraham had been a religious genius or a masterful theologian, but because God had deliberately revealed Himself to Abraham, had made certain promises to him, and because Abraham had believed God and obeyed Him. The God of Abraham is the God Who makes promises and keeps them.

This God of the Hebrews is the only true God. He is a living being, supreme above all others in the universe, creator of all that is, the author of life. All others who are worshiped by men as gods are either creatures of imagination or evil spirits seeking to usurp God's place among mankind.

"No man has seen God at any time," the Apostle John writes in I John 4:12.

The Scriptures speak of God:

—as "the invisible God" in Colossians 1:15.

—as "the king of ages, immortal, invisible, the only God" in I Timothy 1:17.

—as "him who is invisible" in Hebrews 11:27.

This passage in Hebrews says that, "By faith Moses left Egypt, not being afraid of the anger of the king [Pharaoh]; for he endured as *seeing him who is invisible.*"

God is "the blessed and only Sovereign, the King of kings and Lord of lords, who alone has immortality and *dwells in unapproachable light,* whom *no man has ever seen or can see,*" Paul wrote in I Timothy 6:15, 16.

Psalm 104 says that God covers Himself "with light as with a garment."

The Scriptures admonish men, "Let us offer to God acceptable worship, with reverence and awe, *for our God is a consuming fire.*" Hebrews 12:29.

"God is light and in him there is no darkness at all," the Bible says in I John 1:5b. It says also that "The fear of the Lord is the beginning of wisdom." Proverbs 9:10.

The Personal God

The God revealed by the Bible is a personal God, Who reveals Himself to individual men. He deals directly and personally with

men. The prophet Hanani told Asa king of Judah, "The eyes of the
Lord run to and fro throughout the whole earth, to show himself
strong in the behalf of them whose heart is perfect toward him."
II Chronicles 16:9.

Adam, when he had sinned, tried to hide from God in Eden, but
God found him there. Men, in their sin, seek to hide themselves
morally from God. Some say that there is no God, and that gives
them a temporary and delusive relief from concern over the
consequences of their sins. Others tell themselves that God is very
remote and unconcerned with man; that God set the universe in
motion and then went off to some distant eyrie in the heavens to
attend to matters far more important than the affairs of men.
Some say that "God is dead." Scholars especially are prone to
regard it as vanity that God would take any particular notice of
men. Their supposition is that the God of the cosmos could not
be a God interested in fine details. All of these are ways of declaring that man is free to sin and go his own way because God is blind
to sin or so withdrawn from humanity as to be indifferent to
individual acts.

The Bible gives the flattest possible contradiction to this. It
states that "even the hairs of your head are all numbered." (Luke
12:7.) The God who knows the number of the hairs of your head
knows the number of the sins of your heart.

And the God who knows the number of your hairs also knows
the number of the stars. "He tells the number of the stars; he calls
them all by their names." (Psalm 147:4.) Or, as Isaiah puts it, in
majestic poetry: "To whom will you liken me, or shall I be equal?
says the Holy One. Lift up your eyes on high and see: Who created
these? He brings out their host by number; he calls them all by
name. . . .

"Why do you say, O Jacob, and speak, O Israel, 'My way is hid
from the Lord, and my right is disregarded by my God'?" Isaiah
40:25–27.

Man has devised telescopes to probe outward from the earth
into the creation, and with them and by radio search he has discovered some corners of the universe. Only lately has man begun to
know something of the vastness of the creation. In 1955, a photographic atlas of the universe in 200 sky maps was published at the
Palomar Observatory. It was reported then that "Far beyond in
outer space there are galaxies similar to the Milky Way. Sometimes these galaxies group into clusters. Whereas only a scant
three dozen such clusters were known before the sky survey, now

more than a thousand have been found"—1,000 clusters of galaxies.

Congregated in one such system, called the Coma Cluster, are about 11,000 galaxies.

If the Milky Way were observed from an immense distance away, it would be seen as a crowd of billions of suns (some estimate as many as 200 billion), arranged in a flat spiral structure. Its density would be so great as to suggest, to the untutored eye, that they are jammed together, with very little space between them. But we know how perfectly the solar system is arranged around our sun as just a tiny wheel within this massive swarm of suns.

Our solar system is a beautifully ordered mote in a single galaxy —having something less than the prominence of the dot over one *i* in an unabridged dictionary. (Actually, some scratch-pad figures show, the solar system is as prominent in the Milky Way as one dot over one *i* would be on a shelf of 2,850 unabridged dictionaries.)

There are times when the galaxies "collide." One galaxy meets another head-on and they pass through each other and come out on the other side, with no star having brushed another.

"The galaxies within reach of telescopes like that on Mount Palomar probably number in the billions," it was reported in 1963. The atlas of the universe mapped the sky out to a depth in space of 600 million light-years. (A light-year is about six trillion miles.) Isaac Asimov wrote in 1960 that "the 200-inch telescope can make out objects up to an estimated two billion light-years away, and there is no sign of an end of the Universe—yet."

The galaxies *within reach* appear to number in the billions. If each galaxy is a family of billions of stars, we begin to get a notion of the extent of it—billions of billions—yet God knows the number of the stars and He "calls them all by their names."

The God of creation is the God of the cosmos to be sure. He is also the God of the most minute details.

Man has devised microscopes and particle accelerators that enable him to look inward upon the creation, and by them he has sliced matter down to fractions so fine as to make a billionth of an inch sound like an exceedingly crude measurement, but he has not yet managed to pierce to that which is so fine that it does not have clear structure and intelligent design.

An uncle, Dr. Robert H. Phillips, is a nuclear physicist who worked for a dozen years at the Brookhaven National Laboratory on Long Island. He has occasionally given me an evening-long talk on the subatomic world (remember when we used to think of an atom as something terribly small?) and has told me of the precision of nuclear measurement.

Nuclear measurements carried out with a particle accelerator deal in "such sizes as 10 to the minus 25th square centimeters," he told me. "That means that if you put one over one and add twenty-five zeroes—

$$\frac{1}{10,000,000,000,000,000,000,000,000}$$

—then you have written in ordinary decimal system the fraction of a square centimeter that a nucleon occupies in space." That is *one ten-septillionth of a square centimeter.*

"That isn't the very smallest thing that we look in on by any means," he said. "The subdivision of matter certainly reaches to smaller objects than that."

Nucleons are protons or neutrons. "Nobody really believes that a nucleon is the last subdivision of matter," Dr. Phillips said. Some physicists hypothesize quarks as still more elementary particles.

If man looks outward he sees the creative hand of God and he cannot search to the end of it, and if man looks inward he sees the creative hand of God and he has not yet come to the end of it.

Study everything between quarks and quasars and you find structure, motion, order, a lawful stability, arrangement, and design.

Whenever man seems to be near the inner or outer limits of the creation another layer unfolds to his astonished gaze. The God Who made the planets also designed the molecule. He Who formed man also formed the living cells. The God of the whole is also the God of the parts. And He cares particularly for man.

Hear David: "When I consider thy heavens, the work of thy fingers, the moon and the stars which you have ordained; What is man, that thou art mindful of him? and the son of man, that thou visitest him?

"For you have made him a little lower than the angels, and have crowned him with glory and honor. You made him to have dominion over the works of thy hands; you have put all things under his feet . . . . O Lord our Lord, how excellent is thy name in all the earth." Psalm 8.

There is nothing hidden from God. There is no refuge a man can find in which he can hide from the searching eyes of God. "Before him no creature is hidden, but all things are naked and laid bare to the eyes of him with whom we have to do." Hebrews 4:13.

"Nothing is hid that shall not be made manifest, nor anything secret that shall not be known and come to light. . . . Whatever you have spoken in the dark shall be heard in the light, and what you have whispered in secret shall be shouted from the housetops." Luke 8:17 and 12:3.

"His eyes are upon the ways of man, and he sees all his goings. There is no darkness, nor shadow of death, where the workers of iniquity may hide themselves." (Job 34:21,22.) Death will not remove sinners from the face of God; it will bring them to the judgment.

At a time of great decline of faith, even the elders of Israel said, "The Lord sees us not; the Lord has forsaken the earth." Ezekiel 8:12.

Such things as that are said today by seminary professors training young men to be ministers. These statements were contrary to the fact then, and were evidence of the elders' wickedness and blindness, and they are just as false today.

The Bible declares, "Thou God seest me." Genesis 16:13.

"Woe to those who seek deep to hide their counsel from the Lord, and their works in the dark, and they say, 'Who sees us?' and 'Who knows us?' Surely your turning of things upside down shall be esteemed as the potter's clay: For shall the work say of him who made it, He made me not? Or shall the thing framed say of him who framed it, He has no understanding?" Isaiah 29:15,16.

"O Lord, thou hast searched me and known me!" David says in Psalm 139. "Thou knowest when I sit down and when I rise up. Thou discernest my thoughts from afar. Thou searchest out my path and my lying down, and art acquainted with all my ways. Even before a word is on my tongue, lo, O Lord, thou knowest it altogether. Thou dost beset me behind and before, and layest thy hand upon me. . . . Whither shall I go from thy Spirit? Or whither shall I flee from thy presence?

"If I ascend to heaven, thou art there! If I make my bed in Sheol, thou art there! If I take the wings of the morning, and dwell in the uttermost parts of the sea, even there thy hand shall lead me, and thy right hand shall hold me. If I say, 'Let only darkness cover me, and the light about me be night,' even the darkness is not dark to thee, the night is bright as the day; for darkness is as light with thee.

"For thou didst form my inward parts, thou didst knit me together in my mother's womb . . . . Thou knowest me right well; my frame was not hidden from thee, when I was being made in secret, intricately wrought in the depths of the earth. Thy eyes beheld my unformed substance. In thy book were written, every one of them, the days that were formed for me, when as yet there was none of them . . . . When I awake I am still with thee . . . . Search me, O God, and know my heart! Try me and know my thoughts! And see if there be any wicked way in me, and lead me in the way everlasting!"

The Invisible God Made Visible

There is no more awesome and wonderful fact than that God, the Creator, in making Himself known to man, has come to man as man. Of the several means of revelation God uses to make known the truth about Himself, the one that is chief above all is the incarnation: God coming into human society as man.

We are living on a visited planet. That is far more than a New Testament idea. That God Himself—the Creator—would come to Israel as a man is prophesied in the most explicit terms in the Old Testament. Isaiah 9:6 says, "For unto us a child is born, unto us a son is given; and the government shall be upon his shoulder: and his name shall be called Wonderful, Counsellor, The mighty God, The everlasting Father, The Prince of Peace."

Think of that: A man born a Jew—nothing less than Emanuel—God with us.

God made His most complete revelation of Himself to man in a Jew named Jesus. Jesus perfectly showed forth the character of God in His person. He, alone among all men, had no part in sin from birth to death. The Bible says of Jesus: "He is *the image of the invisible God,* the first-born of all creation; for in him all things were created, in heaven and on earth, visible and invisible, whether thrones or dominions or principalities or authorities—all things were created through him and for him . . . . For in him all the fulness of God was pleased to dwell, and through him to reconcile to himself all things, whether on earth or in heaven, making peace by the blood of his cross." Colossians 1:15–19.

Jesus made the invisible God visible to man in His own person. He claimed, in absolute harmony with the Old Testament prophecies of the Messiah, to have lived before His birth at Bethlehem. Jesus said, "I came from the Father and have come into the world. Again, I am leaving the world and going to the Father." (John 16:28.) "Before Abraham was, I am," Jesus said. (John 8:58.) In that, He declared Himself to be God.

He knew this to be true of Himself and proclaimed it openly, a fact that renders the opinion that Jesus was merely "a good man" untenable. If the things He said were not true, Jesus was no "good man."

Jesus said, "truly, truly I say to you, the hour is coming, and now is, when the dead will hear the voice of the Son of God, and those who hear will live."

And, "I seek not my own will but the will of him who sent me . . . the works which the Father has granted me to accomplish, these very works which I am doing, bear me witness that the Father has sent me. And the Father who sent me has himself borne witness to me. *His voice you have never heard, his form you have never seen;* and you do not have his word abiding in you, for you do not believe him whom he has sent." John 5:25, 30b; 36-38.

He said to the disciples: " 'If you had known me, you would have known my Father also . . . .' Philip said to him, 'Lord show us the Father, and we shall be satisfied.' Jesus said to him, 'Have I been with you so long, and yet you do not know me, Philip? *He who has seen me has seen the Father.* ' " John 14:8,9.

"I will not leave you desolate; I will come to you," Jesus told His disciples shortly before His death. "Yet a little while, and the world will see me no more, but you will see me; because I live, you will live also. In that day you will know that I am in my Father, and you in me, and I in you. He who has my commandments and keeps them, he it is who loves me; and he who loves me will be loved by my Father, and I will love him and manifest myself to him . . . . If a man loves me, he will keep my word, and my Father will love him, and we will come to him and make our home with him." John 14:18-23.

The Book of Hebrews begins with these words: "God, who at sundry times and in diverse manners spoke in former times to the fathers by the prophets, has in these days spoken to us by his Son, whom he has appointed heir of all things, by whom also he made the worlds; who being the brightness of his glory, and *the express image of his person,* and, upholding all things by the word of his power, when he had by himself purged our sins, sat down on the right hand of the Majesty on high." Hebrews 1:1–3.

The Old Testament is explicit on the humanity and the divinity of the Messiah. The New Testament, in the declarations of Jesus as well as those of the apostles and writers, is unequivocal on the divinity of Jesus.

You can learn about God by reading the Bible, but God wants more than that for you. He wants you to know Him personally. God specifically offers to come into your life in so definite a way that you will know He has come in; you will know He is there, with you and in you. He wants to walk with you every step of the way through your life. That is your highest privilege as a human being. It doesn't make any difference who you are. "God is no respecter of persons." (Acts 10:34.) The social and class distinctions of the world count nothing with God. If you sit on the lowest rung of public respect and dignity, ignored by nearly everybody, God will come into your life. If you occupy the highest station, God will come into your life. As much is true if you are an ordinary person. After He had risen from the grave, Jesus said, "Behold, I stand at the door and knock; if any man hears my voice and opens the door, *I will come in to him* and sup with him and he with me." Revelation 3:20.

I remember the morning twenty years ago when I asked Him to come into my life on the basis of His promise. He came in that day, and my life was immediately and wonderfully changed—far beyond my own capacity to alter it—and that change has never lost its freshness or its power. God began the change that day, and He remains its continual source and supply. All things are made new.

God's Love and His Fury

Most men have heard that "God is love." The passage that declares this says: ". . . he who loves is born of God and knows God. He who does not love does not know God, for God is love. In this the love of God was made manifest among us, that God sent his only Son into the world, so that we might live through him. In this is love—not that we loved God but that he loved us and sent his Son to be the expiation for our sins. Beloved, if God so loved us, we also ought to love one another. No man has ever seen God; if we love one another, God abides in us and his love is perfected in us." I John 4:7–12.

God created the world and man, and everything else that He created, as the expression of His generosity and love. "God saw that everything he had made . . . was very good." God intends that His creation be joyously perfect. He intends order, harmony, peace, worship, love, and great joy to prevail unchallenged among intelligent beings. There is a glimpse of this primeval state of things in the Bible. God spoke these words to Job:
"Where were you when I laid the foundation of the earth? Tell me, if you have understanding. Who determined its measurements—surely you know! Or who stretched the line upon it? On what are its foundations fastened, or who laid its cornerstone,

> "when the morning stars sang together
> and all the sons of God shouted for joy?"
>
> Job 38:4-7

That is the way it was, and that is the way it ceased to be when Satan brought sin and hatred into God's creation, and persuaded man to turn his back on God.

The beauty, the symmetry, the order and perfection, the sheer loveliness of what God made was all designed to serve the best interests of man and to afford him scope for achievement and discovery, endless provisions, pleasure and joy. It has been terribly impaired by the introduction into its affairs of the active principles of sin and self-will, whose effect is to spread blight and ruin in many different forms over the landscape of God's creation. One such blight is racial hatred, which has caused so much anguish and bloodshed among mankind.

Contrary to a very common notion of it, the quality of God's love is not bland. The love of God is strong. The love of God is discriminate, and it is purposeful. The perfect complement to the love of God—that which throws it into strong relief and shows its purity—is the hatred that God expresses toward that which is evil. God hates sin. He hates evil.

The greater an individual's sensitivity to that which violates what he truly prizes, the less patience he has with it. A love of purity requires by its nature a coequal abhorrence of filth. A symphony orchestra conductor will not rest until he drives everything that mars the symmetry, beauty, and perfection of the music out of the performance. He is intolerant of that which disfigures it musically, and the greater his love of the score the more absolute his intolerance becomes.

Because He is love, God is consistently intolerant of everything that violates His own intention in creation. God hates evil with a pure and furious hatred because He sees that it is constantly at work to destroy what He has made—at work to destroy man, to destroy society, to destroy nature, to destroy civilization, to destroy harmony, to destroy joy. He does not look upon it as man does, that is, relatively, because He sees it not limitedly but in the whole path of its effective ruination.

The intention of Satan is to make moral, spiritual, and physical chaos and wreckage out of as much of God's creation as he possibly can. Satan enlists man in that attempt, by appealing to his lawless lusts and passions. We can see the effects of that all around us, in the nation, in the world.

Man is infected with the moral disease that God calls sin. God is not tolerant of human sin because He knows that if it were allowed to go unarrested it would ultimately destroy everything in its reach.

God loves the man but He hates the sin. It is God's will to separate the man from the sin, but if a man refuses to be separated from his sin, if he exhibits a resolute preference for it, then he must bear the full penalty for it, death. God will put such a man in quarantine forever in a fire prepared for the devil. The Bible declares that sin must be arrested and judged.

God seeks to separate the sinner from the sin, so that He may express His pure love to the sinner and His pure wrath against the sin. That is what He did in sending Jesus to die on the cross for sin. God placed man's sin upon Jesus at Calvary and judged it there with the penalty of death. "He bore our sins in his own body on the tree." (I Peter 2:24a.) The love of God is strong. Strong enough to send His Son to die for sin.

God has spoken and demonstrated His love of man and His abhorrence of sin and in this one act—the voluntary death of the cross.

"Surely he has borne our griefs, and carried our sorrows
    Yet we esteemed him stricken, smitten by God and afflicted
    But *he was wounded for our transgressions,* he was bruised
        for our iniquities;
    Upon him was the chastisement that made us whole
    And with his stripes we are healed . . .
    The Lord has laid on him the iniquity of us all."

                                                    Isaiah 53:4–6

That is why Jesus could cry, "It is finished!" (John 19:30.) The penalty of sin was fully paid.

God's love is expressed in the creation, but it is supremely expressed in the redemption.

God cannot go farther in loving man and in dealing with sin than to die for sin. To go another step would be to tolerate sin. God will never do that. Every man who accepts the blood atonement is cleansed of sin and escapes the wrath that God must, by the deepest necessity of His holy nature, express against sin. The man who rejects the full atonement God has provided for sin, by the blood of Jesus Christ, leaves God with no option but to bar him from His presence and to confine him forever to what the Bible calls "the lake of fire."

The love of God, as well as the wrath of God, is shown throughout the pages of the Bible. It is sheer ignorance to state, as some do, that the God of the Old Testament is a God of wrath, while the God of the New Testament is a God of love. The God of the Old Testament and the God of the New Testament are one. There is no distinction between them.

The anger of God against evil is shown not less in the New Testament than in the Old. The New Testament is full of the expressed fury of God at evil.

The scope of the outpouring of God's wrath against sin is shown in several chapters of the Book of Revelation, and its magnitude is greater than any judgment of God recorded in the Old Testament, including the destruction of Sodom and Gomorrah.

"For the wrath of God is revealed from heaven against all ungodliness and wickedness of men," the New Testament declares in Romans 1:18.

In the Old Testament Moses declared: "The Lord thy God is a consuming fire." Deuteronomy 4:24.

The New Testament declares, "Our God is a consuming fire." Hebrews 12:29.

"Hate the evil, and love the good," the Old Testament enjoins in Amos 5:15a. It is not possible to love the good without hating the evil, because the evil actively antagonizes and runs against the good.

Jesus perfectly mirrored His Father in this respect, too. In Hebrews the Father says of the Son: "You have *loved righteousness* and *hated iniquity*, therefore God, thy God, has anointed you with the oil of gladness above thy fellows." Hebrews 1:8,9.

Jesus' love is seen in the Gospels, and so is His fury at sin and dissimulation. Matthew, chapter 23, records Jesus' address to the religious leaders: "Woe to you, hypocrites . . . ." "Woe to you, blind guides . . . ." "You blind fools . . . hypocrites!" "You serpents, you brood of vipers, how are you to escape being sentenced to hell?"

In the Old Testament Jeremiah prophesied, " 'Woe to the shepherds who destroy and scatter the sheep of my pasture!' says the Lord. Therefore thus says the Lord, the God of Israel, concerning the shepherds who care for my people, 'You have scattered my flock, and have driven them away, and you have not attended to them. Behold, I will attend to you for your evil doings, says the Lord . . . .' Behold, the storm of the Lord! Wrath has gone forth, a whirling tempest; it will burst upon the head of the wicked. The anger of the Lord will not turn back until he has executed and accomplished the intents of his mind. In the latter days you will understand it clearly." Jeremiah 24.

Jesus repeatedly warned men that if they continued in sin they would at last "be thrown into hell, where their worm does not die, and the fire is not quenched." He counseled, "If your hand causes you to sin, cut it off; it is better for you to enter life maimed than with two hands to go to hell, to the unquenchable fire." (Mark 10:43, 48.) He said, "The Son of man"—speaking of Himself— "will send his angels, and they will gather out of his kingdom all causes of sin and all evildoers, and throw them into the furnace of fire. There men will weep and gnash their teeth. Then the righteous will shine like the sun in the kingdom of their Father. He who has ears, let him hear." Matthew 13:41–43.

When there is a fire, true love warns of the fire; love will not say there is no fire. God's love seeks to keep men from a destiny of fire.

The New Testament speaks of a day "when the Lord Jesus is to be revealed from heaven with his mighty angels in flaming fire, inflicting vengeance upon those who do not know God . . . . They shall suffer the punishment of eternal destruction and exclusion from the presence of the Lord and from the glory of his might." II Thessalonians 1:7–9.

Isaiah prophesied that "it shall be known that the hand of the Lord is with his servants, and his indignation is against his enemies. For behold, the Lord will come in fire, and his chariots like the stormwind, to render his anger in fury, and his rebuke with flames of fire. For by fire will the Lord execute judgment, and by his sword upon all flesh." Isaiah 66:14a,15,16.

When it falls upon men, the judgment of God is always the last resort of His faithful dealing with them. He calls to them first in love. He invites them to come to Himself to receive the restoration guaranteed by the sacrificial blood. He warns them of sin and of the judgment He must send upon them for it. He has made every provision for their full liberation from sin.

God will not depart by so much as a shade from His original plan for a perfect and joyous creation. The judgment is a necessary stage in the fulfillment of His great purpose, but the purpose of His love does not end there. At judgment there will be a complete separation of the just from the unjust and a complete, eternal exclusion of the unjust from any participation in the future. When they are put away, God's program will go on. He will banish the curse from His creation. There will then ensue the most wonderful effects.

> "In that day the deaf shall hear
>   the words of a book
> And out of their gloom and darkness
>   the eyes of the blind shall see.
>
> "The meek shall obtain fresh joy in the Lord
>   and the poor among men shall exult
>   in the Holy One of Israel.
> For the ruthless shall come to nought
>   and the scoffer cease,
>   and all who watch to do evil shall be cut off . . . ."

Isaiah 29:18–20

"The wolf shall dwell with the lamb, and the leopard shall lie down with the kid, and the calf and the lion and the fatling together, and a little child shall lead them . . . for the earth shall be full of the knowledge of the Lord as the waters cover the sea." Isaiah 11:6,9.

Both testaments promise a new heaven and a new earth in which no sickness or sorrow or evil will dwell.

The Old Testament says: "For behold, I create new heavens and a new earth, and the former things shall not be remembered or come into mind. But be glad and rejoice forever in that which I create; for behold, I create Jerusalem a rejoicing, and her people a joy. I will rejoice in Jerusalem and be glad in my people; no more

shall be heard in it the sound of weeping and the cry of distress."
Isaiah 65:17–19.

The New Testament says: "Then I saw a new heaven and a new earth; for the first heaven and the first earth had passed away, and the sea was no more. And I saw the holy city, new Jerusalem, coming down out of heaven as a bride adorned for her husband; and I heard a great voice from the throne saying, 'Behold the dwelling of God is with men. He will dwell with them and they shall be his people, and God himself will be with them; and he will wipe away every tear from their eyes, and death shall be no more, neither shall there be mourning nor crying nor pain any more, for the former things have passed away.' " Revelation 21:1–4.

God's love and His fury at sin will not rest at anything short of seeing men perfect and at one with their Creator.

Much more could be said about the nature and character and purposes of God as shown in the Bible. In summary, these primary truths are noted:

God is a living being; a Person. God is a spirit. He is immortal and invisible. God is love. God hates evil. Nothing can be hid from him.

The God of Israel, the only true God, is the Creator. Jesus Christ is the express image of His person, and He showed us by His life and words and acts exactly Who God Is.

The revelation of the invisible and living God is contained in the Scriptures of the Old and New Testaments. Any other so-called revelation of God is either a fiction, or a counterfeit designed to mislead men about the nature and character and purposes of God.

This exclusivity is not an exclusivity of Hebrew achievement or insight or scholarship. It is the exclusivity of Hebrew chosenness. God elected to convey His truth to the world through the Jews. So it is by the Bible, written by Jews, that an accurate knowledge of that which lies beyond the reach of science or the eye of man—the knowledge of God and of the unseen realm of the spiritual and supernatural—may be gained.

Angels

There is an intelligent order of created beings who serve God, called angels. They have to do with God and they also have to do with man. Angels are in many ways very much like men. They possess attributes of intellect and personality and will similar to those of man. Angels can speak. So like men are the angels that it is possible to sit and talk with one and not to know that he is an angel, but to take him for a man. The New Testament says, "Be not forgetful to entertain strangers, for thereby some have entertained angels unawares." Hebrews 13:2.

Angels are spiritual beings. They dwell on the spiritual plane, above nature. They are normally invisible to man. They enter the natural order, visibly and invisibly, but it is not their primary abode. They stand a step higher on the ladder of creation than man.

Man, who is set at the summit of the natural order, was made "a little lower than the angels" in the scale of creation. David wrote, "When I consider thy heavens, the work of thy fingers, the moon and the stars, which thou hast ordained, What is man, that thou are mindful of him . . .? For thou has made him a little lower than the angels, and hast crowned him with glory and honor."

The whole natural order, including man's physical body, is mortal. The angels are immortal. They are not subject to disease or death.

A major difference between angels and men is their mobility. The soul and the spirit of man are perfectly united to his body, and his body in turn is bound to the earth. Thus, as a being, man is limited in his mobility (though he can increase it immensely by inventions that cooperate with the laws of nature).

Angels are in no way bound by the laws of the natural realm. They can travel immense distances, so to speak, at the speed of thought. A physical object must move at a stated rate from one point in the natural creation to another. There is no shortcut; the whole distance must be physically traversed.

A spiritual being is subject to no such necessity. Angels can, at will, enter the natural realm. They can submit to and obey its laws, but they can, at will, leave it and ignore its laws and limitations. Far more significantly, angels can inhabit the natural realm without being observed and without obeying its laws. They move, unseen, among men, accomplishing their appointed work.

Man is almost never aware in any way of the presence of angels, whether it is one angel or a company of angels. What they do is unknown to him. Angels can, if they wish, make themselves visible to men, but they almost never do. When they do, they look very much like men. So much so that it is usually difficult, or impossible, to tell them apart. At times the Bible uses the term man interchangeably with the term angel.

God can open a man's eyes so that he may see angels, but He almost never does. In that case, the eye is allowed to pierce through to see that which exists on the spiritual plane. That is entirely different from an angel coming into the natural order and making himself visible there. When a man's eyes are opened to see the angels, he sees them in the spiritual realm as they are: Though the angels have the form of men they are seen in their splendor and full beauty, and they would not then be mistaken for men.

When angels visit men visibly, they come into the natural realm and show themselves in the physical similitude of men. That which is invisible becomes visible in the natural realm and the angels move among men as men.

In chapter 19 of Genesis, there is an account of a visit by angels to Abraham's nephew Lot:

"The two angels came to Sodom in the evening, and Lot was sitting in the gate of Sodom. When Lot saw them, he rose to meet them, and bowed himself with his face to the earth, and said, 'My lords, turn aside I pray you, to your servant's house and spend the night, and wash your feet; then you may rise up early and go your way' . . . so they turned aside to him and entered his house, and he made them a feast, and baked unleavened bread, and they ate."

These were not men, they were angels. Yet they had feet and they needed to wash them after their walk, and Lot prepared a feast for them "and they ate."

There is no indication at this point that Lot knew that these visiting strangers were angels. He treated them like wayfarers, with the best hospitality of the East. He was entertaining angels unawares.

If angels eat of man's food, as they sometimes do, men have also eaten of angels' food, according to Psalm 78:25, which says that God "rained down upon [Israel] manna to eat, and gave them the grain of heaven. Man ate of *the bread of angels;* he sent them food in abundance."

In their unseen ministry angels are occupied in things that have very practical consequences in human lives. When the prophet Elijah, exhausted with the relentless persecution he suffered from the government, "lay down and slept under a broom tree," the Scripture says "an angel touched him, and said to him, 'Arise and eat.' And he looked, and behold, there was at his head a cake baked on hot stones and a jar of water. And he ate and drank . . . and went in the strength of that food forty days and forty nights to Horeb the mount of God." I Kings 19:5,6,8.

When Abraham sent his servant out to seek a wife for his son, Isaac, from among his kinsmen, Abraham told him, "The Lord, before whom I walk, will send his angel with you, and prosper your way." Genesis 24:40a.

The angels' purpose is to serve God and to carry out His orders concerning men. What angels do to and for men is based entirely on their relationship to God. The angels protect and assist men who serve God. Sometimes they hinder and oppose men who directly defy God's purposes. Sometimes they destroy men. God has a plan in history and the angels have a role in advancing that plan.

I heard Charles E. Fuller, founder of the Fuller Theological Seminary, tell of a highway accident in which the car he was driving went off the roadbed and turned over. He said that as the car turned over, he momentarily saw angelic protectors that completely surrounded him, and he received not a scratch in an extremely dangerous accident. He said that while he was turning upside down he saw himself fully enveloped in light.

Psalm 104 says that God "makes his angels spirits; his ministers a flaming fire."

There are three key words in that Old Testament verse—"angels" . . . "spirits" . . . "ministers." This accords perfectly with Hebrews 1:14 in the New Testament, which says the angels are *"all ministering spirits,* sent forth to minister to men who are the heirs of salvation." The angels are spirits and they are ministers of God sent to men.

The word angel literally means messenger. The angels are messengers of God sent to men.

In the Old Testament, the prophet Zechariah talked repeatedly with angels who brought him messages from God: "And the angel who talked with me came again, and waked me . . . ." "Then the angel who talked with me came forward and said to me . . . ." "Then I said to the angel who talked with me, 'What are these, my lord?' And the angel answered me . . . ." Zechariah 4:1; 5:5; and 6:4, 5a.

In the New Testament, a priest named Zechariah talked with an angel: "Now while he was serving as priest before God . . . it fell to him by lot to enter the temple of the Lord and burn incense. And the whole multitude was praying outside at the hour of incense. And there appeared to him an angel standing on the right side of the altar of incense. And Zechariah was troubled when he saw him, and fear fell upon him. But the angel said to him, 'Do not be afraid, Zechariah, for your prayer is heard, and your wife Elizabeth will bear you a son, and you shall call his name John. And you will have joy and gladness, and many will rejoice at his birth . . . he will be filled with the Holy Spirit even from his mother's womb. And he will turn many of the sons of Israel to the Lord their God. . . .' And Zechariah said to the angel, 'How shall I know this? For I am an old man . . . .' " Luke 1:8–16.

A man who is far more diligent than I at tabulation informs me that angels are referred to 172 times in the Old Testament and 108 times in the New Testament, and there is a consistency of description throughout.

Angels work actively in protecting the people, whether individuals or groups of people, who belong to God. Psalm 91 is the great psalm of divine protection ("A thousand may fall at your side, ten thousand at your right hand, but it will not come near you") and it says: "He will give his angels charge over you, to guard you in all your ways. On their hands they will bear you up, lest you dash your foot against a stone. . . . Because he cleaves to me in love, I will deliver him; I will protect him because he knows my name." (Psalm 91:11,12,14.) The protection of God is for those who love Him and trust Him and worship and serve Him.

"The angel of the Lord encamps round about them that fear him, and delivers them." (Psalm 34:7.) In His charge to Moses God said, " 'Depart, go up hence, you and the people whom you have brought up out of the land of Egypt, to the land of which I swore to Abraham, Isaac and Jacob, saying, "To your descendants I will give it." And *I will send an angel before you,* and I will drive out the Canaanites, the Amorites, the Hittites, the Perizzites, the Hivites, and the Jebusites.' " Exodus 33:1,2.

The military victories of Israel, when the nation was obedient to God, often came through the active intervention of unseen forces. When the huge army of Assyria, which had overrun a series of nations, came to take Jerusalem and the inhabitants had no military power to repel them, God intervened. "And that night the angel of the Lord went forth, and slew a hundred and eighty-five thousand in the camp of the Assyrians; and when the men arose early in the morning, behold, these were all dead bodies." (II Kings 19:35.) "So the Lord saved Hezekiah and the inhabitants of Jerusalem from the hand of Sennacherib, king of Assyria . . . ." II Chronicles 32:21,22.

The Apostle Peter was thrown into prison. His friends prayed for him. "Peter was sleeping between two soldiers, bound with two chains, and sentries before the door were guarding the prison; and behold, an angel of the Lord appeared, and a light shone in the cell; and he struck Peter on the side and woke him up, saying, 'Get up quickly.' And the chains fell off his hands. . . . And he went out . . . . He did not know that what was done by the angel was real, but thought he was seeing a vision. When they had passed the first and the second guard, they came to the iron gate leading into the city. It opened to them of its own accord, and they went out and passed on through the street, and immediately the angel left him." Acts 12:6–10.

In his discourse on God's love for children, Jesus said: "See that you do not despise one of these little ones; for I tell you that in heaven their angels always behold the face of my Father who is in heaven." (Matthew 18:10.) When I was a boy, a relative on my father's side had a large family. One day, a four-year-old child caught fire at the stove and was badly burned. Just before death, the child became radiant and said to his parents, "Oh, don't you see all the angels here!" They saw nothing but the dying child, but they saw that their child was dying in evident joy. Those angels had come as a guardian escort to take the living soul of the dying child from earth to heaven and into the presence of God.

Jesus told of a rich man and a poor man both of whom died. The rich man went to Hades and was in torment. "The poor man died and was carried by the angels to Abraham's bosom," Jesus said. Luke 16:22.

John Wesley, the English evangelist who rode through England alone on horseback for more than forty years, once met a man who told him that he had been hiding beside the road and would have come out to rob Wesley. When Wesley asked him why he had not, the man said it was because of the men riding beside him. Wesley had been riding alone. What the man had seen, Wesley thought, was an escort of angels.

Horses are mentioned in the Scriptures in immediate association with angels. The prophet Elisha saw "the horsemen" of Israel. Later, Elisha's servant's eyes were opened and he saw that "the mountain was full of horses and chariots of fire round about Elisha." Revelation 19:14 says, "And the armies of heaven, arrayed in fine linen, white and pure, followed him on white horses."

Angels are not all equal in occupation or power. There are angels who are set as rulers and leaders over other angels, and they occupy a higher place in the work and plan of God. The Bible speaks of angels and archangels. Two of the latter, who occupy very elevated places in the plan of God, are named. They are Michael and Gabriel.

God described Michael to the prophet Daniel as "the great prince who has charge of your people." (Daniel 12:1.) He would appear to be the leader of the angelic forces assigned to protect the nation Israel. The New Testament book of Jude says that "the archangel Michael, contending with the devil, disputed about the body of Moses." Jude 9.

Because of a burst of anger in front of the people of Israel, God forbade Moses to enter the Promised Land. Instead he died in Moab. Deuteronomy 34:1–5 says: "And Moses went up from the plains of Moab to Mount Nebo, to the top of Pisgah, which is opposite Jericho. And the Lord showed him all the land . . . . And the Lord said to him, 'This is the land of which I swore to Abraham, to Isaac, and to Jacob, "I will give it to your descendants." I have let you see it with your eyes, but you shall not go over there.' So Moses the servant of God died there in the land of Moab, according to the word of the Lord, and *he buried him* in the valley in the land of Moab opposite Bethpeor, but *no man knows the place of his burial* to this day." Undoubtedly because of Moses' sin of anger, Satan came to make some claim regarding the body of Moses, but the archangel Michael contended against and disputed that claim.

The angel Gabriel appears twice by name in the Old Testament and twice in the New Testament, each time on errands of the highest consequence in the plan of God.

The prophet Daniel received a vision setting forth future world history in broad outline. "When I, Daniel, had seen the vision, I sought to understand it; and behold, there stood before me *one having the appearance of a man.* And I heard a man's voice . . . and it called, 'Gabriel, make this man understand the vision.' So he came near where I stood, and when he came, I was frightened and fell on my face. . . . He said, 'Behold, I will make known to you what shall be . . . .'" Daniel 8:15–17,19.

At another time Daniel fasted and prayed. "While I was speaking in prayer, the man Gabriel, whom I had seen in the vision at the first, came to me in swift flight at the time of the evening sacrifice. He came and said to me, 'O Daniel, I have now come out to give you wisdom and understanding." Daniel 9:21,22.

It is this same angel, Gabriel, who appeared to Zechariah the priest in the temple and told him he would have a son. "Zechariah said to the angel, 'How shall I know this? For I am an old man, and my wife is advanced in years.' And the angel answered him, 'I am Gabriel, who stand in the presence of God; and I was sent to speak to you, and to bring you this good news.'" Luke 1:18,19.

It is interesting that the reaction of Daniel and of Zechariah to the appearance of the angel Gabriel was virtually identical. Daniel says, "when he came, I was frightened and fell on my face." "And Zechariah was troubled when he saw him, and fear fell upon him."

The young woman, Mary, had the same reaction. "In the sixth month the angel Gabriel was sent from God to a city of Galilee named Nazareth, to a virgin betrothed to a man whose name was Joseph . . . . And he came to her and said, 'Hail, O favored one, the Lord is with you!' But she was greatly troubled at the saying . . . . And the angel said to her, 'Do not be afraid, Mary, for you have found favor with God. And behold, you will conceive in your womb and bear a son, and you shall call his name Jesus. He will be great and will be called the Son of the Most High, and the Lord God will give to him the throne of his father David. . . .'" Luke 1:26–32.

The birth of Jesus was announced by angels: "In that region there were shepherds out in the field, keeping watch over their flock by night. And an angel of the Lord appeared to them, and the glory of the Lord shone around them, and they were filled with fear. And the angel said to them, 'Be not afraid, for behold, I bring you good tidings of great joy, which shall be to all people; for unto you is born this day in the city of David a Savior, who is Christ the Lord.' . . . And suddenly there was with the angel a multitude of the heavenly host praising God and saying, 'Glory to God in the highest, and on earth peace, good will toward men.'" Luke 2:8–14.

Though they are normally invisible, that does not mean that

angels are weak or powerless. They are extremely powerful, and their power can be applied with force in the physical realm. In terms of what he can accomplish physically, an angel is stronger than a man. Over and over again, the Scriptures emphasize the power of the angels.

"Bless the Lord, O you his angels, you mighty ones who do his word, hearkening to the voice of his word! Bless the Lord, all his hosts, his ministers that do his will." Psalm 103:20,21.

II Peter 2:11 says that angels are "greater in might and power" than men.

The resurrection of Jesus from the dead was attended by angels. A man named Joseph of Arimathea took the body of Jesus and "laid him in a tomb which had been hewn out of a rock; and he rolled a stone against the door of the tomb."

A guard of soldiers was sent to the tomb with orders to make it secure, so the body of Jesus could not be stolen. "So they went and made the sepulchre secure by sealing the stone and setting a guard."

"And behold, there was a great earthquake; for an angel of the Lord descended from heaven and came and rolled back the stone, and sat upon it. His appearance was like lightning, and his raiment white as snow. And for fear of him the guards trembled and became like dead men."

"And when the Sabbath was past, Mary Magdalene and Mary the mother of James and Salome brought spices, so that they might go and anoint him. And very early on the first day of the week they went to the tomb when the sun had risen. And they were saying to one another, 'Who will roll away the stone for us from the door of the tomb?' And looking up they saw that the stone was rolled back, for it was very large.

"And entering the tomb, they saw a young man sitting on the right side, dressed in a white robe; and they were amazed. And he said to them, 'Do not be amazed. You seek Jesus of Nazareth who was crucified. He is risen, he is not here. See the place where they laid him. But go quickly and tell his disciples that he has risen from the dead, and behold, he is going before you to Galilee. There you will see him.' " Matthew 28:1–7 and Mark 15:46; 16:1–6.

That "young man" seated in the tomb on the right side was an angel.

The prophet Daniel was thrown into a pit of lions for defying an edict against worshiping God. King Darius, under whom Daniel served, respected and valued him. The king had not intended to cause Daniel harm, but he had been tricked by a conspiracy of officials into signing the edict that Daniel broke.

"At break of day, the king arose and went in haste to the den of lions. When he came near to the den where Daniel was, he cried out in anguish and said to Daniel, 'O Daniel, servant of the living God, has your God, whom you serve continually, been able to deliver you from the lions?' Then Daniel said to the king, 'O king, live for ever! *My God has sent his angel* and shut the lions' mouths, and they have not hurt me, because I was found blameless before him . . . .' " Daniel 6:19–22.

On the night of Jesus' betrayal, the apostle Peter, in typical haste, "drew his sword, and struck the slave of the High Priest, and cut off his ear. Then Jesus said to him, 'Put your sword back into its place; for all who take the sword will perish by the sword. Do you think that I cannot appeal to my Father, and he will *at once send me more than twelve legions of angels?* But how then should the scriptures be fulfilled, that it must be so?' " Matthew 26:51,52 and John 18:10.

Once Jesus fasted for a very long time. At length it was over, "and behold, angels came and ministered to him," Matthew 4:11 says.

Some clergymen asked Jesus a long and complicated question about a woman married many times. They wanted to know whose wife she would be in heaven. Jesus replied, "Is not this why you are wrong—because you know neither the scriptures nor the power of God? For when they rise from the dead, they neither marry nor are given in marriage, but are like angels in heaven." (Mark 12:24,25.) Angels are not male and female; they do not have offspring. They do not die.

"The sons of this age marry and are given in marriage," Jesus said, "but those who are accounted worthy to attain to the next age and to the resurrection from the dead neither marry nor are given in marriage, for they cannot die any more, because they are *equal to angels* and are sons of God, being sons of the resurrection." Luke 20:34.

The angels are a very numerous company. Psalm 68:17 says, "The chariots of God are twenty thousand, even thousands of angels; the Lord is among them, as in Sinai, in the holy place." Jesus said that, at his call, twelve legions would come from heaven, 50,000 to 60,000 angels. Hebrews 12:22 speaks of "the city of the living God, the heavenly Jerusalem, and an innumerable company of angels." In Revelation 5:11, John writes, "Then I looked, and

I heard around the throne . . . the voice of many angels, numbering myriads of myriads and thousands of thousands."

Except when they move among men as men, angels are repeatedly spoken of in terms of fire, brightness, white and shining raiment, and in terms of the fear that humans feel when they first see them.

Angels have the power to destroy. The two angels who visited Lot told him to get out of Sodom with his family in the morning "for we are about to destroy this place . . . the Lord has sent us to destroy it." Genesis 19:12,13.

On another occasion, "God sent the angel to Jerusalem to destroy it, but when he was about to destroy it, the Lord saw, and he repented of the evil, and he said to the destroying angel, 'It is enough; now stay your hand.' And the angel of the Lord was standing by the threshing floor of Ornan the Jebusite"—a specific angel in a specific place—"and in his hand a drawn sword stretched over Jerusalem. . . .Now Ornan was threshing wheat; he turned and *saw the angel,* and his four sons who were with him hid themselves." II Chronicles 21:15,16,20.

Angels are seen in the Scriptures executing the judgments of God. In the great judgments that are to fall upon the earth, as detailed in Revelation, Chapters 8 and 9, angels are centrally involved.

Jesus promised that He would come again to the earth, and angels would come with Him. Exactly when that coming will be is the best kept secret of the universe. Jesus said the people of the earth "will see the Son of man coming on the clouds of heaven with power and great glory; and he will send out his angels with a loud trumpet call, and they will gather his elect from the four winds, from one end of heaven to the other . . . . But of that day and hour no one knows, not even the angels of heaven, nor the Son, but the Father only." (Matthew 24:30,31,36.) "When the Son of man comes in his glory, and all the angels with him, then he will sit on his glorious throne. Before him will be gathered all the nations . . . ."Matthew 25:31,32a.

The day is coming "when the Lord Jesus shall be revealed from heaven with his mighty angels, in flaming fire taking vengeance on those who know not God . . . ." (II Thessalonians 1:7,8.) "So it will be at the close of the age. The angels will come out and separate the evil from the righteous, and throw them into the furnace of fire; there men will weep and gnash their teeth," Jesus declared. (Matthew 13:49,50.) "For the Lord himself will descend from heaven with a shout, with the voice of the archangel, and with the sound of the trumpet of God, and the dead in Christ shall rise first," Paul wrote in I Thessalonians 4:16. Jesus once told the crowd that was following Him that "whoever is ashamed of me and of my words in this adulterous and sinful generation, of him will the Son of man also be ashamed, when he comes in the glory of his Father with the holy angels." Mark 8:38.

Satan

The Bible declares that God has an enemy: Satan. He is man's enemy, too. Satan is at work today in the world, and in the United States, with an intensity unmatched in our experience, and the Scriptures warn that his activity will be stepped up greatly among the nations, both in degree and in velocity, in the years immediately ahead. Satan desires to organize mankind for its own destruction. Unless we know of him and how he works, we will be caught short and find ourselves unable to cope with the events that descend upon us. To a degree, that is already the case.

Satan does not want you to believe that he exists. His utmost desire is that you think he does not. He will go to almost any length to perpetuate and enforce that persuasion in you. He is your enemy, and it suits his purposes best to have you believe that he is non-existent. One of his primary aims is the destruction of man, and he can work much more effectively to destroy you if you think he is not working at it.

God wants you to know about Satan. The Bible pointedly exposes Satan and exposes his tactics for man's sake. Paul wrote that men must "keep Satan from gaining the advantage over us; for we are *not ignorant of his devices.*" (II Corinthians 2:11.) The reverse of that is: If we remain ignorant of Satan's devices, he will gain the advantage over us. In plain fact, he already has gained such advantage. He has gained such advantage especially over the young people of this nation.

We can know nothing about the existence of Satan apart from the Scriptures. It is the Bible that reveals him to the understanding of man, and we need desperately to know about him because what Satan does, and how he does it, are the concealed factors behind present eruptions of evil in the world.

The Bible is very clear on the point of Satan's origin and person, his purposes, his power, and his domain. It tells a great deal about him at many places in the Old and the New Testaments. Satan is seen at work in Genesis, the first book of the Bible, and in Revelation, the last book, and he is seen at scores of places in between.

There have been many appeals to "tell it like it is," to rip off all the sham and the pretense, to lay matters bare to their roots. That is exactly what the Bible does. It tells it as it really is. It tears away the camouflage, the coverup, and exposes this architect of evil: who he is and how he works.

Satan is a living creature. He is not corporeal. He is a spiritual being, but that does not make him any less real. The fact that he is invisible and powerful greatly serves him in the pursuit of his cause. The idea that Satan is a term for a generalized influence of evil—instead of the name of a specific living personality—is a strictly anti-Biblical idea.

The name Satan does not speak of an impersonal influence. It speaks of a single, identifiable, distinct living being with a will, a personality, and a highly directed intelligence.

One thing we have to do to get a clear view of Satan is to divest ourselves of any caricatures of him as a boiled-live-lobster-red being with a tail and a pitchfork. There is no such creature. Satan wants you to think that to credit his existence you must believe in such an absurdity as that. The difference between the Satan revealed in the Scriptures and all such cartoons is vast. Such conceptions of Satan are a pathetic distortion of the reality they so lightly mock.

The being now called Satan—the name means "adversary"—was at his creation a very beautiful being. His beauty has been corrupted by evil, but he still disguises and presents himself to much of mankind as god. He can do so, because the Bible says that Satan is a god.

The Bible declares that "God is a spirit." It describes angels as "ministering spirits." The Bible calls Satan *the prince of the power of the air, the spirit that is now at work in the children of disobedience.* (Ephesians 2:2.) So Satan is a spirit—that is, an intelligent living being who is invisible to the natural eye.

This one brief portion tells a great deal about Satan: First, that he is a prince. Second, that his domain is centered in the atmosphere of the earth, in the envelope of air in which it is enclosed. Third, that Satan is active, or "at work." Fourth, that his activity is carried out through the lives of fallen or sinful men, who are called "the children of disobedience." It is a stark fact that Satan exercises some degree of actual authority and control over all men who have never become worshipers of the God of Israel.

Satan is a god. The Bible calls Satan "the god of this world." (II Corinthians 4:4.) The statement gives us some idea of the tremendous scope of Satan's activity and power on the earth. It is a literal, precisely accurate description of the position that he occupies with respect to mankind, but it requires reflection to grasp the measure of it.

The appalling fact is that God is rejected now, as He has been through nearly all of human history, as the Lord of mankind. God is not the spiritual leader of most men. Satan is.

Because He made man, God has desired man to obey Him, but man has refused to do so. The Jews were set apart by God as a small, distinct people who were to follow Him with such fidelity that all nations would see His love and power poured out in blessing upon a single people. But they would not. The cry of the prophets is largely the call of a Father to a people whose backs were often turned to Him.

God's Word, His prophets, His Son have all been ignored or despised by those to whom they were sent. The living God, the God of Israel, is not widely worshiped and obeyed among mankind, neither among Jews nor Gentiles.

Satan has succeeded in usurping the place that belongs to God among the masses of mankind. He has substituted his will for the will of the living God in the lives of millions of men. That is why there is so much that is hellish on the earth. Satan has taken the central place that God ought to occupy in the lives of men and has filled it up with other things—including religions.

The Bible makes it clear that it is not God, it is Satan as god, who is followed by most of mankind.

If the living God were worshiped by mankind the earth would be "full of the knowledge of the Lord as the waters cover the sea," as someday it will be. (Isaiah 11:9.) The earth is now filled with conditions that suit Satan, "the god of this world"—strife, treachery, bloodshed, tyranny, upheavals, crime, suffering, addiction, commotions, wars and rumors of wars, death.

Satan is a ruler, and he is consistently spoken of in terms of royal power. As well as being designated "the god of this world," he is called "the prince of this world" (John 12:31) or, as the Revised Standard Version translates it, "the ruler of this world."

As a prince and ruler, Satan has a domain and he also has subjects. His domain, the chief arena of his activity, is the earth and the atmosphere of the earth. His subjects are sinful men, millions of them, whom he has blinded and led astray from the living God—by false religions, by bald denials of God's existence and love, by cults of state that demand entire devotion contrary to the Word of God (notably communism and fascism), by many lies of philosophy, by every form of idolatry.

Satan, the usurper, is wholly conscious of his position as the god of this world. When Jesus faced and met the temptations of Satan, "the devil took him to a very high mountain, and showed him all the kingdoms of the world and the glory of them; and he said to him, '*All these I will give you,* if you will fall down and worship me.'" Matthew 4:8,9.

It was a genuine offer. The kingdoms of this world and their glory are sufficiently in the control of Satan for him to have been able to offer them. Since the primary lust of Satan is to be worshiped, and to take worship away from God, he did not think those kingdoms too dear a price to pay if Jesus would worship him. "Jesus said to him, 'Begone, Satan! for it is written, "You shall worship the Lord your God, and him only shall you serve."'"

Like all other created beings, Satan can only be in one place at a time. He is not omnipresent, as God is, but he manages to seem ubiquitous. Because he exists on the spiritual plane, he is able to move with almost instantaneous speed in the universe. At times he comes directly to an individual on the earth to oppose or to tempt him.

"Resist the devil," the Bible says, "and he will flee from you." (James 4:7.) You cannot resist him, of course, if you do not believe he is there.

Satan's Policy of Secrecy

Satan's purpose is to draw men away from God and to keep men away from Him by every means he can use. In accomplishing this, Satan finds it convenient and strategic to conceal his own identity and his activities as much as possible from human view. He is an enemy, an adversary. Therefore he moves under the cover of secrecy.

Consider the tactics of an enemy in battle. The enemy finds it far easier to send death upon his target if he conceals and hides his own position, so that he may strike by sudden surprise. Sneak attack, it is called. To obtain this advantage, the enemy moves in darkness, by stealth, and takes his position of advantage over the target in a hidden or camouflaged place. He wants the other side to be as unalert as possible, unguarded, unsuspecting, exposed to attack. The enemy will also use deceit and trickery to create a false impression of what and where the dangers are. The less the intended victims know of his existence, his position, his intention, and his power, the greater the advantage to him in bringing injury or death upon them.

These are the tactics of Satan toward man. The less you know about Satan the better he likes it. Your ignorance of his tactics confers an advantage upon him, but he prefers that you do not even credit his existence. If you do not believe that he is, then you will do nothing to prepare yourself, or your family, or your children, against his activities, and by that neglect many are made his victims.

There are three ways by which you can know of Satan and his work: By what the Bible reveals about him. By personal experience. By reading of the personal experiences of others.

Satan is the active adversary of the purposes of God. He is the supreme leader of a rebellion against God.

God is the creator. Satan is the destroyer. The first words of the Scriptures are "In the beginning God created . . . " and every book of the Bible tells us something about the character and purposes of God. Almost from the very start, Satan worked to introduce destruction and misery and sin into the affairs of mankind.

The Author of Idolatry

Satan is a spiritual leader. As the head of the rebellion against God and against the government of God, he works, using every means he can, to see that God is supplanted as the center of man's desire.

He does not greatly care to what secondary object or desire or pursuit a man gives his chief loyalty, just so long as it is not to God, the source of life and of truth. He works constantly to divert man's attention from God, to direct it to something else. It may be to money, property, fame, power, pleasure, the family, success, science, art, a religious idol, a dead saint, a human leader, a false god, a political system, or anything else. Whatever it is that takes first place in a man's life is that man's idol, and Satan is the author of idolatry.

The thing that takes the place of God as first in a man's life is Satan's substitute for God in that life. Find out to what a man's ultimate loyalty goes, and that is his god. That idol is Satan's tool to keep you from God and, by it, to claim you as a member of his rebellion against God.

That thing will keep you from God in your life, unless you break with it as the chief end of your being. The thing may not be evil in itself, it may be good, but it is accursed when it takes the place of God, and it becomes the destroyer of your soul. A man who refuses to serve God and to love Him on the earth will not be allowed to serve Him in eternity. "What shall it profit a man," Jesus asked, "if he gain the whole world and lose his soul?" Mark 8:36.

By the idol—the chief desire—Satan draws a man away from God and betrays him, depriving God of His rightful place in the life of one of His creatures. Satan counts that a triumph. It is his inflexible purpose to secure the allegiance of as many millions of men as he can to *anything* other than to God. By it, he causes them to break the First Commandment.

"Know therefore this day, and consider it in thine heart," Moses said, "that the Lord he is God in heaven above, and upon the earth beneath: there is none else." Deuteronomy 4:39.

God commanded, "Thou shalt have no other gods before me." Deuteronomy 5:7.

If there is anything a man wants more than God, that thing will bar the gates of heaven to him forever. He is an idolater. He has put the creation in the place of the Creator. He is absorbed with a thing, when he ought to be absorbed with a Person.

That is why Jesus said, "No servant can serve two masters; for either he will hate the one and love the other, or he will be devoted to the one and despise the other. *You cannot serve God and mammon.*" Luke 16:13.

That is not a summons to asceticism or deprivation. When God promised Israel "a land flowing with milk and honey," He meant a place of abundance. Psalm 84 promises, "No good thing will God withhold from those who walk uprightly." I Timothy 6:17 charges men not to "trust in uncertain riches, *but in the living God, who gives us richly all things to enjoy.*"

God delights to have men enjoy good things. But He abhors it when men take those things and make them their gods, wresting them to their own destruction. Matthew 6:32,33, sums it up: "Your heavenly Father knows that you have need of all these things. But seek *first* the kingdom of God and his righteousness, and all these things shall be *added* to you." It is when we seek them first, and they become our chief delight, that we are guilty of idolatry. In doing that we make ends out of what were meant to be means.

If we put God first, if we seek Him first, and if we seek Him as earnestly and wholeheartedly as most men seek sundry things, God will see to it that we have everything we need. And we shall be saved from ever having made them our idols and goals.

Satan's purpose—on the earth and among men and in the heavens—is *to oppose God at every point.*

A chief issue on which Satan opposes God is worship. It is right that men worship God. God calls men to worship Him, and Him only.

Satan does not want men to worship God. He prefers that they blaspheme Him, using His holy name as an oath and a curse. He has succeeded in getting vast numbers of men in this way to violate the Third Commandment continually: "You shall not take the name of the Lord your God in vain, for the Lord will not hold him guiltless who takes his name in vain." One of the great, intended uses of the human tongue is to sound the worship and adoration of God, to sing His glory, to utter thanksgiving to Him. Satan endeavors to pervert that faculty—one that separates man from the beasts—and to cause the human tongue to be occupied in speaking out curses. It is no accident, it is by express design, that so much of swearing consists of the misappropriation of God's name. Swearing, when it is deliberate as well as when it is automatic and habitual, is a sign of Satan's dominance over the persons who engage in it.

It is interesting, and significant, that while the name of God is on the lips of millions as a curse and is spoken countless times daily over all the earth—in explicit violation of the Biblical commandment—the name of Satan is nowhere used that way. That is a triumph of Satan's policy. It is a sign of his dominion over the minds and tongues of mankind.

Satan lusts for worship. Because it belongs exclusively to God, he desires it for himself. He would rather have worship than anything else, but because he knows he would not succeed in getting great numbers of men to worship him—if they knew that that was what they were doing—he sets up many objects as alternatives to the worship of God. This is idolatry in its crudest form, and the world is full of it. It makes little difference whether it is a woman coming before a Buddha-figure in the Orient or another weeping at the feet of the figure of a saint in New York, it is idolatry in God's eyes, all of it, and He despises it. It is the breaking of the Second Commandment, the words of which are clear beyond mistaking: "You shall not make for yourself a graven image, or any likeness of anything that is in heaven above, or that is on the earth beneath, or that is in the water under the earth; you shall not bow down to them or serve them; for I the Lord your God am a jealous God. . . ." (Deuteronomy 5:8,9a.) Idols are not to be made, much less to be bowed before. They are an offense to God. All religions that foster images and idols, wherever they may be—in Tibet, India, Europe, in the jungles of New Guinea or Brazil or Africa or anywhere else—whatever the rationale that may go with them, are false and under the active sway of Satan to a significant degree.

Satan stands behind every image and every idol, receiving as unto himself the worship, the respect, and adoration that is directed to them, which belongs only to the living God. Satan promotes the use and worship of idols wherever he can. They are useful to him in one of his chief desires—to rob God of worship.

The use of idols cheats men. It is grotesque for a living being to use his breath to pray to a dead object. The Scripture said of idols, "It is not in them to do good." Jeremiah 10:5b.

The Biblical revelation is at constant war with the worship of idols. Scalding denunciations of every deviation into idolatry are one of the main burdens of the Old Testament prophets. Wherever the Bible is truly influential, wherever the Word of God is proclaimed and honored, there the idolatry of religious statues and objects is minimized. This form of idolatry has certainly been far less prevalent in the United States than in most civilizations, but there is a considerable push now by Satan to bring religious statues and objects into the nation, especially from the East.

Young people, including Jewish young people, are now dabbling in religious idolatry, using Tibetan and Chinese and other images and idols. A close friend told me of a young man who married a Jewish girl who had impressed him in part because she exhibited a sincere interest in her religion. They separated recently, after she brought a Buddha into their house and set it up and started burning candles in front of it.

In the sight of God, a land is "polluted" by its idols, as the Bible puts it. In every place in which an idol is set up, Satan enjoys the presence of a symbol of the dominance of his religious policy in that place. The setting up of an idol is an act of direct defiance against the will of God. The cumulative effect of idols and images is to bring a curse upon the land.

It is bad enough for Gentiles to engage in religious idolatry. It is worse for Jews. For a Jew to use a statue or a charm in religous practices is to fly in the face of the lessons of the whole history of the Jews. Whatever the Gentiles do, the distinctive testimony of the Jews is to be that they worship the living God, not idols.

Moses spoke for God in commanding: "Turn not unto idols, nor make yourself molten gods: I am the Lord your God." Leviticus 19:4.

"You shall make for yourselves no idols and erect no graven image or pillar, and you shall not set any image of stone in your land, to bow down to it; for I am the Lord your God." Leviticus 26:1.

God told the Jews through Moses that if they walked contrary to Him, "Then I will walk contrary unto you also in fury; and I, even I, will chastise you seven times for your sins. . . . And I will destroy your high places, and cut down your images, and cast your own dead bodies upon the dead bodies of your idols, and my soul shall abhor you. . . . And I will scatter you among the heathen, and will draw out a sword after you; and your land shall be desolate, and your cities waste. Then shall the land rest and enjoy her sabbaths." Leviticus 26:28–34.

God never intended, anywhere in all the universe, idols to be set up as religious objects. They steal men's attention from Him and fix it on things that He despises. So profound is the effect of religious idols and images upon a land that the land of Israel could not "rest and enjoy her sabbaths" while the people of Israel disobeyed God and practiced idolatry in it. It was better in God's sight for the people to be taken away and the land emptied of its population than for it to continue to be defiled.

The Old Testament records that "the children of Israel did secretly those things that were not right against the Lord their God. . . . And they set them up images and groves in every high hill, and under every green tree; and there they burned incense in all the high places, as did the heathen whom the Lord carried away before them; and wrought wicked things to provoke the Lord to anger: For they served idols, whereof the Lord had said to them, You shall not do this thing. . . .

"They followed vanity, and went after the heathen that were

round about them, concerning whom the Lord had charged them, that they should not do like them. . .

"Therefore the Lord was very angry with Israel, and removed them out of his sight; there was none left but the tribe of Judah only." II Kings 17:9–12, 15b, 18.

Isaiah speaks of a better time: "In that day men will regard their Maker, and their eyes will look to the Holy One of Israel; they will not have regard for the altars, the work of their hands, and they will not look to what their own fingers have made, either the idols or the altars of incense." Isaiah 17:7.

If you are a Jew, you give Satan a claim on your soul and a basis for activity in your life by using idols and religious objects of any kind. You will bring a curse into your life by them and it will go hard with you.

There is no realm in which Satan is more active than religion. As a spiritual leader, Satan has devised many forms of religion, none of which are able to bring a man into relationship to the living God or release him from the grip of sin. His religions tend to have certain similarities over the world. They are marked by rote and ritual, repetitions and incantations, idols and altars, images and protecting charms.

It is striking, a sign of their supernatural inspiration, that the facial masks carved in Africa, in India, in South America, in Borneo and other places among which there was no possibility of natural communication whatever, are often nearly identical in their design and use in primitive religions.

Look at an ancient temple in Tibet or in Egypt and look also at certain cathedrals in the modern world and you see them similarly figured with stone carvings and reliefs of gods and animals and men—in direct contradiction to the commandment. Satan is the primary author of it all, and that is why so many of them, so remote from one another in place and in time, look so very much alike.

There are those among mankind who do not worship idols but who worship spirits or who worship the devil. There are in this nation those who now openly worship the devil, in such religions as Satanism.

But usually Satan finds it more useful in drawing men astray to hide behind an object or a living person, and to let the worship he is stealing from God be directed to them. For that reason he will cause to be overthrown a system of idol worship when he can successfully replace it with a system of *man worship*. He has done that in China. An evil man is a more useful tool for Satan to set up as an object of worship than an idol, because the man who is worshiped is able to galvanize his followers to Satan's purposes of widespread terror and destruction.

Satan's Policy of Lies

Contradiction of the Word of God is another means by which Satan opposes God among men. His policy is to suppress the Scriptures wherever he can—that is, wherever he can get men to cooperate with him in that purpose. There have been in the past, and there are today, nations in which the possession and reading of the Scriptures is forbidden or restricted by every means available. Such nations are carrying out the policy of Satan against the dissemination of the knowledge of God. Satan hates the Scriptures because they reveal God and because they expose him.

Where he cannot suppress the Scriptures, he contradicts them, distorts them, heaps scorn upon them, causes them to be misapplied, and seeks by every possible means to nullify or severely limit their actual influence. Satan has turned the universities, which once were centers for the study and promulgation of the truths of the Scriptures, into centers where they are mocked and repudiated, with guile, with enmity, with sophistication, and with a false show of scholarly objectivity. Much of the contradiction of the Scriptures in university classrooms is purely gratuitous—dragged in by the preceptor with no relevance to anything but his own arrogant bias—and part of it is a matter of scruple by deceived men. The effect is, as it long has been in this country, profoundly to subvert the Bible's influence among the young, leaving them ultimately without defense against the undermining of their character and morals. Steal the influence of the Bible, once so great, away from the German youth and you have, at the end, a generation of storm troopers and goose-steppers—a youth mobilized by Satan for great destruction. Steal the influence of the Bible, once so great, away from American young people and you have what we are now beginning to have, a generation of militant and articulate anarchists, mobilizing for destruction.

It is the nature of God to speak truth. "God is not a man, that he should lie," Numbers 23:19 asserts. "Has he said, and will he not do it? Or has he spoken, and will he not make it good?" The Book of Titus says that *"God, who cannot lie,"* has promised certain things to man. Jesus said that "Man shall not live by bread alone, but *by every word that proceeds out of the mouth of God."* (Matthew 4:4.) Jesus was directly quoting Moses: See Deuteronomy 8:3b.

"Every word of God is pure," says Proverbs 30:5a.

"Thy word is very pure," Psalm 119:140a affirms.

"The words of the Lord are pure words: as silver tried in a furnace of earth, purified seven times," David wrote in Psalm 12:6.

God cannot lie. His word is truth. In contrast to this, the Bible says of Satan, "When he lies, he speaks according to his own nature, for *he is a liar and the father of lies."* John 8:44b.

It is the nature of Satan to speak lies. He is a liar, but more than that, he is "the father of lies." Satan is the one who introduced lying into the relationships between intelligent beings in the universe, and he still promotes lying today—the breaking of the Ninth Commandment, which forbids bearing false witness.

A lie is designed to deceive. Satan does not present his lies as lies, he presents them as truth. Satan's lies are designed to deceive men about the most important things: about God and the nature of God; about sin and evil; about redemption and salvation; about death; about judgment and hell. Satan's lies are designed to deceive men to their death. He is the father of the religious lie, which contradicts the Word of God and betrays men's souls forever if they believe it. He is the father of the political lie, the big lie, which, when men accept it, leads them to national enslavement or destruction.

In every case where God says something is true and Satan says it is not true or that the opposite is true, what Satan says is a *lie.* Every man who speaks a word contrary to the truth of the Scriptures is a liar. Wittingly or unwittingly, he has lent his mind and his tongue to Satan for the doing of his work. He has lent his tongue to the father of lies. That is why the Scripture says, "What if some did not believe? Shall their unbelief make the faith of God without effect? God forbid! Let God be true, but every man a liar; as it is written, 'That thou mayest be justified in thy words, and prevail when thou art judged.'" Romans 3:3,4.

It is Satan's policy to challenge the word of God directly, and specifically to contradict it. Because God is active in promulgating truth and Satan is active in promoting lies, every man stands between the truth of God and the lies of Satan, and he must decide which to believe.

Satan began his policy of lies in Eden. God told man, "You may

freely eat of every tree of the garden, but of the tree of the knowledge of good and evil you shall not eat, for in the day that you eat
of it you shall surely die." Genesis 2:16,17.

Satan, whose desire for man is death, told the woman, "You will
not die. For God knows that when you eat of it your eyes will be
opened, and you will be like God, knowing good and evil." Genesis
3:4,5.

Satan's purpose was death for man. His method was flat contradiction of what God had said, and he sought to make his lie more
acceptable by adding a promise of knowledge to it. Satan often
tries to sweeten his lies by promising that something good is to
be gained by believing them. His method is rather like that of the
fisherman who baits the hook with something delightful and apparently much to be desired. That is his *offer* to the fish. But it is
not his purpose. His purpose is death.

"The wages of sin is death," the Bible declares. God goes all the
way to the end of sin and shows it to be death so that men, by
seeing the last result of it, may avoid it and be saved. Satan says
another thing entirely. "The wages of sin is" . . .pleasure, he says
. . .or gain, or security, or wealth, or station, or power, or some
other desirable thing. He is careful not to show the end of it, death.

What is the offer of a narcotics experiment? Pleasure, relaxation, escape, transcendent experience—one or more of these. But
at the end it often brings addiction, enslavement, death.

An executive told me of a seventeen-year-old boy in New Jersey
who liked to take a car and race it through town at night at speeds
way above the law. He enjoyed the thrill of it. One Saturday night
he lost control trying to avoid another car, crashed straight-on
into a brick wall, and was found smashed dead. He got the thrill,
and it sent him down into the grave. I read of a sixteen-year-old
boy in Brooklyn who walked over to a woman getting off a bus,
snatched her pocketbook, and ran. A policeman happened to be
walking nearby. He chased the boy, shouted at him to stop, fired
a warning shot, and then, as the boy continued to flee, shot at him.
The aim was high and the boy sprawled on the sidewalk, dead. The
pocketbook slipped from his hand and its contents scattered on
the pavement. "Be sure your sin will find you out," the Bible warns.
"The wages of sin is death." In this case, the payoff came pitifully
soon. If the boy had resisted the temptation to attempt theft, on
the hint of quick or easy gain, he would no doubt be alive today.
In both cases sudden, unexpected death came as the result of

obedience to a lawless impulse. We could shout, "It wasn't worth it. It wasn't worth it." Whatever sin promises, at the end it isn't worth it.

Satan hates what God loves, and Satan loves what God hates. He is utterly opposed to the purposes of God. He is bent on separating man from God, so that God cannot have his created subject to love and worship Him, and so that man will end in moral ruin and destruction.

God is the Creator. Satan is the destroyer.

God created everything that is. Satan has never created anything. He cannot create anything. He has destroyed much. He desires to destroy as much of God's creation as he possibly can. He seeks to enlist man in that pursuit. Man is lending himself to that purpose today as much as ever.

Man, by joining the rebellion of Satan, collaborates in his own destruction. This is unspeakable folly. It is time for man to turn and rebel against Satan. It is time for the young, especially, to refuse to believe his lies, which lead to enslavement, to refuse to indulge in sin, which leads to death. That is why a knowledge of Satan and his tactics is so useful, because it enables man to act intelligently for his own protection against the lies and deceptions of the wicked one, the tempter of men.

It is ever Satan's design to get men to carry out specific parts of his program against God and against the purposes of God.

Satan can do nothing on his own. He could never have gained any influence in the earth apart from securing the willingness of men to obey him and to disobey God, to believe him and to doubt God. He could never have brought death to the garden if Eve had not agreed with him. Satan operates exclusively by gaining the consent of man—to lies, to sin, to every kind of evil.

Satan's unvarying practice is to attempt to make a league with something in the fallen nature of every man, and to use that thing to lead the man first to sin and ultimately to destruction. The thing on which he tries to seize is different in different individuals. He plies the defect to whose touch a person shows himself most susceptible and least resistant. It may not be something as sharp and interesting as greed. It may be something as dull as sloth. I know a young man who showed a genuine interest in the truths of Scripture but who could be counted upon to fail to meet every appointment made with him, regardless of the hour, because he was either dead-tired or dead-asleep. This occurred over a period of years.

Finally, an appointment was made to meet him at six-thirty in the evening for a hotel banquet at which a minister was to speak. My friend did not show up. A call to his home roused him from sleep; but too late for the occasion.

I could have shouted Proverbs 6:9–11 at him through the phone: "How long will you sleep, O sluggard? When will you arise out of sleep? Yet a little sleep, a little slumber, a little folding of the hands to sleep: So shall poverty come upon you like a vagabond, and want like an armed man."

In all seriousness, Satan will use *anything* that he can use to block the purposes of God in a person's life and to advance his own ends. In one it may be pride, in another lust, in another sadism, in another ambition, in another a gnawing desire for gain, in another fear, in another anger, in another a desire for power—and so on and so on, the list is very long. Sometimes it is two or more such things in various combinations. If he can get a man to act upon these perverse things in human nature, he has him on the road to his own destruction, and perhaps to the inflicting of much harm or destruction on others.

If he can magnify such things in the nature of a man to a great degree, he may produce a man whose actions become the very expression of Satan's purposes on earth. Such men become the master tyrants, enslavers, destroyers, and warmakers of history. Servants of Satan.

God made man to obey and worship Him, and He made the world entirely for man's enjoyment and benefit. Satan has come in to ruin man and to wreck the earth, as his way of expressing his implacable hatred of God.

God's desired social order is people helping people—and resisting Satan. Satan's desired social order is people harming people—and defying God. The man who is *socially useful* to Satan is the man who not only commits the sin that destroys his own soul but who communicates sin, who spreads it, who recruits others to it. The man who is socially useful to Satan is the man who spreads suffering and death. Satan gets men to do this by inflaming and aggravating evil propensities in them. They may, of course, resist.

Satan's aim is to overthrow the government of God among intelligent beings in the universe, among angels and among men. To do that, he must have the consent of these beings—not primarily to himself, but to his lies, his temptations, his purposes. In man he obtains that consent by addressing his appeal to defects which he knows are resident in fallen human nature. He seizes upon those defects, stirs them up if possible to overt expression, and by them drives men to do things contrary to the will of God and consonant with his purposes.

Satan opposes the purposes of God—in individuals, in societies, in nations—by every means he can. His desire in each case is to wreck them. He can only go as far as they will let him. Some individuals and some nations cooperate with Satan to that end.

The power of resistance, for every individual and every society, lies in obedience to the truth and conscience. If they cast aside the truth and trample conscience, they leave themselves wide open to Satan's strategy for their destruction.

Satan is right now heavily engaged in the process of attempting to destroy American society. He desires to bring this great experiment in liberty for the individual into chaos, by subverting its population spiritually and morally; and the people, having long ago let down the shield and standard of truth, are running with him in that purpose in larger and larger numbers.

If Satan's frontlash against the social order is a largely irrational, anarchistic, rebellious mutation of Marxism, tied to free-love morals and defiance of law, his backlash may be iron-fisted fascistic repression. The nation is being ripened for the appearance of a shrewd and eloquent demagogue, a man skilled in the manipulation of people's fears and emotions as a means of obtaining power. Though it may rock and shake America, the chances of the frontlash taking over in the nation are extremely remote. The chances of the backlash coming into power on a wave of popular revulsion and fear are far greater. Until now, there have been great balances in American society. They have preserved us from extremisms of the Left and Right, but we do not know how much longer these balances will hold the nation to a middle course of liberty and law and effective reform by democratic processes.

God save this nation from the vile conflict in which the revolutionary Marxists offer to save us from the fascists, and the fascists vow to save us from the Marxists. The Czechoslovaks have been through that cycle since World War II, and they know that it is all darkness and gall.

Men live either in liberty or in tyranny. By far the majority of men in history have had tyranny for their portion. Satan wills tyranny for men. It is as the truths of the Bible break the power of Satan over men that liberty comes to the people.

"Where the Spirit of the Lord is, there is liberty," the Scriptures say in II Corinthians 3:17. God is the author of liberty, and He wills liberty for man. Where men honor God, worship Him, and hold His word in respect, liberty flows to them. The holy Scriptures have been a beacon of liberty wherever they have had real influence with men in the world.

That is one reason why Satan seeks either to keep the Scriptures from men or, failing that, to hold them up to contempt, thereby limiting their influence.

The American society was, from colonial days, a Bible-influenced society. The public standard in this country was, to a remarkable degree, a Biblical standard for quite a long time. Among the early presidents of the nation there were several who rarely let a day go by without spending time reading the Bible. The churches, by and large, upheld the Scriptures and proclaimed their truths.

The effective attack on the Bible as the public standard in the nation began late in the last century, and it gathered great momentum after the First World War. The consequences have been piling up on the nation heavily in the last few years. Satan has been destroying the foundation of the society in order that he may destroy the society.

The public standard of morality in the nation—at least as it is reflected in literature, motion pictures, advertising, and the arts— is now beginning to approximate that of Sodom. Crime, addiction, violence, family instability, and social instability have all been steeply on the rise.

Liberty, order, justice, and conditions that allow human beings a maximum of freedom and happiness are extremely displeasing to Satan, who hates men only less than he hates God. In his adroit parody, "Screwtape Proposes a Toast," C. S. Lewis quotes a devil as saying, "It was a bitter blow to us—it still is—that any sort of men who had been hungry should be fed or any who had long worn chains should have them struck off." The United States has afforded liberty and abundance and safety to millions of men in proportions far above what had ever been known in the world. Satan's strategy for taking these things away has been the continual diminishing of the influence of the Scriptures among the people.

The Scriptures have both a restrictive and a liberating effect. Where they are honored, they restrict sin and misery and evil to a pronounced degree, and they check religious and political tyranny to a pronounced degree. Men are thus made free to expand along lines that are most beneficial to individuals and to society.

The polarization of a free society between extremes is the beginning of its destruction. As a broad consensus on common objectives goes, hatred and anger come in, and violence increases.

Satan, the destroyer, is out to destroy civil order in this nation. He is aiming blows specifically at those things which he knows protect liberty and order and permit the advancement of justice.

The instinct for destruction is almost automatic in persons who are demonically influenced. During the Chicago demonstrations and the police reaction in the summer of 1968, a leader of the demonstrators was asked what he had in mind. "I don't know," he said. "Like maybe destroy the Democratic Party."

The party was far from destroyed, but it was rocked and so was the nation. There are others now who want to destroy the system, destroy the election process, destroy representative government, destroy the courts, destroy the vehicles of free expression—the vital underpinnings of American civil order and justice. They are in a rage against them.

It is always a priority in Satan's program for the spreading of tyranny over a nation to extinguish the voice of the free press. Many works of evil and darkness and suppression can then be carried out without public knowledge and without effective redress. It is worth remarking that the passionate attack on the press came—as it always does, in any nation—from both the far Left and the Right in the 1968 election. The extreme leftists despise what they call "the establishment press." The people standing at the opposite extreme, proposing themselves as the best political remedy to the leftists, notably George Wallace, mounted a bitter attack on the press.

Satan would overthrow the courts, the press, the ballot, elected representation, and everything else from which the people derive their assurance of liberty. It is his program for America. He has his ardent spokesmen for these specific objectives among the population.

Though he is working at it, he cannot do it unless he can get the people to give their consent. In seeking that, he does not stop at lies.

For all their venomous antagonism, the extreme Left and the extreme Right are not two separate programs for the taking over and wrecking of the nation. They are two parts of *one single mechanism* whose ultimate intention is tyranny and whose chief manipulator is the devil, the prince of demagogues.

The two extremes require each other. They feed upon each other. The extreme Right must have the extreme Left as its foil if it is to make headway with the public. Both train their real attack on things that stand between them and total power—the press, the independent judiciary, the electoral system (the yippies wanted to overthrow it and Mr. Wallace wanted to paralyze it), the balance of powers in the government, the law. Both want to distort the police power and make it what it ought not to be. The extreme Left wants to harass and enfeeble or destroy the police power; the extreme Right wants to bloat it into a brutal and authoritarian force. Either way, destruction can have a heyday. Americans must be careful not to allow either half of this single demonic program to betray them into the hands of the other. The devil doesn't care whether he takes over the country with his left hand or his right hand.

Hear the allegory of the Scarecrow and the Soldiers. A certain man—call him John America—lives on a lovely and productive farm on which things have gone well for a very long time. Another man—call him J. Harry Diablos—is bitter about how well things have gone for John. He wants to wreck his place or at least bring it closer to the standard of human misery that has prevailed in much of the rest of the world. So he hires three yippies and a squad of soldiers. He sends the yippies over to the farm to set themselves up as squatters, to poach on the land, to strew garbage around and openly to violate most of the conventions of morality and civility John is used to. They are his scarecrow. When John is sufficiently scared by what he sees, the man brings the soldiers over.

"Look, John," he says, "those derelict yippies out there are a terrible threat to your place. They're making a regular mess out of it. Now, see those smart-looking fellows out there, with the short haircuts and the shiny boots? They're my soldiers. Just look at them, and you know you can trust them. Let my soldiers come onto your place and clean them yippies out." Old John agrees. The soldiers come in and clean the yippies out, but they take over the place.

Satan's tactic for the destruction of American liberty is the manipulation of evil forces in a way that will cause the people to act rashly in alarm, rather than wisely in justice. If he can get them to do that, he can ruin the nation.

Think of a nation as a group of people on a great stage, with a master puppeteer above them. At one side of the stage the puppeteer lowers a frightening apparition and jerks it through a grotesque dance. On the other side of the stage he lowers an open cage. As the people fall away from the apparition and huddle together, the puppeteer swings the apparition violently toward them and invites them to step into the safety of the cage. When they do, he clangs the cage door shut on them.

Demagoguery and destructive anarchism are both essentially devilish phenomena—that is, Satan stands behind them and promotes them as socially useful to his purposes.

He has set the hippies and the yippies up to give ordinary Americans a bad case of cultural shock, bafflement, and fear—yielding eventually perhaps to dumb fury. When he has them worked up to the right pitch, he will present the "answer" in the form of a man or a movement that will arise to save America from the threat of the yippies.

A fascist extremism could not gain a majority of the American vote if it presented itself in just that color. But in taking over, extremism seeks some issue, some single issue, to which a majority of the electorate *will* respond, and it seizes that issue and rides it into power.

Leftist extremists have used this tactic at the universities. They cannot sell their bald program of rebellion and overthrow to more than a minority of the students, so they seek a broader issue with popular appeal on a campus, claim it as theirs, and use it to lift themselves into the leadership of a popular revolt. Then they do what they really want to do, shut down classrooms and drive administrators out of office.

Early in Hitler's regime, before he had consolidated his power in Germany, a group of ministers, alarmed at certain symptoms in the nation, addressed an appeal to the government, warning against what they termed "the new paganism."

It was brilliantly handled. Hitler shortly issued in his own name a grave warning against "the new paganism," as though his underlings had gone wrong and needed to be checked by him. At a later date, he would throw objecting ministers into prison camps. At that stage, however, his tactic was to pose as sharer of their alarm.

All extremism wants is for the people *legally to grant it a share of real power.* It will put on almost any face to persuade them to do that. Once it gets its grip on the jugular centers of national life and power, it will not stop until it has accomplished strangulation.

The extremist burns to murder freedom. He cannot relax until he is able to drop the people's freedom from his grasp, a whitened corpse.

Satan is a practical being. He is interested in obtaining the practical result. The means must therefore be practical and suited to the circumstances. Americans would not now vote into power a fascist extremism that offered itself as plainly that, but they might vote into power a man of just that temper who proved skillful at inflaming their fears.

Satan knows that, and the practical problem is to do something to arouse those fears. Nothing is more useful to him for that than the yippie cult.

As some young people are driven to far extremes of the anarchistic left, some adults react by going farther to the right. One wild-haired yippie may be enough to scare a hundred, maybe a thousand, ordinary citizens into a wrong response. So the yippie is, consciously or otherwise, organizing an army of repression.

That is the yippie's appointed role in Satan's plan for this nation.

When I told a young man I know, who is a yippie in his whole sympathy if not in behavior, that the yippie phenomenon is a tactic of Satan to scare this nation into a fascistic repression, he said, without an instant's hesitation: "Well, ———! *Let them take over!*" He hates the system so deeply that he would rather see it destroyed by an extremism of the Right than go on, he said.

He is a Gentile, but there are also young Jews who are lending themselves today to a program whose ultimate intent is to impose on the United States a midnight of tyranny. It is Satan's program; to cooperate with it is to play into the hands of the enemy of the Jews. Satan desires to fashion an instrument of repression that he can use later to turn with force and fury on the Jews. Every young Jew who, in his rage and revulsion, goes the way of the yippies puts his weight on the side of the national balances that, as it goes down, will help raise the opposite side into power.

A Dealer in Sin

Satan is a dealer in sin. He tempts men and women, teen-agers, children, to sin because it suits his purposes to do so. He knows that if he can get the consent of an individual to sin he has a claim upon that man's soul. He knows that if he can engage a person in sin he can sooner or later destroy that person through his sin, and in the process he can afflict, torment, or destroy other men by it.

Garbage is the rightful domain of the garbage man. Where there is garbage, the garbage man must come. If there is garbage in the wealthiest house in town, or if there is garbage strewing the alley of some slum, the garbage man has the right to come in and claim it and take it. As garbage is the rightful province of the garbage man—so sin is the rightful province of Satan.

Your sin, whatever it is, is Satan's claim upon you. He wants to hold that claim and, if possible, to expand it, to engage you in fuller expressions of sin, because that is useful to him, destructive for you, and hurtful to others. What pleases him yet more is that it reflects in the life of man Satan's own defiance of God.

Men who sin and nations that sin are, to some degree, under the active dominance of Satan and are engaged in doing his will. A man in sin devotes some or all of his faculties, his time, his energy, his money, and his bodily members to the works of sin. He may lend his mouth to blasphemies, his influence to injustice, his hands to theft or violence, his mind to impure thoughts, his money to perversion or organized crime, his service to a false god, his will to purposes of greed, domination, or the imposition of tyranny on others. Whether he does so in greater or smaller measure, he has consecrated himself and his faculties to that extent to Satan's rebellion against God.

Some men give themselves over quite fully to sin. They are the devoted servants of Satan. He uses them to inflict very much harm on their fellow men, some of it seen, much of it unseen.

A writer somewhere allows lust to rise up and occupy his mind and his spirit, and as it does so he transmits it to words on paper. He allows his thoughts, stirred and fire-fed by Satan, to go to excesses of filthy imagination. He does so because he wants the money and because he enjoys the inward motions of lust. Someone else paints a cover for the book that has a pointed sexual appeal. The book goes into a drugstore rack. A high school kid browses among the books, finds a fascination in the cover, buys it and reads it and is led through detailed descriptions of things of which he had not heard or thought before. Excitement and arousal may lead to immediate expression of sin, but it may lead to some damaging adventure in a new form or practice of sin, and it may involve another person, or several others, or many others. It may even lead to the disaster of perversion.

Through the services of a publisher, the writer is brought into contact with thousands of people he does not know, into whose minds he deposits a load of filth. It will be shown to him at the Judgment how many of them were unable to bear it and turned his words into overt sins.

Satan loves to incite the widespread communication of sin, particularly in the realms of immorality and evil supernaturalism, and there are writers and publishers today who serve him abundantly in sowing sin broadcast over the nation. The immediate harvest of it may be money, but behind it there is a harvest of shame, misery, perversion, mental derangement, and, ultimately, grievous social disruption.

The books on perversion—gross perversions of the darkest kinds—now commonly available in paperback book racks across the country offer the most detailed, explicit instruction in unspeakable practices to anyone who reads them. Some who read them will go on actually to engage in them, and by that more lives than may easily be traced can be twisted or ruined. "By one man's disobedience," the Bible says, "many were made sinners." (Romans 5:19a.) The apostle John writes, "He who commits sin is of the devil." (I John 3:8a.) That is why Satan is a dealer in sin.

Men give themselves over to practice sins of various kinds, and also in widely varying degrees. The influence of one man's sin can, at its apex, reach out to affect or destroy a nation or a series of nations. One man, Hitler, lent himself unreservedly to his hatreds and lusts, and because of that graves were dug across the face of Europe. Because of that young men from places as remote as Kansas were drawn off to Europe to fight, and some of them now lie "between the crosses, row on row" in the close-ranked graveyards of youth, the military cemeteries. Out of one man's evil intentions, ultimately millions died.

The Destroyer

Satan runs a kind of universal wrecking company. He takes pleasure in destruction because it mocks the love and purposes of God. Satan loves chaos because God has ordained a lawful and lovely order in the universe and in the relationships of intelligent beings to one another.

Satan's lust is to ruin as much as he can of all that God has made —using God's intelligent creatures, angels and men, to carry out the devastation. He turns those who were meant to be God's subjects into God's enemies and then turns them against God's creation, to become destroyers of His handiwork. If you hated a certain man you could not hurt him more than first to ruin his sons, and then get them to despoil his property.

Sin in man gives Satan the basis on which he can operate in society. The more he can magnify sin in a man, or the more he can draw him out on the line of a particular sin, the more useful that man is to him. To ruin a man Satan must gain the man's consent to sin, or lies, or evil. To ruin a society, he must gain a general consent among the population to sin, or lies, or evil.

Satan loves to pervert and make grotesque the wonderful beings God has made—chiefly man. Since man was made in the likeness of God and is the object of God's redeeming love, Satan delights in ruining men in any way he can—in their souls, or in their spirits, or in their bodies, now, and also forever.

See the miserly man, his frame, as it were, crouched over his money as a tigress crouches over her cubs. See the overly ambitious man, casting his favor, his attention, his smile on those who are over him, who can do him some good; ignoring and cutting short and walking cruelly over those who are below him; loving men for their station, not for themselves. See the angry or bitter man, his face drawn taut with hatred. See the ruined drunkard, slouched in a doorway, sleeping in his urine, babbling out his mindless complaint, able now to live only in hope of another drink. See the overtly homosexual man, dressed like a woman, mincing unnaturally or defiantly, his face white with powder, his eyebrows thinned. Or the homosexual woman, severely mannish, hair scissored short, legs drawn up in pants; men and women living lives of hideous reversal. Of these the Scripture says, "Wherefore God gave them up to uncleanness through the lusts of their own hearts, to dishonor their own bodies between themselves, who changed the truth of God into a lie, and worshipped and served the creature more than the Creator, who is blessed forever. For this cause God gave them up to vile affections, for even their women did change the natural use into that which is against nature. And likewise also the men, leaving the natural use of the woman, burned in their lust one toward another; men working with men that which is unseemly, and *receiving in their own persons the due penalty of their error.*" Romans 1:24–27.

See the far-out, far-gone "flower child" so called, dressing as for a charade, hair grown wild, body stinking from too little washing, talking of love but turning to virulent action, face pale from bad eating and the sickness inside. "Does not nature itself teach you that for a man to wear long hair is degrading to him, but if a woman has long hair, it is her glory? For her hair is given to her for a covering," the Scripture says in I Corinthians 11:14,15.

These are extremes, of course, but they are increasing in their number and in boldness and they illustrate how far Satan will go in twisting men out of all recognition to the likeness of their Creator, if they will let him. As Satan gains more and more headway in our society, such perversions will increase, especially among the young. They will become less exceptional and more and more common. Insanity will increase, and morbidity and disease. In many cases, death will come early.

Every man who will go at last into hell will be a triumph of Satan's policy of sin and death over God's redemptive purpose for that man. Because God wants man in heaven forever, Satan does everything he can to bind man by sin to the opposite destiny.

One of Satan's tactics is to persuade men to disobey God, on the promise that they shall obtain good by it. Another is to tempt and urge men to give reign and expression to their bodily lusts, because he knows that by that he may do much harm.

The tempter knows that if he can get young people to give themselves over for a few minutes to the electric pleasure to be had in an illicit act of fornication, he has a chance of producing a harvest of suffering out of it—a time of shame and fear for a pregnant girl and years of unshared burden in rearing a not-really-wanted child; a sense of guilt and shame for the young man; a dangerous operation perhaps; a suicide possibly; a marriage of necessity that will link for years or for life two persons not suited to each other; above all, a chance at bringing misery or unwantedness or perversion into the life of the child. The consequences, which run on for years, sometimes for generations, are not in any way worth the flashing pleasures of a moment.

Even in those cases where there are no manifest physical or social consequences *there are spiritual consequences to such an act.* The Bible distinguishes clearly between an act of fornication, which it abhors, and the physical love of the marriage bed set within the larger context of a complete and continuing union. That love is a culminating aspect, the most intimate privilege of the full union God has ordained for one man with one woman. It is holy enough, in His eyes, for Him to use human marriage as a figure for the communion that God has with those who are joined to Him.

For an individual to engage in sexual intercourse in any other context wrenches it out of its intended setting and exploits it for momentary purposes, in express violation of God's purpose and in direct violation of His command. "Flee fornication," the Bible says. "Every sin that a man does is without the body, but he that commits fornication sins against his own body." I Corinthians 6:18.

If God's blessing rests upon true marriage, His curse falls upon fornication, and those who engage in it suffer effects in some way. They are inescapable. There is a specific basis for Satanic activity in the lives and persons of those who commit the sin of fornication.

Because He loves man, God shows the thing in its true light. Satan always puts *all* the emphasis on the short-term pleasures. He seeks always to publicize and glamorize and emphasize the pleasure, and to deny or conceal or mock the payoff. "It will not be so in your case," he suggests. "You will escape." But there is no guarantee of that. I was being driven through a pleasant, wealthy town in Connecticut one evening by a reporter and I remember the sadness with which I heard him tell of a young woman, the daughter of a prominent executive, who was found dead in a motel a few miles from her home in that town, the last consequence of a brief fling in premarital sex. The young man who accompanied her on that adventure, fulfilling his own momentary lust by it, could not have dreamed that he was leading her to death so early in her life. The young woman was not murdered by him —not directly anyway. She died in an attempt at abortion. He may not have known of it. The charge, I believe, to which he will have to answer at the Judgment will not be for indulging in unlawful pleasure but for causing the death of a very young woman. Their romantic interlude was one short, deadly fling.

"Be sure your sin will find you out," the Scripture says. Her sin found that young lady out a few months later in that motel room. His sin will find that young man out at some future, inconvenient time. It waits for him at the last great Judgment, where there will be nothing hidden or secret that shall not be brought to light.

Tens of thousands of young women have gone through long, drab years of loneliness and suffering because on one evening years before they agreed to break a law of God.

Satan promotes that kind of thing as hard as he can, by as many means as he possibly can, as openly as the public will allow, and he is doing so now in the American culture on a scale immeasurably broader than anything it has ever known.

Satan is utterly depraved in all his desires, in all his purposes. He is an infinitely cruel taskmaster and tyrant, merciless to a degree not suspected by men, bent on moral chaos, devastation, destruction, and death in as profuse a measure as men will allow him to produce in their society. He is right now sowing the sure seeds of destruction and death and misery throughout American civilization, and we are fools for letting him do it.

Battle for Allegiance

The earth we live on is the chief locale, the theater in the universe, of a challenge by Satan to the supremacy of God over a portion of His creation. Its inhabitants are the objects of what may accurately be called a contest between Satan and God for their obedience and worship. This conflict is so severe that the Bible calls it "warfare," and men are very much at its center.

Satan hates it that any men—that even one man—should worship God and love Him supremely. One of the desires of Satan is to show, if he can, that every man has his price, that no man loves God so well that he will allow nothing to stop him from worshiping and trusting Him. That is why, at one point in history, God allowed a man named Job to stand a severe test of affliction. God knew that Job would not fail or fall.

Though a primary scene of Satan's activity is the earth and the atmosphere of the earth, Satan also has access to God: "Now there was a day when the sons of God came to present themselves before the Lord, and Satan also came among them. The Lord said to Satan, 'Whence have you come?' Satan answered the Lord, 'From going to and fro on the earth, and from walking up and down in it.'

"And the Lord said to Satan, 'Have you considered my servant Job, that there is none like him on the earth, a blameless and upright man, who fears God and turns away from evil?'"

The reply of Satan affords a glimpse of his character. "Then Satan answered the Lord, 'Does Job fear God for nothing? Have you not put a hedge about him and his house and all that he has, on every side? You have blessed the work of his hands, and his possessions have increased in the land. But put forth your hand now and touch all that he has, and he will curse you to your face.'"

What a combination of cynicism, skepticism, accusation, and hatred breathes in that speech!

We are here shown a restriction that was upon the activity of Satan toward the man Job, a restriction that Satan found extremely frustrating. He could not get at Job because God had "put a hedge about him and his house and all that he has, on every side." It was an invisible barrier, set up by the decree of God, and Satan and his demons could not get past it.

Satan therefore accused Job of worshiping God for gain. He asked God to wipe Job out—"touch all that he has, and he will curse you to your face."

"And the Lord said to Satan, 'Behold, all that he has is in your power; only upon himself do not put forth your hand.' So Satan went forth from the presence of the Lord." Job 1:10–12.

Satan now had what he wanted, access to Job, and he was sure he could prove that Job was not a disinterested worshiper of God.

A series of calamities fell upon Job in a single day. These came by the direct activity of Satan, but it is interesting to see their immediate sources. From one side, a party of the Sabeans invaded his property. They stole his animals and slew the servants. From another side, the Chaldeans formed three companies and swept suddenly down upon Job's property in a devastating raid. Men in action, yes, *but Satan in action behind them!* At almost the same time, a fire broke out in the property and shortly thereafter "a great wind came across the wilderness, and struck the four corners of the house," and it collapsed, killing his sons and his daughters. Natural forces, yes, but Satan in action behind them!

"Then Job arose, and rent his robe, and shaved his head, and fell upon the ground and worshiped. And he said, 'Naked I came from my mother's womb, and naked shall I return; the Lord gave, and the Lord has taken away; blessed be the name of the Lord.' " Job 1:20,21.

His words gave the lie to Satan's accusation! Job stood in the test. God told Satan that Job had "held fast his integrity." But Satan was not satisfied.

"Then Satan answered the Lord, 'Skin for skin! All that a man has he will give for his life. But put forth your hand now, and touch his bone and his flesh, and he will curse you to your face.' And the Lord said to Satan, 'Behold, he is in your power; only spare his life.' "

Once more a restriction that was on Satan in the case of Job was removed, but his life was to be left inviolate. Satan filled Job's body with pain and running sores "from the sole of his foot to the crown of his head," and Job went "and sat among the ashes."

At this point Job's wife looked at him and said, "Do you still hold fast your integrity? Curse God, and die."

It was the counsel of Satan from the lips of his wife! Notice especially that the words Job's wife spoke on earth were the very words that had been spoken in heaven! Satan had said that the result of severe loss and affliction would be that Job would "curse God." God told Satan that Job had "held fast his integrity."

Now here—at a critical juncture in Job's trial, and also at the critical juncture in Satan's dispute with God concerning Job—comes Job's wife, standing over him and speaking to him the very desire of Satan! All Satan wanted was that Job curse God. If Job had sunk under his wife's counsel and done that, Satan would have been proved right: Job worshiped God for what he got out of it.

All of her words—"Do you still hold fast your integrity? Curse God, and die"—were put into her mind and into her mouth by the prompting of Satan. Yet Job did not sin with his lips. The end of it was complete vindication for God, complete vindication for Job, and complete defeat for Satan. Satan understood now that there was a man upon the earth who loved God *solely for Himself.*

The Origin of Satan

Satan's program has always been to draw men off from God, as many as he can. He will use any means to that end, especially lies and deceptions. He will, as far as he possibly can, blur the issue, so that men will not understand what their part is in the conflict between God and Satan.

Every man must choose whether he will do the will of Satan, or whether he will do the will of God, and by that choice his eternal destiny is fixed. If he does the will of Satan, he is the subject of Satan, and he will spend eternity with Satan in a lake of fire that God has prepared as the place of Satan's unending punishment.

"He who does the will of God abides forever," the Bible says in I John 2:17.

With two destinies so utterly opposite, to which men must be appointed, God seeks to make the eternal issue clear to man. Satan seeks to make it as vague and doubtful as he can and to keep the question as far as possible from a man's conscious attention. He will scoff at it, deny it, lie about it if necessary, but mainly he seeks to keep it off in the hazy background.

God calls men to decide, because He wants them to come to Him and to enjoy eternal life. "If it seem evil to you to serve the Lord, choose you this day whom you will serve," Joshua called to the people of Israel, making the matter as immediate and urgent as he could, concluding, "As for me and my house, we will serve the Lord." (Joshua 24:15.) There was a choice to be made, between God and false gods, or between the will of God and the will of Satan. God is "not willing that any should perish, but that all should come to repentance," the Bible says in II Peter 3:9a.

Satan wants men to postpone the question, because if they do not choose to do God's will, they—by that very omission—do *his* will. In short, he has them if they do not act decisively.

Satan is glad to have men worry about *anything* other than their relationship to God or their eternal destiny. If they do get on to the subject, his counsel is to put it off until later. "Don't settle it now," is his continuing counsel, given at *any* hour when the subject comes before them.

"Not now." "Not now." "Not now," he says. But what he really means is "Never."

Satan would like to supplant God as the supreme governor and object of worship in the universe and occupy that position himself. He cannot. It is utterly out of his reach. Satan knows that, but it is still his burning and consuming wish, and he pursues it as far as it is possible to him.

He cannot supplant God, so he will seek to wreck as much of the creation as he can, spiritually and physically. He will cause God to be supplanted in the hearts and lives of as many human beings as possible.

A man is the spiritual subject of the spirit he obeys—either Satan—"the spirit now at work in the children of disobedience"— or God. Millions of men are not subjects of God, they are subjects of Satan. They do not do God's will, they do Satan's will.

Yet Satan, for all his power on the earth, is not a universal figure. He is not a kind of wicked equal to God. In his preface to *The Screwtape Letters,* C. S. Lewis put the matter well:

> The commonest question is whether I really "believe in the Devil." Now, if by "the Devil" you mean a power opposite to God and, like God, self-existent from all eternity, the answer is certainly No. There is no uncreated being except God. God has no opposite. No being could attain a "perfect badness" opposite to the perfect goodness of God. . . . The proper question is whether I believe in devils. I do. . . . Satan, the leader or dictator of devils, is the opposite, not of God, but of Michael.

Satan is, within the limits God has set upon him, the chief conspirator behind all evil. In the Scriptures this deliberate enemy of God and man is called, among many other things, the devil, the adversary, Lucifer, the serpent, the evil one, Satan.

In an allegorical description, Satan is spoken of in the Book of Job in these terms: "Upon earth there is not his like . . . *he is king over all the children of pride."* Job 41:34.

Satan, as he is now called, was not at his origin evil at all. The one who now bears the name Satan and the title of devil was in the beginning good. The living being who became the devil was beautiful in every way, in character and aspect.

The prophets Ezekiel and Isaiah tell of the origin and fall of Satan. They tell of the birth of evil desire in him, some of his activities, and they tell the destiny of Satan.

The prophets did this, not by reflection or insight, but by pure revelation, given to them in oral prophecy, subsequently written down.

There are times, in prayer and in prophecy, when a speaker will start praying or prophesying about some local event but will be led by the Holy Spirit to go from that to some far greater theme, entirely to his own surprise. As he prays or prophesies, he receives information and light for the first time on the subject, fully as much as his hearers do. The speaker knows that he has not spoken his own mind, but the mind of God on the matter.

That appears to be the case in these prophecies of Ezekiel and Isaiah. Neither man began to speak about Satan. Each prophet begins by speaking of an earthly ruler. In Ezekiel, it is the prince of Tyre. In Isaiah, it is the king of Babylon. But in each case the prophet is led by the Spirit of God to go beyond those men to the wicked one who stood behind them, prompting them to do evil. In each case the prophet describes God's adversary and man's enemy, the devil.

"You were the signet of perfection, full of wisdom and perfect in beauty," Ezekiel declares. "You were in Eden, the garden of God. Every precious stone was your covering, carnelian, topaz, and jasper, chrysolite, beryl, and onyx, sapphire, carbuncle, and emerald, and wrought in gold were your settings and your pipes; they were prepared in you in the day that you were created."

This passage reveals that the being now called Satan was *a created being;* that he was full of wisdom; that he was a being of great beauty; that he was perfect. It says that he was in the garden of God, and we find Satan there in the account in Genesis.

Ezekiel continues:

"You were the anointed cherub who covers; I set you so. You were on the holy mountain of God, in the midst of the stones of fire you walked. You were blameless in your ways from the day you were created, *until iniquity was found in you.* In the abundance of your trade you were filled with violence, *and you sinned.* So I cast you as a profane thing from the mountain of God, and the guardian cherub drove you out from the midst of the stones of fire."

This portion again declares that Satan was a created being and that he was perfect: "You were blameless in your ways from the day you were created. . . ." It indicates that this beautiful being occupied, by the express appointment of God, a particular station in heaven, "on the holy mountain of God."

The word "anoint" in Hebrew usage means to pour oil upon a person to consecrate that person to God or set him apart for a specific office. God had anointed this beautiful being for a special office in the highest heaven, near the place where God's throne is.

But Satan sinned. He fell in iniquity. He was driven out of his place of high privilege in heaven because of it.

The next verse tells why:

"Your heart was proud because of your beauty; you corrupted your wisdom for the sake of your splendor." Ezekiel thus declares by prophecy that Satan fell because he became proud of his beauty, and that he turned from serving God and began to serve his own vanity and to seek his own glory. He corrupted his wisdom because of his own splendor. That is, he was wise and beautiful, but he let his magnificence carry him into vanity and self-pride and that turned his wisdom into corruption.

This drove him to extremities of ambition and rebellion against God, as Isaiah shows.

Ezekiel describes the beginning of the judgment of Satan:

"I cast you to the ground; I exposed you before kings, to feast their eyes on you. By the multitude of your iniquities, in the unrighteousness of your trade, you profaned your sanctuaries; so I brought forth fire from the midst of you; it consumed you, and I turned you to ashes upon the earth in the sight of all who saw you. All who know you among the peoples are appalled at you; you have come to a dreadful end and shall be no more forever." Ezekiel 28:12–19.

The judgment of the foregoing passage is yet future; it awaits Satan. That is all that Ezekiel says.

Isaiah tells more of how the one called Satan corrupted his wisdom, set himself up in opposition to God, and began to lead a rebellion against God's government in the universe; a rebellion that is now reaching its apex, a fact that is accurately reflected in increasing distress among the nations. It will become more and more severe in the closing decades of this century as the conflict between Satan and God reaches its decisive and most violent stages.

Isaiah begins with the fact of Satan's fall, tells why that happened, details some of its impact upon world history, and tells of Satan's latter end.

"How are you fallen from heaven, O Lucifer, son of the morning!

"How you are cut down to the ground, you who laid the nations low! *You said in your heart, 'I will ascend to heaven, above the stars of God I WILL SET MY THRONE ON HIGH.* I will sit on the mount of assembly in the far north. I will ascend above the heights of the clouds, I WILL MAKE MYSELF LIKE THE MOST HIGH.'

"But you are brought down to Sheol, to the depths of the Pit. Those who see you will stare at you, and ponder over you, 'Is this *the man who made the earth tremble, who shook kingdoms, who made the world a desert and overthrew its cities,* who did not let his prisoners go home?'

"All the kings of the nations lie in glory, each in his own tomb; but you are cast out, away from your sepulchre, like a loathed untimely birth, clothed with the slain, those pierced by the sword, who go down to the stones of the Pit, like a dead body trodden under foot. You will not be joined with them in burial, because you have destroyed your land, you have slain your people." Isaiah 14:12–20a.

Lucifer was not an ordinary servant of God, one of the ranks, so to speak. He was an extraordinary servant of God, created for and appointed to a place of leadership. It is probable that he was the messenger of God to other created beings, their angelic leader within the universal government of God. Lucifer was a creature so beautiful that he was called "the son of the morning."

On the earth and in the heavens, individuals are appointed to various stations in the government of God. Just as Moses and Aaron in their day were set at the head of Israel, and became God's messengers to His people, so Lucifer occupied a high station in the government of God before he fell.

Lucifer decided, on the basis of his beauty, his exalted station, and his perfection, that he would no longer submit to being subordinate to God but that he would make the attempt to set himself above God, to depose God from His throne at the head of the universe, to overthrow His authority, and to bring God into subordination to him. That was the iniquity that was found in his heart. He wanted to take the place of God! That is still the consuming ambition of Satan.

It was a case of the creature desiring to exalt himself above his Creator. This desperate rebellion cast Satan into conflict with God as Satan set out to enlist the obedience and allegiance of intelligent beings to his purposes, and found some that were responsive.

Satan's grand design is to extend his rebellion against God to as many intelligent beings as he can and to reproduce in them aspects of his own nature of sin, thereby claiming them as *his* subjects and servants.

God's design is to enjoy the worship and voluntary obedience of His created beings, to reproduce in them His own character of righteousness, purity, disinterested benevolence (pure love) and to give them the good wine of joy, and life without surcease. God invites men to come to Him, to believe in Him, to worship Him, to serve Him, to receive Him into their hearts and lives, but He honors the freedom of their wills and He will never, never oblige them to do so. He desires willing sons, not automatons. If they go the way of Satan, they go his way forever.

Self-will and self-exaltation began the ruin of Satan. Five times he declared "I WILL" in express opposition to God. Each of those five times, he asserted that he would do something to promote his own interests in defiance of the interests of God.

"I will ascend to heaven.

"I will set *my throne* on high.

"I will sit on the mount of assembly in the far north.

"I will ascend above the heights of the clouds.
"I will make myself like the most high."
That was Satan's program for himself. It was his incredibly audacious bid to overthrow the supremacy of God and to make himself the center of the universe.

He has not succeeded at that. It was an impossible ambition. But he has succeeded in becoming that evil one "who made the earth tremble, who shook kingdoms, who made the world a desert and overthrew its cities," and he is still working at that. And Satan has succeeded in drawing intelligent beings after him in this work of destruction.

God has permitted that, perhaps to prove eternally that the will of every intelligent being is free and that it was open to them to disobey God or to obey Him, perhaps to prove forever that those who serve Him serve Him because they love Him, not because they lacked another option. That, of course, is conjecture.

What is not conjecture is that Satan is a god, and that most of mankind is under his sway. On these facts, the Bible is utterly clear. By far the greater portion of mankind accepts and believes Satan's lies than accepts and believes God's truth. By far the greater portion of mankind engages in sin, at the prompting of Satan, than seeks and attains the righteousness of God. More men worship at the altars of Satan, in the various heathen religions of the world, than worship God. The Bible says that Satan "the god of this world has blinded the minds of the unbelievers." II Corinthians 4:4a.

Satan is the spiritual leader of all men who do not actively and consciously and truly worship and obey and follow the God of Israel, not in some manner that suits themselves, but in the manner that suits Him—"in spirit and in truth."

"God is a spirit," the Bible says, "and they that worship him must worship him in spirit and in truth." John 4:24.

Those who indulge in and practice sin, of whatever form, are not the sons of God. They are the subjects of Satan.

The idea that "we are all the children of God," that all men are God's children, is not at all a Biblical idea. With utter clarity, the Bible divides mankind into exactly two classes: those who are the children of God, and those who are the children of Satan.

We are not, by birth, the children of God. We inherit the nature of sin from our first father, Adam. The whole race of Adam is under the dominion and influence of Satan because of sin. We are "by nature the children of wrath," the Bible says. Ephesians 2:3b.

Since we are not children of God by birth and by nature, we need to become the children of God. We do not have the power to make ourselves that. We become the children of God only by being "born anew." By that spiritual rebirth, the nature of sin and rebellion within us is conquered and God begins to supply to us the power we need to overcome temptation and live lives that are pure, holy, joyous, and pleasing to Him.

This is what Jesus came to do for us. The Scripture says, "He was in the world, and the world was made by him, yet the world knew him not. He came to his own home [Israel], and his own people [the Jews] received him not. But as many as received him, to them he gave power to *become the sons of God,* who were *born,* not of blood nor of the will of the flesh nor of the will of man, but of God." John 1:10–13.

How does a man become a member of any family? By being born to it. A son does not become a member of the Jacobs family by striving to become a member of it. He becomes a member of it by being born into it.

It is the same with the family of God. You must be born into it. It is not by natural birth. It is "not of blood, nor of the will of the flesh, nor of the will of man." You must be *"born of God."* By that rebirth, you receive the power to become a son of God. There is no other way.

Satan, "the god of this world," is the promulgator of the false religious teaching that "all men are the children of God." That is a lie. It stands in direct contradiction to the declaration of the Scriptures. Those who believe it understand themselves to be what, in fact, they are not.

The character of Satan is sin. Sin in men is the reproduction of Satan's character in them. It constitutes Satan's rightful claim upon their souls. *"He who commits sin is of the devil,* for the devil has sinned from the beginning," the Bible says in I John 3:8.

"The reason the Son of God appeared was to destroy the works of the devil. No one born of God commits sin, for God's nature abides in him. . . . By this it may be seen who are *the children of God,* and who are *the children of the devil."* I John 3:10.

One of the lamest and least supportable lies of Satan is that Jesus was hesitant and uncertain about affirming His Messiahship. That common notion is based on two or three Scriptural quotations but it ignores a dozen others in which Jesus explicitly declared and ardently upheld His origin and office against His doubters' attacks.

On one occasion Jesus reasoned with a group of religious teachers: " 'Truly, truly, I say to you, every one who commits sin is a slave to sin. . . . So if the Son makes you free, you will be free indeed. I know that you are descendants of Abraham; yet you seek to kill me, because my word finds no place in you. I speak of what I have seen with my Father, and you do what you have heard from your father.'

"They answered him, 'Abraham is our father.' Jesus said to them, 'If you were Abraham's children, you would do what Abraham did, but now you seek to kill me, a man who has told you the truth which I heard from God; this is not what Abraham did. You do what your father did.'

"They said to him, 'We were not born of fornication. We have one Father, even God.' Jesus said to them, 'If God were your Father, you would love me, for I proceeded and came forth from God. I came not of my own accord, but he sent me. Why do you not understand what I say? It is because you cannot bear to hear my word.

" *'You are of your father the devil, and your will is to do your father's desires.* He was a murderer from the beginning, and has nothing to do with the truth, because there is no truth in him. When he lies, he speaks according to his own nature, for he is a liar and the father of lies.

" '. . . He who is of God hears the words of God. The reason why you do not hear them is that *you are not of God.'* " John 8:34–47.

The Bible declares that Satan is the spiritual head of all men, except those who have turned from sin and been forgiven and accepted by God. That forgiveness and that acceptance is extended to men freely on the basis of the blood of the atonement, and on that basis only. In the Old Testament that atoning blood was shed on the altar for sin and for reconciliation. In the New Testament that blood was shed on the cross when Jesus died for the sins of mankind.

That is why it is written that "He whom the Son sets free is free indeed." That is why Jesus is able to give every man who turns to God through Him "power to become the sons of God," through spiritual rebirth, and membership in the family of God.

In summary, Satan was, at his creation, an angel. He was created as a prince, a leader, of the angels of God, was given a place of high responsibility and privilege, and was endowed with capacities that fully suited him for his work.

When he fell in sin, and iniquity was found in him, he lost his position in heaven, but he did not lose his immense capacity, his intelligence, his quality of leadership, nor even apparently his appearance of beauty. What he did was take them out of the service of God and devote them to the leadership of a rebellion against God.

In presenting himself, when he does, Satan does not present himself as he is, but he presents himself in disguise—that is, he presents himself as what he is not. The Bible says that "Satan disguises himself as an angel of light." (II Corinthians 11:4b.) He never shows himself in his true character, and he hates to be shown to men in that character.

It is a triumph of Satan's policy that so little is known of him in a world in which he promotes and sponsors so much evil and destruction and death. The Bible shows the scope of his influence and power. It says quite flatly that *"the whole world is in the power of the evil one."* (I John 5:19b.) If that has not been apparent, it is becoming more so now, and will become much more so in the years ahead.

In the activities of his rebellion against God and his bid for the destruction of man, Satan is not alone.

Part III

The Thieves
of Forever

The Angels of the Dragon

Just as God has angels who do His will, Satan has angels who do his will. The Bible calls them evil spirits. It also calls them demons and devils.

There is no more terrible reality confronting human existence than that of demons. Demons are the unseen enemies of God and of man; they are ceaselessly at work against the will of God and against all of the best interests of man. The effects of their activity are all around us today, and the Scriptures inform us that these effects are going to be multiplied many times, and at a very rapid pace, at the juncture in history when Israel again seeks to make herself secure in the ancient land. Yet there is no major area of Biblical revelation that is more appallingly neglected than this.

The term demons is very foreign to the American consciousness; remote from the common American concepts of the nature of life and being. We prefer to think that there are no such things as demons. Yet no living person escapes their attention.

Ignorance of demons, just about total in the West, is becoming less and less convenient in our society, because there has been a marked stepup in demonic supernatural activity in this nation in the last several years. We see its effects on almost every hand, but we are blind to its source.

The demons depend for success in their program of disrupting and destroying human life on ignorance of who they are, what they do, and how they do it. The Bible, the accurate guide to the who and what of the supernatural, throws a searchlight of revelation into the darkness in which demons thrive and shows them up.

The Bible tells of the origin of demons, reveals their activities and shows their destiny.

By the knowledge gained through the Word of God demons may be exposed, identified, and dispossessed by men. They may also be intelligently and effectively resisted.

As the head of an organized rebellion against the government of God, Satan leads a host of angelic collaborators. It appears that they number in the millions.

The angels are a divided company. The Scriptures speak, in Matthew 25:41, of "the devil and his angels."

The Origin of Demons

The demons were not created as such. They had their origin among the angels of God, as Satan had. Demons are reprobate angels who follow Satan and do his will.

All of the angels were servants of God until Lucifer, the "son of the morning," rebelled and caused a great split among them. Most held to their loyalty to God. Others abandoned that loyalty and went after Lucifer, or Satan.

The Scriptures speak of the angels who sinned against God. The Bible says that "God did not spare the angels when they sinned, but cast them down . . . and committed them to pits of nether gloom to be kept until the judgment." II Peter 2:4.

Again, the Book of Jude tells of "the angels who did not keep their first estate but left their own habitation." (Jude, verse 6.) The demons are angels who left their first estate, as Satan left his.

The demons are all individual personalities and they have names. Like all spiritual beings, demons are normally invisible to man. They possess the same faculties as angels, but they have put them out to wicked ends. Every evil spirit has a will, intelligence, a personality, and a distinctive character of its own.

When these angels turned away from God and followed Satan, God, by necessity, turned against them. He did so because their misuse of their native capacities began to undermine the safety and tranquility of the universe. If sin were not arrested and judged, it would not cease until it had spread desolation and death throughout the creation.

"Evil spirits" is an accurate descriptive term for demons because they are spirits—invisible living beings—wholly devoted to doing evil.

I have quoted the Scripture that declares that "God is a *spirit.*" Angels are described as "ministering *spirits.*" As fallen angels, demons are described as "evil *spirits.*"

We are told that Satan, "the prince of the power of the air," is "the spirit who is at work in the children of disobedience." Notice that term, "at work." It speaks of direct, personal activity by Satan upon and within individual human beings.

The men and women who are now engaged in conveying so many evils throughout this society are "children of disobedience" in whom Satan and his demons are "at work." Such individuals, whether they know it or not, allow demons to use them to carry forward some of Satan's purposes in the earth.

The work of evil spirits is to do whatever they can to ruin men morally, spiritually, physically, and mentally.

They seek especially, but not exclusively, to ruin human beings morally in the sexual area of life and to ruin them spiritually in the religious area of life. Both of these are critical areas in which, if a person is affected by evil spirits, the results are particularly destructive.

In either of these areas human beings, if they turn aside from the will of God and are overcome by demons, can be ruined not only in this life but for eternity.

The word angel literally means "messenger." The angels are messengers of God. The demons are messengers of Satan who engage in tempting men to do what is evil and in encouraging them to believe what is not true.

The Scriptures reveal that demons have "doctrines," or a system of spiritual teachings that they present to men, contrary to the truth. Demons have false doctrines of salvation, of eternal destiny, of love, of reincarnation, of self-sacrifice, of asceticism, of the way of access to God, and many others besides. Each of these doctrines is a lie, presented as truth. That is why the Scriptures warn us not to be "ignorant of the devil's devices" and not to "give heed to deceiving spirits and doctrines of demons." I Timothy 4:1.

The demons—as deliberate, conscious agents of Satan—are occupied in constant, active rebellion against God. They also engage in conflict against men who are truly God's servants. They come unseen to do whatever they can to hinder such men, to snare them, to withstand or thwart them in carrying out God's will. They are frantic in their detestation of God, and they will stoop to any trick or deceit or treachery or lie to prevent His will from being done on the earth as it is done in heaven.

Their work is not directed solely to men and women who belong to God. They endeavor to get all men to violate the will of God. Demons are particularly bent on the victimization of men. They aim at damaging and destroying human beings—individually, in groups, or, when possible, *en masse*. They will use whatever means are convenient to that end.

Taken together, demons constitute the invisible forces of evil assailing mankind today—assailing individual men, societies, and nations. Their activities are increasing and will continue to increase as the great prophetic events of the end-time occur. Ignorance of who they are and what they do will become more than ever deadly.

Since the mid-1960's, the American society has come under massive invasion and attack by evil spirits. The attack is especially concentrated on youth, and though people see the results of it, they are bewildered by the destructive forces now active among us. Their bewilderment proceeds out of their ignorance.

Spiritual powers and spiritual forces, of good and evil, are at warfare today, and that fact is reflected in the many surprising, untoward, and frequently violent eruptions among men and nations.

The conflict between the will of God and the will of Satan is conducted on several levels. It is conducted on the earth, it is conducted in the atmosphere of the earth, and it is conducted in the lower heavens.

The angels who serve God and the demons who follow Satan engage in conflict. The Book of Revelation gives us a glimpse of this.

"Now war arose in heaven, Michael and his angels fighting against the

dragon, and the dragon and his angels fought." (Revelation 12:7.) The dragon is a figurative term for "the devil and Satan," as the next verse states.

Here are seen two companies of angels under different leaders —Michael and his angels, and Satan and his angels. Michael, an archangel, is a leader of the angels of God, while Satan leads the host of angels called demons, devils, or evil spirits.

This conflict bears upon man, for both angels and demons have to do with men.

The earth, and particularly the atmosphere of the earth, is under occupation by Satan and his angelic legions. That is why Satan is called "the god of this world" and "the prince of the power of the air." With him, among the demons, are other evil princes subordinate to him. They stand together in unrelenting defiance of God's will.

There is a graphic instance of this in the Book of Daniel, the Jewish prophet in the court of Babylon. To Daniel was entrusted a series of prophecies concerning the whole course of Gentile world kingdoms and concerning the destiny of the Jewish people "in the latter days." These prophecies are of momentous character and they are immensely relevant to world events today and to events just ahead. Because they provide a key to these events, Satan did all that he could to oppose Daniel's receiving God's Word concerning them.

After Babylon fell, Daniel continued as a high civil official and a prophet in the court of Persia. Chapter 10 of the Book of Daniel starts: "In the third year of Cyrus king of Persia a word was revealed to Daniel, who was named Belteshazzar. And the word was true and it was a great conflict. And he understood the word and had understanding of the vision."

Because of the gravity of what he was shown, Daniel devoted three full weeks to prayer and partial fasting. In response, a Visitor came to Daniel from heaven.

When this "man clothed in linen" appeared to him, Daniel writes, "I stood up trembling. Then he said to me, 'Fear not, Daniel, for *from the first day* that you set your mind to understand and humbled yourself before your God, your words have been heard, and I have come because of your words. *The prince of the kingdom of Persia withstood me twenty-one days;* but Michael, one of the chief princes, came to help me, so I left him there with the prince of the kingdom of Persia and came to make you understand what is to befall your people in the latter days.' "

The amazing fact is that the Visitor from heaven had trouble getting through!

Daniel's prayer was heard the *first day* and the Visitor was sent on the first day, but when He reached the atmosphere of the earth "the prince of the kingdom of Persia" arose and withstood him for twenty-one days. Daniel engaged in prayer and fasting that entire time.

In this passage God, angels, demons, and men are seen in related action in the conflict.

"The prince of the kingdom of Persia" who withstood the Visitor is the demonic leader of the forces of spiritual darkness in Persia. He is the chief demon appointed by Satan to rule over Persia in the interests of Satan and against the interests of God.

Notice that Michael, a chief prince of the angels of God, came to the side of the man from heaven. This visit to the earth created an emergency for "the rulers of the darkness of this world" and aroused them to a mighty effort to prevent the crucial visitation. Michael came and stood against the prince of the kingdom of Persia—a prince angel contending against a prince demon—and occupied him so that the Visitor was free to continue on His way to Daniel. Here, in the Old Testament, we see the same conflict between the angels under Satan and the angels of God under Michael shown in the New Testament Book of the Revelation.

The man Daniel had a part in this conflict in his day. It was his wholehearted prayer that caused the Visitor to come—"I have come because of your word," He told Daniel—to impart vital information about the future of the Jews.

From this episode it can be seen that there is an interrelatedness between the work of God, angels, men, and demons. It was Daniel's prayer from the earth that stirred heaven to respond, and it was the appearing of the heavenly Visitor that stirred the demons to oppose. This brought Michael to the scene to contend against the prince demon. There was something going on in the earth, something going on in heaven, and something going on in the atmosphere of the earth, and each event bore a relation to the other events and to the conflict.

This episode from Daniel exposes the reality of the intense opposition of evil spirits to the purposes of God. Do not underestimate that conflict, for it is going on today with greater ferocity and it is beginning to affect you, directly or indirectly. It is beginning to affect our nation in pronounced and disquieting ways.

Demons in Hiding

The object of demons is to get men to do Satan's will. Demons work on men—to affect their thinking and behavior—from the outside and from the inside.

A primary function of demons is to tempt men to do evil. Demonic spirits inhabiting the air come to a man and stand, as it were, at the gates of his consciousness. It is in their power to introduce suggestions directly into the minds of men, communicating them from their own evil imaginations to the human mind. By this means they tempt a man or they plant their own thoughts or lies in his mind. Every human being experiences that.

The demons hope, of course, for a successful transference of an evil thought from the spiritual realm into the human realm. That is how "doctrines of demons" get into circulation among mankind. A man is not obliged to accept the thought; he may sweep it aside and give it no leave to occupy his mind.

The mind is a chief target of Satan, and such attacks are designed by Satan to get a man to do that which he knows he ought not to do, or at least to think what is not edifying for him to think.

Temptation is Satan's opening wedge into a man's being. He does not want to stop there. If a man will obey demonic promptings to do evil, Satan will do worse with him by far than merely to tempt him.

In the work of soliciting men to do their master's will, demons are not content to work outside of a man. They prefer to enter into a man and to work from inside his body.

An immensely important fact, of which you may be unaware, is that evil spirits can enter into and occupy the human body and use it as the vehicle for carrying out their own depraved intentions under certain circumstances. They cannot, I hasten to add, do this at any time. They must be given a basis for occupation by voluntary acts of human compliance with the will of Satan.

I would ask you to stop and to read that entire statement again.

It is one of the most important, yet least known, facts with which man has to do. You may have known people in that condition.

When they work from outside, demons can appeal to and importune a man to do some sin, but they cannot make him do so. When they get inside, they obtain a measure of direct control over the man and they can use him for their own purposes. When they inhabit a human being, evil spirits become inseparably identified with the individual in whom they dwell. They are able at times to speak directly and audibly through the lips of that individual.

My awareness of this fact came first in a most unexpected way, during an interview with a professor of psychiatry and religion at the Union Theological Seminary in New York, in April 1964. I had sought the interview for a story I was doing for a magazine, but I had not anticipated its content.

After some discussion of healing in the first three hundred years of the Christian church, the professor told me of a young married woman in a southern state who had become deeply disturbed in her personality, for reasons that were not apparent. She had been to psychologists but had obtained no help. Later she sought the help of a minister, who took a radically different approach to her case and through whose help she obtained relief from her distress, relief that had proved to be lasting.

"I have a tape recording," the professor said, "of the session in which the young woman got relief from her trouble. It is quite remarkable. Would you like to hear it?"

In the next forty-five minutes what was to me an entirely new dimension of understanding of an important aspect of the spiritual and supernatural realm began to unfold. As the tape went round, I heard two voices. The voice of the minister and the woman's voice. But it shortly became plain that the minister was not talking to the woman. He was talking to *another intelligent personality who was in the woman!* He was addressing himself, intentionally and directly, to an evil spirit.

What I remember most vividly is that, about half way through the session, the woman's voice changed. It ceased to be a natural young woman's voice and became an odd, rather high-pitched, whiny, nasal sound.

"You're hurting my head, pastor," her voice said with a kind of nasty, pleading petulance. Three or four times the phrase was repeated.

"I am not touching this young woman's head. I am not hurting her head. I am speaking to you, you foul and lying spirit," the minister said. Two or three times he reproved the evil spirit for lying through the woman's lips.

As I realized later, the demon to whom the minister was speaking was being brought out of hiding within her by stages—was, in short, beginning to be forced against its will to reveal itself as actually present in the woman.

Up to that point, the evil spirit had sought to hide its identity entirely behind that of the woman and to remain undetected. Now, however, the evil spirit knew that it had been discovered and identified by the minister, and it began to speak directly, with no further attempt to hide.

For a while this intruding personality was rather belligerent toward the minister, but as he took authority over it, an evident tremor came into the voice that spoke to the minister and it increased until its tone was that of a nearly hysterical panic.

"You are going to go out of this young woman," the minister said in a strong, even voice.

"If I go out, I will come back in," the high-pitched voice replied.

"No. You will not come back in," the minister said. "You are going to go out today and you will never come back in."

All challenges, all argument disappeared from the responding voice. The voice became considerably weaker, and it was filled with fear and pleading. The evil spirit to whom the minister spoke no longer made an issue of staying or leaving. Instead, it began to bargain for the terms of its departure! The voice begged the minister, in a pitiful manner, not to command it to go to Jerusalem.

The minister took final authority. "You foul and lying spirit," he said, "I command you, in the name of Jesus Christ, to come out of this woman now and not to return."

The young woman, from that moment on, had suffered no more from her perplexing distress, the professor said. He said that what I heard had taken place some months earlier.

What had happened in the final moment was that a demonic spirit, an intelligent agent of evil, who had entered the young woman and had occupied part of her being for many months, causing her much unaccountable distress, had been *discovered, identified,* and *cast out.*

This was a modern-day instance of the casting out of demons. It was the first of which I had ever known, but in the next several years I was to learn of case after case from many different sources, all isolated but often exhibiting the most striking similarities in method, in response and result. It became impossible for me to avoid the conclusion that evil spirits exist and that they sometimes enter into human beings, entirely unsuspected and unseen, and remain until something explicit and forceful and direct is done to get them out.

That conclusion was not easier for me to reach, I think, than for you, but I would ask you not to close your mind or to decide about it until you have read what comes in the pages just ahead.

In the past five years I have heard, from the lips of reputable and intelligent ministers and missionaries, all of the mainline denominations, so many accounts of their own direct experiences in dealing with evil spirits that had taken up residence within troubled individuals—and these accounts, though they were based on experiences as far removed as China from Switzerland, are so remarkably similar in their content—that I cannot doubt their validity.

Demons Exposed

Evil spirits—intelligent, living beings set against the will of God—are not all alike in the particular expressions of their depravity. They are very different. There are spirits who specialize in lying, in filthy thinking, in hatred, in various delusions, in depression, in fear. There are evil spirits of self-destruction, of exhibitionism, of rebellion, of fanaticism, and they produce in their victims' behavior these bizarre effects. There are many more.

While on a reporting trip through the Midwest I met an Episcopal rector in Illinois, who told me of a singular experience in his ministry.

The Reverend Richard E. Winkler said that the six-year-old son of a woman who lived near the church had become dangerously destructive, but physicians could find no cause nor offer any solution. The boy would sometimes strike matches and set fires and he would jump out of the second-story window of his home, bruising himself in the drop.

The boy's mother brought him to the church. "The mother was beside herself," the rector said. "She had to watch the child every moment. Evidently he was possessed by demons of destruction."

As soon as he took the child and put him on his lap the boy kicked and thrashed and struggled like a wild animal. The rector had to hold him down. While several others prayed, the minister began to deal directly with an evil spirit of destruction. He took authority over the evil spirit and, in the name of Jesus Christ, ordered it to leave the child.

"It was wonderful to see," the minister's wife said. "The child changed just like night and day, from a kicking, squalling kid to a peaceful, quiet little boy before our eyes." Now calm and still, the boy needed no longer to be held. The rector talked with the mother a while. Then they left.

Mr. Winkler said that the child had never since set fires or done anything else abnormally destructive. He appeared to be a normal, happy child thereafter.

The wild struggle the boy put up just a moment or two before he was set free is typical of cases of demonic possession. There frequently is such a struggle, and quite often the victims try to hurt themselves or somebody nearby.

"The demons recognize what's going to happen," Mr. Winkler said. "They make a final, desperate bid to hold on to their human victim or, failing that, to harm him."

The rector also told of a church member who had "a daughter who was normal until her college years but something happened in college and she became possessed with several kinds of demons. The mother brought the girl to the altar and when we gathered around to pray for her, the demons threw her to the floor three or four times."

The dean of a seminary near Minneapolis told me of a woman student who had become extremely difficult and unpleasant, and who did not respond to counsel, to discipline, or to warnings of expulsion. The dean and two other faculty members concluded that she was being disturbed by evil spirits and decided to approach her case on that ground.

When she appeared for the interview in which they were to do so, she became violent, tried to get out of the room and showed such extraordinary strength that it took six people to hold her still. The dean said that her strength was way beyond that of any young woman. I have been told repeatedly that inordinate strength is quite often exercised by persons who are troubled by evil spirits;

and that it is usually exhibited just at the point at which ministers are ready to cast the evil spirits out. Though the demons are not physical beings, they are able to apply great force in the physical realm when they occupy a human body, and they frequently do so at precisely the point at which they begin to feel threatened by exposure, identification, and dispossession.

The ministry of Jesus was marked by repeated encounters with individuals suffering from demon possession and repeated acts of authority over the evil spirits, by which Jesus required them to go out of their victims.

The following account from the Book of Mark will give anyone who will read it carefully an insight into this area of reality: "They came to the other side of the sea, to the country of the Gerasenes. And when Jesus had come out of the boat, there met him out of the tombs a man with an unclean spirit, who lived among the tombs; and no one could bind him any more, even with a chain; for he had often been bound with fetters and chains, but the chains he wrenched apart, and the fetters he broke in pieces; and no one had the strength to subdue him.

"Night and day among the tombs and on the mountains he was always crying out, and bruising himself with stones. And when he saw Jesus from afar, he ran and worshipped him. And crying out with a loud voice, he said, 'What have you to do with me, Jesus, Son of the Most High God? I adjure you by God, do not torment me.' For Jesus had said to him, 'Come out of the man, you unclean spirit!'

"And Jesus asked him, 'What is your name?'

"He replied, 'My name is Legion, for *WE are many.'* And he begged him eagerly *not to send THEM out of the country.*

"Now a great herd of swine was feeding there on the hillside, and they begged him, 'Send *us* to the swine, *let us enter them.'*

"So he gave them leave. And the unclean spirits came out, and entered the swine; and the herd, numbering about 2,000, rushed down the steep bank, and were drowned in the sea." Mark 5:1–13.

Notice that Jesus did not deal with the evil spirits as *conditions* but as with *intelligent beings.*

There are some who are fond of saying that, in this, Jesus was merely ceding something to the superstitions of His time, but it is not the case. Jesus made a distinction between a condition—as in certain illnesses—and demonic possession, and He dealt with conditions as conditions, and He dealt with evil spirits as evil spirits, and He knew the difference. Some illnesses He healed as illnesses; others He recognized as physical symptoms of demon possession and He cast the evil spirits out. To confound the two is to leave some people, strangely afflicted or tormented or unbalanced, without hope of relief. To confound the two is also to confuse the matter in a way that is convenient to the hope of demons to remain undetected.

The man who lived in the cemetery was not his own master; he was under the control of demonic spirits, and he showed many signs of that control. The evil spirits had driven him away from human society and had made him a wild recluse.

While the demons possessed him he had more than merely human strength ("the chains he wrenched apart . . . no one had the strength to subdue him"). He was "always crying out and bruising himself with stones." The evil spirits used his voice to cry out and they made him inflict damage on his body.

As soon as Jesus and the man in the tombs saw each other, there was a two-way recognition. The evil spirits in the man recognized Jesus, and Jesus recognized the evil spirits in the man.

As soon as He met him, Jesus fixed His gaze on the man in the tombs and said, "Come out of the man, you unclean spirit."

It is critically important to notice that Jesus *did not address the man.* He went *beyond the man* and directly addressed the unclean spirit.

The man's voice cried out, "What have you to do with me, Jesus, Son of the Most High God?"—the demons knew exactly Who stood before them—"I adjure thee by God that you torment me not."

It was not the man speaking. It was the demons speaking, trying to hide themselves behind the identity of the man, to make it appear that the man was speaking. Evil spirits seek the closest possible identification with the person they inhabit, so that their words and acts will be mistakenly ascribed to the person.

There is more here than the speech of a man. There was instant recognition, not only of Jesus as a man, but of Jesus as the "Son of the Most High God." Men may not know that Jesus is the Son of God—some do, most do not—but every demon knows Who Jesus is. They have no uncertainty whatever about it. The Bible says that "the devils believe, and tremble." James 2:19b.

In this case, the evil spirits were in great fear of Jesus, because He had absolute power over them, so they begged Him not to torment them.

Up to this point they used the first person singular because they still hoped to conceal their true identity. They hoped to make it seem that the *man* was asking Jesus not to torment him.

Plainly, Jesus had not come to torment the man. It was the demons who were doing that.

Jesus did not speak to the man, but He went beyond the man and addressed the demons: "What is your name?"

"My name is Legion," the man's voice answered, "for *we* are many."

The demons, knowing that they had been discovered, changed abruptly from the first person singular to the plural. They were now out in the open, forced to reveal themselves as foreign beings inhabiting the body of the man.

This abrupt switch of terms is quite typical in cases where evil spirits are being dealt with directly. For a while they will speak only of "I" and "me," then suddenly they will refer to the individual they are occupying as "him" or "her," thus making the distinction between themselves and their victim. Or they will speak of "we" and "us." This occurs when they are flushed out of hiding and made to reveal themselves as separate identities.

Verse 12 of this account specifically reveals that it was not the possessed man who was speaking to Jesus, but the unclean spirits in the man. It says: "*They* begged him, 'Send us to the swine, let us enter them.'"

Jesus made them leave the man, but He allowed them to go into the swine. Immediately two things happened.

The man out of whom the demons had gone sat there quietly, "clothed and *in his right mind.*"

The pigs on the hillside, into which the demons went, immediately "rushed down the steep bank into the sea, and were drowned in the sea." The herd ran wild, and the 2,000 swine were destroyed.

When the demons, though unseen to the natural eye, entered the herd of pigs, the man was perfectly sane and rational and calm, but the pigs immediately became self-destructive, as the man had been.

Real demons had gone out of a real man and entered real pigs. When they left the man and went into the pigs, their activity was transferred from the man to the pigs. There can be no more graphic depiction than this of the reality of demons and of the effects of demon possession.

On another occasion a woman, whose young daughter was possessed by an unclean spirit, came to Jesus and fell at His feet. "The woman was a Greek," the Biblical account says, "and she besought him that he would cast forth the devil out of her daughter."

Since she was not a Jew, "Jesus said to her, 'Let the children first be filled: for it is not meet to take the children's bread, and to cast it to the dogs.' " Jesus' ministry at that time was to the house of Israel, not to Gentiles. His words on this were so plain that they might have daunted a less daring faith than hers.

"And she answered and said to him, 'Yes, Lord, yet the dogs under the table eat of the children's crumbs.'

"And he said to her, 'For this saying go your way; the devil is gone out of your daughter.' " Mark 7:25–29.

The following account by the Reverend Derek Prince is taken from an article in *Christian Life* magazine. The minister starts by admitting that some of the troubled people who had come to him for help had not received the relief they sought.

"My prayers, though long and fervent, were ineffective," Reverend Prince says. "My friend . . . never found relief from his inner torment. Through the years there were many other such cases in my ministry of men and women whose hurts were healed, but only slightly. After fifteen years in the ministry . . . the Lord . . . has given me a new type of service which has involved a progressive education in the realities of the spiritual world.

"Early in this experience, a Baptist minister, a friend of mine, phoned to ask if he could bring over a woman who was a member of another Baptist church but who had been under his pastoral care. He explained that she needed deliverance from evil spirits.

"The woman said that she was married and that she had several children. She looked about forty and to all outward appearances was a normal American housewife. The minister told us that she had already been delivered from one demon but that she needed further deliverance from other evil spirits. He placed her in a chair, stood in front of her, and began to demand that the evil spirits manifest themselves.

"With a mixture of interest and skepticism I watched to see what would happen. After a while the woman's face underwent a curious change. Her features became contorted, and a fierce glare shone in her eyes. I could not doubt that some other personality was manifesting itself. At length I asked for the privilege of speaking. . . .

" 'You evil spirit, I'm speaking to you, and not to this woman,' I said. 'In the name of Jesus Christ, I command you to answer me. What is your name?'

"Immediately, with a sound like a hiss, there came out of the woman's lips the one word, 'hate.'

" 'You spirit of hate,' I continued, 'in the name of Jesus Christ I command you to come out of this woman.'

" 'No,' the same voice replied. 'I'm not coming out. This is my house. I've lived here for thirty-five years, and I'm not coming out!' After persistent quoting of Scripture and continued demands in the name of Jesus for the demon to leave the woman, the demon conceded, 'If I come out, I'll come back again.'

"I could think of only one thing to say, 'No you won't come back. You'll come out, and you'll stay out.'

"The astonishing dialogue continued. 'Even if I come out, my brothers are here, and they'll kill her.'

"By this time, I was gaining confidence. 'No they won't. You'll come out first, and your brothers will come out after you.'

"Having apparently exhausted its arguments, the evil spirit tried another tactic. As we watched, the woman appeared to attempt to choke herself. It took the combined strength of the two of us to get her hands away from her throat.

"Eventually the spirit of hate came out. The woman's head fell forward, and there was a brief moment of relaxation. Then the next spirit manifested itself. In all, seven other spirits named themselves and, after much struggling, came out.

"We took turns commanding these spirits to come out. The entire process took more than five hours. The seven spirits that followed identified themselves as: fear, envy, jealousy, pride, self-pity, infidelity, and death.

"A week later, the woman brought her youngest child, a girl of six, to be prayed for. She was a shy, unhappy-looking little girl, who seemed incapable of looking people straight in the eye. At school she had been classified as retarded.

"The daughter's deliverance followed much the same pattern as that of her mother, but was not so prolonged. Several of these evil spirits manifested themselves and spoke out of the daughter. As these spirits spoke, I asked the mother, 'Is that your daughter's voice?'

" 'No,' she replied. 'It isn't anything like my daughter's voice.'

"About a year later, I learned that from that time on the girl's grades at school had shown a marked improvement, and she was no longer classified as retarded."

In the battle against evil, man must deal with invisible intelligences who are devoted to evil. These spirits can be resisted, but they must be recognized to be effectively resisted, and to resist them triumphantly you need God's help.

Casting Demons Out

God has provided the means and the power by which demons inhabiting human beings can be expelled. The Bible speaks of certain "spiritual gifts" that God has given to empower men to engage effectively in the conflict against Satan and the demons.

In his first letter to the Corinthians, the apostle Paul wrote, "Now concerning spiritual gifts, brethren, I do not want you to be uninformed." (I Corinthians 12:1.) In this same chapter, Paul lists nine specific spiritual gifts imparted by the Holy Spirit.

Among the nine is one that has specifically to do with demons. It is the gift of the "discerning of spirits." This gift has been excellently defined as "the God-given ability to detect the presence and ascertain the identity of evil spirits."

The individual to whom this gift is given is enabled first to recognize that evil spirits are present in an individual and second to identify them specifically and to deal with them directly.

The gift has nothing whatever to do with natural insight; it is not in any sense an activity or product of the human mind. It is entirely spiritual in its operation and it is a gift of revelation. The gift comes directly from God by the Holy Spirit to an individual and, by it, God reveals to the individual the presence and the identity of evil spirits dwelling in human victims. The purpose of the gift is to make it possible for persons who are afflicted or tormented by demons to be set free by the casting out of demons.

The common term for this is exorcism. The term is useful enough, but it has become so identified with various practices that have nothing to do with the operation of this wonderful spiritual gift that to use it might be to confound those practices with this gift. There is, for instance, a form of exorcism by religious ritual that has nothing to do with this gift.

Everything that God has ordained in the spiritual realm has its counterfeit in the realm of the demons, and there is a counterfeit discerning of spirits practiced by witch doctors and spiritualists and persons who specialize in magic. Though some of the effects of such a practice may be rather striking or spectacular, it is of no effect whatever in setting a person free of evil spirits. It is Satan's falsification of the genuine gift of the discerning of spirits, designed to deceive the victim.

In giving His commission to the disciples, Jesus said, "And these signs shall follow them that believe: *In my name* they shall cast out devils. . . ." (Mark 16:17.) The casting out of demons was to be a regular part of the ministry of the church to men. In the three years of His ministry in Israel, Jesus engaged in preaching and teaching, healing the sick, and He engaged continually in casting demons out of people. Matthew 8:16 records that "When the evening was come, they brought to him many who were possessed with devils, and he *cast out the spirits with his word.*" Jesus recognized them, identified them, and ordered them to depart from their victims.

It is equally true that the demons recognized Him. They would often make that recognition emphatically known by speaking through the individuals in whom they dwelled.

At one point, "a great multitude from Galilee followed" Jesus, and their number was increased by people from Jerusalem and Idumea and other places. Jesus "told his disciples to have a boat ready for him because of the crowd, lest they should throng him; for he had healed many, so that all who had diseases pressed upon him to touch him. And whenever the unclean spirits beheld him, they fell down before him and cried out, 'You are the Son of God.' And he strictly ordered them not to make him known." Mark 3:7–12.

Jesus knew who they were, and they knew Who Jesus was. The demons would cause the people in whom they dwelled to fall down and the demons would then cry out through them. On the Sabbath Jesus taught in the synagogues. Once "in the synagogue there was a man who had the spirit of an unclean devil, who cried out with a loud voice, 'What have you to do with us, Jesus of Nazareth? Have you come to destroy us? I know who you are, the Holy One of God.' "

It was not the man speaking, it was the evil spirits speaking through the man. Knowing that Jesus had come to destroy the works of the devil, they were in anguish at His presence and in fear that He would destroy them. "But Jesus rebuked him, saying, 'Be silent, and come out of him!' And when the demon had thrown him down in the midst, *he came out of him,* having done him no harm.

And they were all amazed and said to one another, 'What a word is this! For with authority and power he commands the unclean spirits, and they come out.' " Luke 4:33–36.

This ministry of casting demons out was to continue in the church through the disciples, and indeed it did. It is a part of the basic and continuing mission of the church for the alleviation of suffering. We read this account in Acts: "Then Philip went down to the city of Samaria, and preached Christ to them. And the people with one accord gave heed to those things which Philip spoke, hearing and seeing the miracles that he did. For unclean spirits, crying with loud voice, came out of many who were possessed with them." Acts 8:5–7a.

The name and the authority of Jesus is the source of the only power that can conquer demons and cast them out. Evil spirits cannot be dealt with effectively in any other way. Moreover, the name of Jesus and His authority over evil spirits can only be applied and enforced by an individual who truly believes in Him. Invoking the name of Jesus against demons is not a form of magic. That act will only succeed if lawfully applied.

There is an interesting account in the Book of Acts regarding this. It says that "God did extraordinary miracles by the hands of Paul," by which some who were sick were healed and others who had evil spirits were set free. "Then some of the itinerant Jewish exorcists undertook to pronounce the name of the Lord Jesus over those who had evil spirits, saying, 'I adjure you by the Jesus whom Paul preaches.'

"Seven sons of a Jewish high priest named Sceva were doing this. But *the evil spirit answered them,* 'Jesus I know and Paul I know, but who are you?" And the man in whom the evil spirit was leaped on them, mastered all of them, and overpowered them, so that they fled out of the house naked and wounded." Acts 19:11–16.

One man, possessed with a demon, overcame seven young men. You will recall from the account in the previous chapter that while the legion of demons possessed the man in the tombs, he had more than merely human strength and "no one had the strength to subdue him."

The demons in possession of the faculties of a man know when they have been discovered. They do not wish to surrender what they regard as their property, and they will put up a fierce battle not to lose hold of the body of their victim and be cast out.

The mistake of the seven young men was that they attempted to engage in a supernatural activity by imitation. They were practical men. They had observed that the demons could not hold onto their victims when Paul confronted them in the name and in the power of Jesus. Since they were exorcists, and since they wanted results, they decided to try using the name of Jesus, but they used that name in a kind of imitative rote, in an experimental way: "I adjure you by the Jesus whom Paul preaches."

It was a second-hand sort of thing. They did not know Jesus personally, but by reputation. Their use of His name was therefore of no effect.

There is no magic in invoking the name of Jesus in exorcism, but there is power to cast demons out in His name when it is spoken by one who knows Jesus and who has the gift of discerning of spirits and the ministry of casting them out.

There has recently come to my attention a useful book titled *Demon Experiences in Many Lands: A Compilation,* published in paperback by the Moody Press of Chicago, a thoroughly responsible church-related publishing house. It consists of thirty-one separate accounts by missionaries from all over the world of personal experiences in dealing with cases of demon possession and in casting demons out. The accounts come from India, Japan, Korea, Mexico, Ecuador, Colombia, Brazil, Guatemala, Basutoland, Haiti, and many other nations. Each account is signed by the missionary relating it. It is the most extensive and widespread collection of experiences with demons that I have seen in a single volume and it sheds basic light in this much-neglected, exceedingly important area.

In the casting out of demons, the attitude of the person in whom the demons dwell is of utmost importance.

If the demon-possessed person clearly understands the evil of the act the demons have made him do and if he genuinely desires to be free both of the demons and of the sin, it is very much in order for the afflicted individual to receive the ministry of the casting out of demons. Otherwise it may not be wise to go ahead with the casting out, even when it is entirely possible to do so.

The Scripture gives the reason for this. Jesus, Whose understanding of the work of demons in human beings was perfect, said, "When the unclean spirit has gone out of a man, he [the spirit] passes through waterless places, seeking rest, but he finds none. Then he says, 'I will return to my house from which I came.' And when he comes he finds it empty, swept and put in order. Then he goes and brings with him seven other spirits more evil than himself, and they enter and dwell there, and *the last state of that man becomes worse than the first.*" Matthew 12:43–45.

The house of the demon is the body of the man. A man had one evil spirit in him and it was cast out. He was free of the demon and his heart was clean, but empty. He failed to allow God to fill him with the Holy Spirit, so the original evil spirit went back into the man, and the man ended up with eight evil spirits, instead of one.

A man becomes demon-possessed chiefly through his own sin. If he does not truly repent of the sin and turn from it, the demon who is cast out will return, bringing other demons with him. In a man with a propensity to anger there is no point in casting out the demon of anger until it is certain that the man desires to be rid of the sin of anger. If the sin, which gave the demon occasion in the first place, persists, the demon of anger will return.

On the other hand, if the man turns decisively from the sin and refuses again to engage in it, the casting out of the demon will set him free permanently.

The casting out of demons is sometimes an almost instantaneous act. At other times it is possible only after a considerable amount of spiritual conflict and prayer.

A man came to Jesus and said, "Teacher, I brought my son to you, for he has a dumb spirit, and wherever it seizes him, it dashes him down; and he foams and grinds his teeth and becomes rigid; and I asked your disciples to cast it out, and they were not able." Jesus said, "Faithless generation, how long am I to bear with you? Bring him to me."

"And they brought the boy to him, and when the spirit saw him, immediately it convulsed the boy, and he fell on the ground and rolled about, foaming at the mouth. And Jesus asked his father, 'How long has he had this?' And he said, 'From childhood. And it has often cast him into the fire and into the water, to destroy him. If you can do anything, have pity on us and help us.' "

Looking at the boy, Jesus said, " 'You dumb and deaf spirit, I command you, come out of him and never enter him again.' And after crying out and convulsing him terribly, it came out, and the boy was like a corpse, so that most of them said, 'He is dead.' But Jesus took him by the hand and lifted him up, and he arose. And when he had entered the house, his disciples asked him privately, 'Why could we not cast it out?' And he said, 'This kind cannot be driven out by anything but prayer and fasting.' " Mark 9:17–29.

The boy was possessed by one evil spirit who made him deaf and dumb and forced him to fall into fire or water "to destroy him." At times the demon convulsed the boy and at times it made him rigid. These are among the things that certain evil spirits are able to do to their victims.

All demons are destructive, but all are not destructive in the same ways. Often they want to harm or afflict or destroy those they possess. Some drive their victims to suicide. Others do not immediately cause their victims to harm themselves. Instead, they use them to torment, afflict, and even to destroy other human beings. Others drive their victims out of their minds. Many persons, though by no means all, who are held in detention as mental defectives or mental cases are demon-possessed.

King Saul Consults a Medium

Demons work to produce definite effects in human thought and behavior. Such effects can be seen in the life of Saul, the first king of Israel.

He was, the Bible affirms, "a choice young man"—humble, gentle, exceedingly good-looking: "There was not a man among the people of Israel more handsome than he; from his shoulders upward he was taller than any of the people."

There was no royal line in Israel. The prophet Samuel anointed him for the office of king and gave him supernatural signs to make plain to Saul that he had been chosen by God, not man. Soon after this anointing, "the Spirit of God came mightily upon him, and he [Saul] prophesied." I Samuel 10:10.

The young king was greatly blessed by God. He was a modest and unassuming individual, but he was weak and only partial in his obedience to God. He began well but, through cumulative acts of disobedience, Saul lost the blessing. The fateful transition is seen in I Samuel 16:14:

"But the Spirit of the Lord departed from Saul, and an evil spirit from the Lord troubled him."

The course, which had tended upward, now ran steeply downward. Saul ended as a man capable of murder. At the very end, he sank to consulting a medium and that brought swift death to him.

God withdrew His Holy Spirit from Saul and allowed an evil spirit to go to him. This change in the spiritual realm, unobservable to the human eye, brought distinct and drastic changes in Saul's behavior. The first effect was that the evil spirit "troubled him," causing Saul to suffer internal agitation and unrest.

"And Saul's servants said to him, 'Behold now, an evil spirit from God troubles you. Let the king now command his servants, who are before you, to seek out a man, who is a cunning player on an harp, and it shall come to pass, when the evil spirit from God is upon you, that he shall play with his hand, and you shall be well.' And Saul said to his servants, 'Provide me now a man who can play well, and bring him to me.' " I Samuel 16:15–17.

The one selected for this service was a young man named David, whom God had chosen to succeed Saul as king. "And David came to Saul and stood before him, and Saul loved him greatly; and David became his armor-bearer." I Samuel 16:21.

Saul's immediate reaction to David was that he loved him greatly. But soon, under the incendiary influences of the demon, he would show an entirely different aspect.

As young David began to become a respected warrior for Israel, Saul felt the stirrings of jealousy within him. "And on the morrow an evil spirit from God rushed upon Saul, and he raved within his house, while David was playing the lyre, as he did day by day. Saul had a javelin in his hand; and Saul cast the javelin, for he thought, 'I will pin David to the wall.' But David evaded him twice." I Samuel 18:10,11.

Anger and jealousy surged up suddenly within Saul under the immediate influence of the evil spirit. The man who a short while before had held David in great affection made two impulsive attempts to murder David. Under the driving influences of the evil spirit Saul became a man capable of blazing up to a murderous fury. He hurled his spear; if he had killed David he would perhaps have said when asked why—as others have said: "I don't know. Something came over me."

"Saul was afraid of David, because the Lord was with him but had departed from Saul." (I Samuel 18:12.) Saul made further attempts to have David killed: "Now Saul thought to make David fall by the hand of the Philistines." (I Samuel 18:25b.) Later, he made another direct attempt at murder:

"Then an evil spirit from the Lord came upon Saul, as he sat in his house with his javelin in his hand; and David was playing the lyre. And Saul sought to pin David to the wall with the javelin, but he eluded Saul, so that he struck the javelin into the wall. And David fled, and escaped. That night Saul sent messengers to David's house to watch him, that he might kill him in the morning." I Samuel 19:9–11.

Anger, jealousy, rage, hatred, fear, the impulse to murder—all these were produced in the life of Saul by the activity of the evil spirit.

These are not the only effects of evil spirits, not by far, but they are prominent among destructive things that demons stir up within men and prompt them to act upon.

The last step for Saul was a deliberate and desperate encounter with occultism. When Saul had been pursuing the will of God he "had put the mediums and wizards out of the land," because God had commanded that these demonic substitutes have no part in the pure worship of the Jews.

"The Philistines assembled and came and encamped at Gilboa. When Saul saw the army of the Philistines, he was afraid, and his heart trembled greatly. And when Saul enquired of the Lord, the Lord did not answer him, either by dreams, or by Urim, or by prophets. Then Saul said to his servants, 'Seek out for me a woman who is a medium, that I may go to her and inquire of her.' And his servants said to him, 'There is a medium at Endor.'

"So Saul disguised himself and put on other garments, and went, he and two men with him, and they came to the woman by night. And he said, *Divine for me by a spirit,* and bring up for me whomever I shall name to you.'"

Saul chose his words well, for he knew what he was talking about. A medium who is not a sheer fake, who does in fact make "contact" with an intelligent, invisible being, is one who works together with, or comes under the control of, an evil spirit. The art of a medium is the art of direct communication with demons, whether the medium is aware of that or not. Consulting a medium is a shortcut to getting the counsel of Satan upon a matter, though that counsel is usually carefully disguised so that it will not appear to be what it is.

"The woman said to him, 'Surely you know what Saul has done, how he has cut off the mediums and wizards from the land. Why then are you laying a snare for my life to bring about my death?'

"But Saul swore to her by the Lord, 'As the Lord lives, no punishment shall come upon you for this thing.'

"Then the woman said, 'Whom shall I bring up for you?'

"He said, 'Bring up Samuel for me.' " (Samuel, the prophet, had died a short time before.)

"When the woman saw Samuel, she cried out with a loud voice, and the woman said to Saul, 'Why have you deceived me? You are Saul!'

"The king said to her, 'Have no fear; what do *you* see?'

"And the woman said to Saul, 'I see a god coming up out of the earth.'

"He said to her, 'What is his appearance?'

"And she said, 'An old man is coming up, and he is wrapped in a robe.' And Saul perceived that it was Samuel, and he bowed his face to the ground, and did obeisance.

"Then Samuel said to Saul, 'Why have you disturbed me by bringing me up?'

"Saul answered, 'I am in great distress. The Philistines are warring against me, and God has turned away from me and answers me no more, either by prophets or by dreams. Therefore I have summoned you to tell me what I should do.'

"And Samuel said, 'Why then do you ask me, since the Lord has turned away from you and become your enemy? The Lord has done to you as he spoke by me, for the Lord has torn the kingdom out of your hand, and given it to your neighbor, David. Because you did not obey the voice of the Lord . . . therefore the Lord has done this thing to you this day. Moreover the Lord will give Israel also with you into the hand of the Philistines; and tomorrow you and your sons shall be with me. The Lord will give the army of Israel also into the hand of the Philistines.'

"Then Saul fell at once full length upon the ground, filled with fear because of the words of Samuel. . . .

"Now the Philistines gathered all their strength at Aphek. . . . And the Philistines overtook Saul and his sons, and they slew Jonathan and Abinadab and Malchishua, the sons of Saul. The battle pressed hard upon Saul, and the archers found him. . . . Thus Saul died, and his three sons, and his armor-bearer, and all his men, on the same day together.

"On the morrow, when the Philistines came to strip the slain, they found Saul and his three sons fallen on Mount Gilboa." I Samuel 28:3–20; 29:1a; 31:2,3,6,8.

It was but hours between Saul's visit to the medium and his death. He had stepped past the point of no return. The anger of the God of Israel cut him down. That anger is no illusion, nor is the death that it brings a matter of chance. God does act in judgment and men do die on that account. It may be seen in Scripture, and it may be seen in life.

The Hebrew Scriptures uniformly associate every form of spiritual and supernatural and psychic activity not having as its source the God of Israel, with death, and that sentence is carried out more swiftly on Jews than on Gentiles, because all of these things are the most explicit violation of the foremost decrees of Judaism—which are to have nothing to do in any form with any gods (which gods are either idols or demons) other than the God of Israel.

Hear the Word of God: "If a person turns to mediums and wizards [warlocks], playing the harlot after them, *I will set my face against that person, and will cut him off from among his people.*" Leviticus 20:6.

When a Jew has recourse to demons and evil spirits in his religious or supernatural experiments, God is aroused to send death upon him.

"Of all the peoples of the earth, I have chosen you [Israel] alone. That is why I must punish you the more for all your sins." Amos 3:2.

"It is a fearful thing to fall into the hands of the living God." Hebrews 10:31.

Are you a Jew? Avoid mediums, witches, séances, astrologers, fortune-tellers, magic, and every variety of psychic practice as you would avoid fire. Whatever the come-on, the payoff is death.

A Prevalence of Death

At the time in Israel's history when Elijah had arisen as one of the mightiest prophets and workers of miracles the nation had known, a woman named Jezebel ruled as queen in Israel. She was a Gentile. Though she practiced idolatry and worshiped a false god, Ahab, the king, had taken her as his wife. Jezebel was far the stronger personality, and her weak husband ceded much of the management of affairs into her hands.

By these acts, Ahab threw open the gates of Israel to false worship, bringing grief upon the nation and drawing judgment upon himself. It is said that "Ahab did more to provoke the Lord God of Israel to anger than all the kings of Israel that were before him." I Kings 16:33.

Jezebel pursued a bloody career in Israel. Her chief instrument of policy was murder. Since she sat at the head of government, it was an easy thing for her to put this policy into official and therefore fiercely effective operation. She had but to give the order, and murder struck through the sword of government.

There was no political opposition of any consequence in Israel at the time, so her murders did not even have the color of political self-protection. They were the wanton acts of a depraved nature.

What is particularly significant is that her murders and threats of murder were not the product of some burning, generalized lust to kill. Like Saul's assaults upon David, they had a specific target. They were aimed chiefly at individuals who served the God of Israel and occupied essential positions as His spokesmen to the people.

Jezebel was, to put it in its accurate spiritual perspective, the human expression of an evil will set against God's will. The queen was a woman through whom Satan could express, in the practical mode of murder, his furious hatred of God's designs.

The intimate relationship between the evil desires of Satan and the evil acts of men is seen in Jesus' denunciation of certain leaders, to whom He said: "You are of your father the devil, and the lusts of your father *you will do.* He was a murderer from the beginning. . . ." (John 8:44.) Thus He declared that Satan's lusts become men's deeds.

Satan is identified as "a murderer from the beginning." Murder lies in his very nature. Evil spirits are much involved in stirring up murder in human society. But neither they nor Satan can cause murder to erupt until they find an individual who, for one reason or another, is susceptible to their provocations. Some individuals allow themselves to be made the human instruments of Satan's purpose of murder.

When it is possible, Satan inflames individuals who hold the authority of government to carry out murders, because that is the most efficient means and it is the hardest to resist or escape. In our century Hitler became such an instrument, with a spiritual animus aimed straight at a specific target—the people whom God has called His "chosen." If it had been possible, he would have carried out Satan's historic purpose of expunging the Jewish people, as Haman had once attempted to do.

When Jezebel got power, one of her earliest acts was a venture in mass murder. The first Book of Kings records that "Jezebel cut off the prophets of the Lord . . . Jezebel killed the prophets of the Lord." I Kings 18:4,13.

Elijah escaped, and another hundred prophets found refuge in a cave. These survivors lived in fear of their lives and could not move freely.

Later, following the crucial supernatural contest on Mount Carmel in which Elijah called down fire from heaven and commanded the slaying of false prophets who had flooded Israel under Jezebel's patronage, Jezebel sent a messenger to Elijah to inform him that she had sworn that he would be slain "by this time tomorrow." She seemed to be in a position to carry out her threat. Elijah fled.

A man named Naboth owned a vineyard hard by the palace of King Ahab. The king wanted it for use as a vegetable garden. Ahab offered to exchange it for another vineyard or to buy it from Naboth at fair market value. "But Naboth said to Ahab, 'The Lord forbid that I should give you the inheritance of my fathers.' And Ahab went into his house vexed and sullen. . . . But Jezebel his wife came to him, and said to him, 'Why is your spirit so vexed that you eat no food. . . . Do you now govern Israel? Arise, and eat bread, and let your heart be cheerful; *I will give you the vineyard of Naboth the Jezreelite.*'

"So she wrote letters in Ahab's name and sealed them with his seal," directing that Naboth be invited to a certain event and that two false witnesses be planted among the guests to accuse him of something he had not done. Soon, the desired word reached Jezebel: " 'Naboth has been stoned. He is dead.' " Jezebel said to Ahab, " 'Arise, take possession of the vineyard of Naboth . . . for Naboth is not alive, but dead.' " I Kings 21.

When Ahab went down to take possession of the slain man's vineyard—breaking the Tenth Commandment: "neither shall you covet your neighbor's house, his field . . . or any thing that is your neighbor's"—the Lord watched and acted.

"The word of the Lord came to Elijah the Tishbite, saying, 'Arise, go down and meet Ahab king of Israel . . . behold, he is in the vineyard of Naboth. . . . And you shall say to him, 'Thus says the Lord, "In the place where dogs licked up the blood of Naboth shall dogs lick your own blood." '

"Ahab said to Elijah, 'Have you found me, O my enemy?' He answered, 'I have found you, because *you have sold yourself to do what is evil in the sight of the Lord.'* " I Kings 21:20.

The Bible warns that those "who take the sword shall perish by the sword." That law was put into effect in the case of Ahab, the man who sold himself to do evil. By his marriage to Jezebel, Ahab rapidly heathenized Israel. He drew the people into many practices by which they continually broke the commandments and ordinances that Moses received from God.

In taking to himself a woman thoroughly devoted to things God had forbidden, Ahab opened a breach upon Israel through which the will of Satan gained an astonishing ascendancy.

Jezebel's link to Satan was through false religion and false worship. Her involvement with these things had made her an active enemy of God.

By marrying a woman addicted to false religion, Ahab broke faith with God. By allowing her to exercise authority, and by participating in her wicked deeds, he embraced his own untimely and violent death. I Kings 16:30–33 and 22:34–38.

The death of sinners is a harvest for Satan. That is why Isaiah writes, referring to a time when death stalked Israel because of famine and drought, "hell has enlarged herself and opened her mouth without measure" to swallow men. Isaiah 5:13,14.

Hell enlarges itself, increases its toll and population, with every outbreak of deadly violence. That is one reason why demons engage in the work of instigating, promoting, and increasing the prevalence of violent death.

At the moment of death, the state and destiny of a man's soul is fixed forever, beyond the faintest possibility of change. Evil spirits know that. They therefore work to keep a man from reconciliation to God throughout his lifetime. They also seek to spread death so that human lifetimes are cut short.

Every form of murder has the effect of removing souls from life and bringing them to judgment. As the Scripture says, "it is appointed to a man once to die, but after that comes judgment." Hebrews 9:27.

If a man is lost at death, he is lost forever. The Scripture says that "if a tree falls to the south or to the north, *in the place where it falls, there it will lie.* " (Ecclesiastes 11:3b.) Until the tree is cut down, there is every possibility that it may lie in one direction or in another, but when it is cut down, it lies where it has fallen. So it is with a man. See Ezekiel 33:8,9.

The powers of evil under Satan work incessantly to produce murder in human society. Their efforts encompass individual murder and mass murder, genocide and war. If they can, they enlist some persons to engage in widespread programs of murder. At times, murder arises in a kind of mad wave and sweeps through populations, leaving thousands, sometimes millions, dead.

We were appalled in 1969 to witness that obstinate stalemate of wills by which tens of thousands of Biafrans suffered starvation in a politically induced famine.

Apart from wars, waves of murder have arisen in this present century in Europe under Nazism, in Russia under Bolshevism and, more recently, in China in the mass executions during the first years of the Maoist regime and then, in the latter half of the 1960's, in that violent and evil spasm, the great proletarian cultural revolution of the Red Guards. In each of these events, evil spirits were at work to produce human slaughter.

In September 1968, the report came from Hong Kong that:

"Savage fighting between rival Maoist factions in Kwangsi Province in the first half of 1968 cost the lives of more than 50,000 people on one side alone, according to *Tachun Pao*, a newspaper of the April 22 Kwangsi Faction. . . . The paper reported that the hostilities ranged from small clashes to major battles, which, in some instances, were waged with artillery and tanks. The engagements, the paper said, brought brutal massacres of captives. . . . Even a sharp discounting of the paper's report would still indicate a scale of fighting in Kwangsi over a period of months rivaling that of the hostilities of the Vietnam war . . . whole families had been killed if one member was found to belong to the April 22 Faction. . . . In the protracted fighting at Wuchow, opponents of the April 22 Faction killed men, women, and children with machine guns and set large sections of the city afire with napalm."

Murder Exported From the Supernatural Order

Beyond spurring individuals to murder or to suicide (self-murder), evil spirits work on a much larger scale. They seek to intervene in politics at the highest levels to bring about a profusion of murder. There are murderers who never lift a hand in violence.

Sir Basil Zaharoff, one of the most honored and one of the most evil men of his time, specialized in contriving wars among states and prolonging them.

A book was published in 1965 titled *Peddler of Death: The Life and Times of Sir Basil Zaharoff* by Donald McCormick. A concise and lucid summary in *Newsweek* said: "Like many legendary empire builders, slum-born Basil Zaharoff started simply but shrewdly. In the 1880's he sold the navy-scarce Greeks one of his firm's revolutionary new warships. Then, drachmas in hand, he warned Greece's Turkish enemies of the purchase, offering them two submarines. Next, warning Russia of the danger to her Black Sea ports, Zaharoff sold Russia four more subs to cancel the Greek and Turkish threats he had created.

"It was a classic pay-now, kill-later system for which the Machiavellian Zaharoff thought up countless variations in his spectacular rise from a Constantinople pimp to the world's major munitions tycoon. At his zenith, Zaharoff advised generals and statesmen such as Lloyd George, Clemenceau and Briand. He consorted with Rumania's Queen Marie and Russia's royal family, held 300 business directorates and received 298 decorations from 31 nations, including France's Legion of Honor and a British title.

". . . Though Zaharoff rose to society's highest stations, no chicanery was beneath him . . . Zaharoff's incredible business brain excelled at crushing or compromising competitors, negotiating clandestine alliances and creating his own markets in the form of arms scares or actual wars.

"He employed a network of spies and operatives that included high government officials, trigger men and flunkeys specializing not only in bribery, blackmail and murder, but also in respectability. Zaharoff's tentacles reached out to enfold a multitude of enterprises—banks, newspapers, hotels, oil wells, shipyards, mines, factories. By 1913, his submerged empire seemed likely to tip the scales of victory in the coming war. Once the war had started, he stoutly supported the Allies, at least on the surface.

". . . 'I could have shown the Allies three points at which, had they struck, the enemy's armaments potential could have been utterly destroyed,' he boasted during the war. 'But that would have ruined the business.'

". . . When Lloyd George allowed Zaharoff to engineer the Greek invasion of Turkey, the disastrous defeat costing 100,000 Greek lives brought the Prime Minister's government crashing down. . . . When he died in 1936, Zaharoff was a lonely, reviled man. 'Millions died that he might live,' " said an obituary.

Evil spirits found a man, a lover of money and power, of great ability and large vision who did not scruple to maneuver nations toward war by artful manipulations on the highest levels. Zaharoff brought death by violence to literally tens of thousands of his fellow men. What the prophet Elijah said to the wicked king Ahab of Israel, "you have sold yourself to do what is evil in the sight of the Lord," could be said of such a man as this. I Kings 21:20b.

It is interesting to note that Zaharoff began his career in evil in quite a different line before graduating to the larger business of arranging wars.

Now consider quite another case, in which a young man who lost his faith discovers pleasure in bringing death.

The Bible says that a man who has repented of his sins and has experienced the forgiveness of God, who then goes back to his former way of life is like a dog that returns to its own vomit again: "For if, after they have escaped the defilements of the world through the knowledge of our Lord and Savior Jesus Christ, they are again entangled in them and overpowered, the last state has become worse for them than the first. For it would have been better for them never to have known the way of righteousness than after knowing it to turn back from the holy commandment delivered to them. It has happened to them according to the true proverb, The dog turns back to his own vomit, and the sow is washed only to wallow in the mire." (II Peter 2:20–22.) Evil spirits have more access to such a man after he has fallen away than they had before he found repentance. It is therefore not surprising to find that men who have turned from the faith they once had are more apt to do evil.

TRAINED TO HEAL, GI DOCTOR SAYS "I LOVE TO KILL" was the arresting headline on a story from Saigon by Georgie Anne Geyer of the *Chicago Daily News.* She told this story: "I met this congenial young captain—we'll call him Capt. Bob Miller—one night in a coastal city in Vietnam. A doctor, he had been assigned for a year to a combat unit in a forward area. Now his time was over, and he sat in one of those dark, depressingly garish officers' bars and talked unhappily about his future.

" 'If I stay on, they'll put me in a rear hospital,' he complained, 'and then I won't see combat. So I've talked with this buddy of mine, and we're thinking of becoming mercenaries and finding another war.'

" 'Mercenaries?' I asked. 'You'd leave your wife and become a mercenary?'

" 'I don't know if I will, but I certainly would,' he answered. His face in the dim light was thoughtful, determined. It was a square, wholesome American face, topped by a crewcut.

" 'I finally found myself in combat,' he went on. 'I love it. I love to kill.' I must have looked a little startled at his candidness, because he added quickly, 'Oh, I wouldn't go out of the club and just kill somebody. It's the combat that's important.

" 'You see, I never knew what I could do before. I was never able to pit myself against anything and really try myself out.

" 'Now I know. That's why I love war.'

"He paused and mused. 'You know what my shield would be?' he asked finally.

"I couldn't imagine.

" 'A clenched fist,' he answered, 'sinking under the waves with lightning and thunder crashing all around it. You see, it doesn't matter if you sink, as long as you fight.'

"Capt. Miller told me how he had been raised in a strict Fundamentalist church, and how he had lost faith when he went to college. It was a great loss for him, and he never quite got over it.

"Now he had found something else—but that would not last. 'Even if I stay in the service, they won't let me stay in the front lines,' he said.

"The last time I saw Miller we were at a dinner party. In conflict with regulations he had his shoulder holster and gun on. In the midst of other gay toasts, he raised his glass of champagne and said, 'Kill a Communist for Christ.' "

This is the story of a man who had been filled with the lust to destroy: "I love to kill . . . I love war." The young physician had become a friend of death.

There is at least a hint of suicide in what he said. Evil spirits are insatiable for destruction and death and it seems probable that he had been taken over by them to a very high degree.

There is a demonic symbolism that includes strong visual symbols for destruction and death. The doctor's vision of "a clenched fist sinking under the waves with lightning and thunder crashing all around it" is in that category, an expression of the wish of demons to draw more and more human victims down into the vortex of violent destruction.

The following words are from the diary of Ernst Jünger, in which he tells of the last German offensive in 1918:

"The great moment had come. The curtain of fire lifted from the front trenches. We stood up . . . we moved in step, ponderously but irresistibly toward the enemy lines. . . . . My right hand embraced the shaft of my pistol, my left a riding stick of bamboo cane. I was boiling with a mad rage, which had taken hold of me and all the others in an incomprehensible fashion. The overwhelming wish to kill gave wings to my feet. Rage pressed bitter tears from my eyes. . . . The monstrous desire for annihilation, which hovered over the battlefield, thickened the brains of the men and submerged them in a red fog. We called to each other in sobs and stammered disconnected sentences. A neutral observer might have perhaps believed that we were seized by an excess of happiness."

Evan S. Connell, Jr., commenting on this, wrote: "When a soldier drifts into such a condition . . . he is no longer cognizant of fighting to protect his home and family and Preserve the Faith; instead, he is obsessed by a need to kill and to desecrate. Nothing else matters. His concern is no longer with preservation but with annihilation. He despises the world. He renounces his privileges as a human for the deep joy of destruction."

We have here a remarkably clear description of a strange and overwhelming and maddened lust to kill that sometimes seizes whole groups of men in battle situations, and seizes them simultaneously. It is a phenomenon not of themselves. It comes rather from outside themselves and takes hold of them, turning them into raging killers. Something sinister had "taken hold of me and all the others in an incomprehensible fashion," producing a "mad rage."

This is nothing less than the presence of possibly thousands of evil spirits gathered in the air at the site of battle, determined to turn it into a scene of maximum carnage for human beings. "The monstrous desire for annihilation . . . hovered over the battlefield." It "thickened the minds of the men and submerged them in a red fog." Satan's policy of death had been put into peculiarly intensive effect, at a moment when the opportunity for bringing death to many men was ripe, by a concentration of evil spirits—spirits of destruction—at the scene of battle.

There comes a point when men's resort to violence necessitates judgment. Murder was one of the chief causes of the flood that God sent as a judgment on mankind. The Scripture says: "God saw that the wickedness of man was great in the earth. . . . So the Lord said, I will destroy man whom I have created from the face of the earth. . . . The earth also was corrupt before the Lord, and *the earth was filled with violence.* God said to Noah, the end of all flesh is come before me, for the earth is filled with violence." Genesis 6:5a,7a,11,13a.

Noah was "a preacher of righteousness" (II Peter 3:5) and during the very considerable period of time in which he built the ship, he warned the people regarding their increasing and flagrant indulgence in sin.

We are told that "God's patience waited in the days of Noah, during the building of the ark." I Peter 3:20.

We are living in the most violent century in the history of civilization. Our own society has been marked increasingly by violence, and on the international scene the means of violence have multiplied staggeringly. It is now possible for men to think and plan in practical terms for the near-annihilation of whole populations, and they do exactly that in the board rooms of nuclear strategy.

If God judged the world once, He will judge it again. He has revealed in His Word that the world, having once been judged by water, will be judged a second time by fire:

"For behold, the Lord will come in fire, and his chariots like the stormwind, to render his anger in fury, and his rebuke with flames of fire. For by fire will the Lord execute judgment . . ." Isaiah 66:15,16a. The New Testament puts it this way:

". . . The world that then existed was deluged with water and perished" but "the heavens and earth that now exist have been stored up for fire, being kept until the day of judgment and destruction of ungodly men . . . but God is waiting, for the good reason that he is not willing that any should perish, and he is giving more time for sinners to repent." II Peter 3:5–7,9b.

The Thieves of Forever

Satan wants human beings to think his thoughts and do his deeds. The mission of demons is to accomplish that.

What demons aim at specifically is obtaining either *influence* or *control* over the thoughts, the beliefs, and the actions of human beings. Influence is what demons seek to get when they are outside a man. Control is what they begin to get when they enter into a man.

At times you are, inescapably, an object of their attention. The demons know you by name. They would like to have control over your beliefs and actions, but if they cannot initally get it they will settle for influence because it can lead later to control.

A human being is a free moral agent. He may elect to do the will of God, or he may elect to violate the will of God. His spiritual destiny hangs upon his choice.

That is not all that hangs on it. In the world's affairs, the actual carrying out of the will of God or the will of Satan on earth depends upon human choice. When men do what Satan bids them do, they soon get Satan's results in their society. When men obey the will of God, the blessings of God flow into a society through them.

Demons come up against the fact of a man's freedom to choose in their effort to get him to do the will of their master. Initially, therefore, evil spirits must resort to tactics of persuasion, since they are not able to force a man to sin. They must try to goad and coax and coerce a man into doing what he ought not to do.

The strategy of demons is to confront an individual with temptations, hoping thereby to entice him enough to make him *choose* to sin. When he consents to sin, an individual voluntarily puts his will over on the side of Satan. That gives demons some advantage over him. Before long a definite basis for stronger and more intensive demonic activity is created in his life.

The ultimate aim is to draw the individual so far into sin—into the habit of yielding himself to the will of Satan—that he cannot get back out. That is control.

If, on the other hand, an individual refuses to cooperate, the demons find in him no outlet through which the spiritual realm of evil can enter the human realm and get some of its work done by him.

The demons specialize in exporting evil from the supernatural to the natural plane as massively as men will permit. There are no limits to which the demons are not willing to go, if men will let them. Where the Word of God is ignored or disobeyed, they can deposit wickedness and distress in ever greater measures upon a society until at last that society is overwhelmed by evil. The same can be true of an individual life.

In Satan's program for man, lies and temptations are quite often presented together. Evil spirits know that a person who first accepts a lie is more likely to sink under a temptation. A lie softens a man up for sin.

This is a classic technique that Satan has used throughout human history. It can be seen first in his approach to the woman in Eden. It is important to realize that Satan had *no part* in man's affairs up to that point. He desired to gain an entrance into those affairs. What Satan needed was to get the woman to disobey God and to obey him, so that, through her, he might begin to have influence in the world.

The issue before the woman was clear. She had the Word of God on a certain matter and she also had the word of Satan on it. Satan's word was directly contrary to what God had said.

The first thing Satan did was to plant a doubt in the woman's mind concerning what God had actually said. Then he told her a lie.

God had warned the woman that if she ate of the fruit of the tree of the knowledge of good and evil she would die. Satan came and told her she would not die. Supporting this outright lie was the temptation. The Bible says, "And when the woman saw that the tree was good for food, and that it was a delight to the eyes, and a tree to be desired to make one wise," she ate of its fruit.

That is what evil spirits will do. They will present an evil action in a truthless light that heavily emphasizes its immediate satisfactions, gratifications, or rewards. And they will lie about its consequences.

The way Satan took with Eve to get her to do his will is almost exactly the way he will take with you. First he will cause you to doubt the authority and surety of the Word of God. A college professor may assist in that, someone who from a position of apparent knowledge and wisdom will stand up and openly attack the validity of the Scriptures. When doubt is sown, Satan will tell you a lie, directly contrary to the Scriptures. Then he will tempt you to do this, that, or some other evil.

By this process he can take nearly an entire generation into the paths of eternal destruction, if they will let him. It is one of the saddest facts of American life that unnumbered thousands of young people have had their faith in the words of the Bible undermined by the deliberate attacks on it of college professors. All such men, however vaunted, who boldly speak words directly contrary to the Scriptures make themselves liars. That is why the Book of Romans says, "Yea, let God be true, but every man a liar, as it is written, 'That thou mayest be justified in thy words, and prevail when thou art judged.' " (Romans 3:4, referring to Psalm 51:4.) In short, if the time came when every man on earth contradicted the Word of God, that Word would remain eternally true and every man would be a liar. "There is no wisdom nor understanding nor counsel against the Lord." Proverbs 21:30.

Satan is a liar and "the father of lies." From Eden on, his enmity has been hot against the Word of God and he contradicts it and casts scorn upon it now as he did then. Through history he has resisted with fury the early attempts to get the Bible into the hands of the people of any nation in their own language. Our English Bible comes to us from the hands of William Tyndale, who translated the Scriptures into English. He went up in flames at the stake for having made the Scriptures available to the common people.

Satan's move, in any nation where the Word of God is in the possession of the people, is to attack the veracity and validity of the Scriptures. The truths in them stand, when they are appropriated, as a mighty bulwark against all his devices. If he can undermine the people's confidence and trust in the Scriptures, he can eventually do with the population as he wills.

The attack on the Word of God comes in strategic centers and it is particularly directed at the youth, because Satan knows that if he can beguile new generations from truth and lead them into sin, he can, before very long, wreck a nation. These strategic centers are particularly universities and seminaries—universities because they are the prime source of most of the most influential people of the next generation, seminaries because that is where the new ministers and preachers are trained. If you can sabotage belief there, you will soon have the pulpits of denominations filled with men who have no sure standard of righteousness to proclaim to the people, men who cannot distinguish that which is holy from that which is vile. "If the blind lead the blind," Jesus said, "both shall fall into the ditch." Matthew 15:14.

It is a fateful thing for men to contradict and stand against the truths of Scripture. By doing so they invite gross moral darkness to cover a people. The scholarly deniers of God's Word in Germany, led by the school of higher criticism, helped soften Germany up for the eventual moral and spiritual disaster of Nazism. They undermined belief in God and opened the nation wide to the influence of demons. Isaiah described this cause and effect well when he declared, "For the leaders of this people cause them to err, and they that are led of them are destroyed." Isaiah 9:16.

So it is that the attack on the Word of God, designed to delude a nation, most commonly proceeds from the university lecterns and the pulpits. The result of this is to point a nation away from the truth, away from God and into the path of tyranny and disaster.

Behind this, of course, Satan intends for men the personal disaster of eternal separation from God. That is why Micah, in his prophecy against the leaders of the house of Jacob in a time of declension cried out, "The women of my people you drive out of their pleasant houses; from their young you take away my glory for ever." Micah 2:9.

That, exactly, is what the savants do who stand before the young and rob them of their faith in God. If they knew what they did! If they knew the terrible sum of the social and moral wreckage that proceeds from their words! They soften the young up for short-term disaster and salt them for everlasting sorrow. They take away from the young God's glory *forever*.

The Limitation of Demons

Men overcome Satan by loyalty to God. When a significant portion of a nation's population truly worships and obeys the God of Israel, when it honors and upholds His Word, a great limitation is set upon the extent and nature of demonic activity in that nation's territory.

The faithfulness of men to God limits the demons. The infidelity of men to God and to His commandments gives demons more and more freedom to work destructively among them.

Only the nation in which the Bible is honored and believed will fully escape domination by one form of evil or another. *The nation that will not follow God will finally follow demons.*

Many demons engage in virtually incessant, direct, personal activity among men. They tempt them, harass them with evil thoughts, tell them lies, lead them into wrongdoing, influence them away from God and from the Scriptures.

The demons work on men in practical ways to involve them in sin and to keep them from God, but demons are not free to do anything they want at any time. The range of their options and the area of their discretionary activities is very broad, but it is not unlimited.

There are limitations that are set upon them by God, and there are limitations that may be set upon them by men. If it were not the case, they would long ago have succeeded in making an entire chaos out of civilization.

If a lion were placed in a large, fenced preserve, he would be free to attack in any direction but his freedom would end abruptly at the fences of the preserve. He would be free within set limits.

That is somewhat the case with Satan and the demons. They cannot go a fraction beyond limits set on them by God, and God can, and sometimes does, either forbid them to do certain things or command them to do certain things. In that sense, and in that sense only, Satan and the demons remain subject to God.

For quite a long time Satan was not permitted to do anything against God's servant Job. When God took away the hedge He had set all about Job's family and property, the Lord said to Satan, "Behold, all that he has is in your power; only upon himself do not put forth your hand."

God took away a specific part of the restriction He had placed against Satan in the case of Job, but He did not remove it all, and Satan was obliged to move against Job within the limits set by God.

Another limitation that comes upon Satan and his demons as they seek to attain their will on earth is the refusal of men to do evil. Initially, Satan can only tempt and urge an individual to indulge in sin. If the individual refuses, Satan has no more that he can do.

Satan is at the moment having a kind of heyday in America. He is succeeding in promoting crime, sexual indulgence, perversions, violence, occultism, and civil strife to a degree that was impossible until quite recently. Thus his destructive purposes are being carried out upon individuals and groups of men, especially the young, in progressively larger ways.

For a very long time Satan softened up the nation for the present moral and spiritual attack by placing the Bible and its powerful words further and further away from the center of American life. One of the last steps in this long process was to get the Scriptures out of the public schools.

With the Bible's hugely beneficial influence cast aside—its words are an exhortation to virtue and a restraint to sin—Satan is able to promote evil in a way that is both more widespread and more extreme than heretofore. For the "Thou shalt not's . . ." of Mount Sinai, we now have the "Do what thou wilt" of the devil.

There is no apparent sign of any reversal of this swift deteriorative process in our society. Unless there is a dramatic reversal, a large-scale repentance and turning to God, demon activity will increase steadily and become more and more obvious, open, and pronounced in its debilitative and convulsive effects in the United States.

The whole tide of idolatry, immorality, impurity, lawlessness, perversion, and false supernaturalism comes upon a people after they have been persuaded to trade in the truth of God for a lie, and that is happening in America today.

It can be stopped.

Demons are greater than men, but God is greater than demons. God desires to take part with man in the overthrow of Satan's evil works—just as Satan and the demons work to get men to take part with them in the overthrow of God's purposes.

The limitation of Satan's power on earth is based on a joining together of the will of God and the will of man. When that union is lacking, Satan can do nearly anything he pleases (even to organizing such advanced civilizations as those of Germany and China for national ventures in madness). When that union is present, Satan is hindered or thwarted in carrying out his will.

When the sovereignty of God is linked to the obedience of man, the will of God is put into effect, and when that happens Satan is checked.

Satan is well aware that when any man takes hold of God, God will beat Satan down through him. A friend of mine put it this way, "God pushes from His side and man pushes from his side, and Satan is defeated. It doesn't work without the two hitting together."

Daniel is an illustration of that. God was in heaven. From the earth, Daniel prayed to God. God heard his prayer and immediately set the answer in motion. Demonic forces intervened, but Daniel persisted in prayer and fasting day after day while severe conflict was being waged in the atmosphere.

The will of Daniel and the will of God were at one, and at last the power of evil was broken in the matter. Daniel obtained a prophecy concerning the future of Israel that was not for his day, God told him, but "for the time of the end." Daniel 8:19b.

It is not strange that Satan and the prince demon opposed the conveying of that prophecy to Daniel. From the time of Israel's bondage in ancient Egypt on, Satan has attempted repeatedly to do away with God's chosen. He has, at times, been able to arouse rulers and nations to his murderous intent. According to Old Testament prophecies, Satan is going to make another desperate try. When that occurs, the prophecy given to Daniel will be one of the means by which some Jews shall escape his hand.

God is always searching for a man who will stand with Him in the crisis of the world's affairs.

Moses and Gideon were not mighty men in themselves, yet they did mighty deeds in history. God summoned Moses to be His spokesman to the whole Jewish people, and to the whole court of Egypt. Moses had definite limitations that unfitted him for the job, and he shrank from it. Moses was hesitant, "slow of speech and of tongue," and meek. (Exodus 4:10–12 and Numbers 12:3.) But the Lord said, "Now therefore go, and *I will be with your mouth.*"

God was not interested in what Moses could do for Him. God was interested in what He could do *through* Moses. The work of Moses could never be explained in terms of what Moses was. It was Who was with Moses that really counted.

Gideon had behaved very timidly in the face of the enemy. He had no qualifications to be a military leader. Yet God called him to occupy that role and, by placing his whole reliance on God, Gideon overmastered enemy leaders who had vastly larger forces with much experience in battle.

God called each man to serve Him as a deliverer of the Jewish people and put each up against apparently insuperable odds. Purely by faith, both men linked their inadequacy to God's adequacy. Moses brought Israel out of Egypt's bondage in an awesome demonstration of God's power and he took the people through the Red Sea. Gideon routed the enemy army with a tiny force of 300 men by reckoning on the power of God.

I know a man who stutters. God called him to preach. He cannot keep himself from stuttering at times in conversation, but he never stutters when he preaches. God often calls men, not at the point of their strength, but at the point of the greatest weakness. By that they discover the key to the wonderful paradox of the apostle Paul, who said: God's "power is made perfect in [human] weakness . . . for when I am weak, then I am strong." II Corinthians 12:9,10b.

The Old Testament says, "for not by might shall a man prevail." I Samuel 2:9b.

In the conflict between God and Satan, the man who gives himself most wholeheartedly to God is most useful to God in bringing forth His will in the earth. The man who gives himself most completely to sin is most useful to Satan in producing evil in the earth.

If there were two human leaders of considerable eloquence, one proposing evil and one proposing good, and large numbers of men pledged allegiance and service to one or the other, those who followed the former leader and carried out his will would produce evil in their society. Those who followed the other and did his will would produce good in their society.

That is true of men who follow the will of Satan and those who give themselves to God. The former become human agents of the will of Satan. The latter become the human instruments of the will of God.

The consequences in either case are not merely temporal; they are eternal. "Do you not know that *to whom you yield yourselves servants to obey, his servants you are* to whom you obey—whether of sin, which leads to death, or of obedience, which leads to righteousness?" Romans 6:16.

The power of Satan does not begin to be broken in a society until there arises a man or a group of men willing to risk everything and stake everything on the Word and the will of God. God desires to have a people in the earth through whom His truth shall triumph *by their obedience.*

Such men must be abandoned and wholly—yes, even recklessly —given over to God. Such men put God first and thrust everything else into its proper subordination to Him. Oswald Chambers, that luminous British expositor of the Scriptures, put it this way: "The conditions for discipleship laid down by Our Lord mean that the men and women He is going to use in His building enterprises are those who love Him personally, passionately and devotedly beyond any of the closest ties on earth. The conditions are stern, but they are glorious."

Such individuals cannot be suborned by any offer—not for job, for security, nor for life itself. Satan falls before such men, for they have no price.

Men of this sort are free to hurl truth in the teeth of the most popular lies, to call sin by its rightful name, to defy any demagogue. They stand, by faith, on the faithfulness of God. Such men deal mighty blows at the bulwarks of Satan.

Martin Luther showed this quality. "Let goods and kindred go, this mortal life also. The body they may kill, God's truth abideth still," he wrote in his glorious hymn, "A Mighty Fortress Is Our God."

"Here I stand, I can do no other," Luther declared in exalting truth above ecclesiastical tradition. The fear of death could not deter him. That is why he became so chief a force in the breaking of an age-long night of religious darkness in Europe. He dared to stand on nothing but the truth of God, in the face of massive traditions to the contrary and massive opposition. Luther knew that in this he stood against more than men. He made that evident in writing, "And though this world with devils filled should threaten to undo us, we will not fear for God has willed His truth to triumph through us."

The devil is now radicalizing a segment of American youth for destruction. What we need are young people, Jews and Gentiles, who will be radicalized for God's purposes through the Scriptures. As they remain true to Him, God will pour out His love and power upon them and make them a blessing in the earth. Three young Hebrews, Hananiah, Mishael, and Azariah, were captives in Babylon at a time when the king of that vast empire issued a decree that everyone bow down and worship an image of gold set up on the plain of Dura. The three Jews would not bow down to it. Certain officials reported this singular insubordination to the king: "These men, O king, pay no heed to you. They do not serve your gods or worship the golden image which you have set up." The king summoned the young men, gave them one chance to change their minds, and told them, "If you do not worship, you shall immediately be cast into a burning fiery furnace, and who is the god who will deliver you out of my hands?"

The heathen edict was a direct defiance of the commandment of God, backed by the penalty of death.

To this, they answered, "We have no need to answer you in this matter"—in other words, it was not in question what they were going to do; they were *not* going to worship the idol. "If it be so, our God whom we serve is able to deliver us from the burning fiery furnace; and he will deliver us out of your hand, O king. But if not, be it known to you, O king, that *we will not serve your gods* or worship the golden image which you have set up."

They could have secured their lives for a brief act of infidelity to the living God. Instead they were bound and cast into the furnace. At that point the situation changed. The king, when he saw it, "was astonished and rose up in haste. He said to his counselors,

'Did we not cast three men bound into the fire?' They answered, 'True, O king.' He answered, 'But I see four men loose, walking in the midst of the fire, and they are not hurt; and the appearance of the fourth is like the Son of God.'"

Moments later the three came out of the fire, "and the satraps, the prefects, the governors, and the king's counselors gathered together and saw that the fire had not had any power over the bodies of those men; the hair of their heads was not singed, their mantles were not scorched, and there was no smell of smoke upon them." Daniel 3.

The difference between the God of the Hebrews and all other gods became plain at that hour to everyone who beheld it. The power of God to vindicate and save those who put their whole reliance on Him, and who flinch at no consequence, was openly displayed to the court of Babylon.

By the faithfulness of three young Jews, the living God had a testimony in Babylon to put idol worshipers to shame.

He had that testimony only because three young men took an undeviating and perilous stand for truth. To show Himself in power in society, God requires the full abandonment of men to Him. The man who abandons all to God brings God into action in whatever situation he is in.

Part IV

The Challenge
to Self-Possession

Spirit, Soul, Body

The Greeks had one great motto for their intellectual pursuits: Know thyself. The love of wisdom—philosophy—has been praised as the highest form of human achievement through the centuries. Yet neither the Greeks with their many philosophies, nor any of the succeeding nations that engaged in this pursuit of wisdom, from the Romans to our own day, have been able to find this understanding of self. Otherwise there would be no need for the constant rise of new philosophies, and the discarding of others, nor would modern man be at an ever more apparent loss in understanding himself, despite the many modern schools of psychology and psychiatry.

This knowledge of self eludes us, remaining always somewhere beyond our grasp. The attempts of man to arrive at it purely by reason fail, as they do, because there is more to man than reason can account for.

Since the first man lost his communion with God through sin

and thereby lost a true understanding of himself and his reason for being, and since all attempts by man to reach this understanding (who am I, where did I come from, why am I here, and where do I go?) have so obviously failed, the question arises whether it is at all possible for man to understand himself.

There is a way. What man cannot find out, God has chosen to reveal to him.

The Bible says, *"For what man knows the things of a man, save the spirit of man which is in him?"* I Corinthians 2:11.

In these words we are given the clear beginning of an understanding of man. In form the verse is a question, but actually it is a statement of an essential fact. The verse tells us that what cannot be imparted to us by our minds can be given to us by another faculty. A man cannot know the things of a man by the mind, but he can know by "the spirit of man which is in him."

There is no other way to an understanding of man, except through the spirit. Few people would be able to explain this because the very term "spirit of man" is not clear at all to most men. Vague religious notions attached to the term impede, rather than clarify, our understanding. Some men confound spirit and soul and think they are the same.

It is of great importance to understand the makeup of man, the structure of his being.

God created man in His own image, therefore man is tripartite or, more accurately, triune: spirit, soul, and body. In closing his first letter to the Thessalonians, Paul wrote: " . . . I pray God your whole *spirit* and *soul* and *body* be kept blameless. . . ." I Thessalonians 5:23.

That is the sum of what man is. Fail to understand this and it can be guaranteed that you will fail to understand the nature of man.

You may ask what makes it so vital for a man to have this understanding. There are several reasons. Satan is always working to keep man deceived about himself, because by such common deceptions he is able to keep millions of men in bondage and under the power of sin. Some men are drawn, in the vanity of their minds, to estimate man above his true station, even to magnify man against God. Others are led to take such a diminished view of man that they refuse to believe that God would take an interest in such a lowly creature. Either extreme denies man a true understanding of himself. Either extreme denies him an understanding of himself in relationship to God.

To understand how evil spirits work to undermine human well-being, it is necessary to have some grasp of the nature of man: the nature of man as God intended him to be, and the nature of man as he is.

If you were to get a wrong set of instructions with a mechanism with which you were unfamiliar, your understanding of it would not correspond to the actual nature of the thing itself. A wrong understanding of the nature of man—even when that understanding is satisfyingly complex and apparently profound—can, when it is applied in an effort to help a man, do him little good, and it may do him considerable harm.

In this, the good *intentions* of the one attempting to help are of little moment; what really counts is the *accuracy of his understanding* as far as it goes.

Shakespeare was moved to write the exclamatory phrase, "What a piece of work is a man!" Man is, indeed, an incomparable piece of work, created in the image of God, and the Bible teaches very clearly that he is:

Spirit
Soul
Body.

These terms are not self-explanatory, except perhaps in the case of the body, about which most of us have some understanding. To know these three major constituents of every human being by name, but not to know something about them, how they relate to each other and how they function, is not enough.

It is no accident that Paul mentioned them in the order in which he did, for that order places them in their right relationships to each other. The progression as he gives it—spirit, soul, body—proceeds from the innermost to the outermost parts of a man.

For a crude illustration of man's structure, we might think of a peach. The very core of the peach is the nut, which is surrounded by the pit, which in turn is surrounded by the fruit flesh—corresponding in this order to spirit, soul, and body.

That gives you some picture of the elements of a man in their actual arrangement. The soul is set within the body, and the spirit is set within the soul.

The spirit is the very core of man. It is in the spirit that man has his God-given capacity to commune with God, Who is Spirit and

Who must be worshiped in spirit and in truth. It is the shrine in which spiritual life is lived.

The spirit expresses itself through the soul. The soul, in turn, expresses itself through the physical body.

The body is the outer man, the soul is the inner man, the spirit is the innermost man. When all three of these are fully alive and free of sin, and functioning in their right relationships to each other, you have a human being as God made him to be.

But it is not what you find. What you find is human beings with all kinds of impairments and distortions and imbalances, and you find men in whom the wrong part of their being exercises control over their whole being.

Fully to understand the rather simple basics that are set forth above and that immediately follow, it may be necessary for you to read these lines slowly and with deliberate, thoughtful concentration; perhaps to read them carefully a second time. For unless these basics are understood, the applications that follow will not be understood.

Dr. Andrew Murray, a superlative Bible expositor, wrote that *it is through the spirit that man stands "related to the spiritual world."*

Dr. Murray also penned these telling lines:

"The spirit is the seat of our God-consciousness; the soul of our self-consciousness; the body of our world-consciousness. In the spirit, God dwells; in the soul, self; in the body, sense."

Understand these words and you will be well on your way to an understanding of the nature of man.

In this the writer was speaking of man as he was meant to be, not as he actually is. Self dwells in the soul and sense in the body in every case, but God does not dwell in the spirit of a man in sin. The fact is that evil spirits may dwell in the part of a man meant for the indwelling of God.

We tend to think—I know I did for a long time—of the soul as some extremely vague inner principle—a kind of pale ghost that you can't quite put your finger on. That renders the expression "saving the soul" virtually unintelligible because we don't know what it is that is being saved.

The soul is the human being within the body. It is the you within your body. It is the real you. The self.

Your mind, your will, your emotions, and the ability to express personality are all powers of your soul.

The soul includes the mind and the will of a man. Put another way, it includes all the powers of intellect and volition.

A man's personality and his emotions reside in the soul. It can accurately be said that a man's personality is the expression *of* his soul, but a man's personality is expressed *by* his body.

The soul expresses itself through the physical body. The emotions are expressed by facial expressions and physical gestures, and the thoughts are expressed in words and actions. If the emotions of a man's soul are agitated by anger or fear, his face and body will reflect that, or if his emotions are joyful, his countenance will reflect that.

The human soul is the seat of the emotions. The emotions are felt and experienced in the soul, but they are expressed, insofar as they are outwardly expressed, by the body.

So the term "saving the soul" refers to the saving of the essential you—mind, will, personality—as distinguished from your physical body.

Genesis 2:7 shows that man had a body, which God formed out of the dust, before man had life. It was when God "breathed into his nostrils the breath of life" that "man became *a living soul.*"

"A living soul" is what man is essentially. It has been helpfully said that "man *is* a soul, and he *has* a body."

The mouth, the larynx, the tongue, the lips speak—but do the lips really speak? No. It is the man inside the body who is speaking, and his soul is employing his bodily equipment through which to speak. You can use your lips, by an act of will, to form any words you wish. When your lips speak, it is not your body primarily that is talking; it is you, the real you, the inner man, the soul.

The outward members of your body are instruments you use to carry out the intentions of your soul. If, in an accident, you were to lose a forearm you would not be essentially any less yourself. Your soul would be absolutely intact. It would simply have fewer bodily mechanisms to use, by which to express itself.

Though man is tripartite in his makeup, and though each of these three parts is distinct, man's trinity is fused into a perfect union.

The brain, for example, is the seat of the mind. The brain is part of the body. The mind is a part of the soul.

The mind is certainly greater than the brain. The thoughts that come to us come to our minds. They are received, stored, or dispatched by the brain as instructions to our members. *The brain is the command center of the mind for the body.* The brain relates the mind to the body.

Even a dictionary definition helps to show this:

The Random House dictionary defines the word "mind" as "the element, part, substance, or process that reasons, thinks, feels, wills, perceives, judges, etc."

Of the word "brain" it says: "the part of the central nervous system enclosed in the cranium of man and other vertebrates, consisting of a soft, convoluted mass of gray and white matter and serving to control and coordinate the mental and physical actions."

Alternatively, it speaks of the "brain as the *center* of thought, understanding, etc; mind, intellect" (italics added).

The will of the human soul controls the thought processes of the brain, and it is able to direct the brain, to redirect it, to check it.

A thought flies into your mind, seemingly out of nowhere. It may be an idle thought, a creative thought, an unpleasant thought, or an evil thought. It may be about virtually anything from the labels on soup cans to the nature of the universe. When the thought comes to mind, the will can direct the brain to receive it, reject it, ponder it, expand on it, or it can redirect the brain to some other, more useful avenue of thought.

It is through the body that man—his soul—stands related to the external world. His physical senses apprehend—see, hear, taste, touch, smell—the realm of nature, and it is in that natural physical realm—and that realm only—that they are expert. His physical powers enable a man to act upon his environment.

Then there is the human spirit. It is this, above all, that makes man unique. By this part of his being, a man may be in touch with the spiritual realm.

It is the human spirit that gives man his spiritual capacity. It is by this that men may worship God as He desires to be worshiped "in spirit and in truth." Yet this part of man has been ruined by the Fall.

In God's perfect design for man, the human spirit, indwelt and filled by the Holy Spirit and enjoying a full and free communion with the living God, was to govern all the activities and powers of the soul—intellect, will, and emotions. In this plan, man would always act in perfect agreement with the will of his Creator and he would enjoy the fruits of the creation in abundant leisure and in peace.

When man sinned, he was cut off from the life of God. The line was broken between heaven and earth. The communion between the Creator and His Creature was gone. The spirit of man became dead toward God—not dead in the sense that it is totally inactive, but in the sense that it is utterly unable to perform its proper function.

Man, meant to be the express reflection of the beauty and wisdom of God, was made an orphan. Emptied of the life of God, yet still possessing the capacities and energies of his body and soul, man became a menace to himself and to the earth. This is the supreme tragedy of the Fall.

Man's spirit, meant to be the dwelling place of God, became at best dead to God and at worst it became an abode of evil spirits. The intention of God was that man, walking in perfect communion and perfect agreement with Him—the human spirit and the Holy Spirit wholly at one—would jointly rule with God outward from the spirit, through the soul and body, to the whole natural environment. Everywhere man went, then, the will of God would be done.

Instead we see another condition entirely. Man, dead in his spirit and lacking communion with God, carries on in the powers of his soul, which inevitably come under some degree of influence by demons (even in the best of men) or, at the worst, he comes under the actual control of evil spirits and therefore spreads chaos and misery in his environment.

It is the spirit of man, not the soul, that God intended to govern his life! The soul is not capable of governing the life aright. With the soul in charge, the center of man's government is misplaced —from God to self.

Man, created for communion with God, was never meant to walk alone, apart from God, independent of his Creator. Yet that is his condition. He is governed by his soul. Just as confusion besets the body politic when the lines of command are disoriented, confusion has plagued human affairs because of this dislocation.

Yet in his lost condition man, with a very few exceptions, does not seek God. It is God Who seeks man, for He has made a way of restoration for man in his lost estate. He has made a way back to Himself.

The extent of the Fall cannot be measured solely by the lack of communion with God, though this is central, because it manifests itself in countless aspects of our lives. Let us look for a moment at man as he is.

An individual may be primarily or highly developed in any of the three parts of his being: body, soul, or spirit. Or he may be underdeveloped in one or more of these. He may be badly lopsided, as some are.

God intended the balanced development of man in all three sectors, with none to be developed at the expense of another.

A man may be highly developed in his physical body, but be only moderately, or hardly at all, developed in his soul—in his mind and emotions. He may devote a disproportionate share of time to body culture.

By far the great majority of mankind is most developed in the body, the senses. Pleasure and appetites dominate most men and rob them of the dignity God desires for them. For this reason man has sunk below the level of animals many, many times.

We have all met sensual men—men of the senses—whose talk is centered on bodily appetites and needs: They talk a great deal of eating, drinking, of sex, of relaxing and sleeping. They may be men whose minds are thick, but not necessarily so. They may be intelligent men whose interests are centered in the gratification of their senses, even if in a refined style.

I remember a man of the sensual kind saying to me one evening toward the end of a day's work: "You know what I'm going to do? I'm going to go down and git me some tall drinks and then I'm going to git me 'bout the biggest steak in town, and then I'm going to roll into that hay and git me 'bout 15 hours of solid shuteye!" Except for the necessary interruption of work, his chief pursuit in life was in procuring for his senses the next thing they wanted.

Such men are ruled by their bodily appetites inward, in an exact reversal of God's intention that the spirit rule both soul and body.

Another man may be highly developed in his soul—in the department of the intellect, or in the emotions—and remain very underdeveloped in his body. He gives a heavy proportion of his time to cultivating his mind or to cultivating such of the finer soulish emotions as music appreciation. He may bring his soul, where his real powers are, to a very high state of development.

Various aspects of that part of his being—emotions, thoughts, creative genius, artistic talent and so on—may be brought to a point of marvelous sensibility and refinement. Yet even these men cannot understand themselves, because any true understanding must come from the spirit.

There are men whose interests are centered in the life of the intellect. For the sake of pursuing knowledge they may greatly rein in their sensual drives. They live primarily in the mind, not in the body. The extreme of this is the frail, pale, stooped scholar who neglects his body, feeding it haphazardly and giving it no exercise but that which daily routine necessarily imposes. He is highly developed in the mind but sunk in the body.

There are men who strike a balance between intellect and emotions and cultivate them both in very useful ways. There are some more truly rounded men who bring their bodies, their minds, and their emotions all to fairly high states of development. The able athlete with a Phi Beta Kappa key who devotes some of his spare time to chess and Spanish poetry might fall into this class.

In the United States there are large numbers of fleshly men, devoted to their bodily desires, and possibly larger numbers of soulish men, occupied with the uses of their minds or the enjoyment of their emotions, but there are few spiritual men, few who are developed or exercised in this part.

That is not surprising. Man died in his spirit when his first father sinned. He became spiritually dead as far as communion with God was concerned.

It was in their spirits that the first men knew and worshiped God. When they sinned, their spirits became darkened and dead. They no longer had fellowship with God or worshiped Him. They hid from Him.

But in doing the will of Satan and cutting himself off from the life of God, man did not in any sense cut his spirit off from Satan and the demons. Quite the opposite, man gave access to his spirit to evil spirits. If any man who is, as the Bible puts it, spiritually "dead in trespasses and sins" undertakes to develop his darkened spirit, he does so only by the agency and activity of demonic spirits.

Most Americans are dull, inactive, obtuse in this area of their being. Some are not. There are some who are psychically sensitive, as they say, and full of spiritual perceptions and intuitions of various kinds. They may become highly developed and active in their spirits, but it is all demonic.

Such individuals, who possess certain spiritual capacities or powers, are often not aware of that, since demons usually present themselves and their activities as beneficent, even as Satan "disguises himself as an angel of light." II Corinthians 11:14b.

Americans, by and large, have developed the mind and the body but have neglected the spirit. This is not true of many men of India, who have assiduously cultivated and developed the spirit, but have done so almost exclusively through demonic influence.

Some of them, by various rigors, by disciplines, by asceticism and fasts, by neglecting the body, by slavishly repeating certain formulas, obtain powers in the spirit and in the soul and so become wonder men or acknowledged "saints." They have commerce with evil spirits through their darkened but active spiritual part.

Now we see some young people in this nation becoming active in this way. They *know* that there is a spiritual and supernatural realm. They have had experiences in this realm. Some have had encounters with supernatural beings. Whether they know it, or do not know it, these experiences are all demonic in their source.

But unlike most of the older generations of Americans, they are not inactive in this realm—and that is surely a clue to the "generation gap." Adults who have been inactive in this realm cannot in any way comprehend what is happening to the younger people, or why, and they have no way of dealing with it. It is altogether beyond them, and they cannot even begin to guess at the demonic influences that are stirring up and driving the young people—though they see the effects of it.

What is the answer then? Man's spirit is dead in trespasses and he therefore cannot have communion with God until his spirit is "made alive by the Spirit of God," or to use the words of Jesus, until a man is "born again" by the Spirit of God.

As a born-again man abides in the light of God, he will gradually begin to understand himself and his reason for being. He will discover that many if not most of the beliefs, ideas, and opinions he held are to some degree untrue because they were formed by man apart from God, Who alone is Truth and from Whom alone true knowledge and understanding can come. The fear of God is the beginning of wisdom and knowledge. Proverbs 1:7 and 9:10.

There is one more class. It is composed of individuals who are alive and active in their spirits, who truly worship God and know Him. This is true only because they have been reawakened, made alive in the spirit, born again.

Their darkened, deadened spirits have been touched by the breath of God—by the Holy Spirit. They are filled with light in the spiritual part and they enjoy daily fellowship with God.

At some point in their lives, such men become aware that they truly are lost and that unless God saves them they will not be saved. They see their utter spiritual poverty and they call out to God for the regeneration only He can give.

They receive new life from God in the hour they are born again. There is a new joy, a new peace, a new power to live above sin and temptation. They become men as men more truly ought to be—governed by God through the awakened human spirit and exercising their capacities of body and soul in a way that is pleasing to Him.

When Paul wrote, " . . . I pray God your whole spirit and soul and body be kept blameless . . ." he was expressing God's desire that a man's whole being be free of sin, so that he may belong to God and be free of demonic intervention.

Stages and Degrees
of Demonic Control

To the extent that a man becomes involved with demons, to that extent he ceases to be his own master. In the worst cases, a man loses control over certain parts, or over all, of his being. He comes under the power of an alien volition.

There are dramatic instances of this in Scripture and I have seen virtually comparable cases in life. There is the case of the man who came to Jesus and said, " 'Lord have mercy on my son, for he is an epileptic and he suffers terribly; for often he falls into the fire and often into the water.' And Jesus rebuked him, and *the demon came out of him,* and the boy was cured instantly." Matthew 17:15,18.

It was the alien presence of the demon in the boy that seized him and threw him into the fire or into water and tore him with convulsions. As soon as the demon was cast out of him, the boy came into unchallenged and unbroken control of all his faculties.

You are endowed with certain faculties, and God wants you to enjoy full command and control of those faculties. Satan does not. That is why evil spirits seek to cut in on a man's own power over his actions and thoughts and to take them over by as much as they can.

It may accurately be said that demons work to wreck or to damage human beings physically, mentally, morally, emotionally, and spiritually. They have many programs to these ends, and there are many stages, and also many kinds, of demonic activity.

The powers of evil under Satan understand the nature of man quite well. Since man was made in the image of God and was meant to be a perfectly balanced tripartite being—spirit, soul, and body—demons seek to damage or to destroy human beings

>—in their minds and emotions (the region of the soul)
>—in their bodies
>—in their spirits.

Not every individual is made the object of demonic activity aimed at all these areas. Demons may find a person unsusceptible to their strategy for the damaging of his physical being—he may refuse things harmful to his body and be diligent in taking care of it—but may find him open to their strategy for ruining him morally: He may succumb to their temptations. Or they may find him open to their strategy for ruining him spiritually: He may believe their lies.

The demons know the interrelatedness of all the parts of a man's being and if they cannot get a man one way, they are content for the time being to get him in another—knowing that any way they get him will work to the advantage of their over-all program.

Getting a man one way can become the avenue of getting him in other ways later. By goading a man to do what is morally wrong, for instance, demons may adversely affect his emotional or physical well-being.

Evil spirits are skillful at turning an advantage gained in one area into expanded gains—even at parlaying it into death. I know a man who has a physical affliction whose most potent enemy is liquor. Yet he likes liquor. He stays away from it most of the time, but every once in a while he puts a few under his belt, and when he does it takes him down a notch. It is not hard to see that he is being destroyed by quarter inches. Liquor does not have a very big hold on him, but it is enough of a hold to be a death grip.

The stages and degrees of demonic control are so varied that they cannot entirely be categorized. Among the many stages are those that may be described as: oppression, obsession, and possession. Evil spirits oppress some people, obsess others, and actually possess others.

You may know people who are oppressed by demons, yet be unaware of what is troubling them. You may know people obsessed by demons. You may have met people who are possessed by demons.

If you are acquainted with young people today, those in their teens or early twenties, you may know cases of demon oppression and obsession without having any idea of the cause of it.

Such people are under the influence, or the control, of evil spirits in one, or two, or more chambers of their being. There is little that can help them except the power of God. Psychiatrists can do very little, often nothing, to help them. What can be helpful is the pinpointing of their trouble as the work of demonic spirits, if that is actually the case, and an expert dealing with the matter on that level, by someone who is qualified to do so, since demons can be identified and cast out.

The Bible speaks of many kinds of evil spirits, identifying them by their varying propensities and by the effects they produce in those they afflict. There are spirits of fear . . . foul spirits . . . spirits of error . . . perverse spirits . . . unclean spirits . . . spirits of jealousy . . . spirits of whoredom . . . lying spirits . . . spirits of infirmity . . . spirits of emulation.

There are also deceiving spirits, sadistic spirits, scheming spirits, spirits of murder, suicide, destruction, violence, accusation, addiction, malice, hatred, and race hatred. There are spirits of divination, and the Bible speaks many times, and always warns against, "familiar spirits." This is but a very partial listing.

God's purpose in the creation was that the body of a man should be nothing less than the house of God, in which the Holy Spirit dwells. What a wonder that is. What a basis for continuous fellowship between the Creator and His marvelous creature, man.

Satan's counterplan was to wrest that body and those faculties for his own desires. Initially, he uses demons to tempt men and persuade them to devote their faculties to doing what is evil. But his deeper desire is to violate and defile the human body by making it the dwelling place of evil spirits.

Behind both of these is his intention to separate men from God and to ruin them, in this life and in eternity. His policy has succeeded with millions of individuals and it is succeeding *en masse* today.

The important question is how do demons succeed in putting into practical effect Satan's program for man? There has to be a basis for them to do so.

There are four major avenues through which demons gain access to, and a degree of control over, human beings:

> Demons gain control through sin.
> Demons gain control through unbelief.
> Demons gain control through false religion or false worship.
> Demons gain control through alcohol, narcotics, hallucinogens, or other chemical agents.

Demons gain access and control through sin because sin is the will of Satan carried out by human beings. The process begins with temptation—a temptation to theft, to anger, to jealousy, to lust, or anything else—and if a man's will gives way to that sin, *a basis for demonic activity in his life along that line is created.*

Demons gain control through unbelief because unbelief seeks to ignore or deny the central fact of the universe, that God Is. It is an attempt to obliterate the knowledge and fear of the Creator from His Creation. It is the most drastic and elementary and outrageous lie about the nature of the universe. Satan seeks to set up a basis of life that rules God out as totally unnecessary and irrelevant. The Scripture declares that Satan "the god of this world has blinded the minds of the unbelievers" so that they remain ignorant of, and indifferent to, God the Creator during their lives. II Corinthians 4:4a.

An unbeliever's entire life is founded upon a lie, and everything that he does, whether apparently good or bad proceeds out of that lie. The Scripture therefore says that "what is not of faith is sin." Romans 14:23a.

Demons gain control through false religions and false worship of every kind because these are the most express contradiction of the will of God, that He alone be worshiped and that His truth be believed. Satan stands behind every form of religion not revealed by God, and many of the practices of such religions are specifically demonic. They are all designed to lead men into spiritual bondage or keep them in it, and there is no liberating power in them. They are set up to give demons sway over men and they prevent men from finding reconciliation to God.

The role of alcohol and various narcotics and chemicals in making men accessible to the work of evil spirits is taken up, separately, in another chapter.

When temptation is presented to your soul, it is Satan seeking an entrance into your being for sin or for demons. Because of the activity of the human conscience, many men have a very good sense of that which is right and that which is wrong. Yet at times they may become involved in very severe battles to keep from doing what is wrong. At such times, when demonic powers are working hard to draw a man into sin, and when the conscience is aroused to resist, the will of the man is subject to the suasions of opposing spiritual forces, and he must choose between them.

"Resist the devil and he will flee from you," the Bible declares. Temptations are unpredictable in their coming, but they are not permanent. If demons do not succeed in getting a man to sin, if he resists the temptation, the power of it will suddenly be broken and the temptation will be gone. That which is experienced as the breaking of a temptation is, in fact, the demons fleeing in defeat. They will return later with the same or some other line of temptation. The interval may be brief or it may be quite long.

Evil spirits, bent on using men to carry out Satan's will, do not prefer such contests as their mode of operation. They are made too subject to resistance and defeat. They prefer to gain control over a man and over one or more of his faculties, so they can *use* that man, as their victim, to do their will.

From Temptation to Possession

Satan's program is to start an individual off in sin in *any* way he can, perhaps in some very small way, perhaps in some very sudden and unanticipated way, and then, in time, to escalate him in sin, to graduate him to new degrees or depths or forms of sin.

He thus obtains a man's consent to sin by degrees, and if he can take him far enough he can get him into sin so deep that he can't get out of it—except by turning to God in full-hearted repentance.

It is an almost inevitable rule of sin that it pays off at a steadily diminishing rate, so that you have to have more and more of it to get the same result as time goes on. In the same process, its pains and sorrows steadily increase.

There may be, at the start, a considerable reward or gratification in sin. Later, diminishing rewards set in, the sin becomes habitual, and some of the pain begins to be experienced. There may be heavy guilt, depression, oppression, bondage. There may be objective consequences that press in upon or blight a life for years. The area of the sin may be expanded in a number of ways—in frequency, in intensity, in the degree of compulsion, and especially by involving additional people. Finally, the sin may become dominant in a person's life until he is ruled and run by it. Now the person is addicted to sin. He cannot break it. That is the point of possession.

For some individuals, the giving in to demons on a certain line of temptation is the first step that leads to possession. By using temptation to gain an individual's voluntary compliance to sin, Satan may succeed in opening up an avenue of entrance for demons, first into a person's experience, later into his being.

Temptation is the most common work of evil spirits and, as it proves effective, it may be succeeded by the more severe stages of demonic activity aimed at individual men—oppression, obsession, and possession.

No sharp line can be drawn between demon oppression and obsession. Obsession is oppression amplified and intensified. Demon oppression may take many different forms; it is usually experienced in the moods, in the feelings, in the emotional state, and also in the mind. The same is true of obsession; the difference is in degree. Oppression may be cyclic; obsession bears down hard and knows little, if any, relief.

Oppression may take the form of various moods that come over a person. An individual has a spell of gloom or deep melancholy. It may come suddenly or without any apparent reason. It occupies the seat of his emotions and to some extent governs his actions, perceptions, and responses. For a time the individual walks under a cloud of melancholy, or experiences a kind of flooding of his emotions. He may make an important decision affecting his life while under the influence of this emotional oppression.

Human beings were never intended to be ruled or run by transient emotions and moods, but that has become a part of their victimization under the reign of sin and Satan.

I knew a man several years ago who had long been plagued by a particular line of evil thoughts. He did not want them but they seemed to occupy his mind daily. This baffled him, troubled him, and sometimes made him miserable. Then, at last, he cried to God for deliverance. Others prayed with him for that, and the plague of evil thoughts stopped. I met him several years later and he said that he had not been troubled since.

When these thoughts were dealt with at their demonic source, his afflicted mind was cleared. For a man under such mental torment there was no way out, except by the power of God.

When a man believes a lie of any kind—whether it is in the realm of religion or science or philosophy or politics or any other line —and acts upon it as though it were true, he walks in deception and delusion. This becomes especially painful when he thoroughly believes some lie about himself. Some people bear crushing loads of inferiority, for instance, and this false conception obstructs and limits and hampers their lives. It changes their conduct from what it would normally be, and imposes much suffering upon them. Such a state of mind and feelings may be the direct, intentional work of afflicting demons acting upon the thoughts and the emotions.

Satan seeks to introduce various kinds of evils into the human consciousness, and he desires that lies be made pervasive. In this, he uses direct demonic suggestion, and he also uses human communication.

Demons dwelling in the atmosphere charge the air with evil thoughts and present them to men's minds. Suddenly, seemingly from out of nowhere, a surprising thought, or an evil thought or impulse, flies into the mind. We become aware of it with a mild shock of recognition. It is not native to us, it is foreign. It did not originate with us, it was introduced.

Satan wishes to get the human mind down under the power of such conceptions. If a man accepts lies or evil thoughts, he may become a victim and also a transmitter.

There is a massive assault upon the minds of young people in the United States today. Some of it comes from the supernatural realm directly. Some of it comes from individuals who receive various evils by demonic suggestion and then use mass organs of communication to spread them.

This attack on the mind is brought to its highest state when a nation is overmastered by a ruling clique, which uses all the organs of communication to assail the public's mind continually with brutal lies.

You have perhaps read how, for a long time in China, it was virtually impossible for a person to avoid a nearly continual bombardment of the thoughts of Mao in public places. In trains, Mao's thoughts were sung by passengers from song sheets distributed to them. Loudspeakers blared his thoughts into the streets. Tens of millions of copies of his thoughts were disseminated and the Chinese carried them like Bibles. The thoughts of Mao were lies, big lies, but a system had been devised by which such lies could be presented to men's minds with little surcease. Vast populations are thus brought under deception and delusion.

Evil ideas sometimes have a dynamic energy that commands attention and impresses them forcefully upon the mind. That energy lies in the fact that they are demon-originated. There is a genuine degree of "inspiration" in such lies. They are inspired by Satan, not by God.

It became necessary for me, during my reportorial investigation of Daniel Burros, the Jewish Nazi and Ku Klux Klan leader, to spend a day reading through a table heaped with extreme right-wing literature. It was an unpleasant experience because nearly all of it was shot through with lies informed by hatred. The material seemed to be a kind of political pornography.

That night, as I went home, I became aware that certain fascistic conceptions of race superiority and race inferiority, of who was racially good and who was racially evil, had lodged in my mind in a way that actually affected and distorted my perspective, and I could not instantly shake these ideas off. I was a bit alarmed that such ideas as that, under which I had never labored, could prove to be at all tenacious. It took about two hours of conscientious effort before these lies, to which I had been concentratedly exposed through most of a working day, were dislodged. By that I became aware of how it is possible, in societies like Nazi Germany and communist China, for mass delusions to be imposed upon a population, when official lies are poured out incessantly and urgently through all the media, bombarding the consciousness relentlessly. No contrary belief is permitted a public breath to dispute the official "truth."

Our nation, fortunately, is not under the dictatorship of any militant clique determined to enforce its lies by imprisonment and death, so that we do not have a single mass delusion upon us, but if any individual lives under a delusion he is not greatly better off. There are plenty of delusions extant in our society and they are increasing and taking over minds.

Since lies and evil thoughts may come to the individual by direct demonic suggestion (a kind of whisper to the inner ear), or by seeing something evil, or hearing something evil, or reading something evil, Satan uses all these means in mounting his assault upon the mind. Those places from which truth ought to be emanating, such as the pulpits, have given so much ground to various fads of the intellect and to outright lies that they do not have the power to countervail error.

Thoughts, of course, precede actions: an action is formed in the mind before it is carried out. Satan has greatly multiplied the evils now commonly available to the mind—in printed form, in motion picture depictions, in the lyrics beamed out by radio day and night. He intends to produce in actual practice some of that which he is now so assiduously sowing in the minds of millions.

Satan and the demons center much attention on the human

mind, and no one escapes some form of demonic activity aimed at the mind.

One definition of the word "obsess" is: "to dominate or preoccupy the thoughts, feelings, or desires of a person; beset, trouble or haunt persistently or abnormally."

Some of the things that are being shown in popular films today center strongly on the abnormalities of which obsession, and even possession, are compounded, as this morning's copy of *The New York Times* again reminded me: A picture called "Paranoia" is advertised as featuring (and these are in bold capitals) "Debauchery, Perversion, Sadism, and Fright." Another is advertised as showing the actions of "a totally amoral person who shoots heroin (even under her tongue!), cavorts in the nude, lies, steals, makes love to girls, and destroys every man who falls in love with her." Such a litany of unnatural acts! The newspaper's motto, "All the News That's Fit to Print," presupposes that there are some things that are simply not fit to print. The pledge affords nothing to the reader if what is barred from the news columns is blazoned in the ad columns. A double standard of morality is no standard of morality.

But what is more important is that there are at least seven things in those two short lists that are basically demonic and out of which demons are able to bring terrible afflictions for man, including obsession and even possession.

I remember sitting one day in the first-floor office of a man on the West Side of Manhattan and he said, pointing out the window, "Do you see that man walking by?" I saw a tall, rather thin man about thirty-two years old wearing a tan jacket. "Two years ago," he said, "that young man had a full-time job. One day I noticed he showed signs of having dope in him. Pretty soon he had a part-time job. Some days he'd be all right and some days he'd be doped up. Now he doesn't have any job, and he's doped up nearly all the time."

That illustrates, in a graphic way, the steps that lead some individuals from freedom to possession. The man had formerly enjoyed the use of his faculties and could apply them rationally to meet his needs, but now his faculties were necessarily devoted to the procurement and injection of a narcotic. He had become a slave.

People can be obsessed and possessed by things far less material than narcotics but not much less potent in their effects.

Demon obsession takes many forms. It may express itself in

phobias, extreme complexes, fetishes, fixations, perversions, extreme moods and feelings (of a dark and evil character), and acute fears. There are people who labor under these things as truly as the addict labors under the compulsions of dope.

Fear is very often directly produced by the activity of demons and it should be resisted. There can be vague, almost nameless, fears, and there can be knife-sharp, highly distressing fears. They are meant to reduce human efficiency by setting up barriers (unseen but no less formidable) to full, free activity. Fears have a tremendous inhibiting power. When fear seizes a person it can stop him dead from doing what he needs to do or ought to do, and what he would do if fear was not there. Fear is often a form of demonic resistance applied to the soul.

Perhaps the most extreme form of inhibiting fear is expressed in the life of the recluse. Some years ago in New York City the Collier brothers set up thick barriers of newspaper piles inside their town house in Manhattan and left only tunnel-like passages through the piles, to keep them safe from the outside world and intruders. One of the brothers exited and entered through the passages only in cases of emergency or inescapable need. They withdrew from all participation in society and normal life, obsessed by fears.

While crawling out through a passage, the slightly more active of the two recluses tripped a trap, bringing piles of newspapers down on him. Since he could not move, he died there in his own trap. Deep inside the house the other man slowly starved to death. The thing intended by them, in their obsession, to be their means of protection became the means of death. They were betrayed by acting according to their fears.

Evil spirits are expert at persuading individuals to believe some false conception about themselves. By repeating it continually to the consciousness of a victim, they turn it into a fixation. Though the conception is not fact, it becomes as good as fact.

In addition to repeating it, they are able to present a series of outside confirmations of what they tell the person to be true about himself. They may tell a person directly, "You are worthless," or "You are ugly and unloved." They repeat it and repeat it until it is adopted as truth and acted on as objective fact.

From the outside such individuals begin getting confirmations of their disabling misconceptions. People seem to snub them. They are walking in the street and they hear someone say, "Well, look at *her*," and they fit it right into the pattern, as proof of the delusion. A good deal of that may be a seizing upon meaningless or wholly irrelevant details and fitting them right into the picture. Yet demons work together for the discomfort of human victims, and it is entirely possible for a person with a demonically inspired fixation about himself to meet a person who will say something specific to strengthen that fixation. Such a person may speak at the immediate prompting of evil spirits.

In the building in which I formerly lived there was a man about thirty, always neat and presentable in appearance and always silent and glum in expression. I was told by another occupant that he was a brilliant electronics specialist who did not have the confidence to take the work that he was fully qualified to do. Instead he did odd jobs in electrical and radio repair shops for his living. It was clear that the man was living under a terrible weight of inferiority that checked him from ever rising to his normal level of achievement. He was living under a delusion. He was not bound in his body, but he was bound in his conceptions. That bind placed an entirely unnecessary limitation upon his life.

A person like that, who could be making a high salary with some well-established enterprise, virtually skulks from place to place and is very likely to be led to take work in some shabby shop where the owner is of a disposition impossible to please, given to blurting things like "Can't you do *anything* right?" and—*voilà!*—the demon-persecuted man has daily confirmations of his near-worthlessness from the petty shop tyrant under whom he works.

It is a reality little suspected that evil spirits use men to do their work, as far as men will let them. They speak through men. They act through men. Satan is "the spirit who is *at work* IN the children of disobedience."

A bind becomes stronger and harder to break out of the longer the misconception that prompts it is accepted and obeyed, until at last it becomes a fixation.

Another category of demonic activity is driving men: Some men are driven by ambition, and they are driven by it so hard that they inflict much damage, along their upward path, upon other people. Some men are driven to dominate others and, if possible, to hold them in fear. Some men are driven to achieve an almost impossible perfection and, in the process, others are subjected to gross inconvenience and pain. In still more peculiar forms, some are driven to be free of germs and much of their life becomes a labor to that end. Driven men are often, though not always, miserable, and they have an unusual capacity for inflicting misery on others.

It is the privilege of a man to rule over, to govern, his own spirit, forbidding evil passions—anger, envy, hatred, bitterness, jealousy, a lust for power—to reign within him and to use his faculties as their means of expression. If a man gives way to such things as these with scant restraint, he gives occasion to demons to come in and take over parts of his being.

Seizures and Binding

There are many, many degrees of demonic interference with the use of human faculties—from occasional and partial all the way to total.

Some individuals who are afflicted with demons must engage in many of their waking hours in a painful and very difficult struggle for the free and efficient use of their faculties, and often they must somehow limp along with only half, or less than half, of the full use of some parts of their being.

Any kind of seizure of human faculties, by which they are taken over from the primary control of their owner—whether it affects a man in a physical, mental, moral, or spiritual way—may be a result of direct demonic activity.

Demons can and do attack human beings in their nerves and their muscular systems, as well as in their minds. Sudden experiences of acute nervousness, unexplained by any immediate or outward circumstances, can be caused by direct demonic attacks. If this proceeds far enough, it can ultimately lead to nervous collapse.

In this kind of attack, a person's own volition ceases to govern his bodily responses, and he finds that something is happening to him that he cannot control. He would have a better chance at controlling it if he understood its source and withstood it on that basis, claiming back the full control of his bodily resources.

Some people are kept in an almost constant state of nervousness. They rarely get even a few moments of full relief. Demonic suggestions to the mind can also have a part in this.

I was sent to cover a hippie event—mainly an electronic rock concert—on the Mall in Central Park one summer day, and there I talked with a tall young man, pleasant-looking and entirely pleasant in demeanor and also obviously intelligent, wearing a kind of gypsy clothes and some beads. The most obvious thing about him was that he was extremely nervous. This showed in a quavering of his voice and in the shaking of his hands. He had got into some demonic realm in his hippie life and he was already paying a price in high nervousness and tension.

I know another man, a former magazine writer, who can no longer hold a steady job. Since our original meeting three years ago I have met him on the street or in the subway about five times, and I have never encountered him when he was not exhibiting symptoms of the most intense nervousness.

There is a more extreme form of demon control. It is the full, acute seizure, in which evil spirits convulse or throw the body of the man they occupy, or make him do bodily harm to himself or attack others. Seizure is a very good word. It is the seizing of control of a person's muscular and nervous systems from him by another force and employing them against him, against his will. Epileptic fits may be in this category.

I was riding on a bus in upstate New York one afternoon when a woman about twenty-eight years old got on and sat three rows in front of me. About once every forty or fifty seconds a shudder passed through her shoulders, her head would jerk, and she barked once or twice like a dog. In every other way her behavior and movements were ordinary and apparently normal. She was a victim of brief, regular seizures, which must have made her life one of indescribable misery.

The uttering of animal sounds involuntarily is a recurrent phenomenon among some persons under demon control. At one of the big pop-rock summer festivals a group of young people had a barking session.

In taking control over the faculties of men, demons sometimes use them in extreme or violent or speeded-up ways, and sometimes they use them in quite another way: They slow them down or stop their functioning.

Both of these effects can be seen at times in a single individual. There are demons that take control of the faculties of hearing and speech in men and cause them to be deaf or dumb, or both, or to stutter terribly.

On one occasion, Jesus said, " 'You deaf and dumb spirit, I command you, come out of him, and never enter him again.' And after crying out and convulsing him terribly, it came out. . . ." Mark 9:25b,26.

The same demon produced two extreme, but opposite, effects. While it went undetected it had the power to prevent hearing and speaking in the victim. Just as the same demon was to be cast out, it cried out through the victim and convulsed him. When the demon came out, the boy could hear and speak and soon he was in full motor control of his body. This is not to say that all deafness is demonic in its cause, but some deafness is.

The demonic action opposite to convulsions is that in which the evil spirits freeze human faculties, so to speak, rendering them immobile so that a person cannot use them freely. This is best described as binding a person.

Though its sources are unseen, it is as real in its effects as a binding with chains. An extreme form is paralysis. But there are less extreme forms in which the individual is tightened up and cannot express himself freely and fully through his faculties. His facial expression may be frozen, he may be unable at times to smile, or to speak freely, or to move about with ease.

There are some people who are physical cripples, and everyone can see that, but there are other people who are psychological cripples. They cannot use their non-physical faculties any more efficiently or freely than a man with a sprained ankle can use his foot and leg. The interior pain of that condition is, in its way, as severe as the physical pain of the man with the sprain.

Moreover, there can be an interrelation between and among these conditions. A physical crippling can affect the emotions and the mental conceptions of a victim.

In some forms, this binding takes the mode of a deformity of posture. There is a man who regularly passes through my New York neighborhood who is terribly bent over and whose right shoulder is thrust up abnormally high. To look up he has to turn his whole face sidewise, and you see one eye cocked upward. He is extremely religious and will not cross a street without making the sign of the cross several times. His religious fixation is as demonic as his deformity undoubtedly is. He is bound in body and bound in spirit.

The Bible says that Jesus was "teaching in one of the synagogues on the sabbath. And there was a woman who had had *a spirit of infirmity* for eighteen years; she was bent over and could not fully straighten herself. And when Jesus saw her, he called to her, 'Woman, you are freed from your infirmity.' And he laid his hands upon her, and immediately she was made straight, and she praised God. But the ruler of the synagogue, indignant because Jesus had healed on the sabbath, said to the people, 'There are six days on which work ought to be done. Come on those days and be healed, and not on the sabbath day.' Then the Lord answered him, 'You hypocrites! Does not each of you on the sabbath untie his ox or his ass from the manger, and lead it away to water it? And ought not this woman, a daughter of Abraham, *whom Satan bound for eighteen years,* be loosed from this bond on the sabbath day?' " Luke 13:10–16.

Her affliction was not primarily physical. It was primarily demonic, with the physical effect of binding her and keeping her bent. In the most extreme form of binding, the person is rendered virtually inanimate and mute, a victim of the catatonic effect of demonic occupation.

Whether by seizure of binding, the will of the person is not sovereign over certain events affecting his faculties.

Evil spirits may affect, or control, a man's thoughts, his actions, his beliefs, his health, his feelings, his speech, his drives, his passions, or any other critical sector of his life and being.

A man who is possessed by a demon or by demons does not have control of himself in the area in which he is possessed.

Demons of anger and envy and other passions occupy some human beings. When they do, they can cause their own perversion of spirit to agitate and rule the human mind and spirit on a virtually uninterrupted basis.

Persons who are occupied by demons are driven and compelled to do things they know they should not do.

A while ago a boy wrote to a minister with this complaint: "When I catch something alive like a fly or a moth or a mouse I pick it apart. I know this is wrong. I don't want to do it, but I can't help it. Can you help me?"

The boy who wrote that letter recognized that his conduct was virtually involuntary. Some evil had a persistent grip on him that he could not overcome. He was beginning to realize that the problem was bigger than he was, and that is a start. The demons may be more powerful than the man they occupy, but God is more powerful than the demons. And some of God's servants are able to cast demons out of people who have them but do not want them.

Entire Possession

A man who is demon-possessed does not do the will of God, he does not even do his own will. He does the will of Satan. For more than fifteen years a short, raggedly dressed woman in late middle age with iron-gray hair, walked up and down the streets of the neighborhood in which I live nearly every afternoon and evening, shouting angrily in rapid-fire, staccato bursts. She used a rolled-up newspaper as her megaphone. There was an electric quality to her speech, and most of it was in garbled words.

Nearly every day, from early spring until late fall, a man about the same age would come and stand on the corner and endeavor to stop pedestrians, especially women students, and tell them he was messiah. He was there, six days a week, from morning to dark, doing this.

These people were not doing their own will; both were possessed by demons and both were driven daily, for years, to spend themselves on the sidewalks on such futile errands. The regularity of their appearances was metronomic. These are examples of full possession and use of humans by demons.

One night I was out with a group of college students and ministers, speaking from a portable pulpit to a small group of people. A man about twenty-five years old came along, stopped, got down on his back in front of our pulpit and lay flat, and began screaming. After a while, he sat cross-legged and made loud noises. Then he got up and did a kind of dance. Finally, he tried to stand on the pulpit. It was an extraordinary performance until it was interrupted by a policeman who came by and took him around the corner. We then continued, after ten minutes of the most absurd and strenuous interruptions. The mere fact that the words of the Scripture were being spoken publicly at that place had turned this passerby on, so to speak, or had turned the demons in him on and made them put him through a series of wild gyrations designed to drown out what we were saying and seize the public attention. Much of the content of what he shouted, it should be noted, had to do with a Far Eastern religion.

When a demon occupies a man he can use that man, and one or more of his faculties, with which to express himself. It pleases Satan exceedingly when he has made a man over into an automaton of sin, when evil spirits have seized a human body and can use it to act out their passions.

There are varying stages of demonic occupation. Just as paralysis can be anywhere from partial to total—from a hand up to the entire body, involving one part, several parts, or the whole—so it is with evil spirits.

A person may have one evil spirit who possesses him in one area of his being. He may have a number of evil spirits who possess him in that area or in more than one area of his being. Or he may have many evil spirits who effectively possess him entirely. Mary Magdalene, to whom Jesus appeared first after His resurrection, is described as a woman "out of whom he had cast seven devils." (Mark 16:9; Luke 8:2.) When Jesus asked the man in the tombs his name, he said, "My name is Legion, for we are many."

So evil spirits may possess a man in some, several, or all aspects of his being, and in those areas he is overmastered by them and does their will.

Satan's Three-Part Program for the Young

If you were to make a survey of a hundred American adults over thirty-five years old and were to ask them if they believed in the activity of supernatural spirits, a heavy majority would say no. If you put the same question to a hundred Americans between seventeen and twenty-four years old, a majority would probably say yes—and that is a big clue to the generation gap. The older people mainly think there is no such activity. Many of the younger people *know* there is.

We are going to find the key to what is happening to so many young people in this area, and if we do not face that fact, we are not going to be able to meet the difficulties into which they are so rapidly falling. Nor are they.

While with one hand Satan has taken away the truth of God and the joys of true supernatural experience from this generation, he has with the other hand brought upon it a vast new traffic in false mysticism and in contact with evil spirits.

A few weeks ago I was visiting the offices of a company where I have some friends. I had come to know a number of persons there. But I had not met the young Jew (twenty-three years old) in the following brief account, though I had seen him in the place. It was 5:30 P.M. and I was about to leave when a friend said, "Wait. Leonard Marks is sitting in the back corner. He's crying. There's something wrong and he says he wants to talk to you."

"Who is Leonard Marks?" I asked.

"You'll recognize him," he said. "Just go back and talk to him. Maybe you can help him. He had a nervous breakdown a few months ago."

That part of the office had closed for the night and it was dark there. I walked back and found the young man sitting on top of a desk, with tears in his eyes. I recognized him as a bright, vividly alert, energetic young man who had been working as an assistant to several executives.

"What's wrong?" I asked.

What came in answer didn't make sense. "I want to be the flag-bearer on the new Cobra helicopter," he said. "The Cobra is different. It's going to be a force for good. I'm a member of the new generation, and I want to be the flag-bearer on it."

I tried to get him to explain what being the flag-bearer would be, but he said he was a member of the new generation. "I have ideas, new generation ideas, that this company needs," he said. "I want power here." A moment later he talked about becoming "President of the United States." Then he described himself as "a member of the Mod Squad."

"Why did you ask me to come back here to see you?" I asked.

"You know about the supernatural," he said.

"Yes," I said. I talked to him directly and quietly: "Leonard, this thing that's got hold of you is out to destroy you."

His head fell. "Yes, I know that," he said.

A moment later he was talking a stream of nonsense again.

"This is not Leonard speaking," I said. "Leonard is not doing the talking here." His chin dropped to his chest again, and after a moment he said, "No, you're right. It's not me." I was trying to call him from his unreality back to reality. It seemed that he would come out for a moment and be rational, but then lapse back and the delusion that had got hold of him would take over his mind again. He could not get three straight, intelligible sentences out of his mouth.

I knew that something had pulled him off the track and I began to have an idea what it was. "What have you been taking?" I asked.

"I took marijuana on Saturday night," he said. "I haven't taken any LSD. I've had marijuana a few times."

He said he did not intend to take LSD and that he thought he would not take any more marijuana because—and this is especially significant—he now believed it was possible for him "to experience the supernatural without marijuana."

The other side of that, obviously, is that *he had experienced the supernatural by taking marijuana.*

Then he left that theme and began to tell me how he had found it possible to seduce almost any girl by a whirlwind campaign including great personal attention, kindness, carefully selected gifts (ascertaining what she liked and then going to any length to find exactly that thing), doing together the things she liked best to do. The technique was to show every outward evidence of a genuine affection, having in mind, however, the single object of seduction at each step.

He talked about meditation next. He said that he had taken up the practice at home of just sitting, gurulike, and letting his mind wander in daydreams, fantasies. He had read *The Prophet,* he said, and several books on mysticism, psychic phenomena, yoga.

"My father took all the books away from me four days ago," he said.

Later one of the executives told me that everybody liked Leonard, that he had always been a good, quick worker, but that lately he had "gone off on a lot of grandiose ideas." He had taken a memorandum written by one of the executives, revised it, and told a secretary to have it mimeographed and distributed in his new form.

"When did all this begin with you, Leonard? All this meditation and psychic stuff?" I asked.

"It started about a year ago when I watched the Maharishi Yogi on television one night. He was laughing and giggling a lot and, I mean, there was something wrong with him," he said.

"What was the next step?"

"Yoga, mind over matter, psychic energy, books. I sat on the edge of my bed at home, daydreaming, and I got all these great ideas. Listen, if I could put some of them into action it would really be great. I have an idea for a new way of running this company. . . ."

I warned him that if he did not get back to reality he could lose his mind. For almost four years he had been able to hold a good job in an executive office of the company, but then suddenly his behavior and speech had become strangely erratic. The process that threatened his stability was not hard to trace. He happened to see a guru on television. That got him interested in meditation, yoga, the occult, psychic phenomena, and he went out and bought books on these things—nearly every book rack has them—and began to read heavily in these areas. He took marijuana several times.

All of this had been brought into his life—a life that was well organized and on the way to effective participation in adult responsibilities—and in the course of a year it had carried him to the point at which he had had a nervous breakdown and to the point at which unreality had partly seized his mind. He suffered a second nervous breakdown that month. The process had eaten deeply into his ability to think and act rationally, if only at intervals.

Here was a young man who had begun to be undermined in critical areas of his being by factors that are increasingly present in our culture.

In this account I have changed the name, to protect the individual, but the conversations are verbatim. This bright young Jew, obviously full of prospects, stood in danger of becoming a victim of spiritual and supernatural forces—real forces—now loose in our society.

Because he is a Jew, the shock effect of these forces hit him faster and harder than they would have hit a Gentile—for reasons I shall go into later. Under the suasions of the demon religions of the East he had suffered two nervous breakdowns in a year.

Notice three specific things in the life of Leonard Marks which, in his early twenties, had carried him to this point:

First, involvement with the mysticism of the East.

Second, taking marijuana.

Third, the sin of fornication.

There you have it: *Fornication . . . marijuana . . . mysticism . . .* the three-part program of Satan for the young people of this nation today, and he is pushing it from every side in a highly concentrated attack. It is this demonic program whose effects are felt at high school and college campuses all over the nation. And it is this program whose effects on teen-agers and young adults have made them susceptible to violence and disorder.

You cannot go onto the major college campuses without being made aware of this three-pronged push. It is in the campus papers, on posters, in leaflets, in discussion groups, in magazines aimed at young people, in the bookstores, in the demands of student rebels, in the air. And, of course, much of it is also in that favorite medium of the young, the motion pictures.

Each of these three things can open an avenue for demons into the inner being of a young person. All three together provide a basis for a crashing influx of evil spirits, full of potent disintegrative effects.

I use the term marijuana to cover what is broadly called "the drug scene." The big push for marijuana began about 1966, as did the push for LSD and the hallucinogens.

On its heels came the big push for "the wisdom of the East," for "transcendental meditation," for gurus and Eastern mysticism and Hinduism, for the paraphernalia of idolatry and the supernaturalism that goes with it. By 1969, cruder forms of demonic supernaturalism—occultism and witchcraft—were coming conspicuously on the scene.

The big push for the throwing down of parietal rules inhibiting social, and especially sexual, communication between young men and women in college gained considerable momentum in 1967 and 1968.

Anything that increases the possibilities of, and the temptations to, fornication fits into Satan's purposes perfectly, and he supports it with all the zeal and skill of his genius for promotion (advancing apologies and encouragements, contrary to the word of God, from all kinds of supposedly expert sources) because this sin is useful to him in destroying human beings.

Students clamor to be left alone in dormitory rooms long enough and late enough so they can go to bed together if they wish without prospect of interruption or subsequent reproach. Unlimited opportunity for free love ("the practice of having sexual relations without legal marriage or any continuing obligation") is at the core of the demand. Off campus, students live together as man and woman without any commitment to each other for the future.

Any one of these three things—premarital or nonmarital sex, Eastern mysticism, and marijuana or LSD—supplies a basis for direct demonic activity in the lives of those who indulge in them. Combined, they provide the basis for a massive invasion of demonic spirits. Thus students are softened up for the push for anarchism, rebellion, insurgency.

As these three things also reach down into the high schools and the junior high schools, similar conditions of disruption and destructiveness will break out there, as they have begun to do. It is the tragic result of the increasing degree of influence and control that demons have gained in the lives of young people through sin.

Part V

Mysticism, Mediums, Witchcraft, and Magic

A Victim of Magic

Cases of demon-controlled persons show a remarkable consistency whenever and wherever they occur. I have noticed that such cases—whether encountered in New York in the 1960's, or in Zurich in the 1950's, or in China in the 1930's, in Europe more than a century ago, or in the Biblical accounts of almost 2,000 years ago—are strikingly alike in their salient particulars.

A missionary to Europe and a former missionary to China, neither of whom knew anything of the other's experiences, gave me accounts of their dealings with demon-controlled individuals that matched in point after point. And these accounts were consistent, even in some of their least ordinary details, with many others that I read about or heard or saw at first hand.

The pattern of tremendous consistency that ran through account after account reflects the supernatural reality separately encountered by many individuals, widely scattered in place and time. Demons are about the same in their manifestations wherever and whenever they are found. Their powers are used against their victims in ways that have remained the same throughout human history.

A friend of mine, Frank S. Boshold, has just completed a translation into English of an extraordinary document: an account by a German Lutheran minister of his harrowing, and ultimately successful, effort to bring relief to a demon-possessed parishioner.

The account, made by the minister as his official report to the Synod of Württemberg, was later published in Germany under the title *Blumhardts Kampf.* It will be made available in English under the title *Blumhardt's Battle: A Conflict With Satan.* I have permission to quote portions of it here. They show the range of effects that may be suffered in an extremely serious case of molestation by evil spirits.

The writer is Johann Christoph Blumhardt (1805–1880). The victim for whom relief was sought was Gottliebin Dittus. The events described occurred in 1842 and 1843 in Möttlingen, Germany.

"When she prayed at the table . . . she had a fit in which she fell to the floor, unconscious. What was heard was a frequently recurring trampling and scuffing in the bedroom, the living room, and the kitchen. At times these noises lasted all night . . . Gottliebin saw with special frequency the figure of a woman . . . holding a dead child in her arms. . . . This woman, she said, would always stand at the same place in front of her bed and at times would move toward her. . . .

"I decided to make an investigation in the house. I made a secret agreement with the mayor of the town, carpet manufacturer Kraushaar, a sensible, sober, and God-fearing man; and several men of the town council. [We] arrived, unexpected, around ten o'clock in the evening. . . . As soon as I entered the living room, two immense bangs met me from the bedroom. In a short time, others followed. Noises, bangs, and knockings of the most varied kind were heard, mostly in the bedroom, where Gottliebin lay on her bed, fully dressed. . . . In the space of three hours, twenty-five bangs were heard toward a certain spot in the bedroom. They were so loud that the chair leaped, the windows rattled, and sand fell from the ceiling. Villagers at a far distance were reminded of the shooting on New Year's Eve. . . . Everything was checked in greatest detail but no explanation could be found in any wise . . . as soon as something was heard she usually would fall into violent convulsions. . . .

"On a Sunday night I went there again when a number of her women friends were present and silently watched her terrible convulsions. I sat down at some distance. She twisted her arms, turned her head to the side, and bent her body up high. Foam flowed again from her mouth. . . .

"It hurt me to think that there should be no means of help in such a horrible affair. . . . I jumped forward, took her stiff hands, pulled her fingers together with force as for prayer, loudly spoke her name into her ear in her unconscious state and said, 'Fold your hands and pray, "Lord Jesus, help me!" *We have seen long enough what the devil is doing, now we also want to see what Jesus can do.*' After a few moments she awakened, prayed those words after me, and all convulsions ceased, to the great surprise of those present. This was the decisive moment which pulled me into activity for the cause with irresistible power. Before I had not the slightest thought of it."

Pastor Blumhardt, having seen that the case lay beyond the power of physicians to relieve, took the matter on at the level on which it actually was—the level of supernatural conflict. Almost immediately, he became the object of counterattack.

He found that "something hostile in her was directing itself against me. . . . She clenched her fists. . . . close to my eyes as if she wanted to rip out both of my eyes quickly. . . . Finally the whole thing passed when with great force she thrashed repeatedly. . . ."

The writer tells of a later visit: "When I went to Gottliebin's house with my usual companions (because I never wanted to go there without reliable eye and ear witnesses) . . . she herself was lying on her bed, was conscious, and felt no trouble. Suddenly it seemed as if something went into her and her whole body got into motion. I then prayed some and mentioned the name of Jesus. Immediately she rolled her eyes, banged her hands together, and said with a voice which could instantly be recognized as not being hers, not only because of the tone but because of the expression and character of it, 'I cannot stand to hear that Name.' . . . Many threatening words were spoken against me. . . . Those present, including the mayor, received many a knock and fistblow which however were never dared against me as the demons expressly stated that they were not allowed to do anything against me, the pastor, even though they would have loved to. Here and there she tore her hair, threw her head against the wall, and tried to hurt herself in many ways."

The minister cast out fourteen demons on one occasion. "After those fourteen demons were expelled, the number climbed quickly to 175, then to 425. I cannot give a detailed description of the individual scenes since everything happened too quickly. . . . After the last of those battles, quietness came for several days. But at night many figures pressed around the bed of Gottliebin, according to her statement. Also a nurse said she had seen several figures at that time. One night, in her sleep, she felt herself suddenly seized on the neck by a burning hand which left huge burns. When the nurse (her aunt) who slept in the same room had lighted a light, she saw that huge blisters, already filled with liquid, had risen all around her neck. The doctor, who came the next day, could not refrain from marveling at it. The neck did not heal until several weeks later."

One afternoon Gottliebin "heatedly demanded a knife. Her frightened brother and sister would not allow a knife to get into her hands. Then she ran to the attic, jumped on the window sill, and already stood outside in free air, only holding on with one hand on the inside, when the first flash of lightning of the approaching thunderstorm met her eye, frightened and awakened her. She came to and cried, 'For God's sake, I don't want to do that.' The moment of light disappeared and in the returning delirium she took hold of a rope . . . and tied it skillfully around the beams of the attic. She made a noose which easily pulled tight. She had nearly forced her whole head into the noose, when a second flash of lightning caught her eye through the window. As before it brought her back to consciousness. A stream of tears flowed from her eyes the following day when she looked at the noose hanging from the beam. She could never have tied it as skillfully in the best of consciousness.

". . . The patient sank backwards as usual when demonic attacks came on her. . . . Suddenly the wrath and ill humor of the demons broke loose with full strength [against the minister] and many statements like the following were heard, mostly in a howling and wailing voice, 'Now everything is lost! Now everything is betrayed! You disturb us thoroughly. The whole alliance goes to pieces. All is over. Everything is confusion. It is your fault with your constant praying. Woe, woe. You will yet drive us out. All is lost.'

"During the course of the following days it became evident that by far not all the demons had been removed from the patient. . . . She would often lie as dead while her breath was held from within her. . . . Also sometimes she was so paralyzed that she could hardly move a member of her body by her own will. . . . With other spirits

which identified themselves from then on, there seemed to be a
question of what was going to happen to them. . . . They had a
terror of the abyss which they felt near now and said, among other
things, 'You are our worst enemy, but we, too, are your enemies.
If only we could as we would!' And then again, 'Oh, if only there
were no God in heaven!' . . . The patient was tortured incessantly.
Her body would often swell extraordinarily and she would vomit.
. . . She also received frequent blows on her head, knocks in the
side, and in addition suffered from heavy nosebleeding. . . ."

On February 8, 1843, Gottliebin "lay on her bed nearly all day
. . . caught away in her spirit into far regions. . . . It seemed to her
that someone led her with extraordinary speed over land and sea.
She was floating above the surface. She flew through many countries and cities, passed over ships in the ocean whose crews she
could clearly see and hear talk, until she came to a world of islands.
She floated from island to island. Finally she came to a high mountain on whose pinnacle she was set down. On the summit was a
large, wide opening out of which spewed fire and smoke. All
around her lightnings flashed, thunders rolled, and the earth
quaked. In the coastal areas at the foot of the mountains she saw
that cities and villages were overthrown and the dust rise up high.
On the ocean, ships and other conveyances went into confusion
and many of them sank into the water. In the middle of this scene
of horror the demons which had tortured her most up until then
were brought forth. The worst of all, the demon with the immense
book, was the first to be cast headlong into the abyss with great
roaring and screaming. After him about a thousand others followed, all of whom rushed upon Gottliebin as if to try to drag her
with them into the abyss. When all this was over, Gottliebin was
brought back in the same way as she had gone there and awakened,
rather terrified, but otherwise well. I cannot guarantee what she
told here but I was astonished and surprised above measure when
a short time later newspapers reported in detail about the terrible
earthquake which happened exactly on the 8th of February in the
West Indies. . . . I cannot keep silent about what relationship the
earthquake of that time had with the battle here, also the weather
and other things. The drought of the year 1842 and the excess of
rain of the year 1843 were mentioned by the demons. The thing
that horrified me most was that the many fires in cities (the demons put the number at thirty-six) were directly related to the
influence, even the direct work of the demons. One demon especially came to the fore which pretended to have fanned the flames

of Hamburg with special ravenous lust. I asked him what had caused him to do this. He answered with one word, 'Lust.'

"It was shown that things without number in the body of Gottlie- bin had been, to use the only word possible, charmed into her body, all with the intent to put her out of this world. It started with vomiting up sand and small pieces of glass. After a while all sorts of pieces of iron came out, especially old and bent boardnails. Once, after much retching, twelve of those fell into the bowl held under her, right before my eyes. . . . Beside those an unaccounta- ble amount of pins, needles, and pieces of knitting needles came out. . . . I always had several eyewitnesses with me. I insisted upon this without fail in order to prevent evil rumors. [The objects] could be brought out only through prayer. . . . There were so many objects that I could not enumerate them all . . . even living animals came out of her mouth."

Delivering the patient from objects that had been introduced, unknown to her, into her body led Pastor Blumhardt prayerfully to consider how this might be, and the following excerpt shows how perceptive he was:

"During the many battles which I had to go through after the one just mentioned, I thought a great deal about the way and manner in which the magic powers were used. I felt a need to be able to think at least of some explanation for myself. Of course I thought that there are still secrets about the essence of matter which philosophy has not found out with surety. I thought if matter was a conglomeration of a kind of atoms, as already many philoso- phers thought, then magic would be, I supposed, nothing else but a secret art taught by the sinister power, how to dissolve the bonds between the different atoms in order to make the object which is being used unrecognizable, even invisible. Then it enters with other things, for example ordinary food, where the person who exercises this art wants it to go. Then the dissolved bonds are re-established there and the object appears the same as it was before.

"Thus Gottliebin could well remember from former times that once in a while she would immediately feel something strange in her throat or in her body after having eaten a soup or other dishes. Once she tossed a leftover of such a meal to a chicken. Immedi- ately the chicken ran around like mad and after a while fell over dead, as if suffocated. She opened the neck and head of the chicken and to her horror there were a lot of shoenails."

On one occasion blood came "out of both of her ears, both of her eyes and her nose and even out of the upper part of her head. That was the most gruesome thing I have ever seen. . . . At first I did not know what to do, but I collected myself and, after a short, serious sigh of prayer, the bleeding stopped for the time being. . . . On the front part of her head above the forehead, I noticed something and soon a small, bent nail bored itself through . . . from now on the bleeding stopped."

A missionary whose veracity I cannot doubt told me that she had discovered that objects were introduced into the bodies of human victims by the powers of witchcraft, and she showed me half a dozen pieces of metal which she said had come out of the bodies of persons who had come to her for help. The objects are "planted" into the body at least partly to bring damage or death to the victim and perhaps also partly as the token of a kind of claim of Satan upon the individual.

". . . This all leads up to the fact that there are people who have the art of being outside of their bodies, in the spirit, probably not always while completely conscious."

All of this magic has its root, Pastor Blumhardt concluded, in "the sin of idolatry, which by steps leads up to magic and complete black magic."

"Idolatry may be considered every reliance on a supernatural, invisible power, based upon which a man is attempting to obtain either health, honor, gain, or pleasure, as long as this power is not purely divine. . . . Slowly I learned to get a glimpse into the horrible consequences of all of this idolatry. The first effect is that a man becomes more or less bound to a sinister Satanic power. This happens through a demon which wins influence over him because it is enticed through the act of idolatry. . . . A man without knowing it and without noticing it, is bound in spirit by Satan so that the spirit, of course a psychological mystery, can be absent from the body even though the soul, as it seems, is present in the body.

". . . Most of the witches and warlocks to whom are ascribed all kinds of misfortune, disease, plagues of men and cattle, are what they are in this capacity, without their knowledge. The most would be that once in a while they have a feeling of what they do in the spirit without being able to explain this feeling. In any case, they are highly unfortunate people, and from this follows that the accusation of a living person [against a warlock] is unmerciful as a rule and must be rejected. . . ."

The purpose of the plagues and misfortunes that come upon victims because of magic "is none other but to drive these people into a corner so that they in turn will also use superstitious and idolatrous means in order to be caught in the snare themselves." In other words, they try to "change their luck"—to trade in bad luck for good luck by using the various means of magic.

According to one definition magic is "the art of producing a desired effect or result through the use of various techniques, as incantation, that presumably assure human control of supernatural agencies or the forces of nature." With it go magic spells, magic rites, magic words, enchantments, witchcraft, hexes, communication with the "dead," and a wide variety of other practices and means. There is in it, no doubt, very much quackery and fakery, but there is also a potent realm of magic that produces real effects. That which is not fake in it is all very ancient, and it is all demonic and Satanic.

Magic, has, Pastor Blumhardt writes, "a series of steps: On the lowest level are those who, as the saying goes, are being used in magic itself and thus become ensnared without being conscious of it from then on. The highest level is black magic proper in which the person serves Satan with full consciousness and who grants him these powers.

"In the middle between the two categories are those who make a trade out of the use of magic means. . . . Usually they use printed booklets . . . which are revelations of Satan proper."

"This third category of magicians can speak their formulas and do their manipulations for a long time with the seeming consciousness of being benefactors of mankind, even in the reputation of great piety, although always with a bad conscience. But they are being ensnared deeper and deeper through their heathen practices and therefore the danger of becoming black magicians proper comes closer and closer. Closest, although probably still deceived, are those who receive, if I may say so, demons from the devil which become their counselors and which demand the name and age of people looking for help and through which the magicians inquire. These demons appear to them, either visibly or invisibly, through certain means which they use, including mirrors."

In the months before he fatally wounded Robert F. Kennedy, Sirhan Sirhan steeped himself in the lore of occultism and magic. The assassin's prolonged experimentation with mysticism, and his use of a mirror, was detailed in the long aftermath of that jarring event.

In his bedroom, Sirhan spent scores of hours reading about the

Middle East and the occult. He described about twenty books he read during the year preceding the slaying, dealing with metaphysics and the power of the mind.

In an article titled "Sirhan Through the Looking Glass," *Time* reported: "A mirror. Two flickering candles. And Sirhan Sirhan. Alone in his cramped room, day after day, hour after silent hour, Sirhan studied Sirhan. Mail order courses in Rosicrucian mysticism had given him a new creed. They told the disturbed Christian Arab that he could unlock from the mirror image of Sirhan Sirhan the inner knowledge, happiness and power he craved.

"Focusing his mind power on the looking glass, Sirhan soon convinced himself that he could order an inanimate object to move. He rigged a pendulum from a fisherman's weight, and on command, he said, it began to sway. Yet telekinesis—the ability to cause objects at a distance to move through the exercise of will—was a frightening power, and Sirhan feared that he might lose his mind. Once, instead of his own image in the mirror, Sirhan saw a vision of Robert Kennedy, the man he was soon afterward to kill.

"The candles swayed and changed color. . . . One key to the killing," according to the psycholanalyst, Dr. Bernard L. Diamond, "must be found in Sirhan's arcane experiments with the mirror. It was during his self-induced trances, Diamond said, that Sirhan scribbled over and over that 'Kennedy must die.' "

Dr. Diamond, who also holds professorships in law and criminology, described the act as murder in a trance. He said he had made Sirhan relive the killing in his prison cell by hypnotizing him with a coin held eight inches from his eyes. He testified that, as Sirhan fired an imaginary gun "convulsively again and again," his face bore an expression of "the most violent contorted rage."

It would seem probable that, through the devices and rituals of magic, Sirhan unknowingly incurred an alliance with demons who were able to drive him to insanity and murder. His private aberration had public consequences that cut close to the heart of our national life.

Returning to the Blumhardt account: "The demons answer the questions asked of them, of course not without an interest in the reign of darkness. Thus it comes that Christians ask advice at the mouth of Beelzebub (II Kings 1:2–4). Black magicians proper are those who, so to speak, have made a formal pact with the devil. This can happen individually or through joining certain societies whose foundation is such a secret pact. In both cases the signing of the name with blood takes place. This is done by cutting the finger or some other part of the body and using the blood which flows to sign one's name.

". . . What black magicians are looking for is mostly good fortune, lust, money, and protection against bodily dangers. The arts they possess are of many kinds. They are able to provide money for themselves . . . they can kill people hundreds of hours away, and strokes of which often the healthiest persons die can be the consequence of a magic stroke from a shorter or longer distance. They also start fires without being seen. Of course, I have to leave everyone to himself as to what he wants to believe of these things. But alas, the horrible surety I gained of their existence! However, a battle against these sinister powers, begun by faith in Him Who crushed the head of the serpent, could never be but victorious. Our Lord is still greater!"

This assertion about fires checks with an event from my experience. I lived for six years in a large building in New York City in which there were no untoward events until a series of fires began in it. For a period of a little over a month there were frequent fires, sometimes more than one in a day. Each time the fire alarm would clang throughout the building, there would be a scurrying to evacuate, the firemen and their apparatus would come and put the blaze out, usually before any extensive damage was done. The number of these fires went up and up. They broke out on various floors, in various rooms and apartments. Their number reached twenty in not much over twice as many days. An investigation was started but it did not produce any clear-cut leads. Twice a small group of the occupants met for prayer. On the second of these occasions a minister who had come to the building at the request of a tenant said that, while he was in prayer about the fires in the building, he had seen as in a vision a certain individual setting fires. He said that he took authority over that individual in the name of Jesus Christ and bound him in the spirit from setting any more fires. It was, to say the least, a surprising assertion. Yet he made it with quiet assurance, as a man who knew eactly what he was talking about. From that day on, the fires stopped. The source of those fires was not apprehended by the investigators, the whole thing was beyond them. Certainly the source of those fires was driven to set them by the temptations of Satan, and spiritually effective action was taken in prayer to cut in against this demonic prompting to touch off fires.

I am also certain that fire is one of the things that Satan, the destroyer, likes to use against man when he has opportunity. He needs human beings to be the agents of fire. War is full of the use of fire. Though it is true that it was but what they had sown, the firebombing of Dresden in World War II, in which more than 32,000 civilians died in a storm of fire in one night, had just that quality of fiendishness in it that suggests a demonic inspiration.

Returning to Pastor Blumhardt's account: "The impressions I gained in the course of the battle were always immediate and remained not understood for a long time. I left them in their raw state for the time being, but collected them in my spirit until finally they all fit into a horrible coherence. Not until the end of the episode did I get clarity on the whole and on the details.

"Finally I was led to the conclusion to think of a certain Satanic plot according to which all of mankind was to be drawn away after the plan of the devil, slowly, unawares and with deception, in order for the reign of Satan to become more common and the reign of Christ to be destroyed."

As to why Gottliebin Dittus had become so singularly victimized by evil spirits, the minister found the influence of magic or witchcraft present from her earliest childhood on. Gottliebin told of "circumstances from her childhood which point to the fact that she was lain in wait for, in order to implicate her in the net of magic. . . . Soon after her birth she was in danger of being carried away invisibly. Her mother, who died ten years ago, often told her she had the child by her side in the bed and in her sleep she suddenly feared for the child, awakened, did not feel the child and called out, 'Lord Jesus, my child!' Then something fell to the floor at the bedroom door; it was the child. The same thing happened once more in a similar way. . . .

"Soon the child was sent to a cousin who was generally feared as an evil person and who once said to the seven-year-old child, 'When you are ten years old, I will teach you something worthwhile.' This age is usually mentioned as the time of possible initiation into magic. She also said, 'If only you did not have the name of Gottliebin (literally, lover of God or beloved of God) and had different godparents, I would give you great power in the world.' Similar sayings caused the child concern. In her quiet thoughts she always remembered the verse, 'Our Lord is great and of great power and it is beyond understanding how he rules.'

". . . Once in a while sympathetic means ["magic predicated on the belief that one thing can affect another at a distance"] and magiclike medication were used on the child when she was sick. This is why, like others, she was pulled into the net."

But, having been instructed in faith in the living God by her pastor and her parents, the girl shunned everything that tended in the direction of magic. She had been, as it were, marked for involvement in magic and introduced to it and "she was to be misused according to the principles of darkness to plague others. . . . But her spirit . . . withstood the insinuations of darkness through which she drew its hatred upon herself. There resulted, it appears, a sort of tension between her and the sinister realm which, as it has the desire to be unified in itself, went after her as a deserter. Now the question was to ensnare her really into magic, and at that into the deepest magic, because she only seemed safe for the devil in this way; or to do away with her lest through her resistance a disadvantage to the sinister realm result."

As a young woman, with both parents dead, she had the care of a brother and a sister and was very poor. Once she had nothing but some bread in the house and only ten cents "but when she entered her room, the floor was covered with thaler pieces. She was frightened and moved them with her feet in order to see whether they were really thalers." A while later, the thalers vanished. ". . . She preferred, as she said, to remain in the most bitter poverty rather than to be made rich by the devil. . . . Before I knew of the above things, I heard the demons say, 'What a shame that this girl does not want to take anything. We always put it so carefully for her.'

". . . Gottliebin came home once, when once more neither she nor her brother or sister had any food in the house. She was disquieted and discouraged when she entered her living room. To her surprise she saw a man's shirtsleeve full of flour. Besides this, a large coin was wrapped in paper and lay on top of the flour . . . she kept the flour and money not without thanking God for them, although she could not discover the giver even though she asked all around.

"Later, however, she ascribed most of the magic spells which occurred in her to this flour. . . . One demon later on actually said that it all had been Satanic deception and that she should not have eaten this flour. . . . These happenings give the clue, so to speak, to the whole story. To begin with we have to do with a soul which resisted Satan although it already felt his bondage. She felt herself bound to one side, the Satanic, with a certain power and her heart sought for the other side, the divine. . . . Thus the battle began which drew ever widening circles because darkness did not want to give in and because even in the Satanic realm one member hangs together with the others and everything is very closely related. Thus, no matter how insignificant the person was, all of hell could be stirred up by and by."

When Pastor Blumhardt was drawn into the battle he determined not to allow Gottliebin Dittus to "become the victim of darkness at any price. I could only do this by not trying any other means except prayer which held fast to the invisible divine power. Satan was constantly trying to do away with Gottliebin's life, especially when the secret of the Satanic deception became more and more evident. This seemed especially to infuriate the demons. . . . For this reason a removal of the person seemed to become ever more necessary in order that the dark powers could make their survival sure. . . . The attacks on Gottliebin's life became more gruesome every day. As every object smuggled into her body had the purpose of killing her, she also tried much to commit suicide, as a rule, however, without being conscious of it. Beside what was told above, she hanged herself once in the woods with her scarf. Without knowing what she was doing, she carried together stones in order to hang high enough and then she tied the scarf artfully to the tree. She had already hung, when the scarf broke and the violent fall brought her to. On the same evening, without my knowing the above, one demon called out of her, 'What a shame that this girl cannot be killed. She hung herself and the rope had to break.'. . . In all of these and similar things the name of Jesus overcame, sometimes only the mention of the promise in Mark 16:17,18 or Philippians 2:10.

"The desired end of the story came during last Christmas (the 24th to 28th of December of 1843) when everything that had happened before seemed to come together once more. The worst part was that in those days the sinister influence also worked on the half-blind brother and another sister, Katharina, so that I had to fight the most desperate battle with three at the same time . . . they were days the like of which I hope never to live through again . . . . I clearly felt a divine protection so that I did not feel the slightest tiredness or weariness, not even after forty hours of waking, fasting, and wrestling [in prayer]. The brother was free the fastest and in such a way that he could immediately help me actively from then on. . . . The worst attack came on her sister Katharina who had before never experienced the least of such things. But now she raged in such a way that she could only be held with difficulty. She threatened to tear me into a thousand pieces and I could not dare to step too close to her. She made incessant attempts [to harm herself]. . . . She chattered and cried so terribly during that time that one could think of thousands of blasphemous mouths united in hers. The most striking thing was that she remained completely conscious so that one could talk to her and so that she said, when strongly admonished, that she could not act or talk in any other way and to please hold her quite firmly lest anything happen through her. And even afterwards she had the clearest memory of everything, even of the most horrible attempts of murder."

A demon "spoke out of her. [It identified itself] as a prominent angel of Satan, as the chiefest of all magic, which had received power from Satan for this work. . . . It stated that the deadly blow to magic was given now that it had to go into the abyss. . . . Suddenly, toward twelve o'clock midnight, it seemed as though it beheld the open fiery abyss. Then out of the girl's throat roared several times and lasting for about a quarter of an hour, only one cry of despair with such violent strength that it seemed the house would collapse. Nothing more horrible can be thought of, and it could not be but that half of the town's inhabitants got knowledge of the battle. . . . Even though the demon seemed to be all fear and despair, its defiance was, nonetheless, no less gigantic and it demanded of God to give a sign because it would not go out until a sign had been given from heaven that would shake the entire town so that it would not have to lay down its role as commonly as other sinners but, so to speak, go to hell with honors. Such a horrifying mixture of despair, malice, defiance and pride has hardly ever been seen anywhere. In the meantime its expected destruction seemed to be prepared ever more rapidly in the unseen world. Finally the most moving moment came which no one can possibly imagine who was not an eye- and earwitness. At two o'clock in the morning . . . the girl bent back her head and upper part of her body over the backrest of the chair, with a voice of which one could hardly have believed a human throat capable, [and cried] 'Jesus is Victor! Jesus is Victor!'—words that sounded so far and were understood at such a distance that they made an unforgettable impression on many people.

". . . That was the point at which the battle of two years came to an end . . . she slowly came to complete health. All her former illnesses which are well known to the doctors were completely healed . . . her health became ever stronger and more durable. [Gottliebin Dittus became a teacher of children marked by] insight, love, patience, and kindness. . . . Now that a school for small children is to be built, I cannot find a person who would be as suitable as she to lead this school."

Six years later, Pastor Blumhardt wrote of her continued stability, health, and usefulness.

Witchcraft in America

Possibly at no time in this century until the present would the account in the previous chapter have seemed even remotely germane to life in the United States. To many, undoubtedly, it will yet seem to be a horror story out of a distant place and time, hardly relevant to their own concerns. But the startling fact is that, as dreadful as it is in its details, everything in the account bears a direct relation to certain things now occurring in the United States.

For every evil effect described in the foregoing account, there is an occult practice that corresponds to it. A short time ago there came to my mailbox, unsolicited by me, the catalog of a dealer in occult and metaphysical literature. As I leafed through it, I read of promises of mysterious powers and of various practices that bore an amazing correspondence to the things told by Pastor Blumhardt. "These," I remarked, "are the causes of those effects." In short, there are formulas and dark powers in the occult realm that can bring about these terrible results in human lives. There is supernatural power—power capable of producing an impact on individuals and events—behind such practices, and that power derives from their nexus with evil spirits.

There has nearly always been a certain amount of spiritualism, possibly also of witchcraft, practiced in the United States, but for the most part it has been off in remote and obscure corners of our national life and it has rarely enjoyed widespread public favor. Lately, however, we have watched a rising vogue in occultism, astrology, magic, the work of mediums, witchcraft, and the like.

For quite a while it was entirely the fashion in this country to hold that there were no such things as witches—individuals who practice various kinds of magic or black magic—and I dare say that anyone who had ventured to assert, ten or twenty years ago, that there *were* such individuals would have been regarded as hopelessly medieval. Now we are faced with the fact that there are witches who say they are witches.

Though it is still decidedly a minority phenomenon, witchcraft is now practiced quite openly in the United States and it has been getting a fair amount of publicity.

Accounts have appeared in newspapers, magazines, and books in the last two years in which persons who practice some form of witchcraft have told of their activities. The *Daily News,* the New York tabloid newspaper with the largest circulation in the nation, carried a full-page story by Lisa Hoffman, from which I quote in part:

"To moviegoers who saw the chillingly plausible *Rosemary's Baby,* it may come as a disturbing surprise to learn that there really are such things as witches' covens, one of which now operates in an otherwise typical suburban town on the South Shore of Long Island. Long Island holds no monopoly. In fact, [covens exist] elsewhere in New York, in New Jersey, Kentucky, California, Ohio, Washington, D. C. . . . Being what it is, the Craft, as it is known to its practitioners, keeps its membership rolls understandably secret and also the sites of most covens, [each] comprised of twelve couples presided over by a high priestess.

"Don't make the mistake of thinking all this is a piece of arcane flummery. Twentieth-century witches are deadly serious. The chants, the swords, the music, the symbols, the herbs, and the incense are all pretty much what they were in the pre-Christian era of nature cults when the bizarre practice was born.

"The Long Island cult [is] headed by Lady Rowen, 32, and her husband Robat, 34, to give them their cultist names. . . . [They] are white, or good witches [who own] a large collection of books on the occult. . . . The couple, it seems, dropped out of the Church of England thirteen years ago to become disciples of Dr. Gerald Gardner who, until he keeled over on his breakfast tray while reading a book on magic four years ago, was considered the grand old man of British witchcraft.

". . . They were 'remarried' with a ponderous sermon called 'Handfasting.' This boils down to a simple promise to be true to each other for 'as long as love shall last.' If love doesn't last, either party is free to go his own way.

"That expedient philosophy is laid down in *The Book of Shadows,* which . . . contains all the rites, spells, charms, cures, and chants.

'Once in the month,' the book says, '. . . gather in some secret place and adore me who am the Queen of all witcheries. . . .' . . . each new witch copies his own book by hand from his mentor's.

"The Long Island coven holds its rituals in Robat's basement. . . . On Halloween, the major festival among the eight holidays on every witch's calendar . . . the witches, all nude, will begin singing and dancing. . . . Members of the coven say that Lady Rowan . . . has often brewed potions that have cured the minor ills of their children." The writer comments that the witches "seem to share a common faith in reincarnation."

Several months earlier the United Press International newswire carried a story from San Francisco on a wedding rite of a witchcraft cult: "Asking the blessings of Lucifer for a union 'conceived in hell,' Beelzebub, a priest of Satan, performed a marriage ceremony last night using a naked woman as an altar. . . . The dark rite was performed in the small icon-filled black-walled living room of Anton LaVey, 32 . . . who bills himself as the first priest of the Satanic church. It was conducted before a stone fireplace, by the light of candles stuck in human skulls. [Of the nude woman] LaVey explained that the altar shouldn't be a 'cold, unyielding slab of sterile stone or wood. It should be a symbol of enthusiastic lust and indulgence.' The bridegroom, 35, had been married twice before . . . LaVey said it was the first time ever for the diabolical ceremony which he said he concocted from his fifteen-year study of witchcraft, sorcery, and Satanism. The rite consisted of bells, gongs, chanting in a magic language from an old book, *The Equinox,* and some play with a sword and chalice. . . . Stuffed ravens, wolves, owls, and rats looked down from shelves everywhere."

You will notice similarities of usage and belief in the practices of the so-called white and the Satanist witches. Both use chants and swords in their rites and both have a book of mysteries whose formulas they follow. Both make a point of nudity (a practice which Satan has been thrusting forward lately in the United States in several forms) and both twist matrimony into little more than an interim alliance for lust.

The Satanist cult worships the devil. The other coven meets in secret to adore "the Queen of all witcheries"—addressing worship not to God, to Whom all worship belongs, but to a demon spirit. This is the utmost violation of the law given by God to Moses.

Mademoiselle magazine made witchcraft the theme of a "Special

Magical Mystery Issue" whose cover promised: "Sorcery and Sex: A terrific tour of spells, charms, witchcraft, and the mysterious East . . . Yoga . . . India's exciting Tantric art. Chilling occult novel complete in this issue." The issue included an interview with Dr. Harry E. Wedeck, a college professor with an extensive knowledge of the history of witchcraft. Unless witches practiced "white magic," Dr. Wedeck said, "their intentions and operations were evil. Commonly they attempted ruin and destruction, even if they didn't always succeed. On request of their 'clients,' they could blight crops, cause livestock to sicken, even cause diseases in humans."

Are there many witches around now, he was asked?

"In the Far East and India, naturally, but there are some in England, rural France, all over Europe, and everyone knows about Haiti. There are witches in this country, too, though they may not publicize themselves as such." Dr. Wedeck said that "India's full of fakirs and mystic writings and magic," and he remarked, as a matter of curiosity, that "once a fakir in Calcutta predicted the next two weeks of my life precisely."

"It's old. It's all so old," Dr. Wedeck said, observing that he had recently read a book translated from a sixteenth-century manuscript, *Chin P'ing Mei,* which mentioned "witchcraft practices, astrological lore, and spells that were precisely those found in Theocritus and Vergil."

"Vergil to a sixteenth-century Chinese text—that's quite a jump isn't it?" the interviewer said, to which the scholar gave this significant reply: "These beliefs are so pervasive that I feel they are not necessarily transmitted one to the other, but develop independently."

It is important to catch the essence of that. It appears that these practices are *not transmitted* from culture to culture, but that they have sprung up spontaneously and independently. The same practices of witchcraft, magic, divination, and the worship of many gods or spirits are discovered in culture after culture between which there has been no human communication.

Dr. Wedeck rather weakly assigned this repetitive coincidence in practices, reaching across broad barriers of time and space and language, to a similarity in human thoughts. That misses the core of it. The fact is that these practices have their origin outside of the mind of man in a single supernatural source: Satan is their author. They are expressions of his religious purposes for mankind. These products of the genius of one mind are transmitted from the spiritual realm into the human realm.

Demons have access to every culture and it is in their power to communicate mysteries of Satan to individuals in each. These are devil-originated practices that have been separately revealed to various cultures by evil spirits from the earliest history of civilization.

That these practices are often identical is an evidence of their supernatural origin and design. They represent the will of Satan in offering human beings a variety of means by which they may seek help or guidance or something they desire, whether good or bad, from powers outside themselves. These powers are all demonic, and the use of any of these practices or means of worship links a man to the supernatural in a way that suits the purposes of Satan.

Certain it is that nearly identical religious ceremonies and trappings have been found in this century among tribes in South America, in Africa, and in the far Pacific. These tribes have never heretofore had contact with the outside world, but they have had contact with demons.

Witches and witch doctors are priests of Satan and they obtain certain powers from him. It is not surprising, as Dr. Wedeck said, that they often attempt "ruin and destruction," since those are exactly the purposes of Satan.

The interviewer told Dr. Wedeck, "Whenever I've read about witches and even in books like *Rosemary's Baby,* there always seem to be strong links between sorcery and sex—and very sick sex at that," to which Dr. Wedeck replied: "Well, witchcraft often attracted people of unbridled or frustrated sexual appetites. And even if you were possessed of neither, you couldn't be a witch unless you gave yourself completely to it. Which meant involving yourself with your coven—twelve disciples and the devil and the Sabbat [defined as "a secret rendezvous of witches and sorcerers for worshiping the devil, characterized by orgiastic rites, dances, feasting, etc."]. The Sabbat always had a ceremonial orgy, ending in a kind of communion, but sexual in nature, with the devil."

That, to say the least, is explicit. The devil desires worship above all else, and this is devil worship carried to the point of "communion" with Satan in orgiastic sex, through witchcraft.

The same issue of the magazine listed a score of books on witchcraft for young women to read, and recommended for "Absolutely dependable divination: A method you can live by," the *I Ching* or *Book of Changes,* a Chinese oracle. In this system of divination, over 3,000 years old, and now appearing in the United States with much publicity, a person throws three coins six times and then, using the result in connection with a particular section of the book, receives guidance. Divination of any kind is part of a demonically revealed system by which men can put themselves in the hands of a higher intelligence for direction or help. The intelligence activating all devices of divination is that of Satan.

Time magazine did a cover story on the many eruptions of occultism in the American culture. Sybil Leek's *Diary of a Witch* was extensively reviewed in the mass media. These are but several examples out of a great many that have been brought to public attention of late. And witchcraft is just one of many varieties of Satanic supernaturalism that have been moving to the fore.

Public interest in such matters is rising, so much so that according to a report in *The New York Times:* "Harvard University's Coop, a huge merchandising mart on Harvard Square, recently opened a paperback book section for books on the occult. . . . Mr. [Roscoe] Fitts said that there had been an increase in interest in the occult, extrasensory perception, fortune-telling, numerology, and mind-expansion drugs in the last six months, enough to set up a new section that includes titles on witchcraft."

This is not an isolated phenomenon. It is becoming a national one, and the curiosity about such things runs highest among the young.

Witchcraft and magic, in spite of their widely assumed non-existence, are suddenly and prominently with us today. These things have not thronged upon the scene by any mere coincidence.

Satan, who could not foist such practices upon the American public while there was still at least the residue of a Biblical faith among the people, has now found the time ripe to bring these dark mysteries swarming in from the East to a decadent American culture.

It is all timed and carefully planned for the weakening of the society and the damaging of thousands in it, and it will increase rapidly among the people. It will only be reversed if there is an awareness of its source and an awakening to faith in the living God. The present tragedy of America is that it has long left the truths of the Scriptural faith on which many of its founders stood, and to which a majority of the people at least gave assent, and that is why America has lost its way.

In domestic and international affairs the nation staggers as though drunken. Its incapacity to devise effective policies is a reflection of the fact that the nation has cast aside the truth and has gone after lies. The lies the population shows itself willing to swallow get bigger every year.

It is useful to make a close examination of patterns present in various forms of witchcraft, occultism, and false religion. Certain things crop up repeatedly among them. One of these is sex in crude or perverted or public expressions, particularly group sex or sex in religious rites. Sexual sins of the grossest kinds are spawned and promoted by Satan *in direct association with occult practices.* Satan loves to corrupt men sexually. He will do it by wholesale if possible.

Other strands running through the fabric of Satanic religious inventions include: the worship of sundry deities and gods; the obtaining of good luck by charms and the promotion of bad luck for enemies by spells; images; shrines; the sale and use of religious articles and objects; chanting and incantations; festivals; the use of incense or the burning of candles before statues and altars; the use of bells and gongs; beads and prayer wheels; obtaining blessings by purchase; dancing into a frenzy; berobed priests; the participation in mysteries through prescribed rituals; extremes of asceticism and of indulgence (in the Islamic observance of Ramadan, a strict fast is required from sunup to sunset, including sexual abstinence, but at night one may take his fill of the things avoided by day).

These and other things belong to the house of idolatry that Satan has set up for all mankind.

Those are *his* altars, not God's. They are *his* practices. This whole vast supermarket of magic, idolatry, and superstition is his substitute for the worship of the living God and for the placing of human trust in Him. God hates these substitutes with fury because He knows that they are devised as means of separating human souls from Him forever.

To those who have no knowledge of such matters the surge of interest in witchcraft and the like may seem to be a bit of a lark, a mild dabbling in the fantastic, a form of escapism, perhaps, in a crowded and perplexing age. What they fail to understand is that any of these ancient occult practices can open an avenue into the supernatural for a person who becomes involved in them. Young people who have a lively curiosity about, or a hunger for, supernatural reality have not the faintest notion of what they are getting into when they consent to go on such "trips."

Demons are able to produce a very wide variety of supernatural effects for human beings, some of them seemingly quite lovely, others harrowing beyond description. They are real effects and they have real consequences of a practical kind. Practical, that is, from the standpoint of Satan, to whom death, disease, insanity, and addiction in men are wholly practical to his ends.

Any commerce with demons, under whatever auspices or designation, whether avowedly good or openly evil, can be costly and damaging beyond hope of repair for those who venture into it. Even a tentative step into this supernatural realm can be desperately dangerous. Yet now the means of introduction are everywhere readily available to the curious and unsuspecting.

I have said that there is nothing in the account of Gottliebin Dittus that does not have its counterpart in the current literature of magic and sorcery and spiritistic phenomena. Does money appear out of nowhere? Within the last month I have seen books on occultism advertised that boast of exactly this. There is an occult formula or practice for everything from which this woman so greatly suffered. These practices are known to some individuals, not merely by theory, but by direct experience. The Scriptures describe some of these mysteries as "the deep things of Satan" in Revelation 2:24.

Some young people are rushed into the demonic supernatural with startling speed. A friend told me a week ago of a young man he knows at work who participated in an experiment in group occultism. During the exercise he suddenly found himself set in a weird scene, as by a vision: He was walking in a long corridor between two rows of Buddha statues that were alive. This frightened him. He broke the spell of it and came back into reality. Almost immediately he had a different experience. He felt himself to be turned into a snake. He described in vivid detail the sensation he experienced as a snake. There was no physical change of any sort, of course, but his perception of himself was transformed by demons who were able to take him over, at least temporarily, because of his participation in the group exercise.

This young man's alarming experience with the Buddhas that seemed alive took him past the natural perception of a statue as a dead object to the fact that there is a direct relationship between religious statues and evil spirits. A statue is, of course, nothing but a dead object, but some demons identify themselves with particular statues and those demons produce the results that are sometimes obtained by addressing worship or prayers to such statues.

That is why sometimes certain statues, which do not look much different from others of their kind, obtain a special reputation for producing a certain kind of result.

The kind of experience this young man had probably would not have happened in the United States ten years ago, but it is likely to occur more and more as such group occult practices conduct young people directly into the realm of the demons.

Occultism and idolatry go together. There is a direct connection between idolatry and demonic supernaturalism, and Satan is the head of it all. It is all a part of his vast conspiracy to overthrow the worship of God.

Those who practice spiritism, so-called transcendental meditation, various kinds of mysticism, the black arts, magic, communication with the dead, psychicism, witchcraft, and many other kinds of demonic supernaturalism commonly use idols and other religious objects in their practices. All of this, whatever name it may bear, whatever guise it may wear, is Satanic in its origin.

Young Jews, adrift from their heritage, need to become aware of the destruction that they will incur to their minds, their bodies, and their souls and spirits by any traffic with these demonic inventions. To do exactly the opposite of what the Hebrew Scriptures command is to court destruction.

"You shall not practice augury or witchcraft. . . . Do not turn to mediums or wizards. Do not seek them out, to be defiled by them; I am the Lord your God." Leviticus 19:26b, 31.

(When he can get away with it, Satan puts terrible torments into rites of initiation and certain religious rites. Some demonic religions put a child through fire to purge it, a practice the Scriptures vehemently condemn. The purgation maimed many children and burned others to death. It is a Satanic religious devising for the harming of the young.)

"There shall not be found among you any one who burns his son or his daughter as an offering, any one who practices *divination, a soothsayer, or an augur, or sorcerer, or a charmer, or a medium, or a wizard, or a necromancer.*

"For whoever does these things is an abomination to the Lord, and because of these abominable practices, the Lord your God is driving [the heathen nations] out before you. You shall be blameless before the Lord your God. For these nations, which you are about to dispossess, give heed to soothsayers and to diviners, but as for you, the Lord your God has not allowed you to do so." Deuteronomy 18:9–14.

"Do not defile yourself by any of these things, for by all these things the nations I am casting out before you defiled themselves. . . . But you shall keep my statutes and my ordinances, and *do none of these abominations.*

"The persons that do them shall be cut off from among their people. So keep my charge *never* to practice any of these abominable customs which were practiced before you, and *never* to defile yourself by them: I am the Lord your God." Leviticus 18:24–30.

"A man or a woman who is a medium or a wizard shall be put to death. They shall be stoned with stones, their blood shall be upon them." Leviticus 20:27.

If God expressly expelled the Gentiles from Canaan because they had engaged in these demonic practices, and gave the land to the Jews, it is reasonable that if the Jews fell into these same practices, the anger of God would be greater against them for it, who had been told never to do them, than against Gentiles.

The people of Israel did drift into such evil religious practices. "They went after false idols, and became false, and followed the nations that were around about them. . . . And they forsook all the commandments of the Lord their God, and made for themselves molten images . . . and worshiped all the host of heaven, and served Baal. And they burned their sons and their daughters as offerings, and used divination and sorcery, and sold themselves to do evil in the sight of the Lord, provoking him to anger. Therefore the Lord was very angry with Israel, and removed them out of his sight." II Kings 17:15b–18.

The same passage says that "the Lord warned Israel and Judah . . . but they would not listen. . . . They despised his statutes, and his covenant that he made with their fathers, and the warnings which he gave them."

The reigns of two kings at Jerusalem stand in contrast. One was Manasseh, the other Josiah. The character of each man was formed while he was in his teens, and it remained quite constant thereafter.

"Manasseh was twelve years old when he began to reign, and he reigned fifty-five years in Jerusalem. . . . And he did what was evil in the sight of the Lord . . . he erected altars for Baal, and made an Asherah . . . and worshiped all the host of heaven, and served them. . . . And he built altars for all the host of heaven in the house of the Lord. And he burned his son as an offering, and practiced soothsaying and augury, and dealt with mediums and with wizards. He did much evil in the sight of the Lord, provoking him to anger.

"And the graven image of Asherah that he had made he set in the house of which the Lord said to David and to Solomon his son, 'In this house, and in Jerusalem, which I have chosen, out of all the tribes of Israel, I will put my name forever. . . .' But . . . Manasseh seduced them to do more evil than the nations had done whom the Lord destroyed before the people of Israel."

Manasseh followed Satan's religious policy, not God's. It brought much trouble to the nation. The religious sins of the king led him also to sins of violence. "Moreover Manasseh shed very much innocent blood, till he had filled Jerusalem from one end to the other" with blood. II Kings 21:1–9,16a.

The timing of the judgment of God is one thing of which men may rarely be sure. Some men are cut off early in their sins, even in youth, while others continue for what seems to be a long time. The Bible says that God "is not willing that any should perish, but that all should reach repentance." (II Peter 3:9b.) Manasseh reigned for fifty-five years. God knew that Manasseh would ultimately repent of his evil. The Scripture says, "He entreated the favor of the Lord his God and humbled himself greatly before the God of his fathers. He prayed to him, and God received his entreaty and heard his supplication and brought him again to Jerusalem into his kingdom [from captivity at Babylon]. Then Manasseh knew that the Lord was God.

"And he took away the foreign gods and the idol from the house of the Lord, and all the altars that he had built . . . and he threw them outside of the city. He restored the altar of the Lord . . . and commanded Judah to serve the God of Israel. Nevertheless, the people still sacrificed at the high places, but only to the Lord their God." II Chronicles 33:12,13,15–17.

Josiah became one of the greatest kings among the Jews because of his fidelity to the commandments of the God of Israel. In his reign, evil religious practices were swept from the nation and righteousness held sway over sin.

"Josiah was eight years old when he began to reign, and he reigned thirty-one years in Jerusalem. He did what was right in the eyes of the Lord, and walked in the ways of David his father, and he did not turn aside to the right or to the left. For in the eighth year of his reign, while he was yet a boy, he began to seek the God of David his father, and in the twelfth year [when he was twenty years old] he began to purge Judah and Jerusalem of the high places, the Asherim and the graven and molten images. [He] hewed down all the incense altars throughout all the land of Israel." II Chronicles 34:1–3, 7b.

"And the king commanded . . . the priests . . . to bring out of the temple of the Lord all the vessels made for Baal, for Asherah, and for all the host of heaven. He burned them outside Jerusalem in the fields of the Kidron, and carried their ashes to Bethel.

"And he deposed *the idolatrous priests* whom the kings of
   Judah had ordained to burn incense in the high places . . .
those also who burned incense to Baal,
to the sun,
and the moon,
and the constellations,
and all the host of the heavens.
And he brought out the Asherah from the house of the Lord.
And he broke down the houses of the male cult prostitutes
   which were in the house of the Lord,
where the women wove hangings for the Asherah.

"And all the shrines of the high places that were in the cities of Samaria, which kings of Israel had made, provoking the Lord to anger, Josiah removed. . . . And he slew all the priests of the high places who were there. . . . Moreover Josiah put away

the mediums and the wizards
the teraphim and the idols

and all the abominations that were seen in the land of Judah and Jerusalem. . . . Before him there was no king like him, who turned to the Lord with all his heart and with all his soul and with all his might, according to all the law of Moses; nor did any like him arise after him." II Kings 23:4–8, 19a, 24, 25.

These ancient practices of occultism, divination, witchcraft, and false worship have not improved with age, nor have they changed much. The Word of God still stands against them because they are the work of an enemy.

New Gods Rush In

In the Old Testament Book of Judges there is a compelling assertion that says:

"When new gods were chosen, then war was in the gates." Judges 5:8a.

It applied to Israel in a former time—when the people departed from the faith revealed to Abraham, Isaac, Jacob, and Moses—and it applies to the United States today.

New gods are swarming into the American culture. Gods that were never heretofore present in the nation are coming in. For that reason there is spiritual warfare at the gates to the nation and the destiny of the United States will depend on whether the people choose to honor God or to honor the gods. There is no god but the God of Israel. Each of the "gods" is a demon spirit.

Every false god competes for worship with the living God, to steal the honor due only to Him.

In the song of Moses, the leader of Israel remembered how the true God had encircled and cared for Israel and "kept him as the apple of his eye . . . the Lord alone did lead him, and there was no foreign god with him."

Later the nation "waxed fat" in its God-given prosperity: "You waxed fat, you grew thick, you became sleek; then he forsook the God who made him, and scoffed at the Rock of his salvation. They stirred him to jealousy with strange gods; with abominable practices they provoked him to anger.

"They sacrificed to demons which were no gods, to gods they had never known, to new gods that had come in of late, whom your fathers had never dreaded. You were unmindful of the Rock that begot you, and you forgot the God who gave you birth." Deuteronomy 32:10b,12,15–18.

It may be said of the United States that from before its founding and through a majority of its decades one God—the God of Israel —was worshiped within its borders. He alone was the God to Whom the nation looked. The God of the Scriptures was proclaimed from its pulpits. There were no other gods among us.

The religions of the nation were Judaism and Christianity and both proclaim the God of Israel as the Creator. The United States was not a nation of many gods, but of the only God.

Now we have an altered situation with "strange gods . . . demons which are no gods, gods we had never known, new gods that have come in of late."

The land is filling up with gods and also with "abominable practices" and they are coming in from the East as fast as Satan can import them.

There are, in the vast and protean pantheon of Satan, multitudes and multitudes of gods—a god for every occasion, every desire, every need—through which man is invited to seek the help of powers above him and to which man is bidden to give honor or worship.

Satan does not greatly care to whom or to what worship is addressed, so long as it is not to God. If a man will not accept one idol or demon god, perhaps he can be persuaded to accept another. Satan works incessantly to misdirect human worship, turning it from God to objects or demons. All worship that is directed anywhere but to Him is a terrible perversion in God's sight. Wherever it is practiced in the world, by many or by few, idolatry is part of the plan of Satan, whose program is to keep men separated from God.

The Satanic forces of darkness are not deployed uniformly among the nations, and demonic activity is by no means equal in all areas of the world. Some nations are under far heavier demonic occupation than some others, and in those areas the activity of evil spirits is far more prevalent and pronounced than in other areas. There are areas in which Satan and his demons have had much more influence, precisely because of the extent of idolatry and false religion and occultism in those places.

The Scriptures reveal that the work of demons has a geographic aspect. In the Book of Daniel there is a glimpse of the activity of the prince demon of Persia, leader of the forces of spiritual darkness in the old Persian empire.

God recognizes the existence of distinct entities called nations, and the Scriptures declare that He has "determined the times allotted to them and the boundaries of their habitation." (Acts 17:26b.) God deals with these geographic and political entities as nations, and so also does Satan. When, at length, the time comes that these nations give themselves unrestrainedly to Satan, and their wickedness multiplies and reaches the point of the grossest indulgence and perversion, God metes out judgment to them and finally closes the books of history on them.

Just as the territory of Job, the man who loved and worshiped God, could not be invaded by Satan and his demons until the hour that God expressly permitted it, a nation may enjoy a degree of divine protection against the demonic hordes. Though Satan had millions of evil spirits at his command, not one of them could breach the wall of protection that God had placed around Job's territory.

The boundaries of ancient Israel could never be breached by foreign troops sent against the Jews at Satan's prompting, no matter how great their number, while Israel was living in obedience to God. God would not allow them to injure His people. Invasions by men and invasions by demons are not necessarily the same, but remember that the incursions and despoliations on Job's property and family by the demons were carried out in part by human raiders. They were men who were available to Satan because of their attachment to sin.

When Israel broke faith with God the nation's protection was gone. Israel was overwhelmed by superior Gentile military forces. The land was occupied and its people sometimes went into captivity and dispersion.

While the people of the United States honored the God of Israel and gave worship to Him, while they widely accepted the standards of the Bible as the standards of public behavior, this nation enjoyed a very high degree of protection from demonic activity.

Certainly there was far less such activity in this country twenty or fifty years ago than there is today, and there is more such activity in the nation now than there has ever been.

The first step in the Satanic takeover of a nation is to draw the people away from faith in God and in His Word. The next stage is to increase them steadily in the indulgence of sin. The third stage is to lead them into false worship and false supernaturalism. The final stage is usually to bring them under dictatorship. We are in the third stage now.

This nation's rising indulgence in idolatry, false Eastern religions, occultism and spiritualism, and immorality gives Satan the occasion he needs continually to loose more and more demons upon the population.

As the United States has departed from the standard of the Word of God, from which it once derived its moral code and its persuasion of human rights, it has permitted a breach to be opened up through which many demons have rushed, bringing in practices that have long prevailed in distant corners of the earth.

In areas of the world where the name of the living God has been received and honored, the Word of God has had a relatively marked influence upon the people. In those areas, Satan's will has been largely overmastered by the refusal of an enlightened people to obey his bidding in matters of religion and morals.

In other areas, where God's name and His Word have not run, Satan has to a large extent had his way. He has set up counterfeits and substitutes for the worship of Jehovah, the One Who Is eternal, and he has persuaded the people to accept them.

For a long time Satan was not able to do as he would with this nation, any more than he was able to do what he would to Job when he complained that God had "put a hedge about him and his house and all that he has, on every side."

But for more than fifty years now the basis on which this nation enjoyed a certain level of divine protection against the will of Satan has been carefully and thoroughly subverted so that now, at last, the barriers which Satan hated are down and he is sending in his reinforcements from the East.

The region we call the East is the primary center of demonic religious activity running contrary to the revelation made to man by the God of Israel, and it is particularly hazardous for any Jew to become involved with its religious practices and objects.

Demons of the East are coming into the United States now, bringing with them the religious teachings and the occult arts with which they have long deceived the people there. That is why on every hand you see the East . . . the East . . . and observe its ways permeating our culture.

In the copy of the *Times* that was on my breakfast table today, there was a feature story with pictures and a six-column headline: "Tibetan Art, Wrapped in Supernatural and Occult, Is Back In Vogue."

The story reported: "George B. Washburn, head of the Asia House Gallery, said, 'In London, youngsters are fascinated by the supernatural—and Tibetan art is full of the mystical and occult.' "

There is no doubt that it is. Tibet is the region in the East in which the most openly supernatural of the false religions of Satan long prevailed. Of all the religions of the world none was more remote from the United States than that of Tibet, until the gates of this nation were thrown open to the demons of the darkness that ruled for centuries there.

In the comment by Mr. Washburn there is a grasp of that mysterious connection between "the supernatural . . . the mystical and occult" and Tibetan art. Accompanying the story is a photograph of an array of Tibetan religious objects, and this pertinent account concerning "the Jacques Marchais Center for Tibetan Art, a Tibetan temple set on three acres of a terraced Staten Island hillside. The caretaker is Miss Helen Anglade Watkins [who told how] Miss Jacques Marchais [Jacques was also her father's name], an actress who became an Oriental art dealer, built the temple as a center for a study group in Tibetan art and religion. . . . Within a few months she was dead. Her husband, Harry Kaluber, a chemical manufacturer, who financed her project, died soon after."

For a Gentile, Miss Helen Anglade Watkins, handling these cursed objects of idolatry proves not to be particularly dangerous; and, in fact, she regards them purely as pieces of art, having little interest in their religious use or meaning. For a Jew, handling them in a study of Tibetan art and religion proved almost immediately fatal.

Moses told the people, "And it shall be, if you do at all forget the Lord your God, and walk after other gods, and serve them, and worship them, I testify against you this day that *you shall surely perish.*

"As the nations which the Lord destroyed before your face, so shall you perish, because you would not be obedient to the voice of the Lord your God." Deuteronomy 8:19,20.

Moses did not speak on his own authority. Rather, he "testified" to the people of the judgment of God in the matter.

"The idols of the nations are silver and gold, the work of men's hands," the Psalmist wrote.

> "They have mouths but they speak not,
> They have eyes but they see not,
> They have ears but they hear not,
> Nor is there any breath in their mouths,
> Like them be those who make them!
> Yes, every one who trusts in them!" Psalm 135:15–18.

This is a very accurate description of the idols of Tibet, as of the other idols of the East. "Like them be those who make them . . . who trust in them," the Scripture says. That is, let them be deaf and dumb . . . without any breath in their mouths . . . dead.

Such a curse falls more swiftly upon any Jews who use dumb objects in religious uses, because the Jews are specifically called to be a people totally free of idolatry. "Do not turn to idols or make for yourselves molten gods: I am the Lord." Leviticus 19:4.

Moses charged the people of Israel in these words: "We came through the midst of the nations . . . and you have seen their detestable things, their idols of wood and stone, of silver and gold, which were among them. Beware lest there be among you a man or woman or family or tribe, whose heart turns away this day from the Lord our God to go and serve the gods of those nations; lest there be among you a root bearing poisonous and bitter fruit; one who . . . says in his heart, 'I shall be safe, though I walk in the stubbornness of my heart.' . . . *The Lord would not pardon him, but rather the anger of the Lord and his jealousy would smoke against that man, and the curses written in this book would settle upon him, and the Lord would blot out his name from under heaven. And the Lord would single him out from all the tribes of Israel for calamity,* in accordance with all the curses of the covenant written in this book of the law." Deuteronomy 29:16–21.

That is why it is so especially deadly for a Jew to dabble in such things. The living God has given His oath to seek such a man "for calamity."

There have been other areas of the world where the liberating influence of the Word of God has been absent, or unheeded, but Tibet, remotely situated between the Himalayas and the Kunlun Mountains is the highest country in the world: Its valleys sit at 14,000 feet above sea level, its peaks rise 20,000 to 24,600 feet. Until the air age the land could be reached only through difficult passes, some 18,000 feet high, and they were impassable for a good part of the year. For a long time Tibet was effectively sealed off from the testimony of the Scriptures to the one true God, and so the demon-gods of Tibet did according to their will. They introduced supernatural mysteries in Tibet of an especially deep and evil kind.

The communist takeover of that unhappy land imposed restrictions upon the religious practices of Lamaism (a variant of Buddhism combined with elements of an earlier shamanistic religion: a belief in spirits who could only be controlled by shamans, or medicine men), but now the practices and mysteries of Tibet have been brought into the United States by certain individuals who have been particularly susceptible to the influence of evil spirits. *The Tibetan Book of the Dead* and *The Tibetan Book of the Great Liberation* are both available in English.

A few days ago I saw prominently displayed in a bookstore those two titles, and nearby the Bhagavad-Gita, the Hindu Scriptures, *Three Ways of Asian Wisdom*, and *Hinduism, Buddhism and Zen and Their*

Significance for the West. Some of the books had photographs of idols for their covers.

I was startled one morning, while riding out on Long Island by train for a news assignment, to look out of the window and see, spread over the paved surface of a former Amoco gasoline station on Sunrise Highway, a collection of about fifteen giant idols, mostly Buddha figures, some of them ten feet tall, displayed for sale there. It was a weird landscape of the East. It was a sign of the invasion of demonic religious practices and objects into this land. The idols of the East are coming in.

"Against whom do you sport yourselves? Against whom do you make a wide mouth, and draw out your tongue?" the Scriptures ask idolaters and experimenters in false supernaturalism in Isaiah 57:4–8,13,15a. "Are you not children of transgression, a seed of falsehood, *enflaming yourselves with idols under every green tree. . . ?* Behind the doors also and the posts you have set up your symbol. *For you have discovered yourself to another than me* [this is a reference to a spiritual union with Satan and demons], and have gone up. You have enlarged your bed, and made a covenant with them, you have loved their bed, you have looked on nakedness. . . . When you cry out, let your collection of idols deliver you!

"The wind will carry them off, a breath will take them away. But he who takes refuge in me shall possess the land, and shall inherit my holy mountain. For thus says the high and lofty One who inhabits eternity, whose name is holy: I dwell in the high and holy place, with him also who is of a contrite and humble spirit."

This Scripture is both a warning against certain common false religious practices and an invitation to leave them all and to take refuge in God alone. The young person who heeds that invitation will find God an all-sufficient portion for every need of life.

When a nation does not want to be flooded with goods of foreign manufacture it erects what are called trade barriers. Such barriers are set at certain levels, past which such goods cannot go. If those barriers are taken down, the goods can enter into and spread throughout the country. Such a barrier is invisible, except on paper, but it is enforced at the gates of the nation by authorized customs agents.

Whether those barriers are up or down, controls, to some extent, the character of the merchandise which is extant in the nation.

It is possible for a nation to have demon barriers surrounding it, which also are invisible, but past which demons cannot come.

Those barriers are established by God. But they depend on the obedience of the people.

It is not God's will that a people be overrun by demons. It is His will that a people look to Him, refuse and reject all of the devices and lies of Satan, and enjoy divine protection against the works of the devil. To keep the barriers to Satan up, there must be a vigorous obedience to God and a vigorous resistance to Satan. When that is true of a people, new gods cannot enter the gates of a nation.

It is a thoroughly documented fact that many of the early settlers of America came here because of their great desire for a land in which God might be worshiped and honored. They came at personal sacrifice and risk, from advanced civilization to a forbidding wilderness. As they honored God, God honored them. Many of the Satanic religious practices and beliefs, and all that went with them, were shut out of this land. America was singularly free of demons, and of idols.

Obedience to God keeps the barriers to demons up. Disobedience to His will and indulgence in sin opens breaches in them and finally tears them down. God will not deny Satan and his cohorts access to a people who have abandoned the standard of righteousness to which they once adhered and have gone over with enthusiasm to the side of sin.

Every time a commandment of God is broken by humans, a crack is made in the wall of divine protection that surrounds them.

When Israel went the way this nation is now going, the prophet Hosea cried out that "the Lord has a controversy with the inhabitants of the land: There is no faithfulness or kindness, and no knowledge of God in the land; there is swearing, lying, killing, stealing, and committing adultery; they break all bounds and murder follows murder . . . I will change their glory into shame. . . . My people inquire of a thing of wood, and their staff gives them oracles. For a spirit of harlotry has led them astray, and they have left their God to play the harlot . . . Ephraim is joined to idols, let him alone. A band of drunkards, they give themselves to harlotry: they love shame more than their glory. A wind has wrapped them in its wings, and they shall be ashamed because of their altars." Hosea 4:1,2,7b,12,17–19.

Harlotry, in Biblical terms, chiefly refers to a people leaving God and going after other gods.

Because of the high degree of public and private fidelity to the truths of the Scriptures, certain kinds of demonic activity, extremely common in the East, were not present in this nation for a very long time. Satan desired to introduce them and he tried at times to do so, but they could not, in fact, be brought in. The barriers were up.

On August 25, 1926, the liner *Majestic* steamed into New York harbor with a young man and an old woman aboard. The young Hindu, Jiddu Krishnamurti, a twenty-nine-year-old Brahmin born at Madanapalle, India, was being brought to the United States by Mrs. Annie Besant, the eighty-year-old head of the international Theosophical Society, who had discovered him, reared him, and then announced him to be the chosen vehicle through which the great "World Teacher" would again speak to mankind.

Mrs. Besant had got this revelation, she said, directly from the World Teacher. She was a disciple of and successor to Mme Helena Petrovna Blavatsky, one of the founders of theosophy, from whom she had learned communication with supernatural beings in a supernatural world—i.e., communication with demons.

As sponsor and herald, Mrs. Besant was a woman of imposing background. She was born in London but, after turning to theosophy, she devoted herself to India, founding the Central Hindu College in Benares. In 1917 she served in no less a position than that of President of the Indian National Congress. For an Englishwoman to have become a leader in the Indian Nationalist Movement was a remarkable achievement. Of Krishnamurti she said, "I have known since 1909 that he is the vehicle of the World Teacher."

Mrs. Besant asked the boy's father for the privilege of rearing him and got it, though later he tried unsuccessfully to take him back in several court actions. In 1909, Mrs. Besant and her associates began the preparation of the body of Krishnamurti for occupation by the World Teacher, and the signs were almost immediately auspicious. Soon, according to a report in the *Theosophist,* the empty body of Krishnamurti lay at the sacred grove at Adyar, India, while he himself was taken away to Tibet for his mystic initiation, after which he returned to his body at Adyar.

"The Great World Teacher resides physically in Tibet," Mrs. Besant significantly explained, but he periodically inhabits the body of a highly spiritual man who thereby becomes his "voice" or "vehicle."

The World Teacher, or Guiding Spirit of the Universe, was

described as the invisible head of every religion—the Hindu, the Buddhist, and the rest. Mrs. Besant sometimes referred to him as the Lord Maitreya.

He "takes possession of a body chosen by himself" and "in that body he performs his appointed work in our lower world," she said. She also explained that "when the World Teacher manifests himself he takes possession of Mr. Krishnamurti's body and Mr. Krishnamurti goes out of that body."

Preparing Krishnamurti for his vocation was no rush job. From the time of her revelation in 1909, Mrs. Besant and her associates carefully reared the young man to assume his appointed role. He was to be used by the World Teacher to combine all religions into one new, worldwide religion, uniting mankind in brotherhood.

Mrs. Besant met some success in India with her project. When he was twelve years old her protégé wrote a small book on the higher spiritual life, *At the Feet of the Master,* which gained considerable fame and circulation. In an official statement Mrs. Besant explained, "Krishnamurti received his teaching while his body was sleeping in Adyar. He went each night, when he fell asleep, to his Master's dwelling in Tibet, and there received, in very simple language . . . his teaching. These teachings were then published in the little book."

In 1911, a supernatural sign confirmed Krishnamurti's future role when "a great coronet of brilliant shimmering blue appeared above his head" to members of the Order of the Star in the East, founded by Mrs. Besant.

On December 28, 1925, in the grove at Adyar beneath the banyan tree, an assembly of 6,000 delegates from many nations heard Krishnamurti. Near the end of his address, he broke off in the middle of a sentence. According to Mrs. Besant, "then another voice, a voice of wondrous sweetness and power, rang out through his lips," and Krishnamurti spoke in the first person as god. Some of the delegates "bowed down to worship him," a news report said.

"Such manifestations will probably increase," Mrs. Besant wrote, "as the body is taken by its Mighty Tenant, and will, I expect, become fairly continuous as time goes on."

In Australia, theosophists, eagerly awaiting the arrival of the vehicle of the World Teacher, built for him a large and very beautiful Grecian-style white stone stadium that looked out through an eight-columned stage onto the Sydney Harbor.

Then, in 1926, Mrs. Besant decided the time was right to bring her protégé to New York, to launch him onto the American scene. Among those who heard of this plan were Mrs. Hannah Lowe, introduced in an earlier chapter, and the Reverend Thomas Lowe, her husband. They were inwardly grieved to hear of it and deeply stirred to pray. Realizing that the weapons of warfare against demons are "not natural but spiritual," they did not rise up to oppose this plan in any public way, but they set aside time to pray to God that He would frustrate such an incursion into this nation by a spiritual influence so patently counterfeit.

"America is ready to listen," Mrs. Besant declared on the morning of the pair's arrival. "Krishnamurti," she announced, "is the leader of the new civilization."

Krishnamurti was no less direct. "I hope," he said, "to make radical changes in America's religious life. I hope for a new civilization with my coming."

"I do not," he said, "preach repentance or the remission of sins."

By the time of his arrival a good deal of excitement had been generated. A series of news reports cabled from Europe had been splashed at length in most of the New York newspapers. A *New York Times* dispatch from Ommen, Holland, on July 29, 1926, reported that at "last night's campfire, Krishnamurti said: 'Walking over the hills of India last winter my Master, the great teacher, lord of all, appeared before me. Since then he has been with me every day.' . . . The initiated say they can tell the brief moments when the World Teacher uses Krishnamurti's body by the changed expression of his voice."

In London, eyewitnesses gave accounts of "the apparent possession by a spirit of J. Krishnamurti." A retired British Army officer told a reporter that a group of 2,000 persons felt an impulse to adoration as they listened to the young man speak. A physicist said he saw "a huge star over Krishnamurti's head burst into fragments and come raining down" on the slender Hindu. Krishnamurti's arrival was also preceded by reports from Paris correspondents describing the quiet elegance of the Indian's demeanor there, the fashionable and immaculate style of his dress, and his interest in tennis and social teas.

On August 21 the *Evening Post* in New York observed, "No healer of the spirit, communer with the occult or teacher of a new religion ever has come to America with the way so well paved for him as Krishnamurti."

It was with this extensive background of upbringing, occult

experiences, and advance publicity that Krishnamurti and his mentor arrived on their errand to the United States. And it was at the very point of entering the gates of this nation that the whole, elaborate demonic production centered on Krishnamurti began to fall apart.

On shipboard, in New York harbor, Krishnamurti complained of what he called the electrical atmospheric intensity of New York and said he doubted that he would be able to meditate successfully there.

During an interview session on ship at the pier, the atmospheric intensity affected Krishnamurti to the degree that "he became so excited as to reach the stage of incoherence." The next morning, *The New York Times* reported, "The 'holy man' proved to be a shy, badly frightened, nice-looking young Hindu. . . ."

On coming into the nation, Krishnamurti encountered a spiritual resistance great enough to make him doubtful of his mission. There was something in the air, invisible but powerful, that stood against him. Plans that had been laid for him to speak in a public appearance in New York were canceled. The next day Mrs. Besant pulled back somewhat from her earlier assertions, explaining that Krishnamurti had not yet come into full possession of his powers. His body had been "visited," she said, but not "possessed." In interviews that day, Krishnamurti was more composed, rather engaging in a bland sort of a way, somewhat critical of the United States—he said its people did not know art—and entirely unimpressive as a potential wonder man. Stripped of certain powers and also of certain demonic signs that had worked for him in India and in Europe, he appeared now to be nothing more than a rather well-bred young man giving out a few innocuous opinions.

Krishnamurti was taken directly to Chicago for a convention of theosophists and the city made him surprisingly snappish. Told by newsmen that his visit had proved to be a disappointment in Chicago, he said, "I don't care a damn whether the people are disappointed or not. It is not for me to say when the spirit of the Master shall manifest itself through me. This Chicago is too busy and shrieking and noisy and crowded to give me a moment for contemplation or meditation. It is no wonder that nothing has happened."

Note that Krishnamurti complained of *bad atmospheric conditions* prevailing in this country. Those conditions rendered him helpless to show the supernatural effects, that, in other nations, had seemed to confirm his mission, both to his followers and to himself. The atmosphere in this country was not, at that time, host to certain evil spirits of the East. Upon entering this country he was cut off from the spirits who had produced those effects in some of his public appearances.

By now there was a crisis in the camp of the theosophists and the young Hindu went into seclusion. Plans for a public tour were set aside. Mrs. Besant and her prodigy would proceed straight to the West Coast for a time of rest. That night, when Chicago reporters tried to find out what train would carry the pair westward, they were told that that was "none of the public's business." Krishnamurti began at that point to fade from public view as the vehicle of the World Teacher.

Though he had accepted the role and carried it out impressively, Krishnamurti had never been as ardent about it as Mrs. Besant was. In 1929 the elderly lady, who had poured so much of her life and effort into his preparation, was greatly distressed when Krishnamurti flatly renounced all the pretensions that had attended his messianic role. From then on, when he spoke of it in public, it was in a gently mocking way.

Since then he has lived quietly and obscurely for the most part, wandering from nation to nation, writing and making occasional appearances as a spiritual teacher before various groups.

The demons behind the Krishnamurti affair could not at that time break through the invisible barrier that God had set around this nation against the spirits of the East, their false doctrines, and their counterfeit miracles. There were to be no new gods in the gates of America then.

The spiritual conditions that prevailed in this country at that time, more in line with the revealed will of God than those of many older nations, enabled Krishnamurti to come out from under the terrible delusion that had been thrust upon him that he was "the vehicle through which the World Teacher, head of all faiths and inspirer of all religious purposes," would speak to mankind. Until he came to the United States, Krishnamurti had not only believed that to be so and declared it to be so but at times had apparently demonstated it to be so, as when "his voice suddenly changed its character entirely and sounded like that of another person."

The entire episode, from start to end, was wholly demonic, and Krishnamurti was as much a victim of it as anyone. There can be no doubt that Mrs. Besant was entirely sincere in her belief that Krishnamurti was what she declared him to be. Nor is there any reason to doubt that Krishnamurti was sincere in bearing the burdens of that role, with its sometimes supernatural manifestations and signs.

Most of the beliefs and statements and signs in the matter are identifiably demonic. Take, for instance, the statement that the followers of Krishnamurti "believe that there is another unseen world in which dwell a hierarchy of beings, equivalent to angels, increasing in power and wisdom until they approach the seat of the Great Ruler of the Universe." Exactly so!

Without knowing it, these people accurately described the demons. They are equivalent to angels in native endowments, and they are set in an ascending hierarchy, in which some are prince demons controlling larger affairs in Satan's kingdom than others lower on the scale. Satan stands at the summit, supreme in splendor and wisdom among them.

That the Lord Maitreya, or great World Teacher, or Guiding Spirit of the Universe, is the revealer and head of the world's religions is not inaccurate. All of those are names of Satan, which he has audaciously assumed as the god of this world and by which he misrepresents himself to mankind as the supreme being. Occult literature is full of such names as these, among them the Invisible Master, or the All-Powerful Ruler. Such names are useful to Satan in his deeply disguised, counterfeit role as god.

Satan has invented many religions to replace, as far as he possibly can, the recognition and worship of the living God. He is the founder and spiritual head of those religions, each of which is a substitute in its own sphere for the worship of the God of Israel.

Further, it is a central and ultimate purpose of Satan to bring all of these religions at last into one great and powerful amalgam to which all men will be bidden to adhere on pain of death, in the name of unity, universal brotherhood, and peace. Its formation will be such a wonder in men's eyes—all that apparent diversity brought at last into a single and sweeping unity—that only a few men and women, among the Jews and among the followers of Jesus, will recognize it for the Satanic masterpiece of delusion that it is—as full of supernatural powers as it will be—and will refuse to have any part in it. They will never worship or obey demons in any manner, no matter how great the sanctions of it are.

The possession of a human body by a spirit, and the wandering of the human soul from the body, are both among the deepest perversions of Satan. In the East such things are more common than they are in the West. Yet I met a young person in New York

City who knew of such soul travel and who knew of no way of escape from the supernatural powers that had drawn her into it.

The change of voice that Krishnamurti sometimes experienced is a result of a demon seizing control of the human vocal organ and speaking directly through it. That is also why, when Krishnamurti would stop teaching and speak as the voice of the World Teacher, he would go from the third person to the first person in his references to god.

False christs are not uncommon in the East. There may be half a dozen or more of them at one time. The evil spirits who had concocted this false Christ figure were unable to enter Krishnamurti upon the territory of this nation in that guise, in part because faithful intercessors were praying against it. The attempt to thrust this particular spiritual counterfeit upon the American public was thoroughly aborted. Yet we have a very different situation today with the reception afforded such figures as Guru Maharaj Ji.

Indeed, the manner in which the Maharishi Yogi entered the United States and almost instantly had the mightiest of the mass media distributing photographs and magazine covers and stories of him to all the nation indicates how ripe the time was for the demons to introduce this particular apostle of spiritual deception to the United States from India. His visit was an immediate and rousing public success.

In conversations with young Jews in the last three years, I have found a rather marked interest among them in Hinduism and other Eastern beliefs. This is alarming but not wholly surprising: Satan and his demons have made young Jews the particular targets of their strategy to export Eastern religions to the West. Satan hates Jews and seeks to destroy them precisely because God has chosen them. The time is coming, the Bible reveals, when God will use Jews as the messengers of His love to the entire world. Satan would like to misuse them for his own purposes first. Every Jew he can carry decisively into false religions is ruined for God's purposes, and many of God's greatest purposes in history reside in the Jews.

I was sent one afternoon to do a story on a psychedelic fair for the young at an outdoor site in Queens. About a third of the stalls at the fair featured literature, or objects, or demonstrations of Eastern mystical and religious practices. One stall was devoted to the claims of an Indian avatar, or supposed god-in-human-form, who boldly offered himself as savior to humans. The posters and literature were of an especially audacious sort. The man claimed to be health-giver, provider, protector, lord. A young Jew was attending the booth. I asked him how he happened to be there, and he readily told me his story. He was twenty-four years old, obviously intelligent, and until recently had been employed, he said, at a college in New York City.

He told me that one afternoon he had gone to hear a Harvard graduate student just returned from a trip to India. The Harvard man had encountered this avatar and had somehow accepted him, and now he was back in this country declaring him to be his god.

The young Jew said that, as he listened to the Harvard man speak, he was aware that a certain power "came over me." He felt himself being drawn by some strange, compelling force to accept this Indian claimant as his lord.

"I knew I should have resisted," he told me, "but I was being pulled and I seemed powerless." He said he had taken the Indian as his lord and that soon thereafter he had "had some wonderful supernatural experiences."

A short time later he was invited to go to a house in Delaware where followers of this false christ met, and he remained there several days. He sensed something strange, a kind of darkness or unreality about the place. "I knew I should have got out of there," he said. "I should have left, but I stayed." Now, he said, he was much involved in propagating the man's claims and he was happy and satisfied in it. What an occupation for a Jew!

Quietly I told him what I knew to be the fact: "You've been taken over." He did not deny that it was true but he repeated that he was content. That was about two years ago. The Indian has since died.

This was a classic case of demons taking over a human being. God *never* compels or forces a man to worship and follow Him. Satan and the demons do, if they can. Here was a young Jew who was drawn into the net almost involuntarily and who became a victim of the demons of the East. He was helpless to do anything about it now but to go along with it.

There is an active principle—an aggressive life—in all these heathen religious and occult practices and that life is out to bring humans under the dominance of demons.

Every god other than the God of Israel is either a fable or a demon posing as a god. Hinduism is described as a system of innumerable gods, each of whom reveals a characteristic of a single god. That is exactly what it is. The god behind it all is Satan and the many gods are evil spirits and each one shows forth a facet of Satan's character. Hinduism is a Satanically contrived religion of demon gods and demonic religious practices. It is utterly at variance with the will of the Creator.

To the Jews the word came: "I am thy God, Who brought you out of the land of Egypt, out of the house of bondage. You shall have *no* other gods before me."

That is the First Commandment. Honor paid to any other god breaks that commandment. The Ten Commandments—the heart of the Law of God—forbid all commerce with false and idolatrous religions:

"You shall not make *any* graven image, or *any likeness* of any thing that is in heaven above, or that is in the earth beneath, or that is in the waters beneath the earth. You shall not bow yourself down to them, nor serve them: for I the Lord thy God am a jealous God, visiting the iniquity of the fathers upon the children unto the third and fourth generation of them that hate me. And showing mercy unto thousands of those who love me and keep my commandments." Deuteronomy 5:6–10.

The penalty for idolatry in the Old Testament is death: "If there is found among you . . . a man or woman who . . . has gone and served other gods and worshiped them, or the sun or the moon or any of the host of heaven, which I have forbidden, and it is told you and you hear of it; then you shall inquire diligently, and if it is true and certain that such an abominable thing has been done in Israel, then you shall bring forth to your gates that man or woman who has done this evil thing and you shall stone that man or woman to death with stones. On the evidence of two witnesses or of three witnesses he that is to die shall be put to death; a person shall not be put to death on the evidence of one witness." Deuteronomy 17:2–6.

The Second Book of Kings in the Old Testament tells the story of King Ahaziah who "fell through the lattice in his upper chamber in Samaria, and lay sick." The king summoned messengers and said, "Go, inquire of Baalzebub, the god of Ekron, whether I shall recover from this sickness." God saw that, and "the angel of the Lord said to Elijah the Tishbite, 'Arise, go up to meet the messengers of the king. . . .' "

The prophet did as he was told and he met the king's messengers on their way. Later he was taken in to see the king and Elijah said to him, "Thus says the Lord, 'Because you have sent messengers to inquire of Baalzebub, the god of Ekron—is it because there is no God in Israel to inquire of his word?—therefore you will not come down from the bed to which you have gone, but you shall surely die.' So he died according to the word of the Lord which Elijah had spoken." II Kings 1:2,3a,16.

The consequence to Ahaziah of seeking counsel from another god was death. God gave His Word, as the expression of His will, to the Hebrew fathers and prophets, so it might be obeyed. Disobedience to that will brings its due and measured consequences on individuals and on nations. The penalty is not whimsical or inscrutable. It is plainly stated in the Scriptures, and God executes it impartially and lawfully.

Men should be glad for that, for otherwise they would be groping in the dark, stumbling blindly into pits, having no idea of the lawful relation of acts to consequences.

If a road is plainly marked, "Sharp right turn. Danger—Precipice," and if a man ignores that sign and veers left, he will drive over the precipice and plunge to death, but he will not do so unwarned. He need not have died had he heeded the sign.

A Witch on Wall Street

A witch appeared on Wall Street in the spring of 1970. For a few minutes at the lunch hour she practiced an element of magic there. Not long afterward strange events took place at the very point on Wall Street where the witch had stood.

It was on Friday, March 13, that a young woman who works in public relations in New York arranged for the witch to appear on Wall Street near Broad Street in downtown Manhattan to "cast a spell of sexual vitality over Wall Street," as it was put.

Workers on lunch hour crowded around the visitor, who persuaded them to join her in chanting, "Light the flame, bright the fire, red is the color of desire." They unified their voices in that old staple of witchcraft, an incantation to stir passion. A spell was cast, and a curse went into effect.

It was at Wall Street near Broad Street on Friday, May 8, that a mob of 300 or more men in hard hats, mostly construction workers, stormed into the financial district behind a cluster of American flags and attacked student protestors who had gathered on the steps of Federal Hall, where George Washington took the oath of office as President in 1789.

Gangs of men ran through the narrow streets of the financial district, beating and kicking young people as well as other bystanders to whom they objected, including a couple of lawyers whose hair was not short enough to suit them. Some of the men carried heavy, small construction tools. They shouted things like "Kill the Commies" and, while they carried out their brief terroristic rampage, several thousand pedestrians loudly cheered their fist and boot assaults. About seventy persons were injured. When a first-aid station was set up in nearby Trinity Church, the angry workers tore a Red Cross banner from the church gates.

This was all done in the good name of patriotism, but it was the crudest kind of mob action. It was the beginning of an overt right-wing response to overt left-wing radicalism.

I watched news films of this event. The men had paraded down Broadway. When they reached Wall and Broad, their lines suddenly broke from the military order of a march to the headlong disorder of a running mob.

As it happened, the disintegration of the march into a violent outbreak began within yards of the point at which the spell of witchcraft had been cast. The division that exists in a more and more polarized citizenry broke out there that day in street clashes.

It is not possible to trace the relationship between these two events, and therefore nothing dogmatic can be asserted about it. What can be said is that witchcraft and magic are related to the work of demons: They are acts of human cooperation with evil spirits. Such acts may affect events to a degree that is little understood.

"Light the flame, bright the fire . . ." the Wall Street workers had chanted. It seemed innocent enough. Yet in that chant of witchcraft, disguised as something else, there may have been an expression of the design of evil spirits to ignite a flame of national civil disorder.

Some think that there is a latent fascistic impulse residing in a minority of the American public. If that is so, it was at Wall Street on May 8, 1970, that a more or less spontaneous outbreak of that impulse occurred. For the first time in modern American history a mob of brown shirts went into street action. They were not members of some extremist cult but were drawn from the ordinary ranks of laborers. It was a thoroughly ominous event.

The enthusiasm generated by that first day's action led to almost daily demonstrations in the financial district and near City Hall and, by May 21, less than two weeks later, some 80,000 people rallied at City Hall and then marched under massed banners to the financial district.

The marchers in Wall Street may be a shadow of a much larger number of angry men who would be willing to be organized to put down what they already regard as intolerable sedition. Such men are one thing when they move on a free-lance errand of their own in defiance of the law. They are something else entirely when they are organized and put into uniforms and led.

The rule of law, not of men or of mob force, is one that Satan seeks to undermine wherever he can, because he can bring bondage and terror upon masses of human beings when it is overthrown.

The setting was perfect on May 8 for touching off the kind of civil and political turmoil which, when it reaches its apex, sabotages liberty and overthrows law. The demonic mechanism essential to this end is the formation of at least two large factions among the populace, each full of fiery detestation for the other. The manipulation of these factions eventually plunges the civil order into chaos.

In the vacuum of law thus created, a tyranny can seize the state. We have seen the end results of this mechanism in Russia, in China, in Germany in this century.

Now we see forming, in broad outline, two bitterly antagonistic factions in American society, and each can be more or less identified on sight:

One is made up of the radicals and revolutionaries on the left. Their outward marks are often a certain dishevelment of dress, long hair and, especially among the young, the dungarees and blue denim jackets that have become almost a uniform of "the movement." The other faction is made up of people who are angry or alarmed at the manifestations of the radical left. The flag, displayed in every conceivable way, has become their symbol. They fly it, decorate autos and trucks with it, paste decals of it on windows, sew it into their clothing, pin it on their lapels.

My work carries me among both groups and I find that the caricatures of them often break down upon personal contact. Many of the people who wear the clothing of the movement are not fractious or lawless; they are pleasant, decent kids who happen to wear the clothes characteristic of their peers. It is wrong to lump them together as an army of anarchists or youthful bums. It is equally wrong to lump the flag-wearers all together as racists and warmongers. Yet as the long-hair faction grows more hostile and suspicious toward the flag-displaying faction, and the latter becomes more contemptuous and intolerant of the former—each seeing the other as a cohesive enemy group—the possibilities of fratricidal conflict may increase. This becomes especially dangerous when leaders arise to exploit the division, and to depict the other side in terms designed to stir antagonistic passions.

When Abbie Hoffman appears in public, blowing his nose into what looks like an American flag, he administers exactly the kind of shock treatment to the sensibilities of millions of middle Americans that will give opportunity to demagogues of the right to arise, offering themselves and their formulas as the solution to this kind of outrage.

Little need be said of the danger to the Jews inherent in either a right- or left-wing extremism; recent history depicts that danger clearly. Out of intense political turmoil in Germany came the right-wing extremism that made the slaughter of the Jews a matter of national policy. The left-wing extremism that has controlled the Soviet Union for more than half a century has lifted sword and wing over Israel in the Middle East, menacing that small state with its vast power.

Anti-Biblical ideologies often become anti-Semitic ideologies. Such ideologies have arisen in the United States but they have not yet been politically organized. It is folly for Jews either to align themselves with or to seek to exploit such ideologies, in any way.

On Wall Street that day a rather disorderly crowd of young people had gathered at Federal Hall and at least a couple of them had talked of trying to enter and disrupt the New York Stock Exchange. While this was going on, the 300 construction men marched down Broadway from City Hall. Thus the scene was set for conflict and violent steps were taken contrary to a lawful civil order.

It is perhaps more than a mere coincidence that witchcraft had come to that scene first. I do not suggest that those who practiced an aspect of witchcraft there had any intention whatever of creating a spiritual disturbance. The witch, who sought only to draw attention to herself, succeeded in getting a fairly large number of bystanders to join her in uttering an occult incantation. Such chants are a call to demons, whether the persons who utter them intend them to be so or not.

The Scriptures place the severest warnings and prohibitions upon witchcraft and false worship. It is of the devil and it necessarily works against the will of God, and against the well-being of men, whenever it is practiced, even when those involved are not aware of that.

"Do not turn to mediums or wizards; do not seek them out, to be defiled by them: I am the Lord your God," Leviticus 19:31 commands.

"There shall not be found among you any one . . . who practices divination, a soothsayer, or an augur, or a sorcerer, or a charmer, or a medium, or a wizard, or a necromancer. For whoever does these things is an abomination to the Lord." Deuteronomy 18:11,12a.

"Their sorrows shall be multiplied that hasten after another god," Psalm 16:4 warns.

At a time of great trouble for the Jews, the prophet Jeremiah spoke the word of the Lord: "Thus says the Lord of hosts, the God of Israel: You have seen all the evil that I brought upon Jerusalem and upon all the cities of Judah. Behold, this day they are a desolation, and no one dwells in them, because of the wickedness which they committed, provoking me to anger, in that they went to burn incense and serve other gods that they knew not, neither they, nor you, nor your fathers. Yet I persistently sent to you all my servants the prophets, saying, 'Oh, do not do this abominable thing that I hate!' But they did not listen or incline their ear, to turn from their wickedness and burn no incense to other gods. Therefore my wrath and my anger were poured forth, and were kindled in the cities of Judah and in the streets of Jerusalem. . . ." Jeremiah 44:1–6a.

There is no necessary relation between what is *intended* in acts of witchcraft and false worship and what is actually brought about by them. Burning incense to other gods was intended to procure some kind of favor or good fortune; it brought the desolation of Jerusalem.

Scriptural accounts of the activities and powers of magicians and witches suggest that even advanced practitioners of magic, including those who opposed Moses in Egypt, may not be fully aware of the source of what they do or of its ultimate effects. They know that they have certain powers, but they do not fully understand the origin or the whole outcome of using them, at least in many cases.

It is certain that spiritual laws were broken on Wall Street on the day when witchcraft was indulged in there. Perhaps this violation of the atmosphere gave evil spirits opportunity to produce a scene on Wall Street comparable, on a smaller scale, to the scenes they had produced in Germany in the 1930's and in China thereafter —scenes of turmoil, struggle, violence, and injury.

The rule, rarely excepted, is that spiritual transgression precedes the physical manifestations that are its visible result. There are certain spiritual laws and if they are broken or ignored, effects will inevitably succeed. No degree of innocence supplies any shield from the consequences of participating in witchcraft.

Occultism and outbreaks of violence have a relationship. Because it is a spiritual relationship—with one creating conditions conducive to the other—cause and effect cannot be easily traced in the natural order, even when the effects may be clearly seen there. Just as there are laws of physics, whose violation creates disorder, there are spiritual laws whose violation brings consequences. Occultism and witchcraft give particular opportunity to evil spirits to act. Thus, occult practices carried out in one place —spiritual transgressions against the revealed will of God—may cause trouble in that place or in a distant quarter, and the connection between the two may not be commonly suspected at all.

Under demonic prompting, Americans are now engaging in a great many things that will lead they do not know where. Unless there is a sharp reversal in the trend, all of it will have its terrible cost.

Early in the rise of Hitler and Nazism in Germany, occultist elements were actively in play. They were not always openly shown, but a bold clairvoyant named Erik Jan Hanussen, a dealer in astrology and in predicting future events, became known as the "Prophet of the Third Reich."

In the book *Prophecy in Our Time,* Martin Ebon writes that "in the midst of the political churnings, with violence permeating the air of the German capital, Hanussen went on ahead with the opening of his lavish 'Palace of the Occult,' taking up an entire floor at fashionable No. 16, Lietzenstrasse." It was filled with "magical paraphernalia. . . . Golden signs of the Zodiac looked down upon broad, low couches."

At the opening, with "actors and actresses mingling with Nazi bigwigs . . . the 'Prophet of the Third Reich' took his place in the center of his lit-up glass circle; everything else was thrown into darkness." He described a vision "in halting, deep-throated tones of fear and menace:

" '. . . The Storm Troopers move down the Wilhemstrasse. There has been a magnificent victory. The people want Hitler. Victory, Victory! Hitler is victorious. Resistance is useless. But the noise comes closer. Is there a struggle? Shooting? No . . . no . . . it is not that . . . I see flames, enormous flames. . . . It is a terrible conflagration that has broken out. Criminals have set the fire.

" 'They want to hurl Germany into last-minute chaos, to nullify the victory. . . . Only the mailed fist of an awakened Germany can hold back chaos and the threat of civil war. . . .'

"That was on the 26th of February, 1933. On the evening of February 27, at about 9:30, the news-agency teletypes in London, New York, and throughout the world were reporting a flash: 'The Reichstag is burning!'

"Hanussen's spectacular prophecy had come true. With it his own flamboyant success seemed assured, especially amidst the violence that was immediately loosed; the Nazis used the Reichstag fire as an excuse to cancel the elections and embark on the reign of terror that lasted until Hitler's suicide in his Berlin underground bunker, ending World War II, a decade later."

The accuracy of a prophecy may be an indication of its supernatural origin but it is certainly no test of divine origin. Hanussen's prophecy was apparently right, yet its purport was entirely evil.

The Scriptures warn that even when "a prophet or dreamer of dreams" gives a sign or a wonder that actually comes to pass as he said, if the spiritual content is contrary to the Word of God, the prophet is a deceiver. "You shall walk after the Lord your God, and fear him, and keep his commandments, and obey his voice," above the words of all such prophets. See Deuteronomy 13:1-4.

There is truth that will not betray those who receive it in the Scriptures. Isaiah spoke this reasoned reproach to those who faced the temptations of false spiritual practices: "And when they say to you, 'Consult the mediums and wizards who chirp and mutter,' should not a people consult their God? Should they consult the dead on behalf of the living? *To the law and to the testimony! If they speak not according to this word, it is because there is no light in them.*" Isaiah 8:19,20.

When the convulsive events came by which Russia was to be conveyed from one form of tyranny to another and still bloodier form, the mad monk Rasputin moved to the nerve centers of power and manipulated events with all the skill and daring of a considerable cunning. He used certain occult powers to gain decisive influence on the Czarist' side. Statesmen who stood against him lost their positions, and he put feeble and corrupt lackeys into their places. It makes little difference on which side of controversies such individuals stand, or to what intended end they exercise themselves, it is *the fact of their presence and activity,* not their declared purpose, that contributes heavily to the creation of conditions out of which human suffering arises. The danger is not so much from the people who practice these things; it is from the demons behind such individuals and practices—enemies of God promoting spiritual and supernatural transactions that are not of God.

It is well to remember that liberty, once it is lost, may remain wholly out of reach for a very long time. Nations and their populations have sometimes suffered repression and virtual enslavement for decades stretching into centuries. The psychic, occult, and spiritual forces now at work in the United States, with a large degree of public acceptance, are sufficient to plunge this nation first toward anarchy and later into the grip of a Red or a fascist tyranny.

Drugs and the Supernatural

There is a direct and mysterious relationship between certain chemical agents and the supernatural. Certain drugs can carry the user into the realm of the demons. By taking these agents into his body a person opens up avenues into his soul and spirit by which evil spirits may enter and seize a measure of control. He also opens his body, particularly his nerves and muscular system, to demonic interference and to some degree of physical damage.

As a previous chapter has set forth, God wants man to be in full command and control of his faculties. Satan wants to rob man of the full use and control of his faculties, and alcohol, narcotics, and hallucinogens are potent elements for cutting in on a man's own control of his mind and body. He therefore widely promotes their use among populations of the world.

There is a certain class of chemicals and drugs that grow on the earth that have profound effects upon the human system when they are taken into it. I would call them chemical-supernatural agents because these drugs can, and frequently do, introduce people to the supernatural. Talk to twenty young people who have taken marijuana or one of the stronger hallucinogens and roughly half of them will tell you that they know of the supernatural realm. They have had experiences in it, and they talk familiarly of it. It is too easy to dismiss this as a creation of their imaginations. Many of them *have* had supernatural experiences. They know that they have, and they also know the difference between imaginations or nightmares and experiences in this realm. Certain drugs provide a shortcut to the supernatural.

That is no secret; it is an advertised and well known facet of the narcotics experience. William James, author of *The Varieties of Religious Experience,* who is said to have used nitrous oxide as an hallucinogenic agent, wrote: "Our normal waking consciousness . . . is but one special type of consciousness: whilst all about it, parted from it by the filmiest of screens, there lie potential forms of consciousness entirely different. . . . No account of the universe in its totality can be final which leaves these other forms of consciousness quite disregarded," and James stressed that the existence of these forms "forbid a premature closing of our accounts with reality." That, essentially, was what Timothy Leary was talking about when he spoke of "consciousness expansion." It is contended that an introduction to these other forms of consciousness, as they are called, is good, broadening, beneficial, liberating. A closer look will show that it is quite exactly the opposite of these.

It is worth noting that the slogans used in connection with drug experiments and "trips" emphasize mental and spiritual effects. New levels of perception are promised, and it is not an idle boast. A person who gets carried into the demonic supernatural has his consciousness expanded into areas that he never knew existed, areas under the control of demons. There are pleasures of a sort and there are terrors there. Demons are able to produce stunning supernatural effects, unsuspected dimensions of the weird, full of color and radiance and silvered lightning, and they are equally able to produce extremes of terror and chaotic, crashing misperceptions. Therein lies the difference between a "good trip" and a "bad trip."

Havelock Ellis wrote of "the artificial paradise of mescal" (peyote), but that is not quite what it is. It is a counterfeit paradise and that paradise can turn in an instant into a living hell.

The use of certain chemical agents as spiritual agents (expressly in order to be put into contact with the supernatural) is a deeply entrenched practice in certain parts of the world, usually among people of low achievement, slack culture, and little or no education. Some of these agents have been central to the worship of demon cults going back several thousand years.

The United States has been almost entirely free of this tandem of evil until recent years. Lately, there has been a kind of explosion on the American scene of the promotion and use of these chemical agents in association with mysticism or supernaturalism.

Men such as James, Ellis, Huxley were among the few who began to bring the spiritual applications in the use of certain drugs to the Western consciousness several decades ago. Other men did more to bring the ancient practices themselves into the country. Perhaps chief among these was R. Gordon Wasson, a New York banker and a mycologist of recognized distinction, who credits himself with "the rediscovery of the religious role of the hallucinogenic mushrooms of Mexico." He and his wife spent part of 1955 among native cultists in Mexico.

"When we first went down to Mexico, we felt certain, my wife and I, that we were on the trail of an ancient and holy mystery, and we went as pilgrims seeking the Grail," he said in a lecture in 1960. An ancient mystery, yes—but not a holy one. It is filled with cultic practices repugnant to the Old Testament and specifically enjoined by it.

On the night of June 29–30, 1955, the Wassons became probably "the first outsiders . . . to be invited to partake in the *agape* of the sacred mushroom." They had learned from sixteenth-century writers that "certain mushrooms played a divinatory role in the religion of the natives" in Mexico, and they found that "this middle-American cult of a divine mushroom, this cult of 'God's flesh' as the Indians in pre-Columbian times called it, can be traced back to about B.C. 1500. . . . Thus we find a mushroom in the center of the cult with perhaps the oldest continuous history in the world."

Mr. Wasson presented this rite of the demons to the United States in 1957 when *Life* opened its pages to a major article by him called "Seeking the Magic Mushroom." Theodore Roszak later noted that this "splashy and appetizing feature," which provided "detailed illustrations and descriptions of the mushrooms, made all the familiar connections with occult and Oriental religions."

Mr. Wasson lamented that language was insufficient to describe "the nature of the psychic disturbance the eating of the mushroom causes. . . . What we need is a vocabulary to describe all the modalities of a Divine Inebriant." The term is wrong. It is an inebriant, to be sure, but it is the very opposite of divine; it is demonic; and with it go demonic effects and also some of the classic practices of false religion.

Mr. Wasson, banker and mushroom pilgrim, notes that the mushroom enables a man "to travel backwards and forwards in time, to enter other planes of existence, even [as the Indians say] to know God."

Or, as the Greek scholar Mary Barnard wrote in *The American Scholar,* concerning a dozen plants used in religious practices, "Some of them are open doors to the otherworld. . . . They are sacred plants, magic herbs or shrubs . . . magic carpets on which the spirit of the shaman can travel through time and space. . . . The magic plants are vehicles for a special kind of experience adaptable to the use of most religions that acknowledge an otherworld and permit its exploration."

"If there were such a field as theo-botany," Miss Barnard suggests, "the study of these plants and their cults would be the work of a theo-botanist." Of peyote she writes, "The god, being rendered fit for eating, presides over the meeting where peyote is taken and 'sends' the songs sung and the visions seen by the members who partake of this sacrament. The peyote cult is not based on a written or spoken Word, but on the experience of the members during the communion." This is the Satanic counterfeit for the activity of the Holy Spirit. Miss Barnard briefly mentions some of the supernatural aspects of the peyote cult: ". . . the shaman's journey . . . the food of occult knowledge . . . the disembodied soul, the communication with the dead, plant-deities." She notes that they "all converge on this point: that is, on some actual food [usually a drug plant] ritually consumed, not symbolically but for the experience it confers."

A classic myth suggests that the use of these plants for supernatural purposes came by direct demonic revelation. Miss Barnard writes that "The peyote myth tells how an Indian, or several Indians, . . . is lost or wounded and left for dead in an uninhabited desert region. Starving, thirsty, at the end of his strength, he stumbles upon the peyote. A voice tells him to eat it. He eats it and feels his strength miraculously restored. His hunger and thirst are alleviated, and he is able to make his way back to his people, to whom he bears the word of a new god sent to heal their suffering. Usually the Indian hears a voice directing him to eat the plant, or sees a godlike form in the shape of an Indian brave standing where the plant stood; in some versions he is given instructions by Peyote himself on the proper performance of the peyote ritual."

One thing that may be said of any such revelation as that is that it is not of God, but that it *is* demonic. The voice, the vision, and the revelation of the supernatural uses of the drug plant all fall into the category of the activity of evil spirits. Their function is to deceive men, especially to deceive them spiritually. The ritual that goes with the religious use of such drugs is made up of practices that the Bible identifies as false and which it forbids to Jews.

Evil spirits, posing as gods, gain entrance to human beings through the use of such substances.

"The sacred mushrooms of Oaxaca are taken raw, on an empty stomach, like the fresh peyote," Miss Barnard writes. "When the shaman has swallowed the mushroom, the mushroom-deity takes possession of the shaman's body and speaks with the shaman's lips. The shaman does not say whether the sick child will live or die; *the mushroom says.* Some Indians say of sacred plants used by their shaman, that the soul of an ancestor has entered the plant; it is he who takes possession of the shaman and speaks through his mouth." This is none other than possession of the body by evil spirits and their use of the faculties of the one they possess.

The writer lists as among the effects of these drugs: "a displaced center of consciousness seemingly outside the body . . . hallucinations of some sort—visual or auditory or both . . . divination or prophecy . . . occult knowledge conferred by hallucinogenic shrubs and fungi . . . ceremonial communion with the gods or the ancestors . . . [trances in which] the shaman's body is said to be emptied of his soul."

The only "gods" one may ever come into touch with through the use of such substances are evil spirits. Jews especially are enjoined not to deal with "gods" in any wise. To do so is to break faith with the one God, and for a Jew that is to lay himself open to a rapid victimization by demons.

Shamans are sometimes fully aware that they are dealing with evil spirits. Their function is to try to propitiate them.

In a review called "The Magic of Peyote," Dudley Young discussed a book called *The Teachings of Don Juan* by Carlos Castaneda, giving a glimpse into the nightmare experiences that an individual can suffer through involvement with drug plants, especially through a religious involvement. He wrote:

"This book is the record of a young anthropologist's experiences as the apprentice of a Mexican Indian sorcerer. Over a period of four years, Mr. Castaneda paid intermittent visits to Don Juan, first in Arizona, then in Sonora, Mexico. The aim of his initiation was to gain power over the demonic world through the ritualized ingestion of peyote and other hallucinogenic plants." What happened, however, was that the demons began to gain power over Mr. Castaneda. Mr. Young goes on: "Mr. Castaneda's descriptions of his experiences with peyote are both interesting and moving. It made him violently ill and disclosed to him both terror and ecstasy. Towards the end of his fourth year he began to have what the layman might describe as a nervous breakdown, and after a particularly shattering evening with the Don, he abruptly broke off relations.

"Don Juan emerges as an enigmatic, ultimately sinister *guru* figure; ascetic and authoritarian. . . .

"*The spirits of his underworld, contacted through drugs,* can protect and ennoble those they fancy, but destroy those who lack discipline of reverence. The Don was convinced that his disciple was well-favored by the gods, but if this is so, one shudders to think what happens to the ill-favored ones."

Mr. Young says that it was not clear whether Don Juan was "seeking a corrupting kind of power over his disciple," but "Certainly the author's final hallucination, during which he threw a rock at his master who seemed bent on destroying him, would support such a suggestion."

Mr. Castaneda apparently broke with his first misadventure at just the point at which the takeover was about to be completed, and it is a significant sign of the sharpness of his resistance that he threw a rock at the sorcerer leading him on.

Peyote is distinctively used in religious ceremonies and rituals. It is among the best known of the natural hallucinogens. In some places it is used by people desiring to enter into a visionary state.

"Visions and other mystical experiences are part of the regular spiritual diet of the 50,000-odd members of the Native American Church, thanks to what they consider a special gift from God: peyote, a small cactus growing in the valley of the Rio Grande," one report on the plant said. "The Indians of the Native American Church cut off and dry the cactus tops, then eat the 'buttons' in night-long ceremonies to the accompaniment of sacred fire and chanting.

"The faith's adherents believe that the partaking of peyote

brings one into direct contact with God. They also address prayers to it, and consider it to be a protector." Some Indians carry the buttons in beaded bags for good luck.

There is no plant or drug that can put a man "into direct contact with God." The living God does not reveal Himself to a man on the basis of his taking a chemical into his system. Peyote can, however, open up an avenue of contact with an unseen spirit.

In addressing prayers to it, men make it an object of idolatry. In regarding it as a protector (it is exactly the opposite) and carrying it for good luck, they become involved in another phase of Satan's worldwide system of getting men to repose their trust, not in the living God, but in a thing—a talisman, charm, or amulet. By these religious uses it may be seen that peyote is an item in Satan's great arsenal of idolatry.

There have been repeated reports of sex crimes, some against children, committed under the influence of peyote. Peyote is not a blessed substance; it is a cursed substance. It can damage men physically, mentally, spiritually.

Drugs are a means by which Satan can take you out of your own control and begin to bring you under his control. He wants to take controls at the center of your being and make them subject to his spiritual agents, demons. Drug experiences can be the beginning of the seizing of a person's mind and will, a means of carrying him into regions of fantasy, euphoria, terror, passivity, anomie, apathy, lethargy, distorted perspective, mental and spiritual confusion, false worship, insanity.

That would not be terribly important if chemical-supernatural agents were not being widely popularized in the United States. Timothy Leary did much to lead the way as an early "promoter, apologist, and high priest of dope," the mass evangelist of "instant mysticism." It is significant that when Leary formulated his passion for drug-induced experiences into a cult, he called it the League for Spiritual Discovery—LSD. He announced in 1966 that he was founding a "new" religion based on the sacramental use of LSD, peyote, and marijuana.

The Bible warns men against "giving heed to seducing spirits and doctrines of demons." I Timothy 4:1b.

There is a curse that lies upon the earth, and there are things that grow in the earth upon which Satan has made a claim. These plants are inimical to the welfare and health of human beings in a mysteriously numerous variety of ways. The same plant may affect one person one way, another person another way, a third another way, and many other people in many other ways, each different yet all deleterious to well-being.

Such plants are like fountains of evils. When you take one you never know how it will affect you. Its power to do evil is strangely versatile. The effect of these plants on humans goes beyond their chemical effects.

There is a direct link between such plants and Satan. That link may especially be seen in the spiritual and supernatural effects experienced by their use.

There is, for instance, a direct relationship between the use of hallucinogenic agents and the supernatural activity of demons. Such agents can put a man in touch with demons and lead him into a variety of supernatural experiences. Whether these experiences are lovely, or terrifying beyond description, they are all demonic.

Before man did the bidding of Satan and, by it, entered into sin, there was nothing in the whole realm of nature on earth that was bad for or harmful to man. There was nothing in the garden that was contrary to the well-being of man. God told man, "You may freely eat of every tree of the garden" with the one exception of "the tree of the knowledge of good and evil." Man was new and perfectly innocent. His relationship to God was unsullied and utterly free. It was not yet time for such knowledge in the garden.

When God told man of the consequences of the sin of disobedience, one of the things God said was, *"cursed is the ground* because of you. . . ."" Among the effects of that curse was that "thorns and thistles it shall bring forth to you." Genesis 3:17,18.

There had never been any such things in the ground, but now there came out of the ground new and strange plants bearing thorns and thistles.

It would be an extremely unsophisticated and literalist understanding of that statement to think that thorns and thistles were precisely the mode and extent of the curse that fell upon the ground. In the phrase "cursed is the ground because of you" there is the unstated potential for a vast amount of toil, difficulty, pain, and injury to man springing out of the ground.

Things entered into the natural realm as a result of Adam's sin that would never have been there apart from it and that have ever since been bad for man. Some are poisons. They damage a man's physical being if they are ingested, and they may cause death. Others have a different impact. There is something in their mysterious chemistry that causes them to loosen the grip that a man's will exerts on his own faculties—including his mind and his muscular and nervous responses. In some cases these cursed substances quickly carry a man where he has never previously been —into the realm of the demonic supernatural.

That is why it can accurately be stated that demons gain control through alcohol, narcotics, hallucinogens.

They may gain mental control, physical control, emotional control, or spiritual control. By taking these substances a man may undergo changes in consciousness that distort his capacity to judge right from wrong. He may find himself beginning to hold certain convictions about what is true and what is not true, contrary to the Scriptures, but be unaware that he has opened himself up to lies.

With alcohol it can be, and often is, a slow process of deterioration. Or it can be as sudden and disastrous as the head-on collision. Alcoholism can lead eventually to the terrifying hallucinations of delirium tremens: These are more than the effect of natural causes. They are demonic experiences. In the worst state of alcoholism a man is out of his mind, lying in some doorway in unspeakable filth, blabbering out gibberish, pissing through his pants, gone virtually beyond the hope of reclamation. He is no longer truly a man. He is a wreck, as bleak and rotting as a long-abandoned house.

First, jobs are lost; later no job can be kept; then no job can be found. At first, the tremors and slurry speech and graceless behavior are occasional; later, they become frequent; at the end they are always there.

It is fairly common among young people to scorn alcohol and to embrace drugs. "Acid heads" do not admire "juice heads," or heavy drinkers. In a curiously perverse bit of reasoning, some young people justify their taking of drugs on the ground that their parents swill liquor. There *is* a distinction between them, but it is not the distinction commonly thought.

A recent report on medical research by Richard D. Lyons in the *Times* said, "Two New York biochemists reported today what they believe might be the long-sought scientific reason that alcohol can cause behavioral changes ranging from euphoria through drunkenness to hallucinations. Dr. Michael Collins and Gerald Cohen said that the body probably converted alcohol through a series of complicated steps to substances *chemically akin to morphine, peyote, and other opiates and hallucinogens.*"

Their findings were based on test-tube studies and work with cattle tissue. "Dr. Collins said that heavy and chronic drinking was known to produce changes in the nerves and brain ranging from either excitability or anxiety to tremors, delusions and, occasionally, hallucinations." He traced the chemical reaction in the body through several steps to the formation in the brain of an alkaloid named isoquinoline. "This final product then exerts its effect on the brain and nerve endings."

Lyons reported that traces of the alkaloids found in the adrenal tissues of cows led to further research that "showed that these alkaloids were of a type called tetrahydro-isoquinolines," which are "found in desert cacti, most notably in the families that contain mescal buttons and peyote." Dr. Collins pointed out that some members of this alkaloid family may produce "striking pharmacological effects." One provokes convulsions, another is a constituent of opium, he said.

So here in the biochemical laboratory researchers have begun to trace the hitherto hidden chemical relationships of alcohol and some of the most powerful narcotics and hallucinogens.

In addition to triggering hallucinations, these fearful chemicals sometimes induce psychoses. Of 114 LSD users hospitalized in one eighteen-month period at Bellevue Hospital in New York, 13 percent suffered *overwhelming panic,* 12 percent exhibited *uncontrolled violence,* nearly 9 percent had attempted *homicides or suicide.* One out of seven of them had to be sent for long-term mental hospitalization. "Half of those had no history of underlying psychiatric disorder," a physician reported. Some suffered acute schizophrenia. Several "withdrew from society into a totally solipsistic existence."

A West Coast psychiatrist told Gladwin Hill of the *Times,* "We've got an outpatient, huddled in his room near here, who thinks he's an orange, and that if anybody touches him he'll squirt juice." Another man seemed to be in a trance and kept trying to climb the wall, yelling, "I'm a graham cracker," and he thought that his arm had "crumbled off." Such weird ideas necessarily strike us as funny, but to an individual who lives under such a delusion, life is endlessly terrifying. Another report told of a boy who threw himself off a cliff because he believed he could fly.

LSD users have suffered uncontrollable spasms and convulsions, including *grand mal* convulsions typical of the epileptic.

There are delayed reactions, some coming months or even years after LSD has been ingested. One report told of "a young man driving on a highway, a year after his only LSD experience." Suddenly an hallucination seized him. He saw "a hundred headlights coming at him, and he crashed." The hallucination was of a specifically deadly kind and it occurred, without warning, at a time when it could do him the most harm.

The delayed reactions may be still more hidden than that. Taking LSD may be one way to wreck a child before he's born.

The possibility of genetic damage has caused the National Foundation–March of Dimes, whose field of specialization is birth defects, to warn that "it is especially important that men and women in their reproductive years avoid using LSD."

Breaks or other abnormalities in chromosomes are seen in roughly three quarters of persons who take the drug, the *Times* reported.

"Guard your chromosomes" would not be a bad slogan to print on a button. Chromosomes are the tiny, threadlike particles of material buried in the nucleus of every cell, which "transmit hereditary factors from one generation to the next." They carry the instructions that form new life.

In its assault on the body LSD, among many other things, apparently penetrates to the very nucleus of the cell and attacks the chromosomes.

At the University of Oregon Medical School, as Bill Davidson reported in an extensively researched article on "The Hidden Evils of LSD," eight young men, all users, volunteered blood samples for microscopic inspection. Six of the eight were found to have damaged—broken—chromosomes. Two of the six showed signs of "fatal chronic myelogenous leukemia," cancer of the blood.

"It has been known for a long time that certain violent factors, such as atomic radiation and intense X-rays, disrupt and break the chromosomes, causing illness and death from leukemia and other malignancies," Davidson noted.

Dr. Maimon M. Cohen, a geneticist at the State University of New York at Buffalo, tested normal human blood cells in a tube. "He added minute quantities of LSD and studied the chromosomes under a microscope. He was startled and alarmed to see the same kind of chromosomal damage that occurs with radiation. Then he took blood cells from a mental hospital patient who had been treated with LSD. . . . Again, a high rate of chromosomal breakage."

Next he examined the blood cells of three mothers, all LSD users, and their four children, and "the same frightening breakage of chromosomes showed up."

Chromosome damage represents a deep invasion of the inmost chambers of the body. LSD ranks with "certain violent factors, such as atomic radiation" in its battering effect on the chromosomes.

One of the fearful things about LSD is that there is no necessary correlation between dosage and effects. Fragmentation and chromosome damage has been found in those who had had only one dose. The kind of chromosome damage caused by LSD can lead to an abnormality called the *cri-du-chat* syndrome, in which a baby cries like a cat, not a human.

"The results of this chromosome damage may have a delayed effect that may not be in evidence until the second or third generation offspring," warned Dr. Howard A. Rusk, head of the Institute for Rehabilitation Medicine of the New York University Medical Center. Dr. Rusk found that the more immediate effects of the hallucinogens are "on the central nervous system and on the psychic and mental functions" and that these include a "possibility of permanent brain damage."

A dose or two of LSD and a child born to your granddaughter may come into the world crippled for life. What potency that is! What a scheme for the injuring of children not yet born and for the maiming of the race. All of the supposed benefits of drugs— the trips, the kicks, the highs, the hallucinations, the escape from reality into dreamscapes, the illusion of increased powers—are momentary and are offered in exchange for the chance to impose severe damage upon the user and deformities upon future generations.

What kind of an economy is it by which you pop a pill into your mouth now for a brief sensation and others have to pay and pay and pay through all the years of their lives? What is that to you? It is exactly what it would have been if one of your grandparents had, for the sake of some momentary transport, taken a drug so violent in its impact as to have caused you to be born with a gross deformity and to be penalized by it for life. It was your fortune to be born before the curse of drugs had begun to spread across our culture. You have no right to lay such a tax upon members of another generation.

Infants who have a heroin addiction at birth because of the mother's addiction must go through the torment of a cold turkey withdrawal not long after they come into the world. What a monstrous necessity that is, laid upon a guiltless babe!

Among the false religions Satan has devised there are some,

including those centered on drugs, that feature quite sensational effects, including all kinds of interior fireworks shows and a dervish-like frenzy at times—creations of the special effects department of hell, intended to deceive. One thing these tribal religions do not do is to relieve hardship and suffering and poverty and ignorance. They perpetuate them. They intensify them, offering occasional soul flights as escapism. The *real conditions* under which the people live and labor are not changed, except for the worse. If there is superstition, these religions enforce and exploit it. If tribal murder is rampant, these religions provide a base of ceremony and excitation from which it flows.

Another common note is that of possession: the experience of being taken over by the will of the leader or by an outside force.

A reporter I know, a man of unusually forceful character and exceptionally strong will, came to me about three years ago and said that he had an opportunity to take LSD at a house gathering under the supervision of a man who had some experience at it. He asked if I thought he should go ahead. I told him I thought he would be unwise to do so, and explained why.

About a week later he came by and said, "I want to tell you how wrong you were about that LSD. I tried it, and it was wonderful." He told something of the beautiful sensations he had experienced. I felt there was nothing I could say.

Two weeks later he came in quite a different mood. "I took another trip on LSD," he said, "and I thought I was losing my mind. I felt I was coming under the power of this guy who was guiding us. It got so bad I thought I was under his power completely, and the terrifying thing about it was I didn't know if I could ever get back. I'm not kidding, I didn't know if it was possible to come back."

The reporter had lost possession of himself to a large degree during the experience. The big question was whether he could get full possession of himself again.

This experience of a loss of control over one's own person is a very common one. This may be seen in the experience of Frederick Swain, who was one of the first to take advantage of the opportunities opened up by Mr. Wasson's research, and who decided to investigate for himself. He learned that there was a shaman in the village of Huautla de Jiménez in Mexico named Santa Maria Sabina and, with much difficulty, he found his way to where she lived.

"The hut was only one room, with a dirt floor, thatched roof and mud walls. The household consisted of Santa Maria as the head, three men who were her sons, three women, and numerous children, all living in the same drafty room. They all slept, ate, and lived on the floor.

"In one corner of the hut an altar had been set up, with two long candles and a glass vigil in the center, surrounded by bouquets of flowers. A straw mat was spread before the altar and Santa Maria sat on it cross-legged, motioning for me to sit beside her. The candles were lit. Then she pulled a large bowl of freshly picked mushrooms from under the altar. The heads of the mushrooms were brown and rather small, about an inch in diameter. The stems were long and white. . . . She gave me a cup with ten mushrooms. . . . No sooner had we eaten them than the three men behind us began vomiting and spitting. . . . I felt no nausea.

"Within half an hour the mushrooms began to take effect. First there were vivid flashing colors. Then a clammy chill came over me and I began shaking. . . . I pulled my collar tight around my neck and sat there, shaking.

". . . Intricate art motifs appeared in vivid colors. . . . Then they formed a spiral and we traveled down the spiral. . . . Our consciousness changed many times during the night. It seemed we all changed together. I attributed this to the control Santa Maria exerted over us.

". . . Then there appeared before us dancing celestial eagle gods, with all their plumage. . . . They became ecstatic. We too became absorbed with them. It was wonderful.

". . . The dancing soon came to an end and the music stopped. The eagle gods vanished. A new scene quickly took shape. . . . We were in the center of a vast, endless desert . . . the 'Land of Eternal Waiting.' Yes, it was clear to me that we were waiting there eternally. . . . What were we waiting for? I was losing my identity. I felt it might be a hypnotic spell . . . I felt I had lost contact with life on earth.

". . . Silence had become part of me. It seemed years since I had spoken, but I roused myself and forced myself to speak. To my surprise, the Mazatecs answered in English. I swear it. This really was hard for me to believe. It shook me up a bit. There was some kind of telepathic communication between us. We could understand one another, each in his own language. I was later told it sounded to them that I spoke in Mazateca."

At this point demons began speaking directly to the writer through the three Mazatecs, though he did not know it to be the case: "They answered, 'Yes, we really are in the Land of Eternal Waiting. This is reality. This is your true abode. Your life on earth never really happened. It was only a dream: . . . This alone is real.'

". . . We talked for a long while on the subtle nature of reality. . . . They were highly articulate and presented their views with wisdom."

The attack by this point on the visitor had become very severe. He sensed that and, like Carlos Castaneda, who threw a rock at the sorcerer, Don Juan, he found it necessary to take rather violent action to break the grip that had been taken on him.

". . . I would be damned if I would continue sitting there throughout eternity . . . I began to get mad, really hot.

"I turned to them and shouted, 'You're all crazy, and so am I. . . . I announced I was leaving, there and then, though I didn't know where to go. . . . I felt I was being tricked. . . . The situation called for drastic action. I really had to get away if I were going to maintain any sort of emotional balance. I threw back my head and willed myself out of that place by sheer force of concentration. It was as though an explosive charge inside of me ignited. I exploded upwards like a rocket, instantaneously. . . . Later I began to chant in Mazateca, and I moved and swayed to the rhythm of my own chanting. . . . Somewhere along the way, my chanting changed into a song, all in Mazateca. . . . The following day I was told my voice carried through the valley below and was heard all over Huautla de Jiménez. Everyone in the surrounding area heard me.

"I don't recommend the mushroom to anyone, even though they are physically harmless . . . many people would be terrified at the loss of identity caused by the mushroom. . . . Even some Indians are afraid to eat the mushroom."

There are endless variations of these accounts with a great many underlying similarities among them. They show the intimacy of the connection between such drugs and the supernatural realm of demons.

Quite often, marijuana provides the initial introduction into the supernatural, serving as a gateway to a possibly deeper involvement later—either through other drugs or apart from drugs.

A college student in New York City said that it was only after taking marijuana that he became aware of certain hitherto unknown spirit beings he described as "my friends." He said frankly that he did not know whether they were good or evil spirits.

In a report on "The Medical View: Not What the Doctor Ordered," concerning marijuana, *Newsweek* said in part: "Depending upon the personality of the user, marijuana can be a mild hallucinogen. Researchers place it on the lowest rung of the psychedelic ladder, well below mescaline, peyote, and LSD. When inhaled, the drug *quickly passes into the blood stream* and *takes effect on brain centers* in a matter of minutes. . . . A high dose may produce vivid hallucinations similar to an LSD trip." There are effects on the mind, on the body, and on the emotions.

As to physical effects, medical observation has shown that "marijuana can hinder the individual's ability to function. Even small doses produce unsteadiness. Since *spatial perception, as well as coordination, is affected,* a marijuana user may be as dangerous as a drunk behind the wheel."

"A marijuana smoker behind the wheel of an automobile is dangerous," Dr. Donald B. Louria of the Cornell University Medical College writes. "He is in a sense more dangerous—because less liable to detection—than a drunken driver."

Tests have shown that an individual under the influence of marijuana *tends to lose his coordination,* yet he often has *a feeling of omnipotence.*

This is a strategic attack on two centers—the brain and the muscular-nervous systems—having opposite effects of a kind that increases personal hazard. There is some loss of actual efficiency in the bodily mechanisms; at the same time the mind is brought under the impression that there is a higher degree of control. One feels more in command, more relaxed, tremendously able to handle whatever situation is at hand. The misimpression encourages risk-taking at the very time when the mechanisms of the body are less able to cope with the immediate environment. Up goes the inclination for risk and down goes the capacity to handle it, and the margin of danger is increased while the margin of safety shrinks.

One of Satan's most efficient instruments is the narcotics parlay: an innocent flirtation with marijuana now, a deadly alliance with heroin (or some other hard narcotic) later.

It is energetically argued that using marijuana has no connection with, in the sense that it may lead to, the use of stronger stuff. That is a lie—as those who work closely with narcotics victims know.

A study made in New York City in 1968 found that, out of 168 young people who had used marijuana, "at least 40 percent later began using heroin." People who wouldn't think of taking heroin will take marijuana, and some later graduate, for one reason or another, to more potent stuff.

A student friend at Yale who has watched undergraduates become involved with drugs—his older brother's use of marijuana led to a mental breakdown and hospitalization—put it this way:

"An airplane with a hundred seats is about to take off. The loudspeaker promises that the weather is fine and the view excellent, but it also warns the prospective passengers, 'In the middle of your flight, forty of the seats will drop out of the bottom of the plane!' The prospective passengers face the question, 'Is this trip worth taking?' "

Satan is not interested at all in selling you narcotics addiction, any more than he was interested in selling the woman in the garden death. All he aims at is getting a person to take the first bite, or the first puffs, or the first jab, or the first lungful. If you are not a user of any drug, he wants to get you from where you are now —out of the drug scene—over into the drug scene.

If you do get into it, there are a number of ways in which it can turn to your disadvantage, some of them drastic in their effects. But until you take the first step you are not a candidate for any of them.

There are about six million severe alcoholics in the United States. An alcoholic is a liquor addict. The stuff gives him all kinds of trouble but he's got to have it. It is useful to remember that the alcoholic who never takes his first drink never discovers that he is an alcoholic.

You may know four or five people, possibly more, who have used grass or something else who are still able to function perfectly well. That is right. Yet it may not be the case with you! Even if you knew 100 or 1,000, you cannot project that into a guarantee of a similar immunity for yourself.

The fact is that some people can't take the stuff without suffering damage, some can't take it without going out of their minds. If you're one of those, it doesn't make any difference how many people you know who can.

With all of these potent chemicals, the only sure thing is that if you don't bother with them, they won't bother you. *That is the only guarantee you have.* Everything else is playing a kind of Russian roulette with chemicals that may act like small charges of dynamite in your body or in your soul.

Some drugs have a slow, cumulative way of taking toll. You fly now, but you pay later. You may have to pay an enormous amount more than you can afford.

Davidson told of a girl from a well-to-do family in California who took up marijuana at seventeen, went along on it for three years, then tried LSD. "We lay back on the floor and it was a good trip. We rolled on the floor and we laughed and the room filled up with gold fog and we swam through it."

A week later she tried it again. "I began to shake and sweat and I felt like someone was pulling a band tight around my head." Three days later, "I was still trembling and crying all the time and everything still had that nightmare comic-strip look." When the writer saw her, nearly two years later, she had not taken any more LSD but "she was still trembling and unable to work."

The young woman was suffering from more than the direct effects of a chemical upon her system; she was suffering from mental, physical, emotional, and nervous effects produced as a result of taking a devastating drug—a chemical-supernatural agent.

Distorted perspectives are promised—and frequently delivered. They may have a certain novelty, but they can result in a perspective permanently and irreclaimably knocked out of focus.

When that happens, how great the longing in the victim for his right mind, for control of his bodily mechanisms, for perceptions of things as they are—all advantages that had been his, and that have been taken away. Intense desire cannot bring them back.

You would not let a person come along and crack on your skull or break your arm; it is just as unwise to permit this kind of damage to be done to your being. This is mental damage.

"Blow your mind" is another term that speaks of the mental effects of taking certain drugs.

The three words have a certain exactness in describing the explosively damaging effect upon the minds of some victims. The words are an invitation to disaster. You've got one mind. God gave it to you. It is the only one you will ever have, and Satan desires to take it from you, in part or in whole. Nothing could be more self-destructive than to "blow your mind." When you've blown that, buddy, you can never get a replacement.

If you wouldn't put a gun to your forehead and pull the trigger, you will be smart not to take something into your body that can devastate your brains.

Whether or not we are going to have a drug culture depends chiefly on what some young people decide to do now as they are confronted with the greatly increased availability of drugs in the nation.

Barry Farrell, in his essay on the great Woodstock Music and Art Festival of August 1969, spoke of "rock-dope" as a new "American religion" whose believers massed on the hillside at Bethel, New York, as though for a camp meeting of some "electro-chemical church."

It may, of course, be new to much of the United States, but it is a straight throwback to primitive, tribal religion.

They had come as though on a pilgrimage from all over the nation, 300,000, maybe 350,000, some say more. What struck Farrell particularly was how "the great stoned rock show" had "tamed and numbed" those tens of thousands, making them content just to sit there in the mud and rain in what seemed to him to be "bovine passivity."

This is brainwashing on the massive scale of a generation, not by any conspiracy of men, but by a deliberate and elaborate scheme of demons, promoted through the manipulation of fads, through the use of such catchwords and slogans as "Turn on, tune in, drop out," and by the promulgation of a few—a very few—cleverly phrased ideas or seductive promises that are, at base, bald lies.

Taken *en masse*, this is designed to produce a generation of youth whose passivity is such that they can be taken over by malign spirits, or by malign political and social forces set in motion by evil spirits. They "groove" with rock music today. Some other day they may "groove" with the cadences of some vivid demagogue.

We are made observers of the programmed destruction of a segment of the nation's young people, and the program is gaining speed and affecting greater numbers and most of us stand by not knowing quite what to make of it. What will it come to? Misery and sickness and addiction and untimely death for many. Despair and entrapment for others. Mental derangement in some degree for yet many more.

These youth encampments, centered on a bill of musical attractions, bring young people in random variety and numbers into a compact mass. There among them, enjoying a kind of anonymity, are some who possess and are ready to dole out every conceivable kind of narcotic and chemical known to provide kicks or a transient euphoria. Despite the warnings that are broadcast periodically by loudspeaker against certain kinds of drugs, the transmission of the drug culture becomes supremely easy under these conditions. Youths who were not in it are brought suddenly into it.

Among the preponderance of high school and college-age people are some who are younger—a few who are twelve, more who are thirteen and fourteen—who come to see what it is all about. The impression they get as they watch those who are older is that there are certain things a kid must do to be "with it." In this way, some are drawn in early. Some of the worst features of the youth culture are thus quickly spread in the encampment and then, when it breaks up, are diffused more widely in society.

The police, knowing that the handling of such masses would be extremely difficult if they got out of control, are pleased to accept an arrangement that offers a prospect of public order: *Anything goes* within the encampment with no questions asked about what occurs there, if, in reciprocation, the participants keep a satisfactory degree of public order and do not go on rampages. Let narcotics and nakedness and obscene behavior run on as they will within the borders of the festival.

It is not everywhere that a kind of guarantee can be got that for a certain number of hours at a certain place illegality will be protected. Narcotics especially has a field day. Some will be made drug slaves because of it.

Some will mark the beginning of their captivity to narcotics from the time of their attendance at such festivals. At Woodstock and at the Watkins Glen outpouring of July, 1973, the air was sometimes so thick with its sweet scent that all one had to do was breathe in to get some marijuana. Drug dealers calmly circulated through the immense crowd at Watkins Glen, offering mescaline at "$3 a hit" and barbiturates, methaqualone, downers, acid, grass. "At times the scene in the moist darkness resembled a Bosch painting," *The New York Times* reported, "half-naked bodies coated with brown slime moving rhythmically to the music and huddled figures curled sleeping in the mud at their feet in barbiturate or alcohol-induced stupors."

Two days after this festival, I received a call at work from a desperate father, who said that his 16-year-old daughter had gone to Watkins Glen, where she had "gone wild" according to friends on drugs made available to her there, and had not been heard from or seen since 3 A.M. on the closing day.

Though the medical personnel at the site kept an exact count of the injuries and illnesses treated, they lost count of those treated for drug overdoses. What are we coming to as a nation when we afford such unlimited opportunities for evil to work for the early harming and ruining of young lives? Human victims are made during these mass encampments. It is not only what is done during the festival that counts, but its long aftermath, which may do damage beyond any easy calculation.

If addiction spreads widely, as it is likely to do, there will be a visible demoralization of the American culture, as in fact there now is in areas where addiction is high. A terrible blight falls upon neighborhoods where the curse of drugs is rampant. This was not a widespread problem in the United States until quite recently.

Not long ago, deaths from drugs were rare. In Dade County, Florida, there were two such deaths in 1967. In the whole ten-year period ending in 1966 there had been only four such deaths there. In 1968, there were thirteen deaths. In 1969, more than twenty. The *Miami Beach Sun* reported on September 18, 1969, that three teen-agers had died of narcotics in the preceding ten days: Judi Topol, eighteen, was found dead in a car. Army private Stephen Bachanov, nineteen, on leave, died in his sleep in a motel room he had rented with some hippie friends. His mother found Gene Garlick, eighteen, dead in his bedroom. He had been using narcotics for three years.

A story in the *Times* by Paul L. Montgomery began: "Down the circular staircase in the airless basement of the office of the city's Chief Medical Examiner on First Avenue, the day's consignment of drug-abuse fatalities reposed on stainless steel slabs—five young men between the ages of eighteen and twenty-one who had been alive on Saturday and were dead on Sunday."

More than 800 New York City residents died of heroin poisoning in twelve months, including 200 teen-agers from thirteen to nineteen years old.

The young man mentioned earlier in the book who had suffered two nervous breakdowns in a few months was in the supernatural and he knew it. He knew that his experiences in the supernatural were related to his taking marijuana. It was his design to continue in the supernatural, apart from the continued use of marijuana.

Drugs are useful to Satan as the opening wedge into false religion, but they are not at all necessary to its maintenance. Once drugs and hallucinogens have made a person subject to demon influence or control, their continued use is not necessary to the perpetuation of that state. Some individuals are so linked with evil spirits by the use of such chemicals that they are thereafter permanently under spiritual deception and are unable to receive spiritual truth. In Satan's economy they are on a fixed course for hell, with scant chance that they shall ever turn out of it.

Those who engage in demonic supernaturalism directly, without the mediation of drugs, have a certain contempt for those who use drugs in this way—the kind of contempt the refined have for the crude. Satan always has a line of propaganda extant, designed to get men to believe what he wants them to believe and do what he wants them to do, and for a time that line in the West has been the encouragement of the use of drugs.

Now that that program has had a mass success among the young —in a short time pot has been popularized, made a fashion, and brought into tremendous use—there has begun to be a revision in the line. We have begun to hear that spiritual experiences are not dependent upon drugs, that they can be obtained directly through certain religious practices and disciplines.

"Voodoo virtually eliminates the need for reliance on tobacco, alcohol, and hallucinogenic drugs among Haitians, the international drug conference was told by the Haitian delegate, Dr. Emerson Douyon," a *Canadian Press* story from Quebec reported. "He said that voodoo rites and trances satisfied psychological needs of individuals who might otherwise turn to drugs and alcohol. Use of drugs and voodoo trances represent two culturally different means of arriving at the same end, 'escape from self and reality through transcendence,' Dr. Douyon said. Voodoo is a Haitian religion in which the ceremonies lead to collective delirium through movement and the rhythm of drums." It might be added that Haiti is one of the most cursed lands in the world, whose people live under the political tyranny of a witch doctor and in desperate poverty.

A disaffected former disciple of Timothy Leary wrote a long rumination urging young people away from drugs as a spiritual agency and toward purer forms. Now that demonic supernaturalism has been given a good headway, Satan desires to bring in the *systems themselves* by which people may be ensnared in it. Drugs are an expedient in a larger program of filling up the United States with false religion and supernaturalism.

Part VI

Influence

The Media—Marching
to Satan's Music

Supernatural forces of destruction are now making swift headway in undermining the welfare and sanity of many of the nation's young people, with little left to check them, and the media do mighty service in widely communicating the works of Satan among the young.

Last week, I looked up from my desk one night to see the distraught face of an editor before me, a man I have long known. His most prominent characteristics are precision in manner, in dress, and in the expression of thought, and a vast affection for his children. I had met his children and they had impressed me as exceptional for quickness of mind and an almost adult composure. This night he was slightly drunk. I had never seen him drunk before. He told me that his eleven-year-old boy had stayed away from home for several days. It was more than a kid's lark. The boy gave his father reason to think that he might bolt from home again. Fearing that the boy might leave and have no money, he said, "All right, son. I want you to stay, but if you go, here's five dollars for some food."

The boy's response was, "I don't want any of your establishment money."

The speech, of course, could hardly have arisen from any thought-out position. It was a kind of parroting of something the boy had heard. At some point he had come under the influence of ideas that were radically affecting his behavior.

The teen and subteen runaway is a part, a minority part to be sure, of the youth subculture. There is a strategy behind it. Satan knows that a child who is lured away from home can be suddenly exposed to unexpected evils and dangers. There have sprung up in some cities skid rows for young runaways, and among the things to which young people are, in fact, exposed when they wander into them are: the proffered friendship of sex perverts, procurement, assault, narcotics and other dangerous chemical agents, disease, theft, recruitment to crime, close association with a rather wide variety of strange and dissolute characters, including warlocks.

During the time when New York City's East Village was one of the nation's two best-known retreats for runaways it pulled kids in from all over the country. The East Village became a lodestone for the young, and some of the mass media served as the lodestar to guide them to that dismal precinct. For several, the visit ended in violent death.

My work has taken me into these areas. Several visits to the East Village were oppressive in the sights they offered: So many haggard young people living aimlessly on bare mattresses in ratty, dirty, unfurnished flats. Some of them out on the street begging dimes and quarters for slices of pizza to keep them going.

I remember one spring day going into a nest of revolutionary young people in a corner building for interviews. When I came out I saw entering the building, suitcase in hand, a nice-looking young kid, obviously just out of college for the summer, apparently drawn from some far place by what he had heard or read, and I wondered how long it would be before he would be in the demoralized condition some of them were in.

Under the influence of sexual indulgence, drugs, and mysticism, the transformations that occur in the young can be very swift. You see a young person with a clear eye and a clear face, still fresh with the innocence of youth, and a few months later the freshness is gone and you see a thoroughly different person and you wonder how the change could be that great so soon.

It is precisely this triumvirate of sin, along with the romantic propaganda of revolution and overthrow, that supplies the themes of nearly everything that appears in the underground press— tabloid papers written for the young and circulated near many major university centers. They dwell much on grass—marijuana— and drug-propelled "trips" out of reality, and on various aspects of the occult. Photographs and descriptions of orgies have appeared in them and various perversions find a ready outlet in their pages.

The underground papers serve their youthful constituency an unrelieved diet of pot-sex-revolution-mysticism and psychedelic adventure and thereby spread the fashions of the youth subculture, but there are national magazines that are hardly less ardent in seeking out every new excess, even if practiced by a miniscule fraction of the population, and describing it in ample detail for millions throughout the country.

Esquire magazine assiduously digs up fresh modes of aberration among the young and gives them the full blaze of tutorial publicity, especially in its annual campus issue, published a couple of weeks before the opening of the fall college term each year, just in time to inculcate incoming freshmen in the foulest ways of campus and off-campus existence. Let the demons plant some new deviation among 1 or 2 percent of the students at half a dozen campuses, and it is soon seized and conveyed to every town and village in the nation by the media. It is hardly possible any more for a teen-ager to be preserved in innocence; vile corruptions are transmitted to him by print and by film week after week after week.

In one issue *Esquire* printed a long series of side-by-side photographs of male students, showing each face before and after the effects of campus life had registered on it. The contrasts were shaking. The before pictures were of apparently mostly normal, straight young guys; the after pictures constituted a gallery of abnormalcy and degeneracy. Huge transformations had taken place in the interval between high school and college graduations.

The New York Times Magazine for January 26, 1969, carried an article by Arno Karlen reporting on "The Unmarried Marrieds on Campus," men and women living together in "unmarried bliss," except that the author often found these illicit relationships tense and glum.

The writer was not content merely to report on this style of living in an impermanent "arrangement," in which young people seek the advantages of marriage without assuming its responsibilities and without incurring parenthood, if possible.

His article closed with an incredible lament: These "couples" tended to stick together too exclusively in their live-together "arrangements":

"I by no means suggest that the unmarrieds run to the altar," Mr. Karlen hastened to make clear. "I wish more students were shacked up or living together. The best preparation for a relationship is relationships; the best training for a good sex life is sex. We stunt the capacity for both in early life for many people, and they must catch up in their teens and early 20's. I only regret that shifts in the family and in sex roles are not preparing people to enjoy the exploration more. Ventures in sex and sexuality could be a joyful part of a joyful life. They needn't be life-engulfing and glum. I almost wish someone would take much of that unmarried vanguard by the hand and show it the joys of guiltless promiscuity."

It isn't that there is too much sexual laxity and promiscuity, the writer proposes, it is that there is too little!

American society and its stability are beginning to break down under the hammers of violence and a revolutionary discontent, and the family is beginning to disintegrate and to give way to patterns found among cats. The writer publicly wishes that "more students were shacked up," regrets only that there are limitations on the joys of free-lance sexual experience, and almost wishes that promiscuity were the happier lot of those who are merely living in sin.

So it is that the nation's most respected newspaper allows its magazine to become the Sunday pulpit for a plea for more and looser sexual relationships among the young, and another small tap is administered to the crumbling foundation of American social stability.

Misery and joylessness are the inevitable result of this demonically inspired drive to destroy family relationships and to encourage anybody to have sex with anybody anytime. It isn't enough that things are as bad as they are; a word should be spoken for making them worse. This is the wisdom that the Bible describes as "earthly, sensual, devilish," and the mass media multiply it and amplify it a millionfold or more and fill the land with it.

Most of this is justified on the ground that "it's what's happening." It is, of course, part of what's happening. But quite a lot else is happening, and too often what is happening on a rather small (but noisy and gaudy) band of the whole American spectrum is selected for public attention.

In the case of the article above, of course, it was not so much what was happening, as what was *not* happening, that was of primary interest to the writer, who showed himself to be, far more than a reporter, a public enthusiast for immoral indulgence.

Just as the big drive for marijuana reached its first crest, in mid-1967, *Newsweek* did a cover story on pot, including extensive and informative coverage of the marijuana scene. It did not stop there. It also opened two full columns for a complete defense of marijuana on campus by Andrew Garvin, identified as "a twenty-one-year-old graduate of an Ivy League college." His descriptive essay was set up in a feature-column display identical to that given to the magazine's regular columnists, including Walter Lippmann. Garvin's defense of pot as "an additional method of diversion," along with liquor and sex, was a powerful piece of propaganda. Its keynote was hedonism, devotion to pleasure as the highest good. The chance to present a campus view of marijuana in a national magazine went only to an outspoken advocate. Frequently the media confer the advantage on zealots for the side of intemperance.

It is never fair, of course, to judge any publication on the basis of a single article and these news periodicals perform many excellent services, a fact which in no way diminishes the force of what I have said above.

The media are not a luxury in a free society, they are a necessity. They are the chief means by which information on just about everything of major consequence in world and national affairs is made regularly, cheaply, readily, and swiftly available to the public. Since a democracy could not function without an informed citizenry, the news media are an indispensable part of the landscape of a free society. For all their faults, the news media do a magnificent job of keeping the people informed.

Again and again, however, the lowest and basest elements have been chosen as the objects of singular attention in the press. Sometimes the media seem almost to have gone to lengths to find, and expose to public view, the few that have sunk deepest in evil. A rock group known for its appallingly degenerate behavior was given a big spread in *Life*. Not long afterward, one of its members confessed puzzlement about this to a college newspaper writer, who quoted him as saying, "I don't see why they would take four mugs like us, who believe in fornication in the streets, and give us all that ink."

The nation is under an amazing inundation of evil literature, with false mysticism taking its ever more prominent place beside the literature of eroticism, lust, and violence. Moral anarchists, ideological extremists, proponents of resort to violence, and agents of the false supernatural are among the spiritual forces that contribute to the subversion of a society, and they are getting elaborate attention through the media today.

There are spiritual forces that contribute to the stability and justice of a society: They are the ones that stand in line with the mighty truth that "where the Spirit of the Lord is, there is liberty." They are in no extreme shortage in the United States, but they are in obscurity. Their voices do not get amplified by the media in anything like the degree to which these others do. The mass media confer almost all the advantage, and direct most of the attention, to the divisive and disruptive forces, while too often ignoring those that make for cohesion, stability, and a viable unity.

Thus they continually present an artificially distorted, unbalanced picture of reality. The effect is rather like that of one of those peculiar mirrors that elongate or fatten certain features of what they reflect while unnaturally compressing others. That is one cause of what Turner Catledge, who served for almost two decades as the chief news executive of the *Times,* described as "a credibility crisis" now confronting the media.

By reflecting rather too much of one thing, and much too little of another, they give rise to indignation and distrust among the public, many of whose members begin to feel that the media are aligned with things that are strongly contrary to the well-being of their families and the nation. I do not speak here of those extremists who are antagonistic to free media, both in principle as well as in practice, but of a great number of decent citizens of reasonably balanced judgment. Their concern is not unfounded.

In shop windows near midtown Manhattan now there are such magazines as *Naked Boyhood* promising photographs of teen-age boys in the nude. In these windows there must be a hundred or more publications dealing in the boldest and most direct way with various perversions and lusts. Unspeakable filth and illustrated guides to sin and to demonic supernaturalism have lately spilled out onto almost every newsstand, magazine rack, and book rack, where the young can easily get them.

The Scriptures have a word for the men and women who publish and circulate such material as this, laying Satan's snares for the feet of the young:

"Woe to the world for temptations to sin!" Jesus said. "For it is necessary that temptations come, but woe to the man by whom the temptation comes! It would be better for him if a millstone were hung around his neck and he were cast into the sea, than that he should cause one of these young ones to sin . . . it is not the will of my Father who is in heaven that one of these young ones should perish." Matthew 18:7,14 and Luke 17:1,2.

"It is necessary that temptations come," Jesus said. It is necessary because Satan and the demons will see to it. "But woe to *the man* by whom the temptation comes!"

The demons must find human outlets for evils they devise on the spiritual plane. Such individuals make themselves merchants and purveyors of the devil's wares. That is why Jesus said that, though temptations must come, woe to the man *by whom they come.*

Notice that Jesus did not say that it would be better for the *world* if a millstone were hung around that man's neck and he were thrown into the sea. He said that it would be better for *the man.*

At the Judgment, the full bill for the social and personal harm done by the promulgation of such material will be presented to such a man by the omnipotent God. The whole extent of the damage actually done will be fully revealed, and that man's torment in hell will be eternally more intense than it would otherwise have been. Better for that man to be cut off early than for him to go on adding offenses to the ledger from which he will be judged.

In duration, hell is the same for everyone. It lasts forever. It is the fixed abode for eternal beings who have rebelled against their maker: angels and men. But the degrees of punishment in hell will vary. God is just and the Bible makes it clear that He will not mete out the same measure to the master tyrant as to the petty thief, to the ordinary sinner as to the ardent servant and purveyor of sin.

Little of it was in popular currency until about four years ago, but there has been a massive importation lately into America of Eastern religious and mystical ideas, much of it rooted in Hinduism. You can see evidence of it everywhere—on magazine covers, on television, in the book racks, in advertising, in stores.

Not long after the assassination of Robert F. Kennedy, an editor for one of the nation's major publishing houses said to me, "I'm getting out of the violence business." He had decided, on the basis of too many assassinations, to stop publishing books accenting violence.

The editor took his house out of the physical violence line, because he could see the necessity of that, but he did not take his house out of the promotion of *spiritual violence.* It is spiritual violence that gives rise to various forms of physical violence. Sirhan Sirhan is a prime example of that.

The editor's house published, among other things, the story and teachings of the Maharishi Yogi and spread them in an inexpensive paperback edition across the country, where they have, of course, exerted a primary attraction on the young. A book so filled with false and demonic mysticism, contrary to the revelation of God, and contrary to the central truths of the Judeo-Christian tradition, can quickly subvert the minds of young people.

Such a book can carry a young person into the supernatural realm and link him up with demons. If the individual is a Jew it is worse, for it can get him involved with things which the Bible specifically warns the Jews never to have any contact or communication with.

A common excuse for much of this is that it reaches them with "their own thing." In many cases it is not really "their own thing," it is Satan's thing that the demons are spreading among the young.

"Suddenly, Everywhere, Yoga"

If you had asked me at the start of the decade what Satan and the demons were pushing on the youth I would have said:

Marijuana, and other chemical and hallucinogenic agents.

Mysticism and yogism and occultism.

Sexual immorality and pornography.

The idea of revolution, and certain allegedly romantic figures symbolizing violent revolution (especially Che Guevara and Ho Chi Minh).

Wherever you looked you found these things. They were not isolated; they were pervasive; they were suddenly everywhere among the young. It is a sorry fact of our culture that, in the pure pursuit of profits, so many big companies were quick to gear up to push these themes.

The bookstores and book stands, especially those near college campuses, sounded these notes repeatedly in the books that were prominently displayed. On Broadway in New York City, directly opposite Columbia University, there is a very large and very complete paperback bookshop. It has some 10,000 titles in at least 20 subject areas.

One week *half* of the books on display in its two windows accented these themes. The featured titles included: *Venceremos! The Speeches and Writings of Che Guevara; Socialism in Cuba* by Huberman and Sweezy, with a picture of Fidel Castro on the cover; *The Great Rebel: Che Guevara in Bolivia* by Gonzalez and Salazar; *One-Dimensional Man* by Herbert Marcuse (the philosopher of the student rebellion); *Black Rage* by Grier and Cobbs; *Student Power,* including essays titled "Roots of Revolt" and "On Revolution"; *Confrontation: The Student Rebellion and the Universities* by Bell and Kristol; *Confrontation on Campus: The Columbia Pattern for the New Protest* by Joanne Grant; *I Ain't Marchin' Anymore!* by Dotson Rader (a plea for more direct expressions of protest); and *Revolution for the Hell of It* by Abbie Hoffman.

Running through all of these are the themes of revolution, and running through most of them is the assumption that the only way to set things right is by violence. Inside the door of the shop, in places of especially prominent display, I found *Die, Nigger, Die!* by H. Rap Brown and about a dozen titles on Eastern religious mysticism, Buddhism, Hinduism, and Zen. Close to half of the books most prominently featured in this largest of bookstores serving thousands of collegians fell into two of the four major categories listed above—a quite extraordinary concentration in these highly specialized areas for a bookstore that covers so vast a range of subject matter. It shows the ideas that are being programmed now into the minds of people of college age.

Revolution exists first as a concept, as a defined goal, before it is carried into practical action. The theory of Marxism preceded the historical and geopolitical fact of Marxism, with all Russia and all China dwelling under its banners. It is not reasonable to expect that so heavy a dose of revolutionary doctrine as was administered to a generation of students will not produce malign effects. True revolutionaries know how to roll with the tides of events, sometimes hanging back and waiting, sometimes taking daring initiatives. If you trace the lives of some of the communist leaders who rule nations, you will find that they became communists as a result of ideas sown in their minds in their college years. They absorbed those ideas while in college and they have lived by them ever since.

In an article titled "Meet the Women of the Revolution," Peter

Babcox wrote that "there is a quickening disposition among the young that the salvation of our culture is revolution." He spoke with a 27-year-old woman who writes poems of revolution and he quoted these lines: "*I am pregnant with murder.* / *The pains are coming faster now.*"

The public tempo of "the Movement" has subsided, largely because the issue of public discontent on which it seized—the American war presence in Vietnam—is no longer a galvanizing center for it. Many have fallen away from the cause, but a hard core remains and is willing to wait. It seemed that the Woodstock phenomenon was over but it surfaced again at Watkins Glen in mid-1973, with 600,000 attending; the revolutionary bent may also be a stronger undercurrent than we suspect.

Why is it that from New York to San Francisco, from Michigan to Florida, everywhere in the nation among the young, these themes became so markedly prevalent? Is it just a coincidence? Or, is it a plan?

Is it just a coincidence that the revolutionary ideals of Che Guevara became a vogue among young people all over the country? Is it just a coincidence that the name and persuasions of Che Guevara beamed out at the public mind and eye from magazines, newspapers, books, records in such a concentrated way? Or is "the prince of the power of the air, the spirit who is now at work in the children of disobedience," and his army of demonic messengers, able to select and to promulgate themes, ideas, and personalities that suit his purposes?

Is it just a coincidence that astrology and yogism are suddenly everywhere to be seen—on the cover of the women's service magazine at the checkout counter in the supermarket, in the window of the diet foods shop, in the advertisement that comes with the junk mail, and in many places where they confront the American mind in a novel or compelling way? Or is it a plan? Suddenly, everywhere, astrology, mysticism, Hinduism, Buddhism, occultism.

Let me assure you that I do not regard it as the work of any kind of a human conspiracy whatever. The almost unlimited power, the near-omnipotence casually ascribed to human beings by some theories of conspiracy is a product of some combination of ignorance, suspicion, hate, and superstition. Such theories are fables lacking evidence. Behind such theories there is sometimes an animating desire to create human scapegoats. If it were a human conspiracy it could not appear so suddenly and run so far so fast. It simply could not be so pervasive. There is no sinister human cabal that has such limitless access to all the means of publicity and communication as these things so readily enjoy. Instead such things spring up apparently spontaneously and originally in many places almost at once. Fifteen or twenty publishers go heavily into occult subjects in a short time. The attempt to trace the blame to a conscious and organized conspiracy of men detracts attention from where the blame and cause really lie.

The Bible, in assigning blame for evil working, fixes primary attention not on men but on demon powers, not on the earth but in the atmosphere and in the heavens. It reveals that, in contending against evil, men of God "do not wrestle with flesh and blood" —that is, against other men—"but against the principalities, against the powers, against the rulers of the darkness of this world, against *spiritual hosts of wickedness in the heavenly places."* Ephesians 6:12.

Unseen powers of evil, the spiritual hosts under Satan's rule, are able to produce in human society sudden, widespread trends or effects. That they do this is not surprising; it is their vocation. The tragedy is that human beings know so little about demons on one hand and respond so quickly to their evil workings on the other.

Many of the fads and crazes and styles and practices that are being pushed now upon the young people are demonic in origin and expressly contrary to the teachings of the Bible. Satan's policy does not change. Not only are there very evident similarities in what the demons are doing at many points in our society, but some of these things are virtually identical to what demons have done in other societies at former times in history. This is especially so in regard to gross sexual excess and public exhibition. There is nothing new about that; it has been a mark of the last years of once great societies that were soon to be defunct.

Several weeks ago I listened to a radio station whose programs are beamed at a minority audience and heard a disc jockey who, in interludes between records, made incredibly savage and bitter comments. At one point he said, "Che Guevara, that wonderful man. They say he's dead. But I don't say he's dead, because Che Guevara is *alive in me."*

It is certain that Che Guevara, a dead guerilla warfare specialist, is *not* alive in this commentator. What is alive and moving in him is a spirit of destruction who uses the name and the legacy of Che Guevara to stir people up to what they suppose to be emulation.

The man realizes that there is something alive in him that produces certain definite effects in his thoughts, in his feelings, in his speech, and to some degree in his behavior. He craves for destruction. What is alive and working in him is not the late Che; it is an evil spirit who articulates Satan's "solution" to injustice in America in the name of Che Guevara. That solution is to overthrow or wreck the whole system and to replace it with something else, not specified.

In the process individual liberty, and the lawful guarantees upon it, would go into the discard.

The major themes sounded by the underground press also run through the lyrics of popular music performed by the young for the young. The *Yale Daily News* ran a review of a record album under the headline "Stones Release Revolutionary LP." In it the same basic Satanic program—drugs, sex, occultism, and revolution—is thrust upon the young. The article begins with a quotation:

" '*The time is right for palace revolution . . . the time is right for fighting in the streets.* '

"Rock music censors who banned the Rolling Stones' 'Street Fighting Man' are going to have their hands full when they hear 'Beggars Banquet,' the group's latest album.

"Six of the ten songs are blatantly revolutionary, their heavy rhythms pounding, mobilizing, appealing to the people.

"The Rolling Stones came up out of the streets, screaming their rhythm and blues to hordes of shouting teens. Songs like 'It's All Over Now' and 'Let's Spend the Night Together' precipitated many riots, yet those songs contained no attempt at lyrical mobilization as such.

"A few years ago, the Stones stopped touring. Distracted from real hard rock by their drug experiences, they produced 'Their Satanic Majesty's Request.' Many thought Mick Jagger and company were through with the hard stuff for good, in a dream world of acid and flowers.

" 'Beggars Banquet' has proved these people wrong. The Rolling Stones are definitely back in the revolutionary hard rock thing. . . . The inside cover of the album shows the Rolling Stones—hair long and bedraggled, lips painted—in a banquet scene of drunken lust and gluttony." One of the songs in the album is titled "Sympathy for the Devil."

The youth subculture is shot through with the philosophy of Satan. There is ceaseless, incessant, pounding propaganda in the ears and eyes of the young, promoting fornication, mysticism, marijuana, and violent revolution, and we are at the point where young women seek roles as "urban guerrillas" and others feel "pregnant with murder."

This is the wisdom that is "earthly, sensual, devilish" and the purpose behind it is destruction—individual destruction and national destruction.

Satan and the demons have created a quagmire for the young. Now they are urging them to march into it by the masses, and they are supplying the lyrics, the drumbeat, and the tune. The media —motion pictures, records, print—are plugging it hard (with varying degrees of sophistication but with the same basic line of sin). That quagmire—with its come-ons of easy sex, drugs, supernatural experiences, and participation in revolution—is a trap. Many who venture into it, curious to see what it is like, will sink in it and will never get back out.

The Bible promises that "when the enemy comes in like a flood, the Spirit of the Lord will lift up a standard against him" (Isaiah 59:19b) and everyone who comes to that standard will be safe from the works of the devil.

While it is true that the attack on the youth is supernaturally planned, it is also true that the answer to it is supernaturally planned.

The only thing that will break the grip of the supernatural of Satan over the young people today is the supernatural power of God.

The Other Side of the Ledger

The media have this wonderful and terrible power: They can grant, or deny, a public existence to individuals and movements by deciding to report on them or not to do so.

A man stands up on a platform and speaks. An audience hears him, but the media are not present. The next day what he said may be known to two or three times the number of people who heard him, but the event has no public existence beyond that limited circle. For millions, it never happened.

A man stands up on a platform and speaks. An audience hears him, and the media are present—reporters, radio newsmen, television crews. Within hours the event may be made known, quite literally, to millions of people. That is the power of amplification possessed by the media. What they amplify is therefore of some consequence.

For some time now the shrill voices of disruption have been greatly amplified by the media, while certain other voices have hardly been heard. Sometimes these other voices have as much, or far more, legitimate claim to a public hearing, by the ordinary standards of news judgment.

Certain people are recognized as "leaders" by the media, and what they say or do is extensively reported. A tremendous public distribution is thus afforded to the identity, the acts and ideas of these leaders.

Other men with fully equal, or better, claim to designation as "leaders" are rarely, if ever, made known. As far as the broad public is concerned, they do not exist.

In the whole context of American life, advocates of radical positions are granted a disproportionate share of total media time and attention. The owners of more moderate persuasions, from left to right and straight through the broad middle, are not as likely to be seen or heard.

Every day the mass media inject into the mainstream of American life and thought certain influences—events, personalities, ideas.

These have much to do with the formation of the American culture and the trends that affect it. They have a more or less powerful impact on minds and lives, depending largely on the degree of susceptibility that exists at the time in the recipient.

If these daily injections pump so much more of what contributes to the ill-being of the nation than of what contributes to its well-being, accentuating the problems while minimizing the solutions, then trouble has an unusual opportunity to feed on trouble.

In the winter and spring of 1970 many interruptions broke the normal pursuit of business on American college campuses. A stage was reached, after the Cambodian invasion and the shootings at Kent State University, at which finally hundreds of campuses were effectively put out of function.

That phenomenon was, rightly, carefully reported and the nation became wholly aware of it. But another phenomenon occurred in the late winter and early spring that was not widely reported in the media and was entirely ignored by the national press, though it caused the cessation of classes at campus after campus.

You probably never knew it was going on, yet it was surely one of the most remarkable episodes of this century in American higher education.

A kind of benign disruption of campus routine and classes came, spontaneously, as students at many campuses were suddenly and unaccountably affected by a strong desire to pray, to ask God to forgive them for the wrongs they had done to others. As many did so, there followed the welling up of a great joy that was outwardly expressed in thanksgiving, by word, prayer, and song.

At Asbury College in Kentucky, Hughes Auditorium became the focus of this unexpected advent of grace upon a bewildered generation. There was something utterly compelling about the atmosphere in that auditorium. Students were drawn to it, and those who came out after many hours could only say that God was in that place. Visitors who ventured in also found that He was there, the living God manifesting Himself to a needy people.

All classes were canceled. Day after day, night after night, students and faculty members, townspeople, high school youths went in and out of the auditorium for unplanned times of rejoicing in the Presence of God. The revival, which had no human leaders, ran on around the clock, continuously, for a week.

Personal enmities were healed, grudges forsaken, old debts paid, lies and cheating confessed, among many other results. A television reporter from Lexington, Kentucky, told his audience that, in thirty-four years on the news beat, he had never seen anything that had impressed him as deeply as the event at Asbury College. A reporter I know visited the campus several weeks later. He told me that "the atmosphere there was wonderful: It was one big love-in." Yet it was a holy love-in, in which people did what was right, not what was wrong, where reconciliation was the keynote among students and adults.

Within a week the movement had spread to at least twenty other college campuses. Teams of students spread out across the country, from Florida to California, and up into Canada, to tell other students what had happened. More than 600 Asbury students went on the road, conveying the news to as many places as they could.

By any reasonable test, the shutting down of classes on college campuses because so many students are seized with a desire to *pray* is news. One definition of news is that which causes an interruption in the normal course, a break in the routine of life. And when prayer and confession and rejoicing meetings run on for days and nights, and when hundreds of students go out to tell others because they want to spread their joy, it is certainly news. Yet it was largely ignored. It was covered, of course, by local media, newspaper and radio-television stations, but it never got a mention in the national press. As far as the consciousness of the mass American public was concerned, it might just as well not have happened.

The timing of the Asbury revival movement was spiritually significant. It began on February 3, just a few weeks before American higher education was to be thrust by national and world events into its most perplexed and unhappy spring, one that can reasonably be termed a season of student despair.

God knows events in advance and He moves sovereignly in history to anticipate them, to help men who are soon to be caught up in motions of history that are beyond them. Shortly before the outbreak of the Korean War a revival swept through Korea, just as revivals affected large parts of the United States preceding the Civil War.

While division and confusion and despair were afflicting the college generation, along with such devices of the devil as false mysticism and drugs, God visited a campus to set in motion, by the gentle, prevailing Presence of the Holy Spirit, a movement of healing and reconciliation, of release and joy—a movement of such quiet force that it stilled the routine on campus after campus and compelled attention to first things.

It is not possible to tell how far the revival might have run if word of it had been communicated, while it was occurring, in the national media. The movement deserved something more than total nonrecognition.

A witch did not find it hard to get widespread publicity for her activities that spring. In its April 10, 1970, issue, *Life* devoted a three-page spread with five large pictures to Louise Huebner, "The Good Witch of the West," at a time when she was plugging her book, *Power Through Witchcraft*. When she made a self-promoting appearance in New York, the media readily showed up with cameras and microphones—in response to the desire of one witch to promote an occult book.

Certainly I do not want unfairly to criticize any one organ, and it is never conclusive to take a single instance and generalize from it. But it is perhaps an index of the present great imbalance that a national magazine had three pages for a report on the doings of one self-serving sorceress, including a picture of her surrounded by high school students, but none for a quite extraordinary movement, involving at least forty campuses and 600 students who traveled as itinerant heralds of the good news that God is alive and is acting in our generation.

We are living in what is more and more an irrational, hyperexcited and hate-diseased climate, and the many elements that contribute to that condition are given an unwarranted ascendancy over others that are conducive to stability, balance, and health. The nation would be better served if the media would amplify more of the latter. Moreover, the irrational and extremist forces now in motion pose an unveiled threat to the life and freedom of the press. China, Albania, and Greece are living examples of that.

There are many wrecking influences abroad in the nation. Drug addiction is one of them. In the first six months of 1970 the *Times* did a magnificent investigative job, reporting the sources and extent of the narcotics traffic, its terrible effects on communities and individuals, listing the mounting death toll among high school and college students, and reporting the now-admitted failure of hundred-million-dollar government efforts to make any change in it. Money and good will, it has now been found, even when present in enormous measures, are feeble against drug enslavement.

The whole despairing picture, the entire debit side of the ledger, was exhaustively reported. The collapse in Britain of the best-known of the shortcut solutions—supplying free, legal narcotics to addicts in clinics—was set forth. There was hardly a hint that anyone, anywhere, knows anything about a real and effective answer to the problem of addiction.

That is simply not the case. There *is* an answer to addiction. There are programs that are consistently effective in bringing victims out of addiction, not just temporarily, but for the long run. In New York City, and in many other cities, there are groups whose efforts to help addicts come off and stay off drugs have been met with a degree of success that reverses all the expectations (chiefly that a hooked individual will, after a time, go back to drugs again). Many addicts have been delivered permanently from their entrapment by groups working in Harlem, Brooklyn, the Bronx.

These groups, and others like them elsewhere, have worked for the most part in obscurity, unknown to the public because they are ignored by the press.

The imbalance between the amount of public notice granted the problem, as over against the solution, struck me with a certain force a little over two years ago in a matter involving two motion pictures. It came to my attention that a film about drug addiction was on location in New York. Its fascinating peculiarity was that it was a documentary drama in which fifteen of the actors were former New York City addicts, and the commercial picture was being filmed on the very turf in the Bronx where they had gone through their hells of addiction. It sounded like a story to me, so I told my editor of it. He did not want a story about it.

A week later, I was called to the assignment desk and told by an editor whose eyes gleamed with anticipation that a group of twenty-five hippies was on location at Timothy Leary's farm upstate, filming a musical. I was sent there to do a feature on it, and the story ran a couple of days later, with pictures, in the best feature display space in the paper, the front page of the second section. It was an interesting story, to be sure, and I do not suggest that we should not have done it, but its news value seemed marginal and its significance very secondary to that of the other film.

The Bronx film was based on the work of a very small, Puerto Rican church that had achieved, on extremely thin resources and under the leadership of a minister who also held a full-time job, pronounced success in leading addicts back to freedom.

He, and others, know the brighter side of the ledger, the side that says—debt paid, full release. They know of a sure exit from addiction through a powerful spiritual therapy. When it is applied and pursued to a conclusion, it results in an extraordinarily high percentage of total remissions.

As baffling as the addiction problem is, it is not beyond the power of God—even when it is beyond the devices of men to cure. Amid the urban scenes of the worst drug devastations, there are men who have found that God is able to deliver the most helpless victims, permanently. Yet in New York City, where much of this work started and has grown to its present national dimensions, it has been given very scant attention. Such programs are a victim of the large imbalance that highlights the evil with relentless intensity while overlooking the countervailing good—a distortion of the whole reality and one that unfortunately gives that which harms a big edge in the public record over that which heals.

Almost any crier for destruction, almost any individual with a new assault on old standards, a new approach to hitting moral bottom, finds a ready access for himself and his ideas through the media, sometimes with hardly a hint of credentials to support his position as a public force. The possession of a moral or spiritual novelty, or the zeal to espouse and put into action some new excess, is accepted as credential enough.

By seizing too readily upon such manifestations, the mass media communicate one man's perversion or excess to millions at plague-speed.

Fire, when it burns, is not selective. If the media help to fan the flames of social and political extremism, the fires will ultimately burn at the very doors of the media. Part of the stated agenda of extremists on both ends of the spectrum is to bring the free media into check.

This is not a summons to a hear-no-evil, see-no-evil, speak-no-evil complacency. That would be dangerous. It is no call for censorship. When that arises, liberty dies. It is an appeal, in a situation of virtually unlimited liberty, for discrimination, restraint, and especially for a balancing of the ledger so that the red ink of social distress will not get so nearly all of the attention. It is this that will make less credible, rather than more so, the demagogue's plea for imposed restraint, a plea which can already be heard in the land.

Ideas are not all equal. There are, inescapably, bad ideas and good ideas, ideas that are true and ideas that are false and ideas that are evil. If, in the desire for news impartiality, an honest attempt is not made to discriminate among them, the public is victimized.

The power of words is widely underestimated. It was, after all, nothing but ideas, aptly and urgently presented, that carried Germany the way of tyranny and militarism. It was all done with *words*. Bad ideas incessantly promoted can still carry a nation the way of anarchy and revolution, or of repression. And it is words and ideas in which the media specifically deal.

The Influence of the Jews

God desired to have a people who would be separate and distinct from all the other peoples of the earth, a people who would belong exclusively to Him, through whom He would show

His blessing and His power to the world. For that purpose He chose the Jews. The word is not quite strong enough. God did more than choose the Jews. He formed them and made them a separate people, starting with Abraham. They were—by their unique relationship to the living God—to bear a distinctive testimony to the Creator among men. God revealed Himself to them alone.

One of the primary obligations that this placed upon them was that—no matter what any of the Gentiles might do—they were to have no other worship than the worship of the one true God, no other religious practices than the ones given to them by Him, and they were to have no idols or images or icons or any such things among them, ever.

God has never removed the obligation of this exclusivity from the Jews, neither from the Jews as a people nor from any individual Jew. Let a Jew touch an idol or use it in a religious manner and a curse—the active disfavor of God—comes upon his life, and he will feel the effects of it. It is a sin that God will not tolerate in a Jew.

A Gentile can engage in religious idolatry much or all of his life and not be singularly punished for it. A Jew cannot. It is part of the very essence of being a Jew that he will not be as the Gentiles are nor do what the Gentiles do.

Because of their unique position as a people called to belong to God, Jews are more central to the plan of God than Gentiles, and the Jews play a more critical role in history than Gentiles generally do. That is always true in the long run, if not in the short.

More than that, Jews are socially and culturally influential. They cannot avoid being influential as a people. In any society in which they are found, Jews are influential out of proportion to their numbers. They affect the history of the nation they are in and they affect its culture. To a significant extent the history and the culture of the nation will turn on what some Jews do.

It is written into the very nature of the Jews, by the finger of God, to be influential.

The Jews, therefore, as a people, possess an unusual capacity to be influential. That capacity, when it is devoted to God, is the one greatest avenue of blessing and good for mankind. That capacity, when it is devoted to good works, secures immense benefits in the social and cultural realms. That capacity, when it is devoted to evil, is an avenue of cursing and misery for mankind.

Capacity is simply that—capacity. Its effect depends upon *how it is used.*

God knows that capacity is there. He put it there. He intended it to be reserved entirely for Himself, that He might use it as the channel of untold benefit to mankind. Satan knows that capacity is there, and he delights to appropriate it to his own purposes, using it as a conduit through which to pour iniquity on the earth. To do that is especially gratifying to him because it is to seize what God has made for Himself and to use it for contrary ends.

The Jews have a singular ability to take hold of history and of ideas and to shake them profoundly.

Christianity is one of the two most potent forces in world history in the last 2,000 years. A Jew began it, and the Gentiles took it up. The second force is Marxism. A Jew started it, and the Gentiles took it up.

That is influence, immense influence upon the intellectual and political and moral history of mankind. There is a very accurate sense in which the issue that is drawn in the world today is a contest for supremacy between the teachings of Jesus—He said that "the meek shall inherit the earth"—and the teachings of Marx, who said that the violent would take it.

Of all the books, or collections of writings, ever published none has obtained either the currency or the impact of the Bible. It came out of Israel and Jerusalem and it has been spread over nearly the entire earth.

Wherever the Bible has gone it has gripped men and transformed them. There are Africans, Asians, Westerners, South Americans to whom this book is truly the book of books. Though it has been translated into hundreds of languages, the work of making it the universal book goes steadily on, and every year new tribes in the remote and unmechanized corners of the world receive it in translation.

Though much of it is the history of a small people who lived in the ancient world, the Bible never fails to prove relevant and fresh to those to whom it is supplied, even to jungle tribesmen. The miracle of its applicability is in the fact that God inspired it. He honors its message and reveals Himself personally to men who read it as seekers. The Bible is a book of the Jews. Nearly every line of it was penned by Jews, but its message reaches Gentiles over the earth. That is influence.

Jews make up less than 1 percent of the world's population, but they have won 13 percent of all Nobel prizes, and that is an excellent measure of their disproportionate influence in matters of the highest recognized achievement.

Moses . . . Jesus . . . Marx . . . Freud . . . Einstein . . . such Jews
have had a vast impact and influence on the affairs of mankind.
That influence has endured, as with Moses and Jesus, over mil-
lennia. Because of what the Jews were meant to be, some Jews
touch history and culture and ideas in ways that affect the lives of
millions, or even hundreds of millions, of people.

Even where there are severe restrictions upon them, some Jews
rise to great prominence. In the middle of the present century one
Russian achieved the height of influence and circulation as a writer
in the Soviet Union. He was Ilya Ehrenburg, a Jew. His writings
ran to ten million copies in thirty languages in the Soviet Union,
but his effect upon history is not measured by that. As a journalist
and pamphleteer, Ehrenburg rallied the Russians to the anti-German cause in World War II. When the Germans invaded Russia,
there was a disposition among some of the people, weary of life
as they had known it, to look upon the Germans as potential
liberators. Large numbers of Soviet citizens defected to the invaders. Ehrenburg's brilliant anti-German tracts helped arouse a not-
always-enthusiastic Russian people to their heroic resistance to
the Nazi invaders.

Who among the French achieved fame and the highest respect
in letters in the same era? André Maurois, a Jew.

What of writers and novelists of consequence in our own country? Are not an extraordinary number of Jews among them?
Though he is few in number, wherever he is, the son of Israel rises
into the topmost levels of public influence. His exercise of that
influence produces, in our own society, much of the public good
and much of the public woe.

We do not have to look far to find the remarkable influence of
the Jews (who number scarcely six million in a nation of over 200
million population) in the public sector.

Of all the commentators on political events in the nation's public media in the last half-century one achieved a recognized place
as the most respected and most brilliant of the analysts, holding
that place for several decades: Walter Lippmann. Gentiles such as
James Reston and Edward R. Murrow have won eminence, but they
have not risen quite so high nor lasted as long as Mr. Lippmann.
So it is that a Jew occupied the place of preeminence in this field
for close to forty years, and that is influence.

I think I can say objectively, without prejudice due to employ-
ment, that *The New York Times* is at once the best and most influential newspaper published in the United States. Some nominate it

as first in both of these categories in the world. In the nation its circulation among important educators, government officials, and leaders in business, religion, communications, and law is high in every section of the country. A book, *National Leadership and Foreign Policy* by Professor James N. Rosenau, published by the Princeton University Press, showed that 77 percent of the nation's foremost opinion-makers and leaders relied on the *Times*. He wrote: "An examination of the concrete sources upon which national leaders rely for information on world affairs must begin with one fact which stands out boldly among the data—namely that there is, so to speak, an opinion-making bible, *The New York Times*. No other source received even half as many citations." That is influence.

Through all of this century, the *Times* has been published and operated by Jews, who have set its character and mission. It was a Jew, Adolph Ochs, who bought it when it was a pitiful daily of 9,000 circulation and built it into the giant of thoroughness and integrity it has been widely recognized to be. His grandson, Arthur Ochs Sulzberger, runs it today.

Gentiles have had ample opportunity and resources to have taken the places of foremost influence in American newspaper journalism, but in this century the places of recognized preeminence have been occupied by Jews.

In broadcasting and electronic communications, David Sarnoff —a Russian-born Jew who came to the United States as a boy of nine and, in 1906, took a $5.50-a-week job as an office boy with the Marconi Wireless Telegraph Company—changed the habits of the nation. In 1915 he proposed the development of the "radio music box . . . to bring music into the home by wireless." Later he started the first radio network, the National Broadcasting Company, and still later pioneered in the development of television, and he sat at the head of RCA, a corporation with an annual sales volume of over three billion dollars.

It is accurate to say that the most influential and event-shaping role in the election year of 1968 was not played by men named Humphrey and Kennedy and Johnson and Nixon but by a bright, engaging, eloquent young Jew, Allard K. Lowenstein.

It is a rule of American politics that a President in office cannot be denied his party's nomination for a second term, if he wants it, no matter how little enthusiasm there may be for him in the party's ranks. President Truman gave a thorough example of that in 1948 when he was renominated by the Democrats in the face of overwhelming party apathy and misgivings.

Allard Lowenstein set himself the task of overturning that rule, a task that had every appearance of being futile. Mr. Lowenstein was the prime mover in the anti-Johnson movement in the Democratic party, which ultimately won its point in the decision of Mr. Johnson to step aside into retirement.

One evening a few months earlier I covered an event at which I ran into Mr. Lowenstein, who made a few remarks about his consuming wish to see President Johnson retired to Texas. How puny that wish seemed in comparison to the towering realities at the time. Yet Mr. Lowenstein brought if off.

At his retirement in 1969, Earl Warren said that the most important decision of the Supreme Court during his sixteen years as Chief Justice was its ruling that any man's vote should weigh as much in the electoral balances as any other man's—the famous one-man, one-vote decree. It was a Jew, R. Peter Straus of New York, who took hold of that idea when it was only a conception of the way things ought to be. He initiated the legal proceeding and carried it through, and it had an historic effect upon the American election system.

The great peace mobilizations of that year, in which hundreds of thousands of citizens were mustered to protest the war in Indochina, were conceived by Jerome Grossman, a Boston businessman. They were perhaps the most quietly spectacular, massive demonstrations of popular sentiment in the United States in 50 years.

It is particularly in the public sector, in impact upon manners and morals and modes and fashions and ideas, that Jews play a hugely influential role in the nation.

We have seen how profoundly Jews have affected the nation's affairs in this decade. Henry Kissinger rose to the very topmost level of national influence as Mr. Nixon's chief foreign affairs executive. He exercised a significant measure of the authority of the Presidency itself, by authorization of Mr. Nixon. He met with leaders of nations on the highest plateau, took hold of world history and shook it with his two hands, so to speak, and became, in truth, one of the six most powerful men in the world in the 1970's. Millions will quite literally live and die by the initiatives and accords in which Mr. Kissinger was the key figure. That is influence!

Many Americans protested the nation's long participation in the war in Vietnam, some of them quite desperately, but no individual cut so close to the core of the matter as a Jew, Daniel Ellsberg. By his spectacular act of making the secret records of the Pentagon papers available to the public, he shook the nation to its foundation, made the public privy to a long series of actions undertaken in its name, and precipitated a Constitutional crisis.

The Jews have enriched American life to an incredible degree. The influence of Jews in commerce and merchandising and science and music and law and publishing and writing and the theater and in many other areas is not only disproportionately large, it is often of an elevated character. A list would be long. Just in science there is Abraham Flexner, whose landmark analysis of American medical education caused it to be radically changed for the better; Dr. Karl Landsteiner and Dr. Alexander S. Wiener, whose discovery of the Rh factor in 1939 has been called the most important single contribution in our time to man's knowledge of blood; Selman A. Waksman, discoverer of streptomycin, one of the wonder drugs; Albert Abraham Michelson, the first American to win the Nobel prize. There is the monumental influence of Albert Einstein, a genius whose presence gave the United States its lifesaving lead in nuclear power in World War II. The Nazi persecution of the Jews drove him from Germany to the United States and, by that one act, assured the outcome of the war; anti-Semitism is always its own worst mistake.

The once paralyzing scourge of summer that endangered and sometimes crippled the young, poliomyelitis or infantile paralysis ("an inflammation of the nerve cells . . . resulting in a motor paralysis, followed by muscular atrophy, and often by permanent deformities") was ended by the vaccines developed by Dr. Jonas E. Salk and Dr. Albert Sabin. In 1955, more than 57,000 Americans suffered it; in 1968, 57 cases were reported in the United States.

In such things as these the achievements of Jews have affected the whole people for their good.

But it is not always so. There are also Jews who occupy leading roles in promulgating some of the influences that are clearly harmful and disruptive in the American society today. An appalling quantity of moral filth and of false religion has lately been loosed upon this nation in printed form. Part of it is produced in underground operations and their sources are obscure. But more and more is being produced and distributed openly, and the three publishers most openly devoted to advertising and selling material of this kind are of Jewish origin. Of these, there is one who has published more pornographic and erotic material, more perverted material, and more material on false occultism and mysticism than any other house. In the course of a news assignment recently I had to study his operation, and I learned to my sorrow that the publisher is a Jew who became an atheist.

The American culture is under a heavy attack by disintegrative forces that specialize in promoting sexual excess and perversions and religious mysticism, and few men have played a more leading role in this than this publisher. I obtained one of his catalogs and found it to contain an astonishing variety of titles suggesting virtually every form of perversion of which I had ever heard, and some of which I had never heard, as well as radical literature and much occult and mystic material and literature of the black arts. He specializes in the very things that the Bible says offend the God of Israel, things that can inflict gross spiritual and psychological and moral damage upon human beings.

The items in the area of sex are so base that I will not quote them; other items include *The Study and Practice of Astral Projection* (by "the greatest living authority on out-of-the-body experiences"); *Picture Museum of Sorcery, Magic, and Alchemy; Encyclopedia of Occultism* (including "Psychic Science, Magic, Spiritism, Mysticism"); *Introduction to Yoga* and *Tantra: The Yoga of Sex; The History of Witchcraft; Reincarnation in World Thought;* and books on hypnosis, religious mysteries of Tibet, gypsy sorcery, torture and self-torture and sex-torture—all of this and much, much more gathered together and offered to the public by a publisher turned atheist who shows himself in the most active sympathy with the whole list of demonic religious and magical practices. It is, taken all together, an extraordinary disservice to the public. It is said that this publisher is twice a millionaire on the proceeds of this traffic in things the Bible clearly calls sin.

This same tandem, sex and mysticism, is found prominently in the work of another publisher. This morning there came in my mail an invitation to subscribe to the magazine *Avant-Garde*. It included a list of articles the magazine offers. Among these are articles about:

"An Evening with New York's scandalous Orgy-and-Mystery Theater" (the same demonic combination again).

"The First Church of Love—Photographs of a phantasmagorical chapel being built in New York to celebrate sensual pleasure" (again).

"London's Theater of Eros."

"Never-to-be-forgotten stills from the scene in Andy Warhol's film *Romeo and Juliet* in which superstar Viva falls victim to an unplanned gang-rape."

"Move Over, Lady Chatterley—A preview of erotic classics soon to be published in this country for the first time."

The list also included articles on life on a "hippie kibbutz," on "a Baptism-a-thon," two articles on marijuana, "The Prison Poems of Ho Chi Minh," a prediction of "Pornographic Film Festivals at Lincoln Center," and a list of bestsellers in underground bookstores.

The publisher and originator of this magazine—which is taking a lead in openly publicizing and spreading some of the worst of the heathen excesses through the American society—is Ralph Ginzburg.

It has been a particular mark of the worst heathen cultures and the worst Gentile religions of the past that they openly celebrate sexual indulgence, sexual symbols, fertility rites, temple prostitution, seasonal sex orgies, and the sexual abuse and slavery of young women and girls. Such things are now making their bid for an entrance into the American society, so that it may become as heathen and degenerate as any in history.

Nothing could be more heathen and wicked in its conception than such a pictorial subject as "gang-rape." Consider the misery and humiliation and psychological shock of the victim of assault by a gang of attackers. This is what the Bible calls an abomination. It is a thing unfit to be placed before the eyes of an audience of principally young people for, as the magazine suggests, "their delectation." It is for things such as this that the wrath of God comes with fury upon a society. Things such as this lay the American nation open to nuclear holocaust, the blasting sudden death of fire, for if God destroyed Sodom and Gomorrah by fire in a night—*it was precisely an attempt at gang-rape that immediately preceded the destruction of Sodom*—He will not forbid a similar destruction to fall upon this nation if it chooses to go the same way.

The Scriptures, given by God to His chosen custodians, the Jews, hold up a standard exactly opposite to that advanced by this magazine. Wherever that Hebrew book has influenced a non-Jewish people and entered into their lives, it has been a light to lift the Gentiles up out of sex excess, and idolatry, and false mysticism, and all of the other destructive things that Satan promotes and that God hates.

"I will not set before my eyes *anything* that is base," David wrote in Psalm 101:3.

The publisher of this magazine makes it his utmost specialty to set before the eyes and minds of anyone with the money to buy it that which is base and inciting to sin.

The magazine shows the influence in its editorial diet of marijuana, fornication in various forms, and false religion. What is that "phantasmagorical chapel being built in New York to celebrate sensual pleasure" but a heathen altar of the kind the Jewish Scriptures expressly forbid and condemn?

"Pornographic Film Festivals at Lincoln Center" seemed to be a kind of dark prophecy similar to a statement made to reporters following a "love-in" affair: "We'll be holding orgies in Central Park within five years."

Having gone as far as they already have in making sex, violence, and mysticism the theme of many of the books and films of the nation, demons desire to push over the last barriers to restraint and produce open erotic festivals and orgies as soon as they can. They have already succeeded in going more than half of the way.

Another book publisher took a five-column ad in *The New York Times* to advertise four books, two featuring blatantly homosexual themes, another on the Hell's Angels motorcycle gang, and one by LeRoi Jones, the black militant.

Nearly a quarter of a page was devoted to a blurb for a book called *Numbers* by John Rechy: "*Numbers* takes the reader on an unforgettable journey through the limbo of hidden sex between men . . . Its hero, Johnny Rio, is an angel of dark sex . . . He stalks the balconies of the all-night theaters, the erotic beaches and shaded glens of the city's parks. . . ."

A second book, *Sheeper* by Irving Rosenthal, was illustrated by a photo of a bearded man in a turban, with earrings and a kind of gown, holding a vanity mirror. The blurb says: "A 'black book' of the Sixties, celebrating any number of underground cults [and] memorializing the world of drugs and homosexuality. . . ."

There were four books in this larger-than-half-page ad. One detailed the specifics of the life of the male homosexual prostitute; one celebrated underground cults, drugs, and homosexuality; one depicted the violent, cultic life of the motorcycle gang; one aimed at "flinging a passionate challenge at white society in sixteen provocative and bitter new stories . . . in the black man's battle for a black America." Each of these books contains seeds of personal and social derangement. The black-uniformed motorcycle gang, brass-studded with the insignia of its cult, reflects a storm-trooper mentality, a kind of apolitical fascism, devoted to close brotherhood in evil, crime, violence, vengeance, and sometimes torture. Of homosexual acts between consenting parties—not to mention homosexual prostitution—the Bible says: "You shall not lie with a male as with a woman. It is an abomination." It was God Who spoke that to Moses. (Leviticus 18:1,22.) "If a man lies with a male as with a woman, both of them have committed an abomination; they shall be put to death; their blood is upon them." (Leviticus 20:13.) "There shall be no cult prostitute of the daughters of Israel, neither shall there be a cult prostitute of the sons of Israel." Deuteronomy 23:17.

The Bible warns against hatred and bitterness as the destroyer of the man whose spirit is poisoned by it, and as the forerunner of bloodshed and war. The book ad was taken by a Jewish publisher, a man who has made himself a messenger to the nation of perversions, violence, hatred, and lust.

When a man's enthusiasms—in religion, in sexual activity, in militant extremism—run so consistently counter to the truths revealed to the Jews by the living God, when they run so consistently in channels that increase personal and social corruption, we may begin to see that such enthusiasms coincide all along the line with the program of demons to destroy individuals and societies and to trample down the commandments given by God.

A motion picture advertised last year, illustrated by the naked forms of a man and a woman, was said to "go beyond homosexuality into perversion and sadism" and was described as "an ice-cold warning of insidious young evil triumphant . . . a tale of seven delinquent boys who dive to the depths of degradation." It included, the ad said, "an all-out, sordid finale involving theft, blackmail, bestiality, and suicide." So the works of Satan are exalted in the most public way. The slogan of the picture, based on a Biblical quotation, reflected the demonic desire to drive men out of the reach of redemption: "It is written that 490 times you can sin and be forgiven. This motion picture is about the 491st."

"I will not set before my eyes anything that is base," we again hear David declaring.

A book titled *The Exhibitionist* by Henry Sutton, published by Bernard Geis, was described this way by Eliot Fremont-Smith in a review: "*The Exhibitionist* offers teen-age orgy, voyeurism, masochism, lesbianism (quasi-incestuous, between heroine and stepmother), naked dancing, sadistic exhibitionism in front of children, various acts of heterosexual intercourse, animal skin fetishism, an attempt to erotically redirect a homosexual. . . ." This kind of thing is now increasingly and ever more boldly belched out on the public through the presses and the motion picture projectors. Of such things as these is joylessness and moral degeneration compounded for a people.

Liberty gives men latitude to do as they will. But it is possible to run liberty out to an extreme of indulgence at which it turns to bondage. "Do not use liberty for an occasion to the flesh," the Bible warns men in Galatians 5:13. Men who do that use liberty to tie themselves up in cords of personal bondage. Societies that turn their liberty into excesses of sin create the popular demand by which liberty is finally suppressed in the names of public "decency" and "order." The decency they purchase at so dear a price soon turns to totalitarian forms of indecency, and order collapses in disaster.

There is, as there probably always has been, a kind of youth subculture that is not the same as the adult culture of a nation. In the 1930's and 1940's and into the 1950's the culture of teen-age and college-age people was not vastly different from that of the whole population. But lately it has grown so markedly different, so directly at variance with and in contempt of adult society, that the chasm between them is called "the generation gap."

There are new forces, new fashions, new beliefs, new modes of life, and a whole new psychology to distinguish the youth subculture from the adult culture, and if we study the former closely it will be seen that some Jews have stood at the very summit of influence in forming this subculture.

The Origin
of the Youth Subculture

There has been created in the United States a youth culture, or youth subculture, that is distinct from the national culture. It stands opposed to the national culture, not only to what is bad in it but also to what is good in it. Not all the young participate by any means, yet this culture has its grip on a substantial and growing minority of teen-agers and young adults. It is full of powerful attractions which are able to transform a young person from one thing to something very different in a short time.

This distinct youth culture—which will if it prevails change the character of the nation—is composed of many parts. Some of the elements in it are dangerous and destructive. It has sprung up, in part, as a revolt against a national culture that has become fat and sleek and in some ways swinish. Yet the fact that it constitutes a rejection of that culture does not make it exempt from inspection to find out what in *it* is evil.

There are elements in it that are identifiably demonic and that incite the young into doing things directly contrary to the commandments of the Bible.

The present youth subculture, as a phenomenon apart from the larger culture in which it is an island, is a product of the 1960's. It did not take shape all at once; it came by stages. It is interesting to see where it came from.

If there is a single chief, *outward* identifying mark of the many-pronged demonic attack on the stability and well-being of young people today it is hair grown long or wild. It is part of the uniform of youth's great restlessness.

That particular manifestation of youth's desire to be at obvious variance with those who are older started with four young men from Liverpool, England—the Beatles quartet. Long hair was their trademark. As they were lifted up into international celebrity and made known to just about every teen-ager in the English-speaking nations and in Europe, their copious hair was constantly displayed in photographs. The long-hair style flooded in upon the youth through the Beatles' example.

There was apparently no intention other than to have a distinctive trademark as a means of special identification and promotion, but it set the trend among the young.

Now the same style seems to go quite consistently with a whole set of things—like music electrified and amplified almost to the point of pain; a minimum standard of dress and, at least with some, a low standard of cleanliness; passivity toward a regular involvement in productive work; repudiation of authority; lax sexual mores; a certain implicit acceptance of the idea of revolution as a means to a more just order; acceptance of or dependence upon drugs; an interest in the occult and the supernatural and in Eastern religions.

The Beatles, as exemplars, did not stop at hair and hard rock.

As trend-setters for the young they were used, at just the critical moment, to open a wedge into the West for the religious mysticism of the East.

It was their act, as they stood at the absolute height of their fame among the young, of seeking out the Maharishi Yogi for spiritual counsel that, more than any single factor, raised him to renown in the West. Mia Farrow, the actress, reinforced the Indian mystic's vogue a few weeks later, in October 1967, when she went to his Himalayan retreat in search of "a higher spiritual experience." The preceding August the Beatles had sought the yogi out. A news report quoted the yogi as saying, "They came backstage after one of my lectures, and they said to me, 'Even from an early age we have been seeking a highly spiritual experience. We tried drugs and that didn't work.' "

All the publicity and photographs that flowed from these encounters brought the yogi and his concept of transcendental meditation to mass attention in the United States, so that the Beatles became *spiritually instrumental* among the young.

In between the hair and the yogi, one of the Beatles made his gratuitous, but quite accurate, remark that the quartet was more popular than Jesus Christ. It is not the factualness of the remark that is significant; it is the thrust and inference of it.

The Beatles established two principal trends among the young in the West—in hair growth and in getting involved with Eastern religious mysticism. The quartet became immensely influential among young people in half the world. And behind their amazing rise to the utmost heights of popularity and fame stood a Jew.

The Beatles were just one of a great many teen-age quartets working in relative obscurity until they were discovered, altered, and then promoted into a world craze by a young man named Brian Epstein.

Brian Epstein, mastermind of the staggeringly enriching phenomenon that was known as Beatlemania, first encountered them in 1961 as "four scruffy lads in leather jackets and jeans who hung around the [Epstein family's record] store in the afternoons." He made himself their manager and business agent.

By 1964, as their twenty-nine-year-old manager, he had built them into a great attraction and he was running a multimillion-dollar operation with them. Then he launched them out on foreign expeditions. The Beatles conquered wherever they went on whirlwind tours of the United States, Europe, Australia, and Japan. They became, as *Newsweek* later put it, "a global phenomenon."

Variety, the show business paper, said that in only two years Brian Epstein had achieved "a unique impact on the international scene."

I interviewed Brian Epstein during the Beatles' first visit to New York City. I met him at the Plaza, where I found him settled in as plush and spacious a suite as I have ever seen (and I have seen the one the President stays in at the Waldorf-Astoria), a young man sitting on top of the world and quite aware of it. He was making money at an astonishing rate, had scores more booking invitations than he could possibly fulfill, and at that time he controlled by far the hottest property in show business.

On another occasion, when the Beatles were staying at Delmonico's Hotel on Park Avenue, Mr. Epstein came striding through the hallway one evening. I pointed out to him that the tabloid *Daily News* had put the Beatles' arrival in New York in its page one banner headline (an almost incredible prize for a vaudeville act).

"Very, very nice," Mr. Epstein said in a low voice, savoring it. He had at that point everything a man could ask, so it seemed.

For the five young men at the heart of this operation, the quartet and their manager, there came wealth and success in heaping measures. Brian Epstein was a multimillionaire at thirty and he had made the four others millionaires, too. *Newsweek* said that Mr. Epstein led "a revolution in popular music that changed the sensibility of a generation and made John, Paul, Ringo, and George worldwide icons." That is influence!

But note carefully that the Gentile members of the quartet go on today, but that the bright young Jew who promoted them is dead.

Brian Epstein was found dead in bed at his home in Chapel Street on August 27, 1967. "He had earned $14 million in five years," the *London Times* reported, in his dizzying projection of the quartet. And, as the paper said, "he had made five LSD trips in one fourteen-month period." Certainly Brian Epstein was socially and culturally influential on a large scale in the West, yet he became a victim of the very subculture he did so much to form.

Here is the lead of a *London Times* dispatch:

"Mr. Brian Epstein, aged 32, manager of the Beatles, was killed by the cumulative effect of bromide in a drug he had been taking for some time, a Westminster inquest was told yesterday. The coroner, Mr. Gavin Thruston, said death was due to poisoning by Carbrital, due to an incautious self-overdose. He said Mr. Epstein had been taking sleeping tablets for a long time and had 'perpetual trouble with insomnia.' The coroner had 'found a trace of an anti-depressant drug, and barbiturate and bromide' " in the body. Mr. Epstein had discovered them and brought them to their amazing pinnacle, but the quartet had wearied of him and separated from him. *Time* magazine sounded this melancholy note: "When Epstein died last week, the Beatles were some 225 miles away in Wales getting initiated into an Indian mystic cult led by Maharishi Yogi." At Brian's funeral service in a Liverpool synagogue, the magazine noted, "no Beatle was present."

Why Dead?

Why dead? Why did Brian Epstein die at thirty-two? Is there a special, a supernatural, reason why he is dead and the four he made famous and wealthy live on?

When I met him in New York, Brian Epstein had a fresh and almost cherubic countenance, smooth and pink and youthful. Death seemed decades remote, and success lay at his feet, like a servant eager to do his bidding. Yet he was not many months from the grave.

In the wild race that led him finally to insomnia and barbiturates and anti-depressants and LSD and death, young Mr. Epstein probably sought nothing more complicated than fame, success, money, and he got them all by heaps. Yet in making those his ends, he served other causes.

Fame, success, money proved enough to bribe his soul to spend himself and all his energies and genius in the promotion of that meteoric and dazzling, if historically momentary, craze called Beatlemania. In its hour there was nothing quite like it in the Western world—it was certainly "more popular than Jesus"—and its grip on the youth was tremendous. The impact of Brian Epstein's influence fell upon millions of young people and it fell upon them in a way that exploited them, in a way that stirred them to adulation and imitation and frenzy. It was just a trademark that the Beatles wore their hair that way. It was just an oddity that an entire Beatles performance would be drowned out by a chorus of young voices

raised in one continuous, high-pitched shriek. The Beatles gave
them the big beat—in music and in emotions. Out of it all, that
whole vapid, frenzied, tumultuous mania, there began to emerge
certain patterns among the young—a style of dress, an urge toward a kind of animalism, a low running fever of rebellion against
adult-sanctioned authority, a drop-out psychology, a studied neglect of standards of civilized usage, a search for immediate and
short-term sensations in sex and pot and "mind-expansion"
agents and, later, a quest into the mystery religions of the East.
These patterns soon became a culture apart. The Beatles were not
responsible for it all by any means, but they began it, set some of
its most obtrusive styles, rode it like a wild steed; and the Beatles
made the big breakthrough into the West for yogism and Eastern
mysticism. Altogether, trend-setting of potent impact on the
young.

For a time the message that millions of the young were getting
was the Beatles' message—in music, in manner, in lyrics, in dress.
Behind them stood Brian Epstein, the managerial genius of the
Beatles' incredible rise from obscurity. When he found them, the
Beatles were earning $10.50 a night. "One did everything," he
told me that day in the Plaza. "One worked very hard. One shouted
from the rooftops about the group when there was no enthusiasm
for groups. People thought you were mad, but you went on shouting."

The creation and promotion of a sensation among the Gentiles
was the end to which young Epstein consecrated all the energies
and powers of his soul. It was a cause, but it is not the cause to
which the Jews in any wise are called. There is something particularly sad in the fact that at this time in history, with civilization
under the peril of incineration by nuclear fire, with wars erupting
at various places, population levels rising fearfully and famine
stalking the earth, with confusion increasing among the nations,
that at such a time any Jew should occupy himself in promoting
this message to the young—a message that might have seemed
neutral but that actually was bereft of any content in any way useful
whatever to those to whom it was sent, and in some respects it was
evil.

Put all the lyrics that the Beatles screamed and crooned and
moaned into the ears of the young together and you have a
philosophy devoid of character or enduring purpose or temper-
ance or genuine satisfaction. Taken all together it is the counsel
of nihilism, of instant gratification (get what you want and get it

quick), of futile and passive longings, of rebellion, of mystical dreamscapes and picturesque unreality, of psychedelia, of life lived in brief interludes of pulsing tempo and driving excitation on the electronic upbeat, the sex upbeat, the narcotic upbeat, the "speed" upbeat, succeeded by longer interludes of listlessness, hopelessness, stagnancy, apathy, lethargy—alternating cycles of stimulation and depression, neither productive of any good. It is time for a message, but *that* is not the message.

It is the philosophy of demons for young people today, and demons are publicizing it and promoting it massively through many human instruments and through the media. It is designed to fascinate and captivate young people by dangling bright baubles in front of them—invitations to various sensory and spiritual experiences expressed in hard rock, in light shows, posters, buttons, slogans, underground papers, pot, mysticism—and at the same time it is designed to give demons the means of destroying them, either slowly, by installments, or abruptly. A major part of the program is to get the young out of reality, and the ability to cope with reality, into unreality and a disinclination to become meaningfully or constructively engaged with their environment. The step after that is to get them engaged destructively with their environment.

In merely failing to serve God and in serving himself, Brian Epstein fell unwittingly into the service of Satan.

A person does not have to serve demons knowingly to serve their cause; he only has to serve *wrong ends.* If he devotes himself to serving something other than God—making his ultimate goal that which is neither ultimate nor of any real intrinsic merit, and misapplying his human energy—the demons will appropriate it to Satan's cause. That is why it is a mistake to think that by failing to serve God and merely serving self, we do little harm.

First place in every man's life belongs exclusively to God. When a man puts God first in his life, the wisdom and order of God comes into that life and sets it in a vast harmony with all the purposes of God in the universe. It brings him into line with God's whole order of things.

When we put our faculties out to lesser purposes than those for which they were designed, we deny them to God and we put them at the disposal of Satan. You may be more guilty of that than you know, because you cannot see the whole effect of what you do. Millions of humans do the devil's work without having any idea that they do it.

We selfishly reserve ourselves for ourselves and seek our own good, and by doing that we fall into his service. It is not done by intention, but by omission—but such an omission! To omit God in our lives, in our plans, in our pursuits is to omit our Creator, the giver of every good and every perfect gift, and to admit Satan. Why? Because self-service is Satan's first principle: I WILL make my plans, I WILL choose my goals, I WILL run my own life—it is all the echo of Satan's drastic rebellion against God, his adamant refusal to let God be God to him.

The world would have said, looking at the achievements of Brian Epstein, that he was serving his own ends and doing a terrific job of it, piling up the millions for a future that, as it turned out, he did not have.

But if you look at what the Bible says, especially to God's chosen messengers, the Jews, you can begin to see that in going after money and success he was guilty of a monstrous idolatry. "And now, Israel, what does the Lord your God *require* of you, but to fear the Lord your God, to walk in all his ways, to love him, to serve the Lord your God with all your heart and with all your soul. . . ." (Deuteronomy 10:12.) "You shall fear the Lord your God; you shall serve him, and swear by his name. You shall not go after . . . the gods of the people who are round about you, for the Lord your God in the midst of you is a jealous God; lest the anger of the Lord your God destroy you from off the face of the earth." Deuteronomy 6:14,15.

God told the prophet Ezekiel that the people "come to you as people come, and they sit before you as my people, and they hear what you say but they will not do it; for with their lips they show much love, but *their heart is set on their gain."* Ezekiel 33:31.

Their ultimate intention was to get themselves gain. That did not prevent them from coming to the man of God and hearing the words of God, but it blocked them from acting on those words. The idolatry of money had taken deep hold on them—so that what God said was heard but not heeded because it was not in line with the purpose they had settled on themselves. It is a marvel that God will speak but men will not obey because they are busy about something else. If you are one of those who has set your gain as your goal, it would be a good thing to break with it now and to find out what God says, before it becomes ingrained in your character and paralyzes your capacity to respond affirmatively to the call of God.

Brian Epstein became, in a sense, the father of a generation. Today there are scores of groups of similar or imitative mode, many plugging Satan's message, and some are of appalling depravity. With it, Brian Epstein got the kind of package the devil loves to give: fast, short-term thrills and rewards, with enough poison thrown in to send him into the grave at thirty-two. In making success the chief end of his being, Mr. Epstein added much to the babble and confusion and sounds signifying nothing of the age. He undoubtedly possessed a huge capacity for public influence. He exercised it to immeasurable effect, yet never to any godly or elevated purpose.

I said earlier that the fact that the young man I called Leonard Marks is a Jew, rather than a Gentile, had caused his deterioration under the impact of sexual sin, Eastern mysticism, and marijuana to proceed more rapidly. Let me explain that now.

Such things are dangerous for anybody who goes into them, but they are emphatically more so for a Jew than for a Gentile. A Gentile is born and lives under no special or distinctive obligation toward God arising from his origin, his forebears, or his race. If a Gentile engages in sin, in idolatry, in immorality, he is merely doing what the Gentiles have always done.

A Jew is born under a special calling of God. God commanded the Jews to be absolutely different from Gentiles in these respects. Jews, merely by doing what the Gentiles do, violently depart from the special calling that is upon them and pervert their ways before God.

"That is not fair," some may say. "The rules are not the same." It is true that the rules are not the same for Gentiles as for Jews. That makes it important for Jews to find out what the rules are that apply to them and to live by them.

The purpose of God in calling Abraham was to establish a separate people through whom He would start to drive back the influence and works of Satan in the earth and begin to increase His influence and works among mankind.

If the Jews had lent themselves unreservedly to that purpose what benefits the earth would have received by it! Yet is is open to you, as an individual Jew, to cast aside every other consideration and really seek to know what the will of God is for you.

A Jew is particularly to be separate from the Gentiles in regard to false worship, to idols, and to sin. David of Israel declared, "I

love thy commandments above gold; yes, above fine gold. Therefore I esteem all thy precepts concerning all things to be right, and
I hate every false way." Psalm 119:127,128.

A blessing comes upon every Jew who discovers his true
spiritual identity, but Moses pronounced a curse upon Jews who
forsake the distinctive spiritual obligations that Jewishness places
upon them.

A Jew who turns his back on the God of Israel and turns to idols,
to a false religion, to militant atheism, to another ideology, or to
a cause that God despises comes under that curse and leaves
himself open to the intervention of demons in his life.

That is why a Jew who willfully becomes an apostate Jew, a traitor
to his citizenship among God's chosen people, may become a
more forceful and widely influential leader for evil than a Gentile
of equivalent position—even when he does not intend to do evil
at all. Certainly Karl Marx has shaken history and civilization more
profoundly and durably, more to the roots, than any Gentile
philosopher in our time. Marx gave himself, his mental capacity,
his eloquence, his powers to the promulgation of a philosophy and
an ethic contradictory at its core—if not in its aims—to the Scriptures, and out of his possibly good intentions there has proceeded
such a sum of anguish and suffering and death upon millions of
men as cannot fully be totaled up this side of the Judgment, when
all the works of men shall be brought to light. In his staggering
account, *The Great Terror,* Robert Conquest has set out in detail a
documented history of the Russian purges of the 1930's, its system of slave labor and death camps, and the executions and mass
murders, which ran to "a total casualty figure of twelve million
dead" before the adding in of further pogroms, including another
"three and a half million who died in the collectivization itself plus
the similar number sent to camps where virtually all died in the
following years: again, minimal estimates." Thus he got "a figure
of twenty million dead, which is almost certainly too low and might
require an increase of 50 percent or so. . . ." And that is just one
bloody bushel of the fruit of the false philosophy of Marxism,
which still takes its toll of victims daily in the world.

In rejecting the counsel of the Hebrew Scriptures, and in setting
forth his own ideas of how justice might be achieved in civilization,
Karl Marx loosed upon the world a powerful manifesto and program of action that has captured the minds of a great many men,
who have marshaled nations to it. Those nations will yet prove to
be the most murderous enemies of Israel, and the terrible irony

is that there was no room for the God of Israel in the world-view of Karl Marx.

The curse spoken by Moses is still in effect. It applies to Jews who forsake the God of Israel and His truth. "That is not fair," comes the objection again. "The rules are not the same." But it is fair. It is preeminently fair that God has called one people in the world to be His, intending to show His goodness and His power to all mankind through them. What is not fair, to God or to mankind, is that Jews have refused for the most part to allow God to use them in that way, and they have run instead after the follies and excesses of the Gentiles.

A few years ago a man named Alan Freed occupied a position as by far the most popular disc jockey in New York City among the young. There were homes in which the radio dial was set at Freed's frequency and teen-agers would complain if their parents moved it out of alignment. Mr. Freed claimed to have originated the term "rock 'n' roll." That may or may not be true, but he more than any man popularized and promoted the idiom and the groups that performed it in the nation's most populous city. Mr. Freed was a screamer and he went about it in the loudest and most bombastic style and attracted a huge audience of kids. He played music, as one critic said, whose "monotony, inanity, and sometimes suggestive lyrics horrified their parents" and another remarked that some of the content was "crude sex." But it went over big and Mr. Freed was willing to exploit it for all he could get out of it.

His personal appearances at theaters and arenas drew throngs that often ran thousands above maximum standing-room capacities and sometimes the crowds hovered on the edge of riot. I will never forget the scenes in Times Square during a winter school vacation break when Alan Freed moved into the Paramount Theater as master of ceremonies for a bill of young rock groups. A column of kids, standing six abreast, began forming in the early morning and grew steadily until it stretched and twisted for long blocks through the midtown area. Twenty or more mounted policemen and scores on foot patrolled the line, especially near the mouth of the theater, a small opening to receive so many. Day after day the lines moved into the theater for fifteen hours. One afternoon I found Alan Freed backstage in a large, chilly dressing room, wrapped in big turkish towels and sipping a glass of milk, the sensation of the hour in the city, "The Pied Piper of Rock 'n' Roll," as one headline put it.

Freed drove them to hysteria in the theaters. Richard Shepard of the *Times* wrote that "attending an Alan Freed stage show is like having an aisle seat at the San Francisco earthquake." He rolled up record grosses for a week's stand in the big theaters he played. In some places kids stampeded outside and battered down arena doors trying to get inside. In Boston there were so many incidents, including attacks on pedestrians, following an Alan Freed show that he was arrested for "anarchy and inciting to riot." Several cities barred him from returning.

There is something more to rock and roll than just music throbbing in the air. Some of it has spiritual dynamism, and some of it is a throwback to tribal ritual. You can "groove" on it. Go into any of the dark areas of the world, where demonic religions hold sway, and you will find tribes whose members at times dance themselves into frenzy to the vibrations of loud, drumming music. Such music sometimes has an evil energy that produces violence.

This is not a blanket condemnation of the rock idiom; it is not all of a piece. However, it should be recognized that there are spiritual effects attending the use of some of it. Let me quote a paragraph from a story about the religious use of rock music that ran in the *Times:*

" 'The music lets your consciousness expand,' said Joe Frazier, a student at the Berkeley Divinity School in New Haven whose group, the Eschaton, performed at the Yale service. 'It brings out a sense of community and *some fantastic commerce with the spirit and the soul.'* "

That is exactly so. Evil spirits produce such effects in the human soul and spirit through the impulses and vibrations of such music, and some of this music involves a commerce with evil spirits. That is why rock concerts of the more frenzied kind have sometimes been immediately followed by outbreaks of violence. Spiritually, that kind of rock music is an emergence of tribalism in this country.

I don't recall what Alan Freed said the day I talked with him. I only recall an impression of a man vain about who he was and about the hysteria he incited in his youthful followers. Behind it all, of course, there was a business in millions and millions of copies of records.

He was having the reward of his incessant, loud, drumfire promotion of the idiom and its stars, in the ears of the young. They jacked the price up to $4 at the box office that day because they found that the kids would pay it, cut out the movie promised on the marquee, and kept moving capacity audiences in and out of the place as fast as they could.

Mr. Freed, chief salesman of rock music and its lyrics (which came to include free love and drugs in its plain insinuations) in the nation's largest metropolitan market, did not roll on much longer. "PALM SPRINGS, CALIF., January 20," the words rattled off the news ticker in 1965, "Alan Freed, whose career as the nation's leading rock 'n' roll disc jockey was ended by scandal, died today. He was forty-three years old. He had moved to the West Coast after admitting that he took bribes in New York to publicize certain records on his radio programs. . . . He is survived by his third wife."

After Epstein, Alan Freed was the biggest promoter of the new rock mode among the young.

Mr. Freed's big influence among the young, while it lasted, went on the side of such things as: noise and the ceaseless exploitation of momentary vogues; of moaning and groaning over various moods and emotions; the cheap and easy glorification of infatuation and physical love; of a certain recklessness and vulgarity; even of implied escapism through drugs and other things, none of them of any solid worth.

While it worked, the radio and television stations ran with it gladly. Advertisers paid heavily to go along. The whole system of big-audience commercial broadcasting is used by Satan and the demons at times to promote their own programs for the masses. In aiming at nothing but big ratings and money, broadcasting has to have thrills, sensations, vogues, hints of the illicit, and especially mind-blinding noise, noise, noise. This drives out of mass currency anything that might kindle a line of serious ideation or application of thought to circumstances, and Satan is an expert at that.

He seeks always to surfeit the public's attention with vogues and amusements and pleasures that will distract humans from considerations that are important, and continually to fill up their thoughts and emotions with cheap, vivid froth. These things are like balls in the air: Satan throws up one and keeps it going for a while and, as soon as it loses its power to attract attention, he lets it drop and throws up another, having always in purpose to keep enough fresh ones there to hold public attention on an unceasing series of new diversions. It is a game he has been playing for a very long time and the mass media, dependent as they are on gaining and holding public attention, play along with it.

When I was a teen-ager, comedy was one of my special interests, and I remember how the mass magazines kept coming up with big displays on new comic personalities to command attention: There was Zero Mostel (buttering his toast right on up his arm); then there was Henny Youngman (spraying one-liners like machine gun bullets); then Henry Morgan (tweaking the noses of industrial zealots); then Jack E. Leonard (mugging in mock anguish at his own failure to be witty); then Milton Berle (telling the people not to applaud if they liked it, "just throw money"); then Red Skelton, then Morey Amsterdam, then Jackie Gleason, then Bob and Ray, later Jerry Lewis, others. There was always some new phenomenon of hopeful merriment to keep me running or excited or expectant and, sometimes, laughing. The prince of the power of the air knows how to keep the air full of flashing fads and fashions in many lines so that men will not have time to think of things like eternity and where they are going to spend it.

Did Alan Freed ever break into his daily bombarding of the big sound and the big beat at the big audience to read something beautiful that he'd come across, or talk for a few moments of the heritage of freedom, or recommend a worthwhile book to that vast amphitheater of kids whose attention he held hour after hour, day after day? Or was it all just inanity and frivolity and transient sensations and ads, ads, ads, plugs, plugs, plugs, and keyed-up music celebrating the unimportant in the most important-sounding way? The keynote of his success was the frantic commercial exploitation of the young night after night—until a bribe scheme caught up with him and sent him into exile in California where he died at forty-three.

Alan Freed and Brian Epstein rang up fortunes while blatantly promoting rock 'n' roll and all that goes with it to millions in the youth subculture, a subculture that is now filled with demonic devices for the destruction of young people. Both were cut off—Epstein at thirty-two, Freed at forty-three—much ahead of their time.

The rules are not the same for Jews. God has given special rules and special privileges to the Jews, and they wield special influence among the masses of mankind. When they turn their singular capacities and gifts to purposes contrary to the will of God, and convenient to the will of Satan, they walk head-on into trouble.

Part VII

On Being
A Real Jew

Chosen

In a review of a recent book about the Jews a critic pointedly asked: "What of Jews who *do not choose to be Chosen?*"

That is a question of the foremost importance. Since it is God Who has chosen the Jews, the Jew who does not choose to be chosen has an argument with God.

Such a man denies or opposes the wisdom of God. In so doing he incurs consequences upon himself, and he injures the entire human society to a degree that he does not suspect.

It is possible to every man to reject the claim of God upon his life and person, to Jews and also to Gentiles. But there is a substantial difference between the two.

It is natural for Gentiles to live in ignorance of God, unless they have been enlightened about Him through the Jewish Scriptures and have decided that He—the God of Israel—will be their God.

Most Gentiles recognize no true claim of God upon their lives. They live as natural men, trusting in natural and earthly things, ignoring God. They may be caught up in one or another of the many Gentile religious superstitions, properly regarded by the Jews as heathen idolatries. But some Gentiles repose a distinct and hearty trust in the God of Israel, having been awakened to a knowledge of Him by the Jewish Scriptures. They know the God of Israel and they possess and enjoy a saving relationship to Him.

The New Testament states the immutable fact that "salvation is of the Jews." Jesus declared that fact to a Samaritan—a Gentile—woman. The statement is found in John 4:22. "Salvation is of the Jews."

For many centuries the Gentiles have had their full opportunity of salvation through the Scriptures. Paul wrote to his son in the faith, Timothy, and reminded him that "from childhood you have known the holy Scriptures, which are able to make you wise unto salvation, which is in Christ Jesus." (II Timothy 3:15.) It was through the Jewish Scriptures that I was awakened to faith in God.

That happened in a rather unusual way. While in high school I worked summers as a counselor at a camp where well over 90 percent of the staff and campers were Roman Catholic. While the Catholic boys were at Mass in the mess hall, something had to be done with the dozen Jewish and Protestant boys. I was the older of the two non-Catholic counselors, so the head of the camp handed me a copy of the Old Testament and told me to take the boys into the library and hold some kind of a service for them.

I began to look into the Old Testament. I found it an interesting book, much more so than I thought I would, and I settled it in my mind that as soon as the summer was over I would go to a store and buy myself a copy of the Bible. That fall I bought one, and I began to read a chapter a night, and that proved to be one of the most important acts of my life. It led, by a clearly traceable series of steps, to my becoming a believer in the God of Israel. There are several millions of Gentiles in the world who have come to know the God of Israel for themselves through the compelling truths of the Scriptures. They know that they have the salvation that is of the Jews.

The alternative to salvation is damnation.

"The soul that sins, it shall die," the Old Testament says in Ezekiel 18:4 and 20. "The wages of sin is death," the New Testament says in Romans 6:23. Sin and the practice of sin leads inescapably down to death and to hell. "The wicked shall be turned into Hell, and the nations that forget God," Psalm 9:17 declares.

It is no novelty that Gentiles are able to obtain the salvation that is of the Jews. God has always intended it to be so. In His first words to Abraham, God said: "By you all the families of the earth shall be blessed." (Genesis 12:3.) The sweep of that phrase, "all the families," takes in all the Gentile peoples.

The relationship is fixed. Salvation is always *of* the Jews, it is never of the Gentiles. But salvation is never only *for* the Jews. It is for everyone *through* the Jews. All the families of the earth may obtain the blessing of God promised through Abraham the Jew.

If at no time in his life a Gentile turns to the God of Israel and becomes a worshiper of Him, finding the forgiveness of his sins and cleansing from them, his soul has its destiny in hell. A sinful soul cannot be taken into heaven. The Bible says, "It is appointed to man once to die, and after this the judgment." Hebrews 9:27.

Such a Gentile is born in sin, lives in sin, dies in sin and goes to hell in sin. He chooses not to be chosen. The Bible says that "many are called, but few are chosen."

The God of Israel is the God of all the earth. There is no other God. For a Gentile to bypass the promises and commandments of the God of Israel is a fateful choice; but for him it is to continue in his natural course, unenlightened by the living words of the Jewish Scriptures, and therefore unawakened. Since he chooses to live in sin, he shall also die in sin and go to a sinner's reward.

That is one thing. The Gentile is given full opportunity to belong to God, if he will. But the Gentiles are not initially called to belong to God.

For a Jew to ignore or reject the God of Israel is not the same thing. A Jew who "chooses not to be Chosen" does not do so by a mere continuity in sin. He does so by turning his back on what it means to be a Jew, as God sees it. He willfully rejects the role for which he was made as a Jew. He, in fact, does not choose to be a Jew. He knows that he is a Jew by birth, but he rejects the element in that distinctive birth that is of God—the glorious fact that, because he is a Jew, he is chosen to belong to God; to serve Him with all his mind and soul; and to show Him forth to mankind.

If he does not want this element of Jewishness—and most Jews do not—he does not want to be a Jew in the original and pure, the intended meaning of the word: to belong to God, to be one of His people. He chooses *not* to be.

That does not mean that he casts off his Jewish identity in other respects—racial or cultural or even in regard to religious tradition —but that he rejects his Jewish identity at the heart and core, in precisely that point intended by the God Who made him a Jew.

Everything else is merely an *aspect* of Jewishness, a collateral facet of Jewish origin; it is not the thing itself.

It takes the union of two wills to make a Jew: the will of God and the will of the individual. The thing that makes a man a Jew is first that God chooses him to belong to Him and to be His love-servant, and second that he actively chooses to belong to God and to be His love-servant on the earth.

Join the intention of God in setting apart the Jewish people to belong wholeheartedly to Him to the willingness of any individual Jew to have it be so, exactly as God intended it in his own life, and you have a Jew who is a Jew in the sense that God meant in calling Abraham to be a Jew.

Abraham was called and chosen, and he responded to the call of God—to his chosenness—with a hearty willingness to be a Jew. It is very important to realize that Abraham did not start out as a Jew. He started out as a Gentile; he became a Jew by obeying the call of God.

It is a great thing for a man to be called by his boss to carry out some important mission. It would be a great honor to be called by the President to carry out an important mission. It is an incomparably greater honor to be called by God to belong to Him. Abraham grasped that. He did not say no to God. He showed himself willing to cast everything else aside—home, family, job, background, tradition—so that he could pursue the will of God.

He could have chosen not to be a Jew, to remain a Gentile. He could have said that God was asking too much. Abram could have chosen not to be chosen. Instead he chose to be chosen.

Since it is the Creator Who calls him, *the only thing for any Jew to do is to choose to be chosen.*

To refuse to be chosen is to defy God and to exercise an evil heart and an evil will against the purpose of God for Jews. A Jew who does not choose to be chosen rejects God, refuses absolutely to cooperate with Him in the end for which he was born, and brings upon himself a curse.

Moses said that. Moses told the people in plain terms, warning them with the utmost solemnity and urgency: "Behold, I set before you this day a *blessing* and a *curse:* A blessing if you obey the commandments of the Lord your God, which I command you this day, and a curse if you will not obey the commandments of the Lord your God, but *turn aside out of the way* which I command you this day, to go after other gods, which you have not known." (Deuteronomy 11:26–28.) "Other gods" does not refer only to the false deities of the non-Biblical religions; it refers to anything that claims an allegiance that comes before God in a man's life. Silver and gold, achievement and renown can be "other gods," too.

A blessing is the active favor of God toward a man or a nation. A curse is the opposite of a blessing. A curse is the active disfavor of God toward a man or a nation.

Are you a Jew? Do you have any regard for this man Moses, the leader and deliverer of your people? Then hear him. Do not cast his words out of your heart or out of your mind. Do not let Satan tell you that it shall not happen exactly as Moses said. Do not think you shall ever escape the curse which Moses himself pronounced upon Jews who disassociate themselves from the purpose for which God made them.

Moses declared to the people of Israel that "all these blessings shall come upon you and overtake you, IF you obey the voice of the Lord your God. Blessed shall you be in the city, and blessed shall you be in the field. Blessed shall be the fruit of your body and the fruit of your ground. . . . Blessed shall you be when you come in, and blessed shall you be when you go out. The Lord will cause your enemies who rise against you to be defeated before you; they shall come out against you one way, and flee before you seven ways. The Lord will command the blessing upon you in your barns, and in all that you undertake; and he will bless you in the land which the Lord your God gives you. The Lord will establish you as a people holy to himself, as he has sworn to you, if you keep the commandments of the Lord your God, and walk in his ways. And all the peoples of the earth shall see that you are called by the name of the Lord; and they shall be afraid of you . . . and you shall lend to many nations but you shall not borrow. And the Lord will make you the head and not the tail; and you shall tend upward only, and not downward; if you obey the commandments of the Lord your God, which I command you this day, being careful to do them, and if you do not turn aside from any of the words which I command you this day, to the right hand or to the left, to go after other gods to serve them.

"But if you will not obey the voice of the Lord your God . . . then all these curses shall come upon you and overtake you. Cursed shall you be in the city, and cursed shall you be in the field. . . . The Lord will send upon you curses, confusion, and frustration, in all that you undertake to do, until you are destroyed and perish quickly, on account of the evil of your doings, because you have forsaken me.

". . . The Lord will smite you. . . . The Lord will cause you to be defeated before your enemies . . . and you shall grope at noonday, as the blind grope in darkness, and you shall not prosper in your ways; and you shall be only oppressed and robbed continually. . . ." Deuteronomy 28:2–29.

The blessings that God has promised to send upon Jews who obey His voice are spiritual and material, individual as well as national. Anyone who has an acquaintance with Jewish history can see how exactly the words of Moses have proved true. At times when it has seemed not to be so, when it has seemed that Jews have prospered and enjoyed liberty, without serving their God above all else, the curse has rushed suddenly upon them in full measure, as Moses said it would. There has been, there can be, no escaping from it.

For the Jews it is either a blessing above that received by all the peoples of the earth, or it is a cursing above that experienced by the peoples of the earth. The Jews must make the choice between the blessing and the curse.

Moses promised "a blessing *if* you obey." Moses said, "But *if* you will not obey . . . all these curses shall come upon you and overtake you."

Therefore listen to Moses and hear what he says. Believe it and obey it.

"And now, Israel, what does the Lord your God *require* of you, but to fear the Lord your God, to walk in all his ways, and to love him, and serve the Lord your God with all your heart, and with all your soul. To keep the commandments of the Lord, and his statutes, which I command you this day for your good." Deuteronomy 10:12–13.

That, and that alone, is what it really means to be a Jew, to be chosen by God. If you do not want to be a Jew in that sense, *then you do not want to be a Jew,* for it is what God intended in causing you to be born a Jew—nothing less, and nothing else.

If you persist in that quarrel, advising God that He was wrong in calling apart the Jews as a people for His own possession and telling Him that *you* personally want out of it, then you push away the blessing and draw down on yourself the curse pronounced by Moses.

You have not wanted to be a Jew, except in certain secondary respects, and by that refusal you make yourself worse than a Gentile in God's sight.

You can never escape the fact of your birth as a Jew. You cannot change it. Having been born a Jew *you* are under a direct commission from God to fulfill the role of a Jew, and that is to choose to be chosen. It is to love God, to walk in His ways, to serve Him with all your heart. If, born to be a Jew, you do not do so, then you are one of those Jews of whom Moses said that they have "turned aside out of the way."

More hangs on your refusal to be a Jew than your own destiny. If a certain city were threatened by floods and you were appointed the watchman of the dikes and if you refused to carry out your function and got busy at something else, it is true that you would be drowned when the flood came, but it is also true that many others would die by your dereliction.

The Jews' refusal to be the Jews as God intended has cost the world more than can be reckoned. It has cost the world a demonstration of the power and the love of God upon His chosen people.

Even those Jews who, in their refusal to belong to God, have devoted themselves to good works, have cheated the world out of the best good they might have done for it. For those good works, as magnificent as many of them are, are not the answer. Some Jews —they are not many in number but they are immense in their influence and in impact upon human affairs—have, in their refusal to belong to God, introduced evil into human affairs on a scale to match that of the blessings they could have brought had they been obedient to God.

In choosing them to be His spokesmen and prophets to mankind God wrote into the nature of the Jews a certain gauge that makes them influential. Wherever they are, the Jews have an influence upon the culture of a society, and in many of the vital sectors of its life, out of proportion to their numbers. In the United States Jews are influential and powerful in music and letters, publishing and the news media, finance, education, merchandising, manufacturing, the motion pictures, and in many other public sectors. They have not exercised their influence on behalf of that for which it is primarily intended, to make the love and power of the God of Israel known to the world.

It is a high and wonderful calling to be born a Jew and to be chosen to serve God on the earth. If you do not eagerly cooperate with that, if you choose to serve some lesser god than God, or some lesser cause, however good, you will be held accountable for your own refusal to be a Jew and for having, by that choice, denied a knowledge of God to other men in their lifetimes.

It is no small thing for a Jew to refuse to be a Jew. It is to receive a commission from God and then to tear it up and throw it aside as a thing of no value.

What you need is to see how altogether desirable and pleasant it is to be a Jew in the sense that God intended you to be, and how wearying and treacherous and precarious it is for you to decide that, if being a Jew requires you to love and serve God with all your heart, then you do not choose to be a Jew.

You need to see that the blessing of being a Jew is infinitely more desirable and good than the curse of being a Jew who has "turned aside out of the way." The blessing is the active favor of God upon you, upon your ends, upon your life. The blessing leads to eternal life, the cursing leads to eternal hell.

If you are building the tent or palace of your life, even if you are building up an empire on the earth, apart from God's design, it will all be smashed from you at the end. The curse of Moses will descend upon it all finally and you will be found to have built up what you were not meant to build up and to have failed to build what you were born to build.

There are thousands of young Jews today who are giving themselves to various causes, political and social causes of several kinds, some good, some bad, some destructive. If as few as ten young Jews of high school or college age were to decide now to serve no lesser cause but God, if they would act on that decision just as radically, just as wholeheartedly as they do in joining up with causes, if they would ask Him to take over their lives and lead them step by step and make them a blessing, in ten years it would make a difference in American society. God would use them, as He wants to do, not merely as doers of good works, but as prophets and messengers to the people.

Do you object to what God requires of you as a Jew? You are a piece of clay arguing with the potter over why He has made you what you are. You argue that you do not want to be used by Him for the purpose of His original design.

"Nay but, O man, who are you who replies against God? Shall the thing formed say to him who formed it, Why have you made me thus? Has not the potter power over the clay, to make of the same lump one vessel for honor, and another for dishonor?" (Romans 9:20,21.) It would be a good thing for you to remember that no man has ever won an argument with God.

If He wants to make you, a Jew, a pitcher with which to pour out waters to the thirsty, why would you not be willing to be used by Him that way?

The intention of God in calling the Jews to obey Him and to receive His blessing is that the whole world might see, merely by looking at the Jews, that it is good to serve the God of Israel.

Instead, for a very long time, the Jews have given the world an entirely different kind of demonstration, and one that God did not want them to give it. They have demonstrated the *curse,* when they ought to have demonstrated the *blessing.*

They have shown to the world that which does not help the world —a spectacle of a people, called to be blessed and to be a blessing, who have turned aside out of the way and brought a curse upon themselves that has made their history perilous.

They have removed themselves as a people from the covenant-blessing pronounced by Moses and have placed themselves instead under the covenant-curse pronounced by Moses.

They have not shown the world what it is to be chosen and blessed of God, and that is a terrible dereliction, a terrible deprivation to non-Jews. It is so great a failure to fulfill the mission to which they are called that the world now reels and suffers under it.

Tradition and Truth in Conflict

There is no want of religion in the world today, but there is a tremendous lack of spiritual reality. The world is full of religion and religious practices. Religious objects, religious rites, religious rote, and religious relics abound. The Bible speaks of those who "have the form of godliness, but deny the power thereof," and it counsels: "from such turn away."

Religion, more often than not, is the *form* of godliness without the content and without the power. It is truly "the opiate of the masses" because it does not liberate them, does not bring them into a living relationship to God. It succeeds only in keeping them in a kind of dull stupor, not free but hung up on rigmarole. I do not blame young people for not wanting any of it. It is dry as sawdust. You can fill up on it without getting any sustenance out of it.

There is an important, not easily understood, distinction between religion and God. You can have religion, you can have quite a lot of it, without knowing God. Satan does not hate religion; he has invented most of it and has foisted it on the masses to give them the semblance of godliness without the internal reality of godliness. The essence of the religious delusion into which millions of humans have fallen is that by practicing the *form* of godliness, to a lesser or greater degree, they obtain standing with God.

It is not to be urged that young Jews become exceedingly religious and return to all the venerable traditions from which so many Jews have wandered, by choice or by chance. Fidelity to a tradition, even a tradition of very long standing, and loving God with all one's heart are not the same thing. They may stand in direct conflict. The Spirit of God and the words of the prophets are always at variance with the pretensions of religion. The prophet Jeremiah was among many prophets of the Lord whose unpopularity with the religious establishment rose sharply because they proclaimed the message given to them by the immediate inspiration of the Holy Spirit. It was rarely an easy or pleasant vocation to be a prophet of the Lord in Israel. Very often the priests, with their vested interests in the status quo, scorned the messages sent to Israel by God through the lips of His prophets.

If a man determines that he is going to keep the law and the customs and the traditions to show God that he loves Him—that is one thing. It is an elaborate and conscious self-effort.

But if a man loves God with all his heart, he *will* keep His commandments, not as a matter of rule or rote or even conscientious subscription, but as the virtually effortless outcome of that love!

To be born a Jew is to be called by God to be a Jew, but to be born a Jew does not, by itself, give a person standing before God as a Jew. It is when the natural fact of Jewish birth is joined to the spiritual reality of Jewish faith in God that a person becomes a real Jew. There is a natural part to being a Jew and there is a spiritual part to being a Jew, and it takes the two in union to make a Jew a Jew.

A man may be born of the royal line, born to be a king, but if he refuses to take the crown and the scepter he will not become a king, though he was born to it. He will be only *a man who should have been a king* but who has devoted himself to some diminished purpose. It is the greatness of a man to rise to the highest calling that comes to him in life and fill it. God, Creator of the universe, has made no mistake in ordaining and calling a people called the Jews to belong to Him, to be His messengers and light-givers to the world. You will make no mistake in answering that call as it is, out to the full scope of God's intention.

If you are a young Jew who has not yet committed his life to some other purpose, you are especially free to do that. You can begin now to answer the call of God just by telling Him that you want to do so. You will feel that you are not able, and that is right. But are you willing? If you are willing, *God will make you able.* Moses himself did not feel able or equal to God's call, but he was willing.

God called Moses to be His spokesman to the whole Jewish people and to the whole court of Egypt. Moses immediately realized that he didn't have what it takes to be that. "Moses said to God, 'Who am I that I should go to Pharaoh, and bring the sons of Israel out of Egypt?' " (Exodus 3:11.) "Moses said to the Lord, 'Oh, my Lord, I am not eloquent, either heretofore or since you have spoken to your servant, but I am slow of speech and of tongue.' " Exodus 4:10.

But God said to Moses, "Now therefore go, and *I will be with your mouth* and teach you what you shall speak." (Exodus 4:12.) That made the whole difference. You may realize by now that you are too weak to overcome your sins and failings. Why not give God a chance to overcome them in you? You may feel that you are unworthy or unable to be what God wants you to be. In yourself, you are. But God is able to make up the whole difference between what you are not and what He intends you to be as a Jew.

The calling of God is *all* that counts. With the calling come His provisions for absolutely everything you need to fulfill it. "I will be with your mouth."

It wasn't who Moses was that mattered. It was Who was with Moses that really counted.

Moses could never have got the people of Israel out of Egypt without the supernatural power of God. He could never have got the people of Israel across the Red Sea without the supernatural intervention of God. Just by being willing to obey God, Moses brought the power of God visibly into action in human affairs. That is what the Jews are meant to do. Just by being willing to answer God's call, you as a Jew will bring the power of God into action in human conditions that are now in wretched disorder. You will be blessed by God, and you will be a blessing.

I cannot tell you that it will be easy, because I know that it will not be. It was not easy for David, for Jeremiah, for Moses, for

Jacob, for Joseph, for Ruth. But I can tell you that it will be wonderful.

To get a grasp of what the Bible teaches about the distinction between a man who is a Jew in name and a man who is a real Jew, look at the accounts of Abraham and Moses in the Torah.

It all began with Abraham, this matter of being a Jew. So if you want a good idea of what it means to be a Jew spiritually, start with the patriarch Abraham.

A man named Terah had three sons, Abram, Nahor, and Haran. Haran had a son named Lot. The family lived in a city called Ur situated on the Euphrates. Abram married a woman named Sarai, but she was barren and gave him no child. Terah moved from Ur to a place outside the city, and most of the family went with him. Terah died there.

When Abram was seventy-five years old, God spoke to him. This was the beginning of God's supernatural revelation of Himself and of His character to the human race. The message to Abram was very clear and very simple but it was vast in its extent: "Go from your country and your kindred and your father's house to the land that I will show you. And I will make of you a great nation, and I will bless you and make your name great, so that you will be a blessing. I will bless those who bless you, and him who curses you I will curse; and by you all the families of the earth shall bless themselves."

Look at it closely. There were certain things that Abram was told to do, and there were certain things God promised to do as Abram walked in obedience to Him.

The things that God told Abram to do were things that he could do, even if they were not easy things to do.

The things that God promised to do for Abram were the things that he could not do.

The first words that God spoke to Abram were:

> "Go from your country
> and from your kindred
> and from your father's house
> to a land that I will show you."
>
> Genesis 12:1

The first thing God told Abram to do was to *give up everything* he had in the world. Leave it all!

Abram was to make an absolutely fresh start in God. From that day on, everything that Abram had would come straight from God. From that day on, Abram would know that everything came from God.

The call of God is total. To be free to obey God and to become wholly God's man, Abram had to leave his home, his family, his friends, his job, his city, and go out to a place he did not know with nothing but the promise of God to lean on. But if the call of God is total, so are the provisions of God.

As a candidate to become the father of a great nation, Abram was not a very impressive specimen. He was old and had no children. His wife was barren. He was a bad choice from the standpoint of natural prospects, but he was an excellent choice from the standpoint of supernatural prospects. If God did not do it, it would not be done.

Since God chose Abram as a man *through whom to show His power,* it was far better that it be that way. No one would ever think that Abram had done it by himself.

The Jews are a small people among earth's multitudes. The purpose of God in calling the Jews has always been that He might make an open display of Himself and of His power through them. Their weakness and smallness has never been a block to that; it is the best possible aid to it. But their unwillingness and disobedience blocks it entirely.

Nearly everyone who receives and obeys the call of God finds that it gives offense to those who are closest to him and most concerned for his welfare, because it is supernatural rather than natural and it is therefore unaccountable. There is no explaining it in natural terms, and it is not wise to try.

Let a young person prepare himself by natural means for a sensible occupation—lawyer, physician, banker, broker, engineer, teacher, whatever—and the people who are closest to him will be pleased. But let him say, "I am called to be a man of God and do the will of God, whatever that may be," and almost the first question he will be asked is, "And what is the salary for *that?*"

It would not have been wise for Abram to have said to the people around him, "Here I am childless and old, and now I am going to leave my home and work here and go out to some other place and God is going to make a great nation out of me and make my name a blessing to all the peoples of the earth." They would not have been able to understand.

I have rarely known a young person to pursue what he reasonably understands to be the will of God for his life without catching static, and plenty of it, from those nearest to him. They try to figure out in natural terms what is supernatural in origin, and it won't work.

A declared intention to trust the invisible God can set up in relatives the most agonizing apprehensions about the probable welfare of the one they love. I know a young man, now several years out of college, who decided at graduation to follow God with all his heart. His father said to him, "Son, when you come to the time when you have to go out on the street to beg for food, let me know."

He told his father, "Look, Dad, the God I am serving led two and a half million Jews through the wilderness for forty years, and He fed them during that time. That would be about seven and a half million meals a day. Multiply that by 365 for one year, and then multiply that by 40 for the entire time. They never planted or harvested a crop. I believe that the God Who took care of the Jews can take care of me. I am just one person."

This young man has never had a single paycheck since graduation, has never done anything for the sake of obtaining money, and yet he has had plenty to eat, plenty of clothes and comfortable shelter, and today he manages affairs that are probably four times larger than anything he would have had to manage had he set out to make himself a fortune.

In telling Abram to give up everything, God did not intend to make Abram a pauper. He intended to make him a wealthy man, but He intended to make it plain that everything came from Him.

Abram went out as God told him, but he did not quite perfectly obey God's three-part commission:

"Go from your country, AND your kindred, AND your father's house to the land that I will show you." Instead, Abram allowed his nephew Lot to go along with him.

It did not work out well. Abram went out in a spiritual response to the word of God. Lot went out in a natural desire to be with his uncle. Trouble arose because of this breach of obedience, and God had to work it around later for Lot and Abram to separate from each other. Genesis 13:11.

Abram went out in naked faith in the living God. When Abram's caravan had come to Canaan (the land later to be known as Israel), "Abram passed through the land to the place at Shechem, to the oak of Moreh. At that time the Canaanites were in the land. Then the Lord appeared to Abram, and said, 'To your descendants I will give this land.' So he built an altar to the Lord, who had appeared to him." Genesis 12:6,7.

It was Abram's part to go, to leave home and kin behind, and journey into the land of Canaan. He alone could do that. It was God's part to bless him, to make his name great and to make of him a great nation. God alone could do that.

As soon as Abram arrived in the land, God appeared to him supernaturally and told him that He would give that land to his progeny. That is why the Jews are in that land today. It was only a few words that God spoke to Abram, but now they are as fresh in God's purpose as if spoken this morning, and God is still working them out in history.

Abram's acts of simple and trusting obedience to the word of God, his willingness to do what God said, provided the earthly basis for God's acts in history through Israel and the Jews. If Abram had refused to go in sheer and naked faith, there would have been no such basis. Not until you as a Jew obey God in sheer and naked faith will you give Him a basis on which to manifest Himself in your life.

Abram the Gentile became Abraham the Jew because he believed God and dared to take Him at His word.

When the Lord reaffirmed the promises, given first to Abraham, to his son Isaac, God said: "I will multiply your descendants as the stars of heaven, and will give to your descendants all these lands; and by your descendants all the nations of the earth shall bless themselves,

> BECAUSE ABRAHAM OBEYED MY VOICE
> AND KEPT MY CHARGE,
> MY COMMANDMENTS,
> MY STATUTES,
> AND MY LAWS."
>
> Genesis 26:1–5.

Take careful note of that. It is God's statement on the life of Abraham. Yet it is a curious and significant statement in one respect.

Abraham lived several hundred years before the Law and the statutes and commandments were given to Moses—yet he kept them!

If you can discover the means by which Abraham kept them long before they were given, you will get hold of an understanding of what keeping the Law is and what it is not.

What it is not, is human diligence and human effort conscripted to a total attempt night and day to abide by more than six hundred commandments and statutes. Orthodoxy attempts that, more or less, but it cannot succeed at it. The hill is far too steep and the power of human nature falters and fails somewhere short of the top.

We have God's own testimony that Abraham kept the Law in a way that was wholly pleasing to God, so we cannot doubt that he did. It will not do to say that Abraham kept the commandments that had been made known during his lifetime and was not under obligation to keep the others.

If God had said only that "Abraham obeyed my voice and kept my charge" that could reasonably be argued. But God adds to that the great fact that Abraham also kept His *commandments,* and His *statutes,* and His *laws.* The statement is triply reinforced—beyond the fact that Abraham obeyed God's voice and kept His charge—to make it plain that Abraham kept the whole range of God's Law.

By what means did Abraham contrive to keep commandments, statutes, and laws that were not given until several hundred years later? He kept them in the only way God has ever intended them to be kept—not by rote, but out of the heart.

He did not even have to know them to keep them. But he had to know God to keep them.

To use a rude illustration, if the driver of an automobile is convinced of the necessity of safety on the highways, his driving will be strictly lawful, without any strict effort at law keeping.

His demeanor behind the wheel, deeply informed by his desire for safety for everybody, will be lawful and courteous naturally. It will not be necessary to mark the upper speed limits for him along every couple of miles of roadway. Wherever he is, he will find and adjust continually to safety's speed, not because the speed limit is legislated and posted, but because it is his nature to do so.

For such a driver you don't need the law. He keeps it anyway. The law is in him.

The *only way* a man may keep the law and please God in doing so is out of the heart.

To keep the law by effort is a hard yoke, which few are willing to try to bear. To keep the law as an expression of the inner nature is no burden; it is a delight.

It is not necessary to promulgate a long series of hard and

exacting rules for a mother regarding the care of her baby: "Do not drop the infant, do not strike him, do not gag him, do not go off and leave him for the weekend, be sure to give him milk at regular intervals, change him, keep him in an atmosphere where the temperature does not go below 22 degrees or over 91 degrees," and so on. A mother does these things primarily because *the law of infant care is written within her nature.*

She does better than any seventy-five of the best rules you can think up. She loves the baby!

It is not necessary to tell the man who loves God with all his heart to be careful not to go out and murder or rob his neighbor. Because of his love for God, he will not do any harm to his neighbor, but he will do good to him. Why, then, was the law given? Was it to make men good? No!

The law was given to show men that they are bad and that they need a new heart and a new spirit within if they are ever to live lawfully in God's eyes and please Him.

Tradition and interpretation have added much to the law that does not reside either in God's Word or in His intention. Abraham kept the law in its purity, as God intended it to be kept, as you must keep it. But Abraham's keeping of the law, on which God put the seal of His approval, would not pass a close orthodox scrutiny today.

Abraham was ninety-nine years old, twenty-four years had passed since he had entered Canaan at the word of God, but still he had no son by Sarah. He must have wondered at times when God would fulfill His promise. There was no evidence at all in nature that it would or could come to pass.

Then one day "the Lord appeared to him by the oaks of Mamre, as he sat at the door of his tent in the heat of the day." Genesis 18:1.

"He lifted up his eyes and looked, and behold, three men stood in front of him." The Lord and two angels had come to him. Abraham ran to meet them, "bowed himself to the earth and said, 'My Lord, if I have found favor in your sight, do not pass by your servant. Let a little water be brought, and wash your feet, and rest yourselves under the tree, while I fetch a morsel of bread, that you may refresh yourselves, and after that, you may pass on—since you have come to your servant.'"

One might wonder if the Jewish tradition of hospitality had its beginning here, and in the Biblical injunctions to treat strangers and sojourners well.

The heavenly visitors told Abraham, "Do as you have said." Abraham's hospitality went well beyond the morsel of bread of which he had spoken.

"Abraham hastened into the tent to Sarah, and said, 'Make ready quickly three measures of fine meal, knead it and make cakes.' And Abraham ran to the herd, and took a calf, tender and good, and gave it to the servant, who hastened to prepare it. Then he took curds, and milk, and the calf which he had prepared, and set it before them, and he stood by them under the tree while they ate." Genesis 18:2–8.

It is fully evident that Abraham did not keep a kosher kitchen. Abraham, the man who pleased God, served a meal of "curds, and *milk, and the meat of the calf*" and he set it before the Lord! He served the milk and the meat to God, Who had come and appeared to him with two angels, and *they ate it.*

Here is where tradition and truth clash hard, and one or the other must give way.

Three times the Bible says plainly, "You shall not seethe [boil] a kid in his mother's milk." (Exodus 23:19 and 34:26; Deuteronomy 14:21.) That is the word of God.

To build that up into a system for the absolute separation of kitchens and utensils, keeping meat and dairy products apart, is to go way beyond the word of God. Abraham kept the law and the statutes of God in serving cakes and curds, milk and meat to his visitors.

His visitors said to Abraham, "Where is Sarah your wife?" He said, "She is in the tent."

"The Lord said, 'I will surely return to you in the spring, and Sarah your wife will have a son.' And Sarah was listening at the tent door behind him." Genesis 18:9,10.

Genesis 21:1–4 says: "The Lord visited Sarah as he had said, and the Lord did to Sarah as he had promised. And Sarah conceived, and bore Abraham a son in his old age. . . . Abraham called the name of his son who was born to him, whom Sarah bore him, Isaac. And Abraham circumcised his son Isaac when he was eight days old, as God had commanded him."

The three visitors, as I have noted, were the Lord with two angels. They appeared to Abraham as "three men." Their next destination was the evil city of Sodom. Abraham accompanied them on their way toward Sodom, but the angels went on ahead. Genesis 18:22 says, "So the men turned from there, and went toward Sodom; but Abraham still stood before the Lord."

Abraham began to plead with the Lord to spare the city of Sodom from destruction if He found as many as ten righteous men in it.

When the angels arrived at the city to be destroyed they found Lot there. Genesis 19:1 says, "The two angels came to Sodom in the evening; and Lot was sitting in the gate of Sodom." There is a contrast here between the man who goes out in God's will and the man who goes out in self-will. Abraham's journey had brought him into the presence of God; Lot's journey had brought him to the most dangerous place on earth.

God's standard is perfection: A man who keeps the Law would be a perfect man. Earlier in the same year in which the Lord and the angels appeared to Abraham and promised him a son by Sarah, the Lord alone appeared to him. Genesis 17 says, "And when Abram was ninety-nine years old, the Lord appeared to Abram, and said to him, 'I am the Almighty God; walk before me and be you perfect.'

"... And Abram fell on his face, and God talked with him, saying ... 'Neither shall your name be Abram any more, but your name shall be Abraham, for a father of many nations have I made you. ...'" Genesis 17:1–4.

It is a wonderful fact that Abraham kept the law, without knowing the law. The commandments, the statutes, and the ordinances of God were shown by him, not in writing, but in the way he lived.

"Walk before me and be you perfect," was God's word to Abraham. No man can ever do that on his own native resources. It would ordain a terrific and unceasing struggle against his own inward nature. What he needs is *a new inward nature.*

It is absolutely necessary—indeed, God requires—that a man have a thoroughgoing inward transformation as the first means of getting right with God and living in a way that is truly pleasing to Him. A man must have a new nature within if he is ever to live lawfully in God's eyes.

A man receives that new nature when he is given a new heart, a new spirit, when he is circumcised in his heart. He is then born again. The new spirit that comes into a man is of God, and that spirit is able to keep the law because *its nature is to do so.* When that happens, the great struggle against sin, the great struggle to measure up to the law ceases. The new spirit that God implants within the man is of God and the man therefore keeps the law of God. That is the inner secret of Abraham's godly life.

Do you know how Abraham was made righteous in the eyes of God? Immediately following God's promise to Abraham that he should have descendants as the stars for number, the Torah says Abraham "believed the Lord, and he reckoned it to him as righteousness."

By faith in God and in the word of God, Abraham was made righteous. A man can do no greater thing than to believe God, to obey Him, to trust Him actively, to love Him. To do anything less denies God the primary place at the center of human life that He rightly claims as Lord and Creator of the universe.

The New Testament upholds the divine authorship and the perfection of the Mosaic Law in every respect. "Think not," said Jesus, "that I am come to destroy the law, but to *fulfill* it." The work of Jesus was to make available to all the inhabitants of the earth, including its preponderance of Gentiles, that inward transformation by which they are enabled to keep the Law in the way that Abraham did—not by rote and rigor and sweat and memorization—but by believing God, by exercising faith in Him, by receiving Him, by loving Him supremely.

Paul, the master teacher of the early Christians, gave us a tremendous clue when he wrote:

"We know that *the law is spiritual,* but *I am carnal,* sold under sin." Romans 7:14.

It is impossible for a natural man to keep the spiritual Law! Only a spiritual man can keep the spiritual Law. And he does not do it by any tremendous effort of his will, by any mighty cranking up of his own flawed and insufficient nature.

There are two entirely different natures here. The Law of God is heavenly, spiritual, perfect. The fallen nature of man is earthly, carnal, "sold under sin." The two do not match.

It is no use exhorting a Model A Ford to fly. See it roaring down the runway, coming as fast as it can, in a great rush toward the takeoff, its hood rattling. It will not get far off the ground! If it is ever going to fly it will have to be taken into the workshop and be made over into an airplane and given wings. It simply is not in the nature of Model A Fords to fly. And it simply is not in the nature of natural men, no matter how hard they may try, to keep the spiritual Law. When a man has a new heart and a new spirit within him, his new heart and new nature matches the spiritual Law and keeps it for him. For the first time a man finds within him that which is adequate to meeting the challenge of the spiritual Law.

How clearly I recall the unending struggle in which I once engaged against certain sins of which I morally disapproved but which I found my strongest efforts inadequate to overcome, except on a hit-or-miss, now-you-win, now-you-lose, basis. I was the victim of my fallen nature and I could not get permanently up above it. It was not because I did not try. I tried hard, but I could not make it.

All that stopped the day I was born again. Suddenly I found there was no more battle—but there was victory! And it was effortless, unfailing victory.

I could not *get* up above it by trying, but now I *was* up above it. My human nature could never keep the moral law, because it was impossible to it. But my new spiritual nature kept it for me.

That is not very flattering to a man, to be sure. It robs him of a certain false sense of heroism in the struggle. But it works! I far prefer effortless and continual victory over sin to great effort and stumbling defeat.

What God desires of Israel is not slavish conformity or great rigors of soul but ardent heart's love and devotion to Him. The large distinction between the most arduous religious devotions and practices of God's people, the Jews, and the kind of service that God really wants of them is made clear in Chapter 58 of Isaiah:

> "Cry aloud, spare not, lift up your voice like a trumpet; declare to my people their transgression, to the house of Jacob their sins. Yet they seek me daily and delight to know my ways, as if they were a nation that did righteousness and did not forsake the ordinance of their God. They ask of me righteous judgments, they delight to draw near to God. 'Why have we fasted,' [they ask] 'and thou seest it not? Why have we humbled ourselves, and thou takest no knowledge of it?'
>
> "Behold, in the day of your fast you seek your own pleasure, and oppress all your workers. Behold, you fast only to quarrel and to fight and to hit with the fist of wickedness. Fasting like yours this day will not make your voice to be heard on high.
>
> "Is it such a fast that I choose, a day for a man to humble himself? Is it to bow down his head like a rush, and to spread sackcloth and ashes under him? Will you call this a fast, and a day acceptable to the Lord?
>
> "Is not this the fast that I choose:
> To loose the bonds of wickedness,
> To undo the thongs of the yoke,
> To let the oppressed go free,
> and to break every yoke?

Is it not to share your bread with the hungry,
and bring the homeless poor into your house;
when you see the naked to cover him,
and not to hide yourself from your own flesh?
"Then shall your light break forth like the dawn, and your
healing shall spring up speedily;
Your righteousness shall go before you,
The glory of the Lord shall be your rear guard.
Then you shall call, and the Lord will answer;
You shall cry, and he will say, Here I am.
"If you pour yourself out for the hungry,
and satisfy the desire of the afflicted,
Then shall your light rise in the darkness
and your gloom be as the noonday.
And the Lord will guide you continually,
and satisfy your desire with good things;
And you shall be like a watered garden,
like a spring of water, whose waters fail not.
"And your ancient ruins shall be rebuilt;
You shall raise up the foundations of many generations;
You shall be called the repairer of the breach,
the restorer of streets to dwell in."

Isaiah 58:1–12

Signs, Symbols, and Reality

It is very much the bent of human nature to substitute
the symbol of a spiritual reality, or the agency of it, for the reality
itself. God rejects, and He will never accept, such a substitution.
Thus some Christians regard the act of water baptism as having
some mystic virtue in itself—as if the conformity to an outward rite
would ever substitute for that inward transformation, of which
baptism is the appropriate sign.

The symbol is thereby made to take the place of the spiritual reality (of which it is to be an outward, visible evidence) but it will never work!

Even the claim of descendancy from Abraham can become a vain and empty boast. John the Baptist, when he was preaching, said: "Do not presume to say to yourselves, 'We have Abraham as our father,' for I tell you, God is able from these stones to raise up children to Abraham. Even now the axe is laid to the root of the trees. Every tree therefore that does not bear good fruit is cut down and thrown into the fire." (Matthew 3:8–10.) At one point some men came to Jesus and said, "Abraham is our father." Jesus said to them, "If you were Abraham's children, *you would do what Abraham did.*" John 8:39.

Nowhere does the Old Testament indicate in any way that spiritual standing before God is conferred upon Jews automatically as the offspring of Abraham. The prophets, from Moses onward, are unanimous in crying out against and warning against such presumption, because it deceives those who hold it into thinking they are something they are not.

God said that the Jews of Moses' day, every one a lineal descendant of Abraham, had "corrupted themselves" and had "turned aside out of the way which I commanded them," and so would be blotted out cf His book.

The prophet Ezekiel wrote, "The word of the Lord came to me: 'Son of man, the inhabitants of these waste places in the land of Israel keep saying, "Abraham was only one man, yet he got possession of the land; but we are many; the land is surely given us to possess." Therefore say to them, Thus says the Lord God: You eat flesh with the blood, and lift up your eyes to idols, and shed blood; shall you then possess the land? You resort to the sword, you commit abominations and each of you defiles his neighbor's wife; shall you then possess the land? . . . They will know that I am the Lord when I have made the land a desolation and a waste because of all their abominations which they have committed. As for you, son of man, your people who talk together about you by the walls and at the doors of the houses, say to one another, "Come, and hear what the word is that comes forth from the Lord." And they come to you as people come, and they sit before you as my people, and they hear what you say but they will not do it; for with their lips they show much love, but their heart is set on their gain. And, lo, you are to them like one who sings love songs with a beautiful voice and plays well on an instrument, for they hear what you say, but they will not do it.' " Ezekiel 33:23–26,30–32.

The people were very diligent in attending services, but they did not go to hear the word of God and obey it. They went to enjoy the beauty of the liturgy! They liked the form, but they rejected the content.

The people made their claim in Abraham to the possession of the land, but they did not do as Abraham did, and God said that they would not possess the land. Neither tradition, nor lineage from Abraham, nor going to services, all of which they had, was enough.

A man who is a natural descendant of Abraham must also be a spiritual son of Abraham by truly believing in the God of Abraham, Isaac, and Jacob and by living as Abraham did. Such a man walks by faith; trusts God, not things; loves God and serves him with a whole heart. That man is a Jew.

Of the Jews of Moses' generation exactly two—Joshua and Caleb —came through the wilderness and got into the land of milk and honey. All the rest died short of it.

When the people of Israel, led out of Egypt by Moses, came to Canaan, the good land which God had promised to give them, a man was selected out of each of the twelve tribes to go in and "spy out the land." The twelve returned. Ten of them "brought to the people of Israel an evil report of the land, saying, 'The land, through which we have gone to spy it out, is a land that devours its inhabitants; and all the people that we see in it are men of great stature . . . and we seemed to ourselves like grasshoppers, and so we seemed to them.' " Numbers 13:32,33.

"Then all the congregation raised a loud cry; and the people wept that night. And all the people of Israel murmured against Moses and Aaron; the whole congregation said to them, 'Would that we had died in Egypt! Or, would that we had died in this wilderness! . . . our wives and our little ones will become a prey; would it not be better for us to go back to Egypt?' . . . And Joshua the son of Nun and Caleb the son of Jephunneh, who were among those who had spied out the land, rent their clothes, and said to all the congregation of the people of Israel, 'The land which we passed through to spy it out, is an exceedingly good land. If the Lord delights in us, he will bring us into this land and give it to us, a land which flows with milk and honey. Only do not rebel against the Lord; and do not fear the people of the land, for they are bread for us; their protection is removed from them, and the Lord is with us; do not fear them.' But all the congregation said to stone them with stones. Then the glory of the Lord appeared at the tent of meeting to all the people of Israel. And the Lord said to Moses, 'How long will this people despise me? And how long will they not believe in me, in spite of all the signs which I have wrought among them?' " Numbers 14:1–11.

Of the Jews over twenty years old only the two, Joshua and Caleb, got into the land. All the rest died outside the land in the wilderness. God told Moses that Caleb would be allowed to go in "because he has wholly followed the Lord." Deuteronomy 1:36b.

Joshua and Caleb got in because they took an Abrahamic position of faith regarding the promise of God. The rest failed to take such a position of faith. If the Jews of Moses' day did not get into the land of promise, the land their forefather Abraham had sojourned in, it is a gross delusion to think that Jews who are not the spiritual children of Abraham will ever get into heaven, where their father Abraham now is.

The human propensity to try to have the symbol do for the substance is reproved in the Book of Revelation when God addresses the church at Sardis: "I know your works. *You have the name of being alive,* and you are dead." Revelation 3:1b.

They had the name of life, but they did not have the life itself. There are millions of people in the world today who have the *name* of Christians, but who are no more Christians in the sight of God than statues are. They suppose that going to church and keeping up with certain rites, which do not change the inner man, make them Christians. They have never realized that an individual becomes a Christian only by a new birth.

Religious Jews, those who have not been washed onto the bleak shores of unbelief by tides of modern secularism, are especially prone to this substitution of symbols, traditions, and rites for the true content of their faith. This has been the case for a very long time, and the prophets of Israel and Judah cried out against it with consistency and ardor. Hear Joel: "Yet even now, says the Lord, *return to me with all your heart,* with fasting, with weeping, and with mourning; and rend your hearts and not your garments. Return to the Lord, your God, for he is gracious and merciful, slow to anger, and abounding in steadfast love, and repents of evil." Joel 2:12,13.

"Rend your hearts and not your garments." At some point, men in the act of true heart's repentance for sin tore their garments. It was a spontaneous expression of what was taking place within them. This was observed and—since true repentance brings peace with God, joy and communion with the Creator—the tearing of garments became a kind of ritual practice, perhaps in the hope that repeating it would produce an inward result. It could not do so. Yet the form goes on, until the Spirit of the Lord raises up a prophet to remind men once again of the content, without which the form is a ritual husk.

Churches and synagogues tend very much to try to satisfy the people by serving up the husks—the *right* husks, not the wrong husks, but nevertheless husks. The synagogues serve up Jewish husks and the churches serve up Christian husks, and the people are supposed to get by on that diet in a time of desperate spiritual need.

A man would not object to a feast of fruits being brought to him in a large bowl, but if on future occasions the *bowl* were to be brought back empty and set before him to be admired as the bowl in which the feast had formerly come, he could not be greatly blamed if he grew a little weary of the bowl. Even if the bowl were a very beautiful one, he might not care to have it brought to him week after week. After a while he might ask, "Why do we have only the bowl? Why do we not have the fruits as well?"

Why do so many churches have the form but not the power? That is why some young people are not attracted to their religion. It does not meet their needs. History, tradition, and form, all useful things in their place, are never a satisfying substitute for content.

God Himself is the true content of the Abrahamic faith! God revealed Himself to Abraham and told him to make *Him* the basis of his life. Except in those brief seasons when his faith wavered, Abraham leaned on God and expected all benefits and results to come from Him. The key to Abraham's life was that he lived in conscious, daily, entire dependence on God. That stance allowed God to be God to him. Abraham did not try to play the role of his own providence. He did not seek to be "the cause of his own effect."

With God as the content of one's faith, the activity of God—not merely the influence of God but His direct activity—is seen and experienced in one's life, in small ways and large ways, day by day.

Gideon became one of the leaders of Israel in the new land. Chapter 6 of Judges begins: "The people of Israel did what was evil in the sight of the Lord, and the Lord gave them into the hand of Midian. And the hand of Midian prevailed over Israel, and because of [the attacks of] Midian the people of Israel made for themselves the dens which are in the mountains, and the caves and the strongholds. Whenever the people of Israel put in seed the Midianites and the Amalekites and the people of the East would come up and attack them . . . and destroy the produce of the land as far as the neighborhood of Gaza and leave no sustenance in Israel, and no sheep or ox or ass. . . . And Israel was brought very low because of Midian, and the people of Israel cried for help to the Lord."

God heard the cry of His people and almost immediately put into effect a supernatural program of help for Israel.

"When the people of Israel cried to the Lord the Lord sent a prophet to them"—that was the first step—"and he said to them, 'Thus says the Lord, the God of Israel: . . . I delivered you from the hand of all who oppressed you, and drove them out before you, and gave you their land; and I said to you, I am the Lord your God; you shall not pay reverence to the gods of the Amorites. . . . But you have not given heed to my voice.' "

The people of Israel had, very largely, lost both the form and the content of their faith and were without the blessing of God.

The young man Gideon was under the oppressor, too, and he was carefully hiding his meager provisions from the Midianites. As a boy he had heard of the things God had done for Israel.

Shortly, "the angel of the Lord came and sat under the oak at Ophrah." The angel spoke to Gideon and said, "The Lord is with you, you mighty man of valor." It was a strange salutation to a youth who was acting timidly. "And Gideon said to him, 'Oh my Lord, if the Lord is with us, why then is all this befallen us? And where are all the miracles that our fathers told us of?' And the Lord turned to him and said, 'Go in this your might and deliver Israel from the hand of Midian; have not I sent you?' "

That was all Gideon needed for the task—the word of the Lord.

Gideon was not, in himself, a mighty man. He was weak and he felt powerless. But God told him to "go in *this your might* . . . have not I sent you?" The strength of Gideon was to be the power of God openly displayed through Gideon.

Gideon knew the historic tradition, passed down by the elders, that at times God had acted mightily for Israel, but he saw just the opposite in his own day, and he could not make the two things jibe. Was God dead? It was a great question that he asked—*"Where are all the miracles that our fathers told us of?"*

Gideon wanted to be doubly sure that God would be with him, so he asked God for a sign. He said he would put a fleece of wool out. " 'If I find dew on the fleece only, and it is dry on all the ground, then I will know that you will deliver Israel by my hand, as you have said.' And it was so. When he arose early the next morning and squeezed the fleece, he wrung enough dew from the fleece to fill a bowl with water."

Even with that supernatural evidence of God's intention, Gideon was not wholly convinced. "Then Gideon said to God, 'Let not your anger burn against me, let me speak but this once. Let it be dry only on the fleece, and on all the ground let there be dew.' And God did so that night; for it was dry on the fleece only, and on all the ground there was dew."

The enemy came up against Israel "as locusts for multitude; for both they and their camels were without number, and they entered into the land to destroy it."

Gideon blew the trumpet and rallied an army of 32,000 men to meet this host. "The Lord said to Gideon, The people who are with you are too many for me to give the Midianites into their hands—lest Israel vaunt themselves against me, saying, *My own hand has saved me.*"

God did not propose to deliver Israel by natural means but by supernatural means. She would prevail not by her own might but by an open show of His power. So the army was cut from 32,000 men to 10,000 men.

"And the Lord said to Gideon, The people are yet too many...." So this time the muster was cut back to three hundred men, a number that would never allow for any confusion or doubt about Who had done what.

To strengthen Gideon's faith for the attack on the invaders, God told Gideon to steal down into the camp of the enemy by night.

"And the Midianites and the Amalekites and all the people of the East lay along the valley like locusts for number." Gideon went down and entered the camp and "when Gideon came a man was telling a dream to his comrade; and he said, 'I have dreamed a dream, and lo, a cake of barley bread tumbled into the camp of Midian, and came to the tent, and struck it so that it fell, and turned it upside down, so that the tent lay flat.' And his comrade answered, 'This is no other than the sword of Gideon the son of Joash, a man of Israel; into his hand God has given Midian and all the host.'

"When Gideon heard the telling of the dream and its interpretation, he worshiped."

As rumors run quickly through a military camp, this dream quickly spread through the ranks of the Midianite host, sowing a fear of Gideon in the ranks.

Chapter 7 of Judges tells how the three hundred Israelite men, each armed only with a trumpet and a jar with a torch in it, were divided into three companies. They "stood every man in his place round about the [enemy] camp" at night and they "blew the trumpets and broke the jars . . . and they cried, 'The sword of the Lord and of Gideon!'

"When they blew the three hundred trumpets, the Lord set every man's sword against his fellow and against all the army; and the army fled. . . ." The battle turned into an utter rout. God had intervened to deliver Israel from her oppressors.

The whole program of deliverance was supernatural from start to end: God sent a prophet to speak His Word to the people; the angel of the Lord visited Gideon; God gave Gideon the supernatural sign of the wet and dry fleeces and the supernatural confirmation of the dream overheard; God gave Gideon a strategy for the battle. Finally, "The Lord set every man's sword against his fellow." The casualties were on the enemy's side.

The content of Israel's faith had again showed Himself in response to the cry of the Jews to Him. It was a glorious hour, but very soon the attempt was made to institutionalize the victory wrought by God through Gideon.

"Then the men of Israel said to Gideon, 'Rule over us, you and your son and your grandson also; *for you have delivered us out of the hand of Midian.*' Gideon said to them, 'I will not rule over you, and my son will not rule over you—the Lord will rule over you!' "

That, for all its brevity, was a very great speech. The people invested the credit for their deliverance not in the content of their faith, but in His human instrument. Gideon reproved them for this idolatry, rejected their misplacing of the credit in man and pointed them to the living God.

Gideon rose to this occasion with strong loyalty to God and an admirable restraint, but Gideon was not entirely free of this troublesome human bent to substitute form for content. He asked the people for the gold earrings they had seized from the Midianites, and they gladly gave them to him. "And they spread a garment and every man cast in it the earrings of his spoil . . . and the purple garments worn by the kings of Midian. . . . And Gideon made an ephod of it. . . ." (An ephod is defined as "a richly embroidered, apronlike vestment having two shoulder straps and ornamental attachments for securing the breastplate, worn with a waistband by the high priest.") This ephod must have been made after the specifications given in Exodus 28:2–8, and it was no doubt a very beautiful piece of religious wear. But it soon became an object of idolatry. It was placed on public display, and it drew Jews from all over to gaze at it. The Bible says, "And Gideon made an ephod of it and put it in his city, in Ophrah; and all Israel played the harlot after it there, and it became a snare to Gideon and to his family." The ephod became a *religious object,* and the people came to it, and once again men substituted a thing for the glory of their God.

The people of Israel did not need a religious museum with a beautiful ephod in it; they needed only to continue to put their daily trust in the God Who had delivered Israel out of bondage to the Midianites. God despises this propensity for idolatry in the human race because it seeks to reduce Him to the level of someone or something.

Once, while Israel was journeying under Moses, the people became impatient with their lot and spoke seditiously. "Then the Lord sent fiery serpents among the people, and they bit the people, so that many people of Israel died. And the people came to Moses, and said, 'We have sinned, for we have spoken against the Lord and against you. Pray to the Lord, that he may take away the serpents from us.' So Moses prayed for the people. And the Lord said to Moses, 'Make a fiery serpent, and set it on a pole; and every one who is bitten, when he looks upon it, shall live.' So Moses made a bronze serpent, and set it on a pole; and if a serpent bit any man, he would look at the bronze serpent and live." Numbers 21:4–9.

Why did this figure of a bronze serpent set on a pole save the people who looked at it? There is a reason: The people had been bitten by serpents, a Scriptural figure for sin and Satan. Bronze or brass is a Scriptural figure for judgment, consistent through the whole Bible. The bronze serpent on the pole was a figure of *judged sin.* A look at the figure on the pole took away the penalty of death!

Sin must be judged, and it would either be judged and punished in those who had committed it, or it would be judged in the figure on the pole.

Those who looked to the figure of judged sin on the pole found that the judgment that should have fallen on them was taken away. They lived.

The power of the figure lay entirely in the fact that it was a faithful representation of what was to happen later, for it typified the suffering and death of the Messiah.

Isaiah says, "It was the will of the Lord to bruise him . . . when he makes himself an offering for sin, he shall see his offspring, he shall prolong his days; . . . he shall see the fruit of the travail of his soul and be satisfied; by his knowledge shall the righteous one, my servant, make many to be accounted righteous; and he shall bear their iniquities." (Isaiah 53:10,11.) This prophesies the death of the Messiah, by the will of God, as an offering for human sin, the raising of Him to life again, and the efficacy of His death in making sinners to be accounted righteous. The prophecy accords precisely with the New Testament word that says of Jesus: "He bore our sins in his own body on the tree." I Peter 2:24a. Christ was made "to be sin for us, who knew no sin, that we might be made the righteousness of God in him." (II Corinthians 5:21.) Jesus became *judged sin* on the cross. Anyone, Jew or Gentile, who looks to Him will find the reality of the amazing fact that the penalty for his own sin, death, has passed upon the Lord. Anyone who looks to Jesus will live, even as the Israelites who looked to the bronze serpent on the pole lived.

There are, not literally but spiritually, fiery serpents among the young people today, stinging them with sin and with death. One day word came on the radio that Fairleigh S. Dickinson III, 19-year-old freshman son of a wealthy and cultured family and a graduate of the Kent School in Connecticut, was found lying unconscious in a dormitory room at Columbia University and was taken to St. Luke's Hospital and pronounced dead. He had taken a dose of LSD and inhaled the fumes from some burning opium a few hours before he died. His family gave him the best advantages the American culture offers; they sent him off to college, not knowing they would see him soon in a coffin. A report in the *Times* makes it clear that young Dickinson was very much a member of the LSD-rock music scene, with its emphasis on dreams and mystical experience and freaking out. The devil promised one thing but delivered something different. Instead of "kicks" and "trips," he got sudden death.

There comes a point, as demons work destructively among the young, at which nothing—no advice or cultural advantage or psychological aid or parental counsel—can break the grip of demonic influence upon a kid. The fiery serpents were more powerful than their human victims, and the demons are more powerful than men.

For a supernatural affliction, a supernatural answer is required. The people of Israel were helpless before the fiery serpents until they confessed their sin and looked at the bronze serpent God told Moses to make. The instant they did that, the power of death over them was broken.

It takes the power of God to break the power of demons.

The basis of God's intervention against Satan on behalf of man is the death of Jesus on the cross. When nothing else will work, when all hope fails, Jesus is able to come in and break the power of demonic influence in a life and set the person free. I do not say that because it is my religion, I say it because it is a supernatural fact. I have seen the powers of narcotics addiction overcome and its helpless victims set free, when nothing else could do it, by the personal appropriation of the saving work done on the cross, and by calling on the name of Jesus. It may look weak to men, but the demons know it is their undoing.

The bronze serpent that Moses lifted up on the pole had no power or virtue in itself. It saved the lives of those who looked to it, not because of what it was, but because of what it represented. Hundreds of years later we read of this same bronze serpent in the Old Testament. It appears in the Biblical summary of the life and work of King Hezekiah of Judah, a godly ruler who rooted out false worship:

"Hezekiah was twenty-five years old when he began to reign, and he reigned twenty-nine years in Jerusalem. . . . And he did what was right in the eyes of the Lord, according to all that David his father had done. He removed the high places, and broke the pillars, and cut down the Asherah. And *he broke in pieces the bronze serpent that Moses had made,* for until those days the people of Israel had burned incense to it." II Kings 18:1–4.

God had commanded it. Moses had made it. Hezekiah destroyed it. When the plague was over, the object should have been destroyed. Instead, it was preserved and placed in a special niche in some religious museum, where the people burned incense to it. It became a relic, a religious artifact.

Form, ritual, tradition, symbols—none of this must be allowed in any way to displace the living God. Religion is full of such things. The less men have of God in their lives, of the experience of His power and presence, the more they look to things that are dead in themselves.

Because they are lifeless things, religious practices that lean on them, rather than on God, become burdensome, repetitious and dull to the young—form without content.

Among these false props is the boast of natural descendancy from Abraham—if it is made apart from the exercise of a faith like Abraham's in the living God. Circumcision, too, falls into the category of mere outward subscription to ritual if it is not followed up by a life befitting circumcision. The Old Testament makes this clear.

Circumcision—Outward
and Inward

Circumcision, the cutting of the flesh, was commanded by God for the Jews. It was to be the outward sign of an inward reality.

Of what is the rite of circumcision a symbol or sign? There need be no doubt on the point, for the Scriptures declare it repeatedly.

It was to Abraham that the commandment of circumcision was given: "And God said to Abraham, 'As for you, you shall keep my covenant, you and your descendants after you throughout their generations. This is my covenant, which you shall keep, between me and you and your descendants after you: Every male among you shall be circumcised.

" 'You shall be circumcised in the flesh of your foreskins, and *it shall be a sign* of the covenant between me and you. He that is eight days old among you shall be circumcised; every male throughout your generations, whether born in your house, or bought with your money from any foreigner who is not of your offspring. Both he that is born in your house, and he that is bought with your money, shall be circumcised. So shall my covenant be in your flesh an everlasting covenant.' " Genesis 17:9–13.

At the very outset, circumcision, the distinctive mark of the Jews, was not limited to Jews but was applied to any Gentile brought into the house of Israel by purchase. Immediately, the covenant blessing promised to the Jews was made available to the Gentiles. From the start, all the nations of the earth were to be blessed through Abraham.

Later, Moses speaks specifically of circumcision. The teacher of the Law reveals its meaning and its spiritual nature:

"And now, Israel, what does the Lord your God require of you, but to fear the Lord your God, to walk in all his ways, to love him, to serve the Lord your God with all your heart and with all your soul, and to keep the commandments and statutes of the Lord, which I command you this day for your good? Behold, to the Lord your God belong heaven and the heaven of heavens, the earth with all that is in it; yet the Lord set his heart in love upon your fathers and chose their descendants after them, you above all peoples, as at this day. *Circumcise therefore the foreskin of your heart, and be no longer stubborn.* For the Lord your God is God of gods and Lord of lords, the great, the mighty, and the terrible God, who is not partial and takes no bribe. . . . Your fathers went down to Egypt seventy persons; and now the Lord your God has made you as the stars of the heaven for multitude." Deuteronomy 10:12-22.

Circumcision removes a covering of skin from a part of the human anatomy that is reproductive, that has the capacity to transmit life to another generation.

Circumcision, in its inward reality, is a kind of cutting out and removing of a covering over the heart—spiritually, not physically —that impedes the free and ardent exchange of love between the heart of man and the heart of God. That which impedes it is cut away and cast off permanently. When that great love is fully in action, the Jews are able to carry out their mission to the world and to reproduce in others their own devotion to Jehovah.

What a day it will be for mankind, staggering in thickening moral darkness, when the Jews are circumcised in their hearts! For individual Jews, those who care, that can occur now if they desire.

Moses, in his discussion of the dispersion and the regathering of the people to the land, specifically promised this to Israel: "And when all these things come upon you . . . and you call them to mind among all the nations where the Lord your God has driven you, and return to the Lord your God, you and your children, and obey his voice in all that I command you this day, with all your heart and all your soul; then the Lord your God will restore your fortunes, and have compassion on you, and he will gather you again from all the peoples where the Lord your God has scattered you. If your outcasts are in the uttermost parts of heaven, from there the Lord your God will gather you, and from there he will fetch you; and the Lord your God will bring you into the land which your fathers possessed, that you may possess it; and he will make you more prosperous and numerous than your fathers. *And the Lord your God will circumcise your heart and the heart of your offspring,* so that you will love the Lord your God with all your heart and with all your soul, that you may live." Deuteronomy 30:1-6.

This great inward transformation is connected by Moses, in

point of time, to the end of the dispersion and the repossession of the land of Canaan by the Jews. So we can see that we are now living in a day when God will circumcise Jewish hearts.

Circumcision of the body alone, when it is not accompanied by a full-hearted and consuming love of God, is an outward sign not matched by its corresponding inward reality. That makes it of no avail. It is a form without content.

Jeremiah exhorts Israel in this same respect, "For thus says the Lord to the men of Judah and to the inhabitants of Jerusalem: 'Break up your fallow ground, and sow not among thorns. Circumcise yourselves to the Lord.'"

How? Jeremiah makes it clear: *"Circumcise yourselves to the Lord, remove the foreskin of your hearts,* O men of Judah and inhabitants of Jerusalem; lest my wrath go forth like fire, and burn with none to quench it, because of the evil of your doings." (Jeremiah 4:3-4.) Again the prophet addresses himself to the same absolute necessity: "Behold, the days are coming, says the Lord, when I will punish all those who are circumcised, but yet uncircumcised— Egypt, Judah, Edom, the sons of Ammon, Moab, and all who dwell in the desert that cut the corners of their hair; for all these nations are uncircumcised, and **all the house of Israel is uncircumcised in heart."** Jeremiah 9:25-26.

Such is the condition of the Jew who is only ritually and physically circumcised: He is counted among those who, in the sight of God, are "circumcised, but yet uncircumcised."

The New Testament speaks of circumcision in precisely these same terms:

"Circumcision indeed is of value if you obey the law, but if you break the law, *your circumcision becomes uncircumcision.* So if a man who is uncircumcised keeps the precepts of the law, will not his uncircumcision be regarded as circumcision? Then those who are physically uncircumcised but keep the law will condemn you who have the written code and circumcision but break the law. *For he is not a real Jew who is one outwardly, nor is true circumcision something external and physical. He is a Jew who is one inwardly, and real circumcision is a matter of the heart, spiritual and not physical. His praise is not from men but from God."* Romans 2:25-29.

So the testimony of the Scriptures—in Moses, in the prophets, and in the New Testament—is absolutely unified on this point. The sign without the corresponding inward reality is null and void.

"Circumcise therefore the foreskin of your heart, and be no longer stubborn."

"Rend your hearts and not your garments."
Ritual religion, no matter how true the origins on which it rests, is never pleasing to God because it is a facade. It is the container without the content. Such religion is never really satisfying to men because it does not afford them a living relationship with God. The nation Israel, apart from that spiritual circumcision that enables its people to serve God with all of the devotion of their hearts and souls, is, no matter how scrupulously it hews to religious forms, dead to God.
As a young Jew you are not called to rote, but to reality.

Charter of Freedom

On Commencement day at Radcliffe near the height of student unrest, Miss Susannah H. Wood prayed:
"We do not feel like a cool, swinging generation—we are eaten up inside by an intensity that we cannot name.
"Help us to prepare a kind of renaissance in our public and private lives. Let there be born in us a strange joy, that will help us to live and to die and to remake the soul of our time."
Let there be born in us a strange joy!
There is a joy that is beyond all the power of words to catch. When David brought the Ark of God to Jerusalem, he was filled with great joy. "And David danced before the Lord with all his might. . . . So David and all the house of Israel brought up the ark of the Lord with shouting, and with the sound of the horn. As the ark of the Lord came into the city of David, Michal the daughter of Saul looked out of the window, and saw King David *leaping and dancing* before the Lord; and she despised him in her heart."
Religious processions are supposed to be solemn affairs, and kings ought to bear themselves as though they had been starched, and Michal, who was David's wife, came out to scold David for what she considered an unseemly display of religious hilarity.
"That was a fine show you made out there today, David, leaping around in front of all the people—you the king of Israel!"
"And David said to Michal, 'It was before the Lord, who chose

me above your father, and above all his house, to appoint me as prince over Israel, the people of the Lord—and I will make merry before the Lord.' " II Samuel 6:14–16,21.

"I will make merry before the Lord!"

David had a joy in him that day that could not be contained within the limits of any ceremony. It was not that he thought he ought to dance—he couldn't help dancing! He had so much joy in his heart that it had to come out at his feet.

The Ark of the Lord, representing the presence and power of the living God among His people, was being brought into a city that would someday be the capital of the world. In terms of spiritual history, it was a tremendous event.

God had chosen Jerusalem. David could look back to the day, not many years before, when it had been in the hands of the Jebusites. He had gone up to take it against the natural odds, and the Jebusites had said, "You will not come in here, but the blind and the lame will ward you off."

"Nevertheless, David took the stronghold of Zion, that is, the city of David. . . . And David built the city. . . ." II Samuel 5:6a,7,9b.

He took the future capital of Israel and built it up and now he had brought the Ark into it and that is why he "danced before the Lord with all his might."

The kind of joy David had that day comes only out of a close identification with the purposes of God—an identification in which you are given something bigger to do than you can possibly do and on which you risk everything. The joy comes as you see God intervening to make possible the impossible thing he has told you to do.

When it is done, you know absolutely that if God had not acted, it would not have been done. The joy of David was the joy of seeing God in action. It was also the joy of knowing God.

If he is ever going to experience that kind of joy a man has got to take radical action. Not the kind of radical action that is causing so much commotion lately, but action that is just as radical in a different direction.

Gideon is a wonderful example of that. God called Gideon to be the leader of the Jewish people at a time in history when they were living under extremely heavy oppression by heathen nations, so that they "made for themselves the dens which are in the mountains and the caves" and hid in them. Judges 6:2b,3.

The situation was terrible. How was it going to be changed? The first thing God told Gideon to do was to act against his own father's false gods.

"That night the Lord said to Gideon, 'Take your father's bull, the second bull seven years old, and pull down the altar of Baal which your father has, and cut down the Asherah that is beside it. . . .' "

"So Gideon took ten men of his servants, and *did as the Lord had told him;* but because he was too afraid of his family and the men of the town to do it by day, he did it by night.

"When the men of the town rose early in the morning, behold, the altar of Baal was broken down, and the Asherah beside it was cut down. . . . And they said to one another, 'Who has done this thing?' And after they had made search and inquiry, they said, 'Gideon, the son of Joash has done this thing.' "

It was, in their eyes, the profanation of their religious altars and objects, a grave offense.

"Then the men of the town said to Joash, 'Bring out your son that he may die, for he has pulled down the altar of Baal and cut down the Asherah beside it.' " The Asherah was the symbol of an ancient Semitic goddess. Gideon was in great trouble.

The destruction of his Baal altar and Asherah appears to have brought Joash to his senses, for he said, "If he is a god, let him contend for himself, since his altar has been pulled down." Judges 6:25–31.

Gideon started by destroying the false altars of the false gods in his own backyard. It was the beginning of a career that was shortly to see him put the enemies of Israel to rout and to bring immense relief to the Jews.

It was a good place to start. It may be where you should start. The God of Israel demands entire exclusivity of devotion to Himself, and He commands Jews to have "no other gods." What have you got—what books, what images, what occult devices, what medals or anything else—that represent religion or divination apart from the God of Israel? Whatever it is, in articles or in practices, it is a sign of allegiance to a false god, and the Scriptures require you to get rid of it.

Gideon acted against the religious tradition of his family and against the religious practices of the town, but notice this: The action that Gideon took was not his own idea of what should be done about the situation that confronted him. It wasn't even something that he wanted to do. It was something that he did not want to do. He did it because God told him to do it. He took specific action according to nothing but the Word of God.

You can do that. The Bible is the book of your people. You ought to have a personal copy of a convenient size with type that is large enough so you won't have to squint to read it. As you read it, ask God to help you bring your life into line with it. There is more cure for what ails you, more cure for what ails this society and the world in this book than in anything else.

Gideon was a radical, but he was a radical for God. God needs, and He wants, young men of this same caliber today, who will have nothing whatever to do with anything which the Word of God forbids and condemns, who will act in explicit and joyous obedience to the holy Scriptures, letting all traditions contrary to it fall where they may. There are specific promises of the Scriptures for young men like that. God acts in observable ways in response to the faith of such men.

As a military leader, Gideon was as successful as anybody has ever been—but what methods he used! He went out against a huge enemy army with three hundred men, armed only with trumpets and empty jars and torches. There wasn't a sword among them. They were outnumbered by thousands to one. Gideon had a secret weapon: the promise of God that He would go into action on Gideon's behalf at the crucial moment. So the three hundred men blew their trumpets and broke their jars and shouted, and the whole enemy army panicked, broke, and ran. It was a complete rout. Israel was delivered from years of extremely intense oppression.

The pulse beat of Gideon's method was God-in-action.

The Jews are not called to serve any cause, however high-minded, other than the cause of bringing God into the affairs of mankind. It is the privilege of the Jews to know God personally and to be His spokesmen. There is nothing more exhilarating and filled with adventure than that.

"Of all the peoples of the earth, I have chosen you alone," God says of the Jews in the Bible.

"*I chose your sons* to be Nazarites and prophets—can you deny this Israel? asks the Lord." (Amos 2:11.) Can you deny that?

God has chosen Jewish young men to be consecrated to Him and to be His prophets. Since God has chosen that, all you have to do, if you are a young Jew, is decide that you will agree with that calling and cooperate with it with everything you've got.

If you do that there is no question that you—like David, like Gideon—will bring God into action in the situation you are in.

The old have, for the most part, already made their life commitments and they are not very likely to change. It is the young—those in their teens and early twenties—who still have the option of making genuine choices. If that is your case, you still have the opportunity to respond to this call, to make it your life's vocation, allowing nothing secondary to claim your energies. I cannot give you the specifics of it. The specifics for David were entirely different from the specifics for Gideon, and the specifics for you will be different from either of them. God alone has the specifics. They fit you perfectly because God knows you perfectly, and He knows exactly what His plan is for you.

There is only one thing I can tell you about them. God has something bigger for you to do than you can possibly do. That was true with David, with Gideon, with Moses. The reason is that *anyone* can do what is possible to him. That doesn't take God. What God gives you to do will absolutely, somewhere in its course, require His direct intervention if the thing is to be done. Your part is faith. When you see God in action, doing the impossible through you, you will taste joy and you may know something about the way David felt when he brought the Ark into Jerusalem.

What is faith? The best definition I know is: "Faith is a *voluntary act* of trust in God."

Another is: "Now faith is the assurance of things hoped for, the conviction of things not seen." Hebrews 11:1.

Gideon trusted the invisible God to come into visible action, and he staked everything on it. That is faith.

The Scripture says that "the just shall *live* by his faith." (Habakkuk 2:4b.) Faith is the principle by which all the great patriarchs of Israel, beginning with Abraham, lived.

Faith, as a basis for life, is radically different from any other basis, because it proceeds confidently on the basis of "things not seen." Faith risks everything on the veracity of God.

When a man does that, God acts on his behalf. Oswald Chambers has put it this way: "When we choose deliberately to obey Him, then He will tax the remotest star and the last grain of sand to assist us with all His almighty power."

When Jesus sent the disciples out to preach, He said, "Heal the sick, raise the dead, cleanse lepers, cast out demons. You have freely received, freely give. Take no gold, nor scrip, nor copper in your belts, no bag for your journey, nor two tunics, nor sandals, nor a staff; for the laborer deserves his food." Matthew 10:8–10.

The whole principle of that was faith. No man can raise the dead or cast out demons or cleanse lepers by his own power. They were to go out trusting God to do all that through them, and they were to go out trusting God to provide their needs for food and shelter and everything else daily. That is faith, and it is freedom.

A man must not be divided in faith:

"No one can serve two masters; for either he will hate the one and love the other, or he will be devoted to the one and despise the other. You cannot serve God and mammon," Jesus said in the Sermon on the Mount.

"Therefore I tell you, do not be anxious about your life, what you shall eat or what you shall drink, nor about your body, what you shall put on. Is not life more than food, and the body more than clothing? Look at the birds of the air: they neither sow nor reap nor gather into barns, and yet your heavenly Father feeds them. Are you not of more value than they?

"And which of you by being anxious can add a cubit to his span of life? And why are you anxious about clothing? Consider the lilies of the field, how they grow; they neither toil nor spin. Yet I tell you, even Solomon in all his glory was not arrayed like one of these. But if God so clothes the grass of the field, which today is alive and tomorrow is thrown into the oven, will he not much more clothe you, O men of little faith?

"Therefore do not be anxious saying, 'What shall we eat?' or 'What shall we drink?' or 'What shall we wear?' For the Gentiles seek these things, and your heavenly Father knows that you need them all. But seek first his kingdom and his righteousness, and all these things shall be added unto you.

"Therefore do not be anxious about tomorrow, for tomorrow will be anxious for itself. Sufficient unto the day are the troubles thereof." Matthew 6:24–34.

This is a charter of freedom because it is true, and God will back it up entirely in your experience as you make it the basis of life.

Most men devote themselves to providing for themselves and their families. Since they have to look out for themselves to be sure they get enough of what they want and need, they are not free because they are obligated to be the source of their own supply.

But as God *adds* all these things to a man as the man lives for Him, a man is free. God is the source of his supply.

There is a better cause for a young Jew to give his life to than tilling the money patch. Materialism can fulfill many human needs, but it can never satisfy the deepest hungers of the human spirit.

The failure of materialism as a life cause is its total incapacity to meet or to answer the ultimate questions. It is mute on those things. It is embarrassed by them.

As a way of life, materialism takes what is only a means and makes it into an end. It is idolatry. I recently saw a large sign in an automobile dealer's window: "Buick—Something To Believe In." Israel had its golden calf; we've got the new Buick.

Henry A. Kissinger caught the essence of this when he said that "the worldwide revolution of youth—especially in advanced countries and among the relatively affluent—suggests a spiritual void, an almost metaphysical boredom with a political environment that increasingly emphasizes bureaucratic challenges and is dedicated to no deeper purpose than material comfort." The nerve is missing.

Yet to reject materialism as a life pursuit may be to incur a binding poverty that makes life hard and narrow and bitter. To break with materialism is a step, but it is not enough. The spiritual void is still there.

It is not until God is at the center of a man's life that spiritual and material things fall into their right relationship.

The terms of it are that you "seek *first* the kingdom of God and his righteousness" in everything and He then adds along the way all the things that are necessary for your life.

This does not work, I hasten to add, as a principle of self-service nor as a warrant for a life of idle ease. That perverts the foundation of the promise. If you try to make it work on that false basis, you are as likely as not to fall into a life of abject poverty and unmet need, of scrounging around for bare sustenance, of great economic stringency and limitation. That is not freedom; it is another kind of slavery.

The point is not that God is going to serve you. You must serve God and, as you do that, He *will* provide for you.

How do you know that He will do it? You have to take Him at His Word. "Man shall not live by bread alone, but by every word that proceeds out of the mouth of God." Matthew 4:4.

The God revealed in the Scriptures is a personal God Who knows your needs in detail. "What is man that thou art mindful of him, and the son of man that thou dost care for him?" David inquired in Psalm 8:4. There is an affirmation in the question: *"Thou art mindful of him." "Thou dost care for him."*

"Are not two sparrows sold for a penny?" Jesus asked. "And not one of them will fall to the ground without your Father" knowing it. Matthew 10:29.

"I have been young, and now am old," David declared. "Yet I have not seen the righteous forsaken or his children begging bread." Psalm 37:25.

There is another translation of Matthew 6:33 that says of material things, "God will give them to you gladly if you put him first in your life."

God acts in response to faith. He gives in response to being asked—if the person doing the asking truly belongs to Him. It is when you give yourself to God unreservedly and serve Him with all your heart that God will provide everything you need.

It may amount to quite a lot. Have you heard of George Mueller, the great British man of faith who took in orphans by the hundreds, loved them, refused ever to tell anyone of his needs, and trusted God for all the provisions necessary for all those child ren?

One morning the larder was absolutely bare. All the children had come down for breakfast and were seated at the tables. Mueller, knowing there was nothing for them *yet,* bowed his head and gave thanks to God for the food that was about to be set before the children for breakfast—from he knew not where—and as he raised his head from the prayer, a loud knocking came at the door. A baker had arrived with a load of sweet bread and milk.

A young woman named Lettie Cowman, an ardent believer, conceived a great desire to provide the Scriptures for the people of the Orient. She took it to God in earnest prayer and bought a small notebook in which to enter contributions for the purpose. The first entry was 25 cents. Before very many years had passed, $5,000,000 had passed through her hands and the Scriptures had poured into the Orient. It was impossible, but she did it by faith. She tapped the resources of God, which are infinite.

The faith and trust God requires is not a passive thing; it is a deliberate and voluntary and active expression. It is a delightful thing, a liberating thing, to serve God and count on Him, and then to see Him fulfilling His promise to supply all of a man's needs day by day by day, year after year after year.

There is nothing illusory about that provision. It is real—real food on the table, clothes on the back, money in the purse, shelter, and many other necessary things.

My own experience of trusting God for my needs began in a small way. I was in the Army, had just embarked on the life of faith before being drafted, and I needed to take a bus ride to the other side of Baltimore and I did not have a nickel. "Be anxious for nothing," the Bible says, "but in everything by prayer and supplication with thanksgiving let your requests be made known to God." (Philippians 4:6.) Faith rose and I just told the Lord silently that I needed bus fare two ways, and as soon as I did I was filled with assurance that the Lord would provide it.

Half an hour later He did, through the man in the bunk next to me who decided that he should take half a dollar out of his pocket and hand it to me. That half-dollar made me happier at that moment than $10 could have some other time.

The next time the need was a little bigger. I wanted to go to a place in the country, about eight miles from the end of the last bus line running in that general direction. So I went out to the last stop, got off, sat down by the edge of the road and prayed, "Lord, here I am. I need to get out to the farm. I don't have any way. I ask you to get me there."

I did not have the slightest doubt that this prayer would be answered and I sat there suffused with a confident faith that God would supply. It was not long before a car pulled over to the side and stopped. The driver had seen me somewhere before, and stopped to find out what I was doing there. I told him I was going to the farm, which is where he happened to be going, so I got in and he drove me the rest of the way.

These are small things to be sure, but they gave me the basis for continuing to trust the Lord in larger things. They were the start of my education in faith.

A few years ago I was sent to cover some integration troubles in Mississippi. I did not have a driver's license and the nearest airport was sixty miles from the place where the news was. It was not hard to go in trust. As I got off the plane I bumped into a fellow from Michigan I had once met and he drove me to the spot, which was two miles from where he was heading.

Toward the end of the assignment I was in a motel room and I became aware that the Lord was telling me to pick up my bags and leave, though I had no way to get to the airport. I cannot tell you exactly how the Lord communicates such a direction, since it is not in words, except to say that it was very clear that the exact moment for departure had come. As I stepped out into the night there were two men putting bags into the trunk of a car. I walked over with my two bags and heard one of them mention the name of the airport. "That's where I need to go," I said. "Climb aboard," the driver said with a hearty joviality, and we were off.

One other detail. When I got to that motel, they not only did not have a room, they had people quadrupled up in rooms. But I was there on faith, and while I was standing at the desk, somebody called and said he would not be using his room that night and would not object to it being used, so I was handed the key. I believe I was the only guest in the motel that night who had a room to himself.

There were several other remarkable provisions on the trip. Just as perfectly timed, such as the total stranger who came over to me in the crowded diner the next morning—to me of all the people in the place—and offered in a delightful drawl to drive me around the town that morning. I have no idea why he did that, but for the next three hours I had a private chauffeur.

The Bible is your charter of freedom from want. It is also your charter of freedom from sin.

Sin is a problem, because no one caught in it is free. "Every one who commits sin is a slave to sin," the Bible says in John 8:31. That is plain enough, and if you are honest, you know it's true. You sin because you don't have the strength or the power not to, even though you know it's wrong.

Maybe you have tried resolutions. Starting tomorrow, "I will . . ." or "I will not . . ." The resolutions express your idealism, but you don't keep them because you can't keep them. You don't have the power.

Every once in a while you hear people say they live by the Ten Commandments or the Sermon on the Mount, or both. That is nonsense. No man can live by either if he tries to live by them as rules. Most people who say that can't name the commandments anyway, and they could not quote six verses from the Sermon on the Mount.

It takes new life to live them! It takes power to live above the power of sin.

When Paul was sent out to preach, the Lord told him he was being sent "To open their eyes, and to turn them from darkness to light, and from the power of Satan to God, that they may receive forgiveness of sins." Acts 26:18.

My own experience of this new life, and the power over sin and freedom from it, began shortly after I read these wonderful words:

"He was in the world, and the world was made by him, and the world knew him not. He came unto his own, and his own received him not.

"But as many as received him, to them gave he *power to become the sons of God,* even to them that believe on his name, who were born, not of blood, nor of the will of the flesh, nor of the will of man, but of God." John 1:10–13.

When I first saw those words they hit me with considerable force. I knew that I was not a son of God, but the Bible said God was able to give me "power to become a son of God." About three days later I received that power.

Jesus Christ came into my life, and sin went out of my life. That is not to say that I did not ever sin again, but the power that sin held over me, despite my best efforts to overcome it, was broken. Sin could no longer compel me to do its bidding. As long as you lack power over sin, you are not free.

Read what Isaiah says: "Come now, and let us reason together, says the Lord, though your sins be as scarlet, they shall be as white as snow; though they be red like crimson, they shall be as wool." Isaiah 1:18.

No matter how much of a hold sin has on your life, that situation can be suddenly and utterly reversed. There is entire forgiveness with God.

Every man needs a direct, personal relationship to God. That begins in an encounter with the living God. In this first encounter, God extends pardon for sin, imparts new life, and sets a person in a new relationship to temptation—above it, not under it. That cleansing, and the realization that God has done a miracle inside you, brings joy with it.

Then, there is a direct, personal experience of the Holy Spirit. This direct dealing of God with individual men and His bestowal upon them of His Spirit goes back to the chosen men of Israel. We have seen how, when the prophet Samuel took the horn of oil and anointed David, "the Spirit of the Lord came mightily upon David from that day forward."

Earlier, Samuel took a vial of oil and anointed Saul, and the prophet told Saul, "as you come to the city, you will meet a band of prophets coming down from the high place with harp, tambourine, flute, and lyre before them, prophesying. Then the spirit of the Lord will come mightily upon you, and you shall prophesy with them and *be turned into another man.*

". . . When he turned his back to leave Samuel, *God gave him another heart;* and all these signs came to pass that day. When they came to Gibeah, behold, a band of prophets met him, and the spirit of God came mightily upon him, and he prophesied among them. And when all *who knew him before* saw how he prophesied with the prophets, the people said to one another, 'What has come over the son of Kish? Is Saul also among the prophets?'" I Samuel 10:5b,6,9–11.

Saul could not have prophesied to save his life before God sent His Spirit upon him, made him a new man and gave him a new heart—and did it all in a day. No wonder the people who knew him were amazed.

The Book of Judges tells of Gideon and of Samson: "And the

woman bore a son, and called his name Samson; and the boy grew, and the Lord blessed him. And the Spirit of the Lord began to stir him in Mahaneh-dan, between Zorah and Eshta-ol." Judges 13:24,25.

The Spirit of the Lord changed Saul quite suddenly. It was at a particular point in time and at a particular place. The same is true of Samson. At a certain time, in a certain place, "the Spirit of the Lord began to stir him," and he became a deliverer of his people.

If you are a young Jew these things are particularly applicable to you. Moses said of the Jews: "For the Lord's portion is his people, Jacob his allotted heritage."

> "He found him in a desert land,
>   and in the howling waste of the wilderness;
> he encircled him, he cared for him,
>   he kept him as the apple of his eye . . .
>   the Lord alone did lead him
>   and there was no foreign god with him."

Deuteronomy 32:9,10,12

The prophet Joel said:

> "Be glad, O sons of Zion,
>   and rejoice in the Lord, your God.
> You shall eat in plenty and be satisfied,
>   and praise the name of the Lord your God,
>   who has dealt wondrously with you.
> And my people shall never again be put to shame.
> You shall know that I am in the midst of Israel,
>   and that I, the Lord, am your God and there is none else.
> And my people shall never again be put to shame.
>
> "And it shall come to pass afterward,
>   that I will pour out my spirit upon all flesh;
> your sons and your daughters shall prophesy,
>   your old men shall dream dreams,
>   and your young men shall see visions.
> Even upon the menservants and the maidservants in those days
>   I will pour out my spirit."

Joel 2:23a,26–29

The transformation that comes with forgiveness of sins brings a new joy. C. S. Lewis, the English writer, who knew this transformation in his own experience, wrote a book about it. He called it *Surprised by Joy.*

In the Book of Galatians, Paul writes: "Now the works of the flesh are plain: immorality, impurity, licentiousness, idolatry, sorcery, enmity, strife, jealousy, anger, selfishness, dissension, party spirit, envy, drunkenness, carousing, and the like. I warn you, as I warned you before, that those who do such things shall not inherit the kingdom of God." Galatians 5:19–21.

It may be that you are involved in one or more, or many, of these things. If so, it is not altogether surprising. You have yet to be transformed. The Spirit of God has not yet come to you to change your life and give you a new heart.

The Bible very clearly explains that "That which is born of the flesh is flesh, and that which is born of the Spirit is spirit." John 3:6.

If you have been born of the flesh only—that is, by your natural parents—then you *are* flesh, and it is natural that you would be in some of these things. When you are born of the Spirit—that is, born of God, and given power to become a son of God—you will be put on an absolutely new basis. You will be a different person. That difference will not only surprise other people, it will surprise you.

There are certain things that go with this change. "The fruit of the Spirit is love, joy, peace, patience, kindness, goodness, faithfulness, gentleness, self-control." Galatians 5:22.

While some of the former things—impurity, idolatry, party spirit, and so on—characterize your life now, these things—love, joy, peace—will begin to characterize it then. You will know that the difference has not been by your own effort, but by what God has done for you.

Then you will be able to say, with the Psalmist, "When the Lord restored the fortunes of Zion, we were like those who dream. Then our mouth was filled with laughter, and our tongue with shouts of joy; then they said among the nations, 'The Lord has done great things for them.' The Lord has done great things for us, whereof we are glad." Psalm 126:1–3.

Then you will know what it is to sing to the Lord upon your bed by night. You will have some idea of what made David dance that day.

Such supernatural encounters are by no means things of the past. I have interviewed a great many students and ministers and missionaries and others who have told of their own entrances into the dimension of the supernatural through the leading of the Holy Spirit. They tell of healings and casting demons out and many other things.

Here, however, I would like to introduce you to a name that will probably be new to you—that of Charles Grandison Finney, a lawyer who became one of the greatest preachers of righteousness this nation has ever known.

There have been in American history a number of evangelists, heralds of the Scriptures, who, because of the extent of their public ministry and the crowds they drew, have become quite well known. Finney was not an evangelist, he was a revivalist. Because he did not practice mass evangelism, he did not win the popular attention the others have had.

I had never heard of Finney until late one afternoon, sitting in a car with a Jewish friend, I heard him mention Finney in passing and remark that he was a lawyer. It may have seemed a casual remark to my friend, but somehow the brief mention of Finney's name made a deep impression upon me. I knew that I would have to find out something about him. What a mine of gold I struck when I did!

Finney was reared in Oneida County, New York, in the early 1800's in an area that was then largely a wilderness. In 1818 he entered a law office at Adams, New York, to study law and he became a successful attorney. He had no religious upbringing and, while finishing high school, went for a while to a church where an aged minister who had "a monotonous, humdrum way of reading what he had probably written many years before" bored him beyond measure.

"To give some idea of his preaching, let me say that his manuscript sermons were just large enough to put into a small Bible. I sat in the gallery, and observed that he placed his manuscript in the middle of his Bible, and inserted his fingers at the places where were to be found the passages of Scripture to be quoted in the reading of his sermon. This made it necessary to hold his Bible in both hands, and rendered all gesticulation with his hands impossible. As he proceeded he would read the passages of Scripture where his fingers were inserted, and thus liberate one finger after another until the fingers of both hands were read out of their places. When his fingers were all read out, he was near the close of the sermon.

"Anyone can judge whether such preaching was calculated to instruct or interest a young man who neither knew nor cared anything about religion," Finney later wrote, describing himself as "almost as ignorant of religion as a heathen." But God had another way of reaching the heart of Mr. Finney. "In studying elementary law, I found the authors frequently quoting the Scriptures, and referring especially to the Mosaic Institutes, as authority for many of the great principles of common law," Finney wrote. "This excited my curiosity so much that I went and purchased a Bible, the first I had ever owned; and whenever I found a reference by the law authors to the Bible, I turned to the passage and consulted it in its connection."

In the course of his exposure to Moses and the Law and the Scriptures, Finney encountered the great promise, "Ask, and you shall receive, seek and you shall find, knock and it shall be opened to you. For every one that asks receives, and he who seeks finds, and to him who knocks it will be opened. What father among you, if his son asks for a fish, will instead of a fish give him a serpent; or if he asks for an egg, will give him a scorpion? If you then, who are evil, know how to give good gifts to your children, how much more will the heavenly Father give the Holy Spirit to those who ask him!" Luke 11:9–13.

His exposure to the truths of the Bible soon brought Finney to the consciousness that he was a sinner and that he "needed a great change in my inward state."

Soon he found that he could not "long hesitate between the two courses of life presented to me"—to belong to the world or to belong to the living God.

He did not exactly know how to go about seeking, but he prayed for help and understanding without seeming to get very far. The important thing, of course, is that he was seeking. "I had no opportunity to pray above my breath," Finney wrote, "and frequently I felt that if I could be alone where I could use my voice and let myself out, I should find relief in prayer."

One morning, he wrote, "At an early hour I started for the office. But just before I arrived at the office, something seemed to confront me with questions like these: indeed, it seemed as if the inquiry was within myself, as if an inward voice said to me, 'What are you waiting for? Did you not promise to give your heart to God? And what are you trying to do? Are you endeavoring to work out a righteousness of your own?' . . .

"North of the village, and over a hill, lay a piece of woods, in which I was in the almost daily habit of walking, more or less, when it was pleasant weather. It was now October, and the time was past for my frequent walks there. Nevertheless, instead of going to the office, I turned and bent my course toward the woods, feeling that I must be alone, and away from all human eyes and ears, so that I could pour out my prayer to God. . . . But when I attempted to pray I found that my heart would not pray. I had supposed that if I could only be where I could speak aloud, without being overheard, I could pray freely. But . . . I was dumb; that is, I had nothing to say to God; or at least I could say but a few words, and those without heart.

"Just at that point this passage of Scripture seemed to drop into my mind with a flood of light: 'Then shall ye go and pray unto me, and I will hearken unto you. Then shall ye seek me and find me, when ye shall search for me with all your heart.' I instantly seized hold of this with my heart . . . I was as conscious as I was of my existence, of trusting at that moment in God's veracity. Somehow I knew that that was a passage of Scripture, though I do not think I had ever read it. I knew that it was God's word, and God's voice, as it were, that spoke to me. I cried to Him, 'Lord, I take thee at thy word. Now thou knowest that I search for thee with all my heart, and that I have come here to pray to thee, and thou hast promised to hear me.'

"I told the Lord that I should take him at his word; that he could not lie, and that therefore I was sure that he heard my prayer, and that he would be found of me.

"He then gave me many other promises, both from the Old and the New Testament, especially some most precious promises respecting our Lord Jesus Christ. . . . I continued thus to pray, and to receive and appropriate promises for a long time, I know not how long. . . . Before I was aware of it, I was on my feet and tripping up the ascent toward the road. The question of my being converted had not so much as arisen to my thought; but as I went up, brushing through the leaves and bushes, I recollect saying with great emphasis, 'If I am ever converted, I will preach the Gospel.'

"I soon reached the road that led to the village, and began to reflect upon what had passed; and I found that my mind had become most wonderfully quiet and peaceful. . . . I walked quietly toward the village, and so perfectly quiet was my mind that it seemed as if all nature listened. It was on the 10th of October, and a very pleasant day. I had gone into the woods immediately after an early breakfast; and when I returned to the village I found it was dinner time."

Finney had found the living God. He had that day received the forgiveness of his sins. His slate had been wiped clean through the blood of Jesus Christ. Forgiveness is a central theme of the Bible, from Genesis on, and it is always through blood. The Holy Spirit had imparted to Finney the truths of forgiveness from the Old and New Testaments, and he had believed them and received them, and the result was that "all sense of sin, all consciousness of present sin or guilt, had departed from me. . . . The repose of my mind was unspeakably great. I never can describe it in words. The thought of God was sweet to my mind, and the most profound spiritual tranquility had taken full possession of me."

This was the start of Finney's lifelong experience with God, but there was yet another transaction—an outpouring of the Holy Spirit upon him, or a baptism in the Spirit.

"I went to my dinner, and found I had no appetite to eat. I then went to the office. . . . I took down my bass-viol, and . . . began to play and sing some pieces of sacred music. But as soon as I began to sing those sacred words, I began to weep. It seemed as if my heart was all liquid. . . . I wondered at this and tried to suppress my tears, but could not. . . . There was a great sweetness and tenderness in my thoughts and feelings . . . my heart seemed to be liquid within me. All my feelings seemed to rise and flow out; and the utterance of my heart was, 'I want to pour my whole soul out to God.' The rising of my soul was so great that I rushed into the room back of the front office, to pray.

"There was no fire, and no light, in the room; nevertheless it appeared to me as if it were perfectly light. As I went in and shut the door after me, it seemed as if I met the Lord Jesus Christ face to face . . . it seemed to me that I saw him as I would see any other man. He said nothing, but looked at me in such a manner as to break me right down at his feet. I have always since regarded this as a most remarkable state of mind; for it seemed to me a reality, that he stood there before me, and I fell down at his feet and poured out my soul to him. I wept aloud like a child, and made such confessions as I could with my choked utterance. It seemed to me that I bathed his feet with my tears; and yet I had no distinct impression that I touched him, that I recollect. . . . I returned to the front office, and found that the fire that I had made of large wood was nearly burned out. But as I turned and was about to take a seat by the fire, I received a mighty baptism of the Holy Spirit. Without any expectation of it, without ever having the thought in my mind that there was any such thing for me . . . the Holy Spirit descended upon me in a manner that seemed to go through me, body and soul. I could feel the impression, like a wave of electricity, going through and through me. Indeed it seemed to come in waves and waves of liquid love; for I could not express it in any other way. It seemed like the very breath of God. I can recollect distinctly that it seemed to fan me, like immense wings.

"No words can express the wonderful love that was shed abroad in my heart. I wept aloud with joy and love; and I do not know but I should say, I literally bellowed out the unutterable gushings of my heart. These waves came over me, and over me, and over me, one after the other, until I recollect I cried out, 'I shall die if these waves continue to pass over me.' I said, 'Lord, I cannot bear any more'; yet I had no fear of death.

"When I awoke in the morning the sun had risen, and was pouring a clear light into my room. Words cannot express the impression that this sunlight made upon me. Instantly the baptism that I had received the night before returned upon me in the same manner. I arose upon my knees in the bed and wept aloud with joy, and remained for some time too much overwhelmed with the baptism of the Spirit to do anything but pour out my soul to God. It seemed as if this morning's baptism was accompanied with a gentle reproof, and the Spirit seemed to say to me, 'Will you doubt?' 'Will you doubt?' I cried, 'No! I will not doubt; I cannot doubt.' He then cleared the subject up so much to my mind that it was in fact impossible for me to doubt that the Spirit of God had taken full possession of my soul. In this state I was taught the doctrine of justification by faith, as a present experience. . . . My sense of guilt was gone; my sins were gone; and I do not think I felt any more sense of guilt than if I never had sinned. . . . Nor could I recover the least sense of guilt for my past sins."

Finney had received the great inward change every man needs, circumcision of heart. He was forgiven and cleansed of sin, and then he was baptized and filled with the Holy Spirit.

The thought occurred to him that "I should be obliged to leave my profession, of which I was very fond [but] I no longer had any desire to practice law."

"I had, no more, any pleasure in attending to law business. I had many very pressing invitations to conduct lawsuits, but I uniformly refused. . . ."

Finney "soon sallied forth from the office to converse with those whom I should meet about their souls," and he did so with wonderfully good effect. He found that young people were "converted one after another, with great rapidity" and that the work of the

Holy Spirit "spread among all classes, and extended itself, not only through the village, but out of the village in every direction." Finney would call the believers together daily for prayer. "One morning I had been around and called the brethren up, and when I got to the meeting-house . . . Mr. Gale, my minister, was standing at the door of the church, and as I came up, all at once the glory of God shone upon and round about me, in a manner most marvelous. The day was just beginning to dawn. But all at once a light perfectly ineffable shone in my soul that almost prostrated me to the ground. In this light it seemed as if I could see that all nature praised and worshiped God except man. This light seemed to be like the brightness of the sun in every direction. It was too intense for the eyes. I recollect casting my eyes down and breaking into a flood of tears, in view of the fact that mankind did not praise God. I think I knew something then, by actual experience, of the light that prostrated Paul on his way to Damascus. It was surely a light such as I could not have endured long."

Finney's experiences with the living God were, of course, no part of the standard, cut-and-dried church practices to which most of the religious sort adhered, and he found that it did not pay to speak to them of them. "I soon found that it would not do to tell my brethren what was passing between the Lord and my soul. They could not understand it. . . . I soon learned to keep quiet in regard to those divine manifestations, and say but little about them."

Nor did Finney, who was very shortly to become one of the most effective preachers this nation has known, submit to the formality of theological education. He knew far more about God and about the truths of the Scriptures by first-hand experience than most men acquire in a lifetime of learning.

"Having had no regular training for the ministry I did not expect or desire to labor in large towns or cities, or minister to cultivated congregations. . . . I went out to the northern part of Jefferson County, and began my labors at Evans' Mills, in the town of Le Ray."

Nor did Finney use any of the standard methods of preparing to preach sermons. "I began, as I said, to preach in the stone schoolhouse at Evans' Mills. The people were very much interested, and thronged the place to hear me preach. . . .

"I had not taken a thought with regard to what I should preach; indeed, this was common with me at that time. The Holy Spirit was upon me, and I felt confident that when the time came for action I should know what to preach. . . . The Spirit of God came upon me with such power, that it was like opening a battery upon them. For more than an hour, and perhaps for an hour and a half, the word of God came through me to them in a manner that I could see was carrying all before it.

"When I first began to preach, and for some twelve years of my earliest ministry, I wrote not a word; and was most commonly obliged to preach without any preparation whatever, except what I got in prayer. Oftentimes I went into the pulpit without knowing upon what text I should speak, or a word that I should say. I depended upon the occasion and the Holy Spirit to suggest the text, and to open up the whole subject to my mind; and certainly in no part of my ministry have I preached with greater success and power. If I did not preach from inspiration, I don't know how I did preach. It was a common experience with me, and has been during all my ministerial life, that the subject would open up to my mind in a manner that was surprising to myself . . . and whole platoons of thoughts, words, and illustrations came to me as fast as I could deliver them. . . . I find that such sermons always tell with great power upon the people. . . . I preached out of doors; I preached in barns; I preached in schoolhouses; and a glorious revival spread all over that region of the country."

Men whose lives were touched and changed in the revivals that occurred wherever Finney went were seeing God in action through a man. Finney was the instrument, but the power of the method came directly from God.

"Let no man think that those sermons which have been called so powerful were productions of my own brain, or of my own heart, unassisted by the Holy Ghost," Finney wrote.

Such uncommon procedures and such results were bound to arouse opposition, and they did. Ministers, wedded to their formal concepts of what was right and what was wrong, reproved him for being so unlike them. One divine was "indignant at the manner in which I let down the dignity of the pulpit. . . . He insisted upon it that I should not be allowed to preach till I had a ministerial education; that I should stop preaching and go to Princeton and learn theology, and get better views of the way in which the Gospel should be preached. . . . I seldom felt that I was one of them, or that they regarded me as really belonging to their fraternity."

In a genuine revival, the work of God proceeds with very little regard to the efforts of man. Finney's preaching sparked revival, but Finney did not by any means manage the revivals that occurred; nor did anyone else. At Utica, "the largest hotel in the town became a center of spiritual influence, and many were converted there. . . . Indeed, both in this place and in Rome [N.Y.], it was a common remark that nobody could be in the town, or pass through it, without being aware of the presence of God; that a divine influence seemed to pervade the place, and the whole atmosphere to be instinct with a divine life."

Finney went on through nearly all the rest of his life preaching from place to place—at Philadelphia, Boston, and New York, among the larger cities—and also spending part of every year teaching at Oberlin. Finney walked in power all his years. His preaching against slavery struck men to their hearts.

As a note appended to his memoirs says, "Notwithstanding the abundant and exhausting labors of his long public life, the burden of years seemed to rest lightly upon him" in his eighties. "He still stood erect, as a young man, retained his faculties to a remarkable degree, and exhibited to the end the quickness of thought, and feeling, and imagination, which always characterized him. . . . In these closing years and months . . . the quiet power of his life was felt as a benediction upon the community [Oberlin]. . . . He died, August 16th, 1875, lacking two weeks of having completed his eighty-third year."

Except by a few, this man of God has been virtually forgotten and his burial place is consequently obscure. There is an old weathered stone there on which these words are engraved: "The Lord our God be with us, as He was with our fathers, let him not leave us nor forsake us." The words are taken from King Solomon's prayer recorded in I Kings 8:57 of the Old Testament.

There are some who suppose that God desires a dull, pleasureless, rigorous life for man, full of petty restrictions. That is very far from the truth. John Wesley put it well when he said, "Sour godliness is the devil's religion."

God has filled the earth with things that give great and lawful pleasure to man. He is the author of pleasures. There is no true pleasure that would be possible apart from its creation by Him. "Every good and perfect gift is from above, coming down from the Father of lights." James 1:17.

"No good thing does the Lord withhold from those who walk uprightly," Psalm 84:11 declares.

"Thou wilt show me the path of life; in thy presence is fulness of joy; at thy right hand there are pleasures for evermore," David wrote. Psalm 16:11.

God wants you to have pleasure, now and throughout eternity, but he is not willing that your pleasure be gained at anyone else's sorrow and expense. He is not willing that your pleasure be gained at your own sorrow and expense.

Satan has never been responsible for the creation of any true pleasure. His only role is to take the pleasures created by God and to twist them or pervert them into that which will lead to the destruction of man.

Satan doesn't have any interest in pleasure for humans, except as a means of bringing them pain. He uses pleasure as a convenient tactic in his strategy to increase human misery. That is his sole interest in pleasure.

God looks over the whole long course of the consequences rising out of an act, and if there are bad effects and evil consequences in it, He makes that plain, to keep humans from suffering those effects. God has the whole state and welfare, both now and for eternity, of your soul in view, not some quickie pleasure that lasts a few minutes and later stings and stings and stings.

The principle that Satan presses upon man is *self-gratification.* He will always counsel a man to act on appetites, impulses, desires without considering the last effects. That is one of the chief lines of his propaganda and you see it everywhere. Are you angry? Are you jealous? Do you have lust? Are you consumed with ambition? Go ahead, he urges, act *now.*

The promptings of immediate self-gratification, without regard to consequences, are an echo of Satan's counsel to the woman in the garden. God said that if man ate of the fruit of the one tree, he would surely die. Satan said the opposite, "You will not surely die."

"Forget that God said you will die if you eat of this tree," was his counsel. "I say you won't. Now look, you see how good the fruit looks? And if you eat some of it, it will make you wise."

Behind this counsel were his specialties, lying and murder. Satan truly knew that, if she ate of it, she would die. His message was, disobey God and you will accrue advantage by it. His message has not changed.

In the final analysis you are going to have to take God's Word on it or Satan's. Consider, for instance, the sin of fornication. It is a key sin in Satan's plan for the destruction of human beings. He knows that fornication, if it is not repented of and quit, will shut heaven to an individual forever. He has a guarantee of that.

"Do not be deceived," the Bible says, "neither fornicators, nor idolaters, nor adulterers, nor homosexuals, nor thieves, nor drunkards, nor revilers, nor extortioners shall inherit the kingdom of God." I Corinthians 6:9,10.

The Book of Revelation solemnly declares that "murderers, fornicators, sorcerers, idolaters, and all liars—their lot shall be in the lake of fire that burns" forever. Revelation 21:8.

That is what is behind Satan's incessant promotion of the sin of fornication. You already know what Satan says about it. I would ask you to hear and consider God's Word and to see that it is entirely for your good:

"My son, do not forget my teaching, but let your heart keep my commandments, for length of days and years of life and abundant welfare they will give you. Trust in the Lord with all your heart, and do not rely on your own insight. In all your ways acknowledge him, and he will direct your paths. Be not wise in your own eyes; fear the Lord, and turn away from evil. It will be healing to your flesh and refreshment to your bones.

"My son, do not despise the Lord's discipline or be weary of his reproof, for the Lord reproves him whom he loves, as a father the son in whom he delights. Then you will walk on your way securely and your foot will not stumble. If you sit down, you will not be afraid; yea, you shall lie down and your sleep shall be sweet." From Proverbs, Chapter 3.

Demons find the one thing that a man wants more than he wants God, and they use that thing to wreck him. Samson was called to be a judge and deliverer of his people. He was born according to a promise given to his parents by God, set aside as "a Nazarite to God from birth," blessed by God as a youth and prepared for service. After "the Spirit of the Lord began to stir him," he began to strike telling blows against the tyranny of the Philistines.

There was a prospect of liberty and safety for the Jews. This created a crisis in the camp of Satan. Something would have to be done about the Samson problem. Samson was found to be susceptible to the allurements of a harlot. By that sin, he was stopped in mid-career, lost his eyesight, and was taken captive as a slave. He loved the pleasures of sex more than he loved the will of God, and though he ultimately repented and scored one last victory for Israel, he died in it. His life was a tragic failure.

If there is something, if there is anything, that a man wants more than God, Satan will find that thing and place it before him as his own personal idol.

Other men, among them Abraham, Joseph, Moses, and David,

though they may have faltered at times in the life of faith, grew stronger in their loyalty and love for God as their years increased.

They discovered the glorious truth that "all things work together for good to those who love God, to those who are called according to his purpose." Romans 8:28.

There is, in Jews more than in Gentiles, a concern for the welfare of mankind and for the state of society. If you subtracted the sum total of Jewish philanthropy from the American culture, a great many people would be considerably worse off than they are.

These are things of great social utility yet short of the purposes of God and they are entirely unable to meet and answer effectively the social and moral and political crises of today. Indeed, some of the philanthropists' own sons and daughters are being swallowed up in evil causes.

Young Jews are becoming absorbed in causes that fail their followers, fail mankind, and betray both—devoting themselves to evils worse than materialism: to false crusades and false cults, false religions, false mysticism, false supernaturalism, idols and demons.

The pot-sex-protest mode that is becoming increasingly prevalent is not the way to liberty that it claims to be. It is the way to bondage, destruction, and death.

What God wants young Jews to have, and young people generally, is the real thing, not Satan's terrible counterfeits.

To get to this ultimate reality, a personal encounter with God Himself through the Holy Spirit, an experience of His love and supernatural power that cannot be argued away, you have got to be willing to make a clean break with sin and with all demonic substitutes, and give yourself radically to the God of Israel.

To be free, find out what God wants you to do and do it.

If you discover the joy that only God can give, your own life will be wonderfully changed and you will be able to help remake the soul of our time in ways of which you cannot now even guess, because they are beyond you.

Hear these words: "Ho, every one who thirsts, come to the waters; and he who has no money, come, buy and eat! Come, buy wine and milk without money and without price. Why do you spend your money for that which is not bread, and your labor for that which does not satisfy? Hearken diligently to me, and eat what is good, and delight yourself in fatness.

"Incline your ear, and come to me; hear, that your soul may live; and I will make an everlasting covenant with you, my steadfast, sure love for David.

"Seek the Lord while he may be found, call upon him while he is near. Let the wicked forsake his way, and the unrighteous man his thoughts; let him return to the Lord, that he may have mercy on him, and to our God, for he will abundantly pardon. "For my thoughts are not your thoughts, neither are your ways my ways, says the Lord. For as the heavens are higher than the earth, so are my ways higher than your ways and my thoughts higher than your thoughts. "For you shall go out in joy, and be led forth in peace. The mountains and hills before you shall break forth into singing, and all the trees of the field shall clap their hands." From Isaiah 55.

If you have never heard the mountains singing, or seen the trees of the field clapping their hands, do not think because of that that they don't. Ask God to open your ears so you may hear it, and your eyes so you may see it, because, though few men ever know it, they do, my friend, they do.

About the Author

McCandlish Phillips has been a reporter on the staff of *The New York Times* since 1955. His byline appears regularly over deft human interest and color stories, vignettes of city life, and anecdotal profiles of famous men. He is best known for two stories—one on a Jewish Nazi, the other on a Jewish Marine. The first was his famous 1965 exposé of Daniel Burros, a member of the American Nazi Party and New York State head of the Ku Klux Klan, whose career in spreading viciously anti-Semitic hate literature ended violently when Phillips revealed his hidden Jewish birth and upbringing. The other was a front-page biography on the short life of Pfc. Richard Marks, a prep school boy who joined the Marines and died in a tank in Vietnam.

McCandlish Phillips was born at Mount Vernon in 1927, reared in Boston; New York; Cleveland; Huntington, Indiana; and Brookline, Massachusetts—an upbringing that ran the full cycle from rural wheat farm to teeming city street.

He worked for the *Boston Sport-Light,* the *Brookline Citizen,* and the United

States Army, before joining the *Times* as a night copy boy in 1952. He wrote his way to the staff and "soon he was one of the best reporters on the paper," as Gay Talese recounted in *The Kingdom and the Power*.

He has covered the whole run of general news—parades, strikes, riots, trials, United Nations affairs, political campaigns, and he has concentrated lately on the New York City cultural news beat.

In 1960, Phillips became the first *Times* reporter to receive the newly established Meyer Berger Award of the Columbia University Graduate School of Journalism, for excellence in reporting and writing the news in the tradition of the late Meyer Berger of the *Times*.

In a column about him in the New York *Herald Tribune*, author Dick Schaap wrote:

"McCandlish Phillips is not the typical American newspaperman. He keeps a Bible on his desk and, between assignments, he reads from it . . . . A slender six-feet five-inches tall, a friendly and gentle man, McCandlish Phillips is, obviously, an uncommonly decent human being. He is, also, an uncommonly gifted newspaperman."